# THE MEDIA IN BRITISH POLITICS

D1486119

# The Media in British Politics

*Edited by*
Jean Seaton
*and*
Ben Pimlott

# Avebury

Aldershot · Brookfield USA · Hong Kong · Singapore · Sydney

Published by
Avebury
Gower Publishing Company Limited
Gower House
Croft Road
Aldershot
Hants GU11 3HR
England

Gower Publishing Company
Old Post Road
Brookfield
Vermont 05036
USA

**British Library Cataloguing in Publication Data**

The Media in British politics.
  1.–Mass media—Political aspects—Great Britain
  I.–Pimlott, Ben   II. Seaton, Jean
  320.941     P92.G7

**Library of Congress Cataloging in Publication Data**

The Media in British politics.
  Includes bibliographies and index.
  1. Press and politics—Great Britain—History—20th century.
  2. Great Britain—Politics and government—20th century.
  I. Pimlott, Ben, 1945-   II. Seaton, Jean, 1947-
  PN5124.P6M44 1987    302.2'34'0941    86-31842

  ISBN 0-566-00930-7

# Contents

List of contributors     vii

Introduction    *Jean Seaton and Ben Pimlott*     ix

PART I   PRESS AND BROADCASTING IN POLITICS

1   Leaders   *Colin Seymour-Ure*     3
2   Class   *Howard Davis*     25
3   Voters   *Martin Harrop*     45
4   Elections   *Jenny Craik*     64
5   Local press   *David Murphy*     90
6   The Lobby   *Peter Hennessy and David Walker*     110

PART II   MEDIA REVOLUTION AND POLITICAL CHANGE

7   The struggle for 'balance'   *Jean Seaton and Ben Pimlott*     133
8   Reporting atrocities   *Jean Seaton*     154
9   News management and counter-insurgency   *Fred Halliday*     183
10   The media and politics in Northern Ireland   *Paul Arthur*     201
11   Media policy and the Left   *Denis MacShane*     215
12   Newspapers and the new technology   *Brian Whitaker*     236
13   Goodbye to *The Times*   *Peter Kellner*     249

Index     255

# List of Contributors

**Paul Arthur** is Senior Lecturer in Politics at the Queen's University, Belfast. His books include *Government and Politics of Northern Ireland*.

**Jenny Craik** is Lecturer in Communications at Griffiths University, Brisbane.

**Howard Davis** is Senior Lecturer in Sociology at the University of Kent. He is author of *Beyond Class Images* and co-author of *Western Capitalism and State Socialism*.

**Fred Halliday** is Professor of International Relations at the London School of Economics. He is the author of *Arabia without the Sultans, Iran: dictatorship and development, The Making of the Second Cold War;* and co-author of *The Ethiopian Revolution*.

**Martin Harrop** is Lecturer in Politics at the University of Newcastle upon Tyne. He is co-author of *Comparative Government: An Introduction* and co-editor of *Political Communications: the General Election Campaign of 1979*.

**Peter Hennessy** is a Visiting Fellow at the Policy Studies Institute and Editor of *Contemporary Record*. He is co-author of *States of Emergency* and *Sources Close to the Prime Minister,* and author of *Cabinet*. A regular commentator on British politics on radio and television, he has worked as a journalist for the *Financial Times, The Times* and other newspapers.

**Peter Kellner** is Political Editor of the *New Statesman*. He is co-author of *Callaghan: The Road to Number Ten* and *The Civil Servants: An Inquiry into Britain's Ruling Class*.

**Denis MacShane** is Assistant General Secretary of the International Metal Workers' Federation in Geneva. He has worked as a reporter for the *Financial Times* and other newspapers, and is a former President of the National Union of Journalists. He is the author of *Using the Media,*

*Solidarity: Poland's independent trade union, François Mitterrand,* and co-author of *Power! Black workers, their unions and the struggle for freedom in South Africa.*

**David Murphy** is Lecturer in Sociology at the University of Manchester Institute of Science and Technology. He is the author of *The Silent Watchdog: The press in local politics.* He has worked as a local reporter in Bolton.

**Ben Pimlott** is Professor of Politics and Contemporary History at Birkbeck College, University of London. He is the author of *Labour and the Left in the 1930s* and *Hugh Dalton.*

**Jean Seaton** is Senior Lecturer in Sociology at the Polytechnic of the South Bank, London. She is co-author of *Power without Responsibility: The press and broadcasting in Britain.*

**Colin Seymour-Ure** is Professor of Government at the University of Kent. He is the author of *The Press, Politics and the Public, The Political Impact of the Mass Media, The American President: power and communication, David Low,* and co-author of *Studies on the Press.*

**David Walker** is chief leader writer on the the *London Daily News.* He is co-author of *Media made in California: Hollywood, politics and the news* and *Sources Close to the Prime Minister;* and author of *Municipal Empire.*

**Brian Whitaker** is a journalist working for the *Guardian.* He previously worked for the *Sunday Times.*

# Introduction

There are two main schools of thought concerning the relationship between the media and the political process. The first, liberal traditionalist, presents the media simply as an instrument by which the powerful and sinister in society may be checked, and holds that press freedom is best guaranteed by the absence of government involvement. According to this view, 'freedom' and 'non-interference by governments' are so closely related as to be virtually the same thing. Hence private or capitalist ownership and control should be seen, not as a cause for suspicion, but as the best guarantee of liberty. Where a state monopoly is deemed necessary or happens to exist (as in broadcasting), freedom is best served by ensuring a proper balance between alternative opinions as expressed through the workings of a democracy.

The second school, while preferring freedom in the liberal sense to the non-freedom of authoritarian regimes, nevertheless sees the media primarily not as a restraint on rulers but, in effect, as their servant. Thus, in modern Britain, the media should be regarded as the agent of consensus: directed towards producing the agreement, acceptance or acquiescence of the masses towards policies and attitudes which are not of their making nor necessarily in their interest. This view, in direct line of descent from the Marxian theory of false consciousness, has been presented in various forms by Stuart Hall, Raymond Williams and James Curran and by the Glasgow Media Group.[1] Related to this school is a third, more quizzical and less implicitly moral, approach: that the media should be seen neither as a temple of liberty nor as a cudgel of oppression but as an instrument of political negotiation, neither good nor bad, to be used or abused by those who seek to influence public opinion. Thus Anthony Smith has argued that television, in the political arena, operates as a 'megaphone' through which political leaders may project their voices – but which is neither monolithic, nor persuasive in itself.[2]

The aim of *The Media in British Politics* is to examine aspects of these opinions, which appear consciously or unconsciously in many writings, and to explore some of the territory between them. It is not comprehensive. It does not, for instance, examine in any detail recent dramatic changes in the technology of broadcasting and (especially) news-papers.[3] These changes, which require close study, are happening too fast to permit any verdict that will not be rapidly overtaken by events.

The essays in this volume consider the media-politics interaction on a broad canvas, and with an historical dimension. The emphasis is on areas which have, so far, received surprisingly little attention from students of the media. As will be seen, the view taken of politics is a wide one and a strong theme is that 'politics', 'culture' and 'entertainment' do not exist in independent departments.

It might be argued that non-political media coverage is politically more important in the long run than overtly political material because of the role of the media in establishing or modifying acceptable values. There is the additional point that obviously political – especially propagandist – writing or broadcasting sets up a resistance in the potential audience. To give one example, it is reasonable to suppose that the practice of giving blacks positive or heroic parts in television soap operas will have more effect on attitudes to race than an equivalent amount of time devoted to the subject of race in party political broadcasts. To give another, it has often been suggested that stereotyped images of 'ideal' womanhood (as, for example, in advertising) reinforce particular attitudes to the proper role of women in society. Such influences, whether intended or not, work precisely because the recipient of the signals is not aware of any attempt at political persuasion.

In addition, of course, there is a fusion of covert and overt material. Thus the special power of innocence associated with culture and entertainment has not gone unnoticed by politicians. If entertainers are unconscious politicians, politicians increasingly seek to be entertainers, either directly or by association. Following the American example, British political leaders have increasingly sought endorsement by celebrities, whose appeal is supposed to have no political bounds.

The cult of the media celebrity is, indeed, one which politicians have watched with fascination; and it is one which provides a salutary reminder of the broad effects of the media on politics. Unlike the heroes of antiquity, the heroes and heroines of the media do not champion anything or anybody in particular. Personally, celebrities may lead complicated lives. Politically, all the pressures on them are to avoid contention. If, as sometimes happens, they adopt a strong moral stance, it is on the side of the consensus. In general, however, passivity on moral dilemmas is to be preferred, on the highly practical grounds that a celebrity – actor, compère, presenter – is not in the business of causing offence. Media personalities tend, therefore, to be in favour of virtue and against sin, and to exude a deceptively neutral good will.

Such a stance, so it may be argued, is contagious. The media are not solely responsible for the politicians' habit (especially at election time) of talking in bland generalities; but they foster it. In the absence of the modern media with its instant access to a vast, largely passive public, the instincts of political leaders are to talk to their followers; the mass media on the other hand, encourage them to talk directly to everybody and to follow the entertainer in avoiding controversy. Colin Seymour-Ure has noted the tendency among political contenders for office in the United States to seek to emulate the disengagement of the media personality, the ratings-enhancing knack of being 'well-known for well-knownness'.[4] It was a technique, pioneered by F.D. Roosevelt's fireside chats in the 1930s, that reached its apotheosis when Hollywood came to the White House in 1981. The elision of politics and entertainment has been a growing phenomenon in Britain as well.

Chasing the consensus is not the only way to manage the media, and there have been some (industrialists and union leaders as well as politicians) who have found abrasiveness or harshness an alternative tactic – though one which, in media terms, merely constitutes another form of entertainment. In the culture of cosiness, an occasional sharp note is enlivening and can be contained. The main impact of the mass media upon the politician in pursuit of votes, since before the days of television or even radio, has been to place presentation above content, good nature above righteous indignation, mildness above radicalism.

Perhaps this is a good thing for our system of government. One school of democratic theory has always applauded the anaesthetising of controversy. The contemporary political 'centre' in Britain, with its trumpeted rejection of the alleged 'slanging-match' between the major parties, echoes the writings of American sociological writers such as Daniel Bell,[5] who argued in the early post-war period that a decline in political contention should be regarded as a happy sign of national health. The same idea was implicit in the arguments of those in Britain in the mid-1970s who claimed that political authority was being undermined by competitive bidding.[6] In the first case apathy, and in the second moderation, were presented as desirable goals. It may be, therefore, that the ability of the media to induce these conditions should be seen as a benefit.

That is a matter of opinion. What is beyond dispute is that the public's perception of politicians, as of some other powerful people who seek publicity, has been changed by the growing extent and sophistication of the mass media – and, to a degree that was never true in the last century, has tended to merge the different categories of well-knownness. Political leaders have always been famous: but our intimate awareness of their quirks and mannerisms, their facial expressions and accents, is a novelty that is a direct product of the mass media and has important consequences.

Media-manufactured reputation is brittle: a minor poet may hope for an after-life of growing recognition, but a major politician, like a pop star, is almost immediately forgotten. Such fame is also sanatised. Like the wiggles of a pop star, the fulminations of a politician pass through a cleansing, bureaucratic sieve before they reach the armchair viewer. It is the invisible army of producers, directors and researchers, not the politicians or the public, who determine what the citizens may see, by selecting performers and editing performances. Few market-places, indeed, are more weighted than that of the media: all politicians need the media, but the media does not need all politicians. It is a point which journalists, who do not regard politicians with deference, never let the politicians forget.

The filtered intimacy of television is thus both the means to fame and success for politicians (as for entertainers), and an illusion, giving an impression of directness yet hiding from the viewer the disciplines and restrictions that bind the speaker almost as effectively as a script. A traditional justification of public service broadcasting used to be that radio and television could probe the 'news behind the news' – revealing truths through direct interviews in a way that newspapers could never achieve. The doyenne of televised current affairs, Grace Wyndham-Goldie, even argued that a virtue of television was the opportunity it gave to politicians to demonstrate their communicating skills.[7] The ancestor of this view was the pre-war BBC belief in the microphone as lie detector. Broadcasting, it was held, revealed speakers in their true colours and sorted out the genuine from the insincere. The self-deluding nature of such assumptions appears palpable today – and yet, paradoxically, the 'naturalness' of the final product has manifestly increased.

The recent decision not to admit public television into the Chamber of the House of Commons may owe more to fear of embarrassment (empty benches, inactive Members) than to fear of distortion. Yet few MPs doubted that such a change would have a profound effect. Indeed, no better illustration could be given of the importance of the media in British politics than the argument put forward by one Labour Member, returning to Westminster in 1983 after an absence of four years. Viewing the depleted numbers on his own side, he suggested that the televising of Parliament might have a salutary effect in increasing attendance at debates – MPs would be more inclined to appear in the House, he reasoned, if there was the incentive of appearing on television.[8] In such a way, the medium might cease to be the message – having long since ceased to be a mere means of communication – and take an immediately observable part in the daily working of the legislature. But the question then becomes, whose hand should hold the camera?

This book contains two sections. The first examines general aspects of the media in the political arena: the use and attempted use of the media by leaders (and vice versa), the electoral impact, the working of the lobby, the influence of the media on class and class perceptions, the means by which political information is shaped and disseminated, locally and nationally. The second section contains essays on historical and contemporary aspects of media influence and media management. Colin Seymour-Ure, focusing on politicians, shows the ways in which modern political leadership and media management are inextricably bound up. Every crisis has what he calls a 'media sub-plot', and the media, by setting the agenda, frequently determines what counts as a crisis. Leadership itself, the importance of issues, and – of course – political success, are all defined by the media. The 1984-5 miners' strike was fought out on television by contrasting media personalities (MacGregor and Scargill) as much as in the pit villages; and the Social Democratic Party would have been stillborn without a media hype. 'After 1983', writes Seymour-Ure, 'media appearances made TV a kind of surrogate office for the SDP leader, David Owen.' Television conventions favour some kinds of leadership over others – thus, a middle-of-the-road party with little emphasis on policy and a strong emphasis on personal celebrity fitted prevailing news values like a glove. But the relationship between politicians and the media has become more than one of mere intimacy. There is now an identity: to be a political leader is to be *part of* the media, an unpaid performer with a prescribed routine.

For some time, sociological studies of the influence of the media have concentrated on the supposed 'meaning' of a particular message, especially in the case of television programmes. Thus the Glasgow Media Group have assumed that a receptive audience will tend to absorb the 'meaning' uncritically. Howard Davis, examining the salience of class, points to evidence that an individual's understanding or use of media political messages is strongly affected by social factors, as well as by recent political experiences. Davis argues, not only for the centrality of class in any analysis of the media's political role, but also for the importance of the media in the maintenance and formation of class attitudes. Here, television is of particular interest because other media (in particular, newspapers) are stratified and segmented along class lines, whereas most television programmes aim at a broad, cross-class public. The characteristic 'personality' of the television message – white, middle-aged, middle-class, masculine, metropolitan and liberal pluralist – presents a unified set of values which people in different social groups relate to in different ways. Hence, the identity of some groups is reinforced by television far more effectively than the identity of others. At the same time, the traditional bases for group identity – family, work, religion – change with such rapidity that the role of the media as a unifying force is given added importance.

The 'reinforcement' thesis was derived from a simple theory of social-category-based voting which appears extremely dated in the volatile 1980s. Its popularity among social scientists Davis attributes to its simple, counter-intuitive and generalisable nature. (He might have added that research funds are more readily obtainable to finance large projects that are simple, counter-intuitive and generalisable.) Harrop argues that in order to understand the impact of the media, we need to look for the long-term effect: one episode of *Crossroads* may change nothing, but twenty years of it may influence attitudes profoundly. The main effect of the mass media may be to set the conditions and establish the climate in which opinion is changed and formed, rather than directly to alter particular opinions.

In a democracy the potential significance of the media is always greatest at election time. When contenders for power are separated by a narrow margin of support, their presentation by journalists and broadcasters becomes a critical factor in determining the history of the nation. In Chapter 4 Jenny Craik argues that changes in the media have increased the importance of the campaign period. The result is to put enormous, arbitrary power into the hands of a few people – mainly in television – who are deciding what the public are to regard as important while remaining competitively concerned about ratings and the need to entertain.

The main emphasis of this book is on the national media. In the case of newspapers, however, it is the local press that receives the greatest public attention. For the majority of politicians – MPs as well as councillors – the local press provides the only available forum most of the time. What determines the way in which they are presented, and indeed the way in which local affairs generally gets reported? David Murphy provides a sharp analysis of the tight contraints at work. Politics, he suggests, is seldom the main influence: the main motive of local and provincial editors is to obtain the maximum number of words for the largest possible readership at the lowest cost. Hence most 'political' news is made up of barely altered press releases; news that might take up journalistic time or might cause offence tends to be avoided. 'Investigative' journalism – as in the mythology of the newshound – is a luxury which only the nationals can afford. Hence a great deal of corruption and potential scandal locally goes unreported, because the price or risks of pursuing it are too high. Recently, however, there has grown up a corrective: an alternative press, made possible by the new technology, where journnalists can write the stories their employers dare not print. Since this alternative press provides one route into national newspapers, the journalistic profession has been saved from the utter sterility into which it might otherwise have sunk.

Craik shows how the media define politics. Peter Hennessy and David Walker look at the way in which political information is gathered and handled. Much 'hard' political news is the product of ritual rather than investigation: through the antiquated (and disintegrating) institution of the lobby. As Hennessy and Walker indicate, the function of the lobby system is to serve the Prime Minister and the government and to deceive the public about the true source of the news that is being offered and the way it is manipulated. The lobby, however, does not serve merely the authorities: it also makes the lives of journalists easier. It is, in short, a club or cartel for the mutual benefit of news disseminator and news gatherer and in which 'public interest' plays only a subsidiary part. The parliamentary lobby is not unique: similar relationships exist between specialist journalists and their subject matter in (for example) industrial relations reporting.[9] The parliamentary lobby, however – as Hennessy and Walker demonstrate – is a particularly discreditable example both because of its national significance and also because of the cynicism of its operation. They make the particularly important point that the lobby is not only anachronistic in itself – it also encourages anachronistic reporting, by steering journalists towards big Westminster political stories and away from the investigation of Whitehall, which has long since become the main locus of power.

The second part of the book looks at particular cases, and the varying ways in which the concepts of fairness and bias have been understood or ignored. In our own essay on the development of the notion of political 'balance' in broadcasting before the Second World War, we have tried to show the accidental and piecemeal way in which the idea progressed – and the way in which battles between interested individuals or bodies about the handling of news could (as in the case of broadcasts to Germany in 1939) in reality be symbols for more important conflicts in a wider political arena. The acceptance that 'balance' was desirable in a democracy – a principle fought for and eventually won in the coalitionist conditions of wartime – was also an acknowledgement that there could be no objective truth in politics. Jean Seaton's essay on the treatment by the BBC of the Nazi death camps is another attempt to examine the way in which conservative newsgatherers respond to truths that do not accord with their own preconceptions. The question was not (as some historians have imagined) whether the news was 'believed', and when. Rather, it was a matter of priorities (military news came first) and of uncertainty – derived from memories of First World War sensationalism – about the wisdom of disseminating atrocity stories.

Jean Seaton's essay is partly about the constraints imposed by broadcasting conventions. Fred Halliday looks at media conventions as developed since the Second World War, in another context: the reporting of conflict in Oman. Halliday's conventions, however, involve deliberate and subtle news management, amounting to censorship and control, in order to hide the extent of British military involvement. The

notion of free and objective reporting vanishes altogether and is replaced by a tradition of conscious manipulation. Oman is a single case.
The implications of Halliday's argument, however, raise important
questions about the relationship between foreign policy and foreign reporting in general.

The reporting of domestic conflict is the subject of Paul Arthur's
study of the media in Northern Ireland. The function of newspapers in
the province, Arthur argues, is almost entirely to reinforce opinion, not
to question it: there is no paper that seeks to address both Catholic and
Protestant communities or build a consensus between them. Even the
BBC became, from its inception, effectively the official voice of the majority.

What might be done to correct imbalances, cater for minorities, ensure better and fairer reporting? These have not been problems which
have greatly concerned Conservative politicians, and until recently the
idea of a 'media policy' was not one which received much attention in
the Labour Party either. Denis MacShane looks at the vacuum and considers how it might be filled. Interest in media reform in the labour
movement, he suggests, has yet to engage the serious attention of those
who might be in a position to carry it out.

Any survey of the prospects for the role of the media in politics is
likely to be pessimistic. Broadcasting has seen the most rapid
technological changes over the longest period – with a tendency to
erode what is left of the public service principle. Yet the most dramatic
and potentially dangerous development has been the thunderbolt that
struck the British newspaper industry in 1986, when new technology,
with the aid of powerful interests, finally broke resistance to innovation. One of the most alarming aspects of the recent demonstration
of baronial power has been the evidence it provides of the dispensable
nature, not only of printers, but of journalists as well. Brian Whitaker
(himself a former *Sunday Times* reporter who resigned over the Wapping lockout) considers some of the consequences of the print revolution. Peter Kellner, who ceased writing for *The Times* for similar
reasons, develops the letter he wrote at the time of his own resignation:
an important document at a key turning point in the history of the
British press.

A different kind of turning point is provided by the 1987 election
(which took place after the essays in this book had gone to press). Mrs
Thatcher's third successive victory strengthens the arguments, in
particular, of Seymour-Ure and Harrop. On the one hand, there was
an even greater tendency than in the past to focus on the personal as
distinct from political attributes of contenders; on the other, the result
showed that the electorate was more impervious to media stimuli than
some people imagined.

Certainly it was a television election *par excellence* with every political party arranging its whole campaign around the so-called 'photo opportunity'. One interesting development was the transformation by the Labour Party of the televised party political broadcast from a dull and patronising form into skillfully emotive documentary. Meanwhile, news and current affairs coverage came to resemble a compendium of classic party politicals – more earnest and stylised than before with the politicians rather than the producers apparently in control of the medium. It has long been the practice of many provincial newspapers to deal with the problem of 'balance' in elections by giving all candidates equal space regardless of what they do or say and permitting them to use their allotment as they see fit. In 1987 this spread to television. In the ritual debates, the parties supplied their own chosen speakers, carefully keeping out of view those they felt to be the least electorally appealing. On the news programmes, the cameras obediently followed the party leaders' whistle-stop tours, the sole function of which, of course, was to feed the cameras.

Yet the campaign had little obvious effect on voters' preferences. Although the Conservative television campaign was widely considered to have been poor, and Labour's to have been much better, the coverage failed even to bring Labour back to what Professor Ivor Crewe regards as Labour's 'natural base' of 35 – 38 per cent of the vote, or give the Alliance (granted equal exposure for the first time) its expected advance. 1987 lends weight to Harrop's argument that the effects of the media are to be seen more in the long- than the short-term. Labour's alleged 'extremism', an old issue, was apparently a significant influence on voters' decisions; 'City scandals', a new one frequently mentioned in the election, barely registered. It is possible, however, that the media campaigns had hi... .rectly, Labour may have saved itself from the ... ı place. Indirectly, the portrayal of the parties ... ubtedly influenced post-election politics, restor... ...m and – not least – increasing pressure for ... ...s of the Alliance. It was the 'Tweedledum ... ...sion of the Liberal/SDP dual leadership or ... ...rovided the strongest impetus for a chang ... . Alliance to compete on an equal footing ... ...ontests which modern televised British ele...

Britain does not have a st... ...theme of many of the contributions to this ... ...lf-censorship – a product of a range of pol... ...ures – frequently provides an effective subs... ...because it is seldom recognised. For any individua...., ...t critical pressures are those of career prospects, salary and job security – and, with all of these, the relationship between quality and objectivity, on the one hand, and 'success' on the other, is often tenuous, to say the least. Acceptability to editor, management and proprietor is always the first criterion.

This is not new. The press has always been partisan and subject to financial constraints and there have been press barons since the last century. If, however, as some suggest, the interdependence of politics and the media is growing, and if – because of the growing sophistication of the electorate, or the immediacy and ubiquity of television – the role of the media in shaping political attitudes is even greater today than in the past, then discussion of the part played by the media in British politics needs to become a matter of urgent national debate.


## Notes

1.  S. Hall, *Culture, Media, Language: Working Papers in Cultural Studies*, London: Hutchinson, 1980. Raymond Williams, *Communications*, Harmondsworth: Penguin, 1973. James Curran, *The British Press: a Manifesto*, London: Constable, 1979. Glasgow University Media Group, *War and Peace News* Milton Keynes: Open University, 1985.
2.  Anthony Smith, *The Shadow in the Cave: a study of the relationship between the broadcaster, his audience and the State*, London: Allen and Unwin, 1973.
3.  Chapters 12 and 13 offer some preliminary arguments.
4.  Colin Seymour-Ure, *The American President: Power and Communication*, London: Macmillan, 1982.
5.  Daniel Bell, *The Coming of Post-Industrial Society*, New York: Basic Books, 1973.
6.  See, for example, James Alt, *The Politics of Economic Decline*, Cambridge: Cambridge University Press, 1977, and for a useful discussion of the effects of this view, see Krishan Kumar and A. Ellis, *Dilemmas of Liberal Democracy*, London: Tavistock, 1983.
7.  Grace Wyndham-Goldie, *Facing the Nation: Television and Politics, 1936-1976*, London: Bodley Head, 1977.
8.  B. Gould, 'Televising Parliament' in *The Political Quarterly* no. 3, 1983.
9.  Jean Seaton, 'Trade Unions and the Media', in B. Pimlott and C. Cook (eds.) *Trade Unions in British Politics*, Harlow: Longman, 1982.

# Part I

# Press and Broadcasting in Politics

# 1 Leaders
## Colin Seymour-Ure

### The growing intrusiveness of media

What are we to say about the relations between mass media and political leadership? The two are so utterly entwined. All political behaviour is conditioned to some extent by the means of communication through which it is carried. Leadership, whether based on command or persuasion, depends especially on effective communication. Ever since the introduction of universal suffrage and the development of mass circulation newspapers, mass media have been the dominant intermediary between leaders and led, supplanting the bombast of the hustings and the argument of squib and pamphlet. But not only have they provided leaders with a medium of persuasion and the public with a basis of judgement. A leader's image in the media has also become a key ingredient in his reputation with the narrower group of people – in party, say, or Parliament – with whom he has to work and upon whom his tenure may depend. Whatever the judgement of history on his short premiership (1963–64), Sir Alec Douglas-Home deserves to be remembered as the first party leader whose resignation, after his defeat in the 1964 general election, was caused partly by colleagues' poor opinion of his television image.[1]

British television had begun to 'open up' to politics in the late 1950s. The turning-point was the broadcasters' decision in 1959 to report the general election rather than, as before, to ignore it from fear of the electoral and broadcasting laws. Until then, the scope for political leadership on the air was limited to the party political broadcasts, rationed out and produced by the parties themselves, and rare 'ministerial broadcasts', when the Prime Minister would talk sonorously face to camera in some national crisis such as Suez, or the Chancellor of the Exchequer would expound the Budget, and the Opposition would exercise their 'right of reply' (granted at the broadcasters' discretion).[2] From those days to 1983, when the Prime Minister could appear more rattled by a Bristol housewife's question on a phone-in show than at any other point in the election campaign, or when negotiations in industrial disputes like the miners' strike in 1984 seemed at times to be conducted live on television, is a long distance indeed.[3]

From being confined by a narrow, mechanistic view of political balance and (perhaps wisely, until the 1950s) by a timorous attitude to controversy, radio and TV have abandoned the role of marginal reporter and clattered into the marketplace. Increasingly television is not just the reporter of leadership exercised in some other arena – party, trade union, constituency, Parliament. Television now, like the press, which historically combined the role of observer with that of participant in party politics, has become itself an arena in which politics is carried on. Since TV is overwhelmingly the medium with which audiences spend most time, and which most creates the illusion of bringing audience and televised subject together, such a development must surely be transforming the relation between mass media and political leadership.[4]

The extent of this change can be marked in politicians' behaviour (though one must beware being too categorical since, again, politicians have always sought to manage their public communication in the manner appropriate to the time). Starting with Harold Wilson, prime ministers have experimented with new forms of media contact going beyond the Downing Street/lobby correspondent arrangements that dominated political reporting from at least the 1930s.[5] Wilson yearned for a cadre of columnists like those with whom American presidents have sometimes established a close rapport, and he appeared on a number and variety of TV programmes beyond the measure of his predecessors. Heath tried open, 'presidential' press conferences (unhappily); Callaghan aped Jimmy Carter by holding the first prime ministerial phone-in – but did not repeat the experiment. Mrs Thatcher, like Wilson, played the TV channels against each other and granted interviews as rewards. In Bernard Ingham she had a Press Secretary with a more important role, and certainly a much more publicised one, than that of anyone since the post was established in its modern form in 1945. Beyond that, Thatcher had advice from advertising and marketing specialists, notably Tim Bell (initially of the highly successful advertising agency, Saatchi and Saatchi); Gordon Reece, who 'packaged' her for the 1979 election and continued to help at critical periods even after he went to work in the USA; and Christopher Lawson (formerly a director of the Mars Bar Company).[6] In the 1983 election, communication tactics seemed to be dominated by adman's language ('We must watch for signs of palate fatigue' – i.e. a particular Thatcher image must not begin to cloy).

Such arrangements are a natural response to the opening-up of TV and radio and to the proliferation of programme formats and channels. Prime ministers (and other leaders to a less extent) now need advice not simply on what to say – once the chief if never the exclusive consideration – but also on how to say it (Mrs Thatcher had coaching) and on when, where and how often.[7] Leaders out of office, correspondingly, are more tempted than ever before to blame the media for their predicament, like those who killed the messenger of bad news in ancient times. Media are especially liable to attract hostility in industrial disputes: for example, they were a favourite whipping-boy of Arthur Scargill in the 1984–85 miners' strike.[8] More generally, 'blaming the media' has for long been a kneejerk reaction to misfortune by the Left, both at large and among particular factions. Michael Foot's memoir after the 1983 election typified the habit, and it was a favourite theme of Tony Benn.[9]

The other side of the coin was the launch of the SDP. Here was a new party, so the Left critique went, whose very creation was the product of the media. Broadcast executives, instinctively sympathetic from years in the centrist atmosphere of public service broadcasting, were feeding the Gang of Four great gulps of free air-time, and like-minded journalists were dishing out column inches. The SDP itself would not have put it that way. But certainly the style of the launch in 1981, down to the emphasis on telephones and credit cards in the initial membership drive, reflected a determination to exploit up-to-date communication techniques in every practical way.[10]

From whatever perspective one views the SDP, the launch of a new party which, in alliance with the Liberals, would capture 25 per cent of the votes in a general election two years later, would have been immeasurably more difficult in the days before TV had opened up to politics. Before World War I and perhaps through the 1920s, it might have been done, but much more slowly, with laborious grassroots work and the funding of a daily paper.[11] In the 1940s and 1950s it would probably have been impossible: papers by then were too expensive to found, and broadcasting was shut off.

Whether politicians are in or out of office, then, the new intrusiveness of broadcasting has accentuated the tendency to blame the media when things go badly. How often is there a political crisis which does not have a media sub-plot? The Falklands crisis had its sub-plots: 'managed news' (no quick TV pictures); the alleged 'cover-up' of *Belgrano* details; the unsuccessful prosecution of Clive Ponting, an Assistant Secretary in the Ministry of Defence, for leaking details two years later to the Labour backbencher, Tam Dalyell.[12] Policy crises have sub-plots: Cabinet discussion of welfare policy in 1983 was jeopardised by the publication, as 'plans', of CPRS papers which the government claimed were simply 'options'; sterling crises generally involve the intangible factor of 'confidence', so easily damaged by media, like yoghourt by the wrong yeast. Operational crises have sub-plots: the arrival date of Britain's first cruise missiles was leaked to *The Guardian* in 1983 by a clerk, Sarah Tisdall, who was imprisoned for six months under the Official Secrets Act. Crises of personnel have sub-plots: Cecil Parkinson, a rising star in Mrs Thatcher's Cabinet, was obliged to resign in 1983 after press disclosures about his private life.

Media and political leadership can never have been more entwined. But the very twining makes a thicket for analysis. It is a typical problem of media research – like, for instance, that of effects on audiences. It would be equally absurd to suggest either that media have no definite impact at all, or that their impact is uniform and decisive. Of the great brambling ground in between, what can usefully be said? The realistic answer may be that this is a subject for case studies, and that broader generalisations must be trite or extremely tentative. With that in mind, the rest of this chapter explores one possible approach – but less a finely structured framework than, say, a bulging plastic bag.

### Media and the arenas of leadership

From the viewpoint of news media, political leadership consists in persons saying or doing things. These may be denoted by a place (the House of Commons), by an event (a by-election), by membership of a group (the TUC; the Cabinet) or by tenure of an office (prime minister). All such places, events, groups and offices may be defined as *arenas* in or from which leadership is exercised and which may attract the attention of media.

As the previous discussion has emphasised, media are themselves arenas. By reporting a politician's speech, a newspaper carries the news delivered in one arena to another, probably larger, that is constituted by the newspaper's readership. If the politician writes an article for the paper, as the party leaders do in general election campaigns, the paper is an arena in a more direct sense. It is in this latter sense that the expansion of political radio and TV has been so great. In phone-ins, radio and TV talk-shows, documentaries, current affairs magazine programmes and still, occasionally, the face-to-camera address, politicians continually broadcast in circumstances where the microphone and camera are not eavesdroppers but are the sole *raison d'être* – and where the style of communication appropriate to broadcasting needs no adjustment to the needs of some other arena.

Such is the spread of media that the corresponding notion of 'leadership' must clearly extend beyond the idea of 'office'. A person in office is a Leader with a capital 'L'. Office involves open, formal, explicit, acknowledged leadership. Office-holders are appointed or elected; leaders (small 'l') emerge.[13] Clearly there are many arenas to which the idea of office is irrelevant, yet in which leadership through media is exercised. Although Tony Benn was an MP and member of the Labour Party National Executive Committee in opposition after 1979, it would surely be misleading to attribute the scale of his public prominence to those offices, and his media coverage did not concentrate on them. Throughout the 1970s Enoch Powell similarly commanded media attention on a scale unrelated to the office of a backbench MP.

A broad general definition of leadership may therefore be formulated as the occupancy of any position (not just an office) from which the political attitudes and behaviour of a group may be influenced towards specific objectives.[14] In office, a Leader may have *executive* and *managerial* functions – supervising a party machine, managing a leadership group such as the Shadow Cabinet, running an election campaign. In government, of course, executive functions will be a major preoccupation. Beyond that, leadership may have an *ideological* or *policy* function, from the all-embracing grasp of an ideology such as socialism to the sharply focused campaigns of many pressure groups. In government, arguably, 'ideology' recedes and 'programmes' come to the fore. Lastly, leadership includes *symbolic* and *expressive* functions. Enoch Powell's leadership in the early 1970s consisted in his capacity to express attitudes towards immigration evidently shared by thousands of people who felt that party orthodoxy excluded them.[15] Tony Benn, similarly, expressed a form of parliamentary socialism not as widely represented at Westminster as among activists in the constituencies. The phrases clinging to politicians evoke attitudes they symbolise: Mrs Thatcher was 'the Iron Lady'; espoused 'Victorian values'; was 'not for turning'; claimed 'There is no alternative' (to her economic policies). Winston Churchill, as war leader, symbolised a national will (but not, as the 1945 election showed, in domestic politics). Middle-class Labour leaders sometimes adopt symbols to identify with the working class; upwardly mobile Conservative leaders become indistinguishable from those born to privilege.

All these leadership functions can be affected by the behaviour of media. In general, the managerial and executive are likely to be affected least, since they will depend on lines of communication within the organisation concerned. Media may also affect another set of leadership categories: the *stages* of leadership. Leadership is a process, and in addition to the activity of *'leading'* itself, media may be crucial to the stage of *becoming* a leader – especially to the emergence of the non-office-holder – and to that of *stopping* leading (or leaving office).

Whatever the activity or stage of leadership concerned, it will be carried on, as has been said, in an arena. Media rank arenas, for purposes of allocating coverage, in three ways. First, they decide whether to treat an arena as political or not. Obvious political arenas are discussed in relation to Figure 1.1 below – parties, pressure groups, the Cabinet and so on. But which are the major social arenas that national news media habitually do not treat as political – and often claim should 'keep out of politics'? A rough list might include the following:

> The royal family
> Church of England
> Armed services
> Police
> Courts
> Theatre and arts
> Showbiz and pop music
> Universities
> Scientific and medical research
> Financial institutions ('the City')
> Industrial and commercial corporations
> TV and press (exc. overtly political programmes and publications)
> Sport

Press coverage of many of these subjects – most obviously sport and finance – is physically separated from political news and features. In others the occasional political story, such as the attempt to mobilise the actors' union, Equity, or political interventions by the Archbishop of Canterbury, may be presented as attempts to politicise what ought properly to be regarded as non-political activities. Perhaps the chief reason for this deep-rooted attitude is the failure of the national press to distinguish the idea of the non-political from the non-partisan.

The second type of ranking is among the political arenas. In choosing which to cover, and how much, media continually rank arenas in terms of status or power. They offer their audiences, in effect, a hierarchy of leadership arenas. Figure 1.1 suggests, on a selective and completely impressionistic basis, how such a hierarchy might look.

The Prime Minister and Cabinet get most attention. Parliamentary arenas of all kinds do rather well; constituency arenas rather badly. Major TV programmes are not only useful arenas in their own right but often get reported elsewhere too. It is not uncommon for a breakfast-time interview with a minister on the Radio 4 *Today* programme to be reported in the news bulletin on the same station half an hour later.

But while media routines, amongst other reasons, assure some arenas steady coverage, the attention given to others fluctuates. Among the former, if an incumbent Leader of the Opposition, or a Cabinet minister, seems weak, the media response (certainly in the short run) will not be to ignore him but to use his weakness as a justification for evaluating him negatively. Among the variable arenas, an incumbent may suddenly command attention because of events in another arena, for example. When the Liberal Party found itself narrowly holding the balance in the 1974–79 Parliament, David Steel as Leader became much

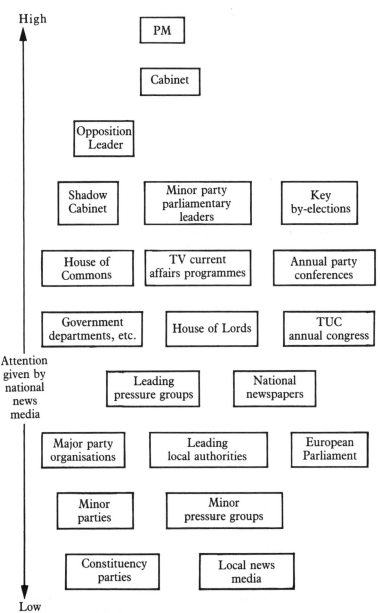

*Figure 1.1  Notional ranking of political leadership arenas*

more newsworthy. After the SDP broke away from the Labour Party, individual MPs who joined it gained more attention than they had as Labour backbenchers.

Figure 1.2 thus offers another hypothetical scale. At one end are arenas such as the Cabinet, whose problem is to ensure themselves good media coverage. At the other are those who have to struggle for coverage at all. The further you are towards this end, the more likely will your publicity depend on general interest news values and not the specifically political. This might be termed the Vanessa Redgrave or Cenotaph effect. Much of the coverage given to Vanessa Redgrave as a parliamentary candidate for the Workers' Revolutionary Party in the 1979 general election, consisted in pictures of her latest film *Yanks* ('From wide-screen kisses to XXXX – it's all part of the scene these days for Vanessa Redgrave, Oscar-winning actress and parliamentary candidate': *Sunday Mirror*, 22 April 1979).[16] As to the Cenotaph, it became a matter of heat in the SDP as to whether its Leader, David Owen, should line up alongside the Prime Minister, Opposition Leader and Liberal Party Leader on Remembrance Sunday. In 1983 he was excluded. In 1984, after a public row, he was reinstated. The lure, of course, was the presence of the TV cameras. A previous example of the Cenotaph effect was the furore created by Michael Foot appearing, as Labour Leader, not in a traditional dark coat on this highly charged ritual occasion, but in what was alleged to be a disrespectfully informal, light-coloured, short top coat. This was an early step along his road to the 'Worzel Gummidge' scarecrow image (echoed by his amiable mongrel dog) that looked so poorly in a Leader in the 1983 election campaign.[17]

These different kinds of media ranking are most unlikely to coincide with the self-images of people in the arenas themselves, nor with their images of each other.[18] The factors governing the attitudes and behaviour of the media may overlap with, but are certainly not identical to, those which govern politicians. There is argument within arenas themselves about whether they are, or should be, political. In the labour movement, this has sometimes focused on the question whether a particular union should affiliate to the TUC. In sport, the Olympic Games, at first not widely seen as political outside the Soviet bloc after World War II, have become an overt propaganda instrument, with boycotts and alternative games in Moscow and Los Angeles. Rugby football and cricket have become embroiled in the politics of anti-apartheid. To many people on the Left, and axiomatically to Marxists, a definition of politics which excludes armed services, police, courts and large concentrations of economic power is ludicrous; and a ranking which attaches importance to bourgeois institutions like the House of Commons simply contributes to mystification.

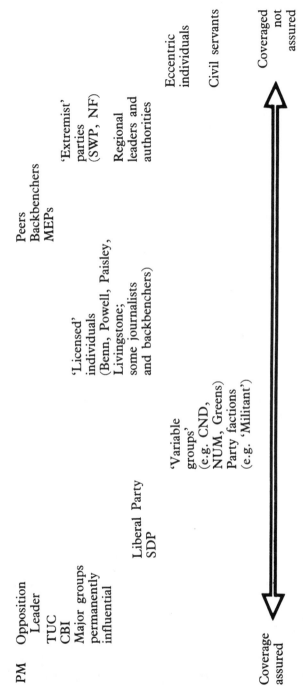

*Figure 1.2  Notional scale of media coverage of selected arenas*

Apart from that, leadership is a dynamic process, in its nature competitive. Individual arenas naturally tend to believe that they should get more – and often qualitatively different – attention. Parliamentarians hanker for a mid-Victorian Golden Age, with citizens agog for every word of their debates. (But press coverage never was as good as it used to be.) Pressure groups elbow each other for leverage in the Whitehall and Westminster of the 1980s; political PR firms are a growing feature of the parliamentary scene.[19] By definition, pressure groups are sectional and self-interested, unlike parties, which thrive by finding common ground. Some groups, such as those with a clear focus of pressure and a limited category of membership, like the National Farmers' Union in its dealings with the Ministry of Agriculture, find media useful only for general public relations or leverage in a wider context like arguments about membership of the EEC. But for many groups whose chief or only weapon is the government's fear of public opinion or the wrath of its own backbenchers, media are indispensable. Certain social welfare groups, such as Shelter and the Child Poverty Action Group, have not had big organisations but existed, in a sense, largely in and through the press and the current affairs TV programmes. Pressure group leaders such as Des Wilson and Frank Field become specialists in publicity.

Again, where would CND be without the media? CND 1960-style was the first postwar movement to exploit the televisual potential of the march, perhaps drawing on the experience of popular protest at the Suez invasion in 1956. Marching *to* the Aldermaston nuclear weapons research establishment *from* London (1958) provided a less dramatic climax than going in the other direction, so from 1959 the tributaries of marchers swelled a stream that gushed to join the fountains in Trafalgar Square.[20] CND 1980-style worked in a more sophisticated TV age and against a background of TV images of the anti-Vietnam War movement in the USA. The symbolism of peace camps, of the Greenham Common women, of linking hands to encircle a nuclear base, involved a more subtle imagery than the steady trudge from Aldermaston.

CND would claim no more than other groups to get the media coverage it wants. Like the Labour Party, it is bound to feel that, regardless of the amount of its publicity, the content is unsympathetic. The nature, extent and causes of an anti-Labour bias in the press are too large a topic for inclusion here. But to put it simply in terms of arenas, Labour lacks reliably sympathetic arenas in the popular press corresponding to the Conservative broadsheets, the *Daily Telegraph* and *The Times*. Aside from straightforward partisan preferences, Labour might argue too that its leadership pyramid includes arenas such as the NEC and the party bureaucracy that are persistently underplayed by comparison with the parliamentary arena. (Conservative Central Office might also feel that it does not have the publicity which would reflect its true importance in the Party.)

Lastly, there are differing views within and between arenas about the extent of their *needs* for publicity. Senior civil servants are against publicity: the 'open government' lobby believe they should be exposed to more of it. Cabinet ministers are against publicity for the process of decision-making (except when a minister wishes to advance a particular cause by leaking, or defines his role generally as what Headey calls an 'Ambassador Minister') – but they are in favour of the 'right sort' of publicity for their actual decisions.[21] The 'open government' lobby, again, favours publicity for the decision-making too, in particular for the system of committees without which the Cabinet could not function at all.[22] Political parties want intense publicity during election campaigns and for their annual conferences. The Labour Party wants publicity stressing its ideological, collectivist character; the Conservatives, by comparison, are happier with the politics of personality and individualism. Small parties, the Liberals and SDP, want publicity as nourishment – to give them muscle to match their voting strength.

## Leadership within arenas

If the publicity for leadership arenas does not fit exactly what leaders want, what inferences may be drawn? Consider leadership first within particular arenas. The initial problem for the aspiring politician is actually to get into an arena recognised by media as political. For a subversive politician it might be desirable to work in stealth, but not for others. Sometimes people manage to turn a non-political arena into a political one: pressure groups, for instance, get politicised, as happened in the late 1960s with race relations groups and in the 1970s with some feminist organisations. Or a Peter Hain will arise and build a group like 'Stop the Seventies Tour' to exert political pressure (about sporting contact with South Africa) in a conventionally non-political arena. David Bellamy and others have succeeded comparably on environmental issues. For the young, the obvious path is to join an established organisation. For those who come to politics later – which often means people whose energies have been concentrated on a career in business – a sideways leap from business leadership to political leadership is attractive. For those the House of Lords is a desirable arena. For people hoping for more influence, a parliamentary seat is better. In either case, a preceding public leadership role must surely be a help not a hindrance: better still, perhaps, if one has a brand name of some kind such as Sainsbury or Ferranti.

A public leadership role is greatly assisted by regular access to media. Those few with the resources as well as the aspirations – Victor Matthews (*Express Newspapers*), 'Tiny' Rowland (*The Observer*) and

Robert Maxwell (the *Mirror Group*) being examples in the early 1980s – may buy into a newspaper. Cecil King tried hard to exert leadership – over the Prime Minister, Harold Wilson, as well as Labour and the electorate – from the boardroom of the *Mirror Group* in the 1960s. Broadcasting is less pliable. Controls on content make radio and TV, even now, less available than the press for fighting a political campaign.

In a more direct way than through ownership, however, media are often the base on which a political career is founded. Many a journalist has exercised political leadership without moving from the arena of his newspaper. One can quote a string of great editors such as A.G.Gardiner (*Daily News* 1902–21), C.P.Scott (*Manchester Guardian*, 1871–1929, though he moved into the parliamentary arena too for some years) and Geoffrey Dawson (*The Times* 1912–19, 1922–41) among the dailies, and J.L.Garvin (*The Observer*, 1908–42) and Kingsley Martin (*New Statesman*, 1930–60) among Sundays and weeklies.[23] In broadcasting, the leadership potential of interviewers such as Robin Day and Brian Walden – even of newscasters like Alistair Burnet – has been considerable since the days of Richard Dimbleby, whose apotheosis was fittingly reached in his hushed reporting of the Coronation ceremony in 1953. In a sense, it is recognised by the bestowal of honours (Sir Robin...).

In a rather different way, some broadcasting figures take on a populist and perhaps more potent, tribune-like role which echoes that of journalists like W.T.Stead and Horatio Bottomley. These are the people such as Gilbert Harding, Malcolm Muggeridge and Mary Whitehouse, whose skill lies in touching certain popular feelings or prejudices; and, in later versions, the likes of Esther Rantzen and Jimmy Saville, who 'fix things' literally or figuratively. In extreme cases such as Harding and Muggeridge, their familiarity on and with TV makes them almost 'office-holders' in that arena. The same might be said for the leaders of small parties such as the SDP. After 1983, media appearances made TV a kind of surrogate office for the SDP Leader, Dr David Owen.

Two points need stressing in this. First, leadership may be seen, from the viewpoint of media involvement, as a process of emergence, after someone has entered an arena. Media can help or hinder the process, for they provide other people in the arena with a gauge of a colleague's performance: they help build (or destroy) a reputation. Secondly, a Leader's emergence will be cemented, for media, if it culminates in office. As one would expect from the nature of news values and procedures, media have a very strong bias to office. Just as media attention may be a gauge of a Leader's success for his colleagues, so the attainment of office is a gauge of success for the media: 'Fleet Street talks of Ministers' end of term reports.'[24]

Office thus involves reciprocal licence: a licence for the holder to ex-pect publicity, and for the media to purvey it. It is a relation of ex-change. Office-holders – ministers, for instance – can predict that if they follow certain routines, such as press releases and conferences, speeches and travel, media will use them in their own routines. Media know, too, that conventions about the private person do not attach to the office-holder; that the minister's whole life, virtually, can be justi-fied as fair game. (Of course, the limits of the licence may be under constant criticism on either side. *Private Eye,* for one, lies at the boundary.)

On more practical ground, office often involves a wider range of ac-tivity than non-office-holding leadership. Office-holders running something – even the AA or the CBI, let alone a ministry – have some-thing to do. A recurring problem for the Leader of the Opposition is that, in this sense, he has little newsworthy to do at all. When the Com-mons are not sitting, he lacks even the floor of the House as a regular focus of attention. That is one of the attractions of travel for Party Leaders out of office. If you cannot run a government yourself, it is no bad thing to visit people who do. In building his public image, it was important for Neil Kinnock to be seen, however briefly, mingling with Leaders in Washington and the Kremlin. Opposition Party Leaders flocked to the Kremlin for the domino obsequies of Brezhnev, Andropov and Chernenko in 1982–85. (Dr Owen, indeed as a medic, was able to give early intelligence of Chernenko's medical condition at Andropov's funeral.)

The non-office-holder must find some other licence if he is to attract publicity which will help him to emerge as a leader in his arena. With-out it, publicity will seem fortuitous or irrelevant to his ambitions. He will be liable to the Vanessa Redgrave effect. In addition, moreover, he will have to overcome (or adjust to) at least two other features of media coverage of politics.

The first of these barriers is a *stereotype/individual* continuum. It is linked to the particular news value according to which people become newsworthy if they are unpredictable within a certain range of what is expected. A classic example is the emergence of Ken Livingstone, whose early coverage as Leader of the Labour-controlled GLC in 1981 depicted him as the latest in a tradition of left-wing bogeymen – 'Red Ken'. The first personal tabs of identity seemed the result of a groping by news media for the elements of personality: a frenetic 'Livingstone the newt-lover' phase. A fuller personality emerged, largely as the re-sult of regular appearances in TV and radio arenas; but politically the stereotype endured for several years.[25] On a collective level, the same comment may be made about a whole group such as the Green Party. Entering the arena of parliamentary politics in some force in the general election of 1979, the Party acquired a licence to media attention. But who on earth were they? In the course of the campaign some of the answers became clear. Early on, however, journalists appeared to work to a rather 1940ish stereotype of bearded poets and vegetarians, with perhaps a touch of naturism.[26]

Collectivist values reinforce the stereotype tendency. There is a *collective/individual* continuum which is a similar barrier for an emergent leader. The Conservative, Labour and Alliance Parties each, in their distinctive ways, attach a value to *collective* leadership. This is partly a matter of group dynamics and the aggregative nature of the political party in a parliamentary system; partly, for Labour, of a collectivist ideology (reflected strongly in its rhetoric and its self-image as a 'movement'); and partly of response to a collective Executive in government – the Cabinet. The Prime Minister herself is technically no more than 'first among equals'. In a parliamentary arena, the discipline sustained by party competition acts equally as a general brake on individualism. Civil servants, too, operate in a collectivist departmental organisation and retain public anonymity. More than anyone else in the world of government and politics, surely, the civil servant is subject to a grey and featureless stereotype.

The aspiring parliamentarian, then, is subject to a range of pressures towards uniformity. Their effect must be all the stronger because the media bias to office, and the news value of personalisation, mean that publicity in fact focuses quite disproportionately (looked at from the parties' point of view) on each individual Party Leader. This is true for Cabinet, Opposition and minor parties alike, and between elections and at them. If the Shadow Cabinet spokesman on, say, Agriculture, does not carry instant recognition he (or she) can take comfort from the fact that the Minister does not either.[27]

Where, then, may the aspiring parliamentarian find his 'licence' for publicity? He can seek, first, some modest office within the parliamentary arena: chairmanship – even simple membership – of one of the more newsworthy select committees, such as Foreign Affairs or Defence. He may be lucky in the ballot for Private Members' Bills; exploit the procedural opportunities for publicity, like 'Question Time'. (But in all this he must remember that publicity can be counterproductive to his reputation.) Secondly, he can seek to turn the Vanessa Redgrave effect to advantage: for reputation in a non-political arena can sometimes help to build a reputation in a political one. (Most of the Workers Revolutionary Party candidates in 1979, after all, did not get as much publicity even as Vanessa Redgrave.) Still today, many parliamentarians have a distinguished background in some other occupation, which helps to pick them out in the Westminster crowd. Increasingly this may include connections with pressure groups – across a far wider spectrum than the trade union movement, which formerly would have been the chief example.

There is also a process by which a Leader can emerge through assumption of a kind of informal 'office'. While Edward Heath was toiling to assert his authority as Conservative Leader after Harold Wilson's runaway electoral victory in 1966, the veteran Conservative Minister, Duncan Sandys, became known as 'Shadow Leader of the Opposition' because of his more effective Commons manner. Again, Westminster seems still to be a place where age is credited with wisdom. 'Prime Minister emeritus' seems to be an office recognised by media, with ready attention given in the 1980s to Lord Stockton (Harold Macmillan), Lord Home, Lord Wilson and Mr Heath. An elderly politician such as Lord Shinwell (long before his hundredth birthday) can attract far kindlier attention than in his days of political vigour. Moreover, the elements of leadership may be acquired, in the form of media attention, by a certain distancing from one's party. If a group looks like joining hands, media will be quick to give it a name – making a whole new arena. What were the 'Gang of Four' – Roy Jenkins, David Owen, Bill Rodgers, Shirley Williams – if not office-holders in a new arena, which duly broke off formally from Labour to launch their own party in 1981? The collectivist urge in party politics is always subject to counterpressure in which, because of its context, the line between dissent and disloyalty is often fine and contested. Whether a group remains informal ('Wets', 'Bennites') or is institutionalised like Francis Pym's Conservative Centre Forward group in 1985, or the endless series of groups in and around the Labour Party, faction will be seized on by the media. It is a truism, too, that Party Leaders frequently have in their background, as did Churchill, Macmillan and Wilson, episodes of rebelliousness which are as much a manifestation of leadership as is later loyalty. Westminster provides plenty of opportunities for symbolic distancing (including a vote against one's party, though not all are so explicit as that). So, too, does Cabinet membership. Tony Benn gave a masterly performance in remaining a Minister in Jim Callaghan's Cabinet while signalling effectively to media his reservations about important aspects of its policies. The original 'Wets' in Mrs Thatcher's government were Cabinet Ministers, though progressively they were weeded out.

Political arenas obviously vary enormously. What goes for Westminster may not go for others. But the importance of office, formal or informal, and the need to acquire a 'licence' to publicity are surely common factors.

## Multiple arenas and movement between arenas

It should be clear from some of the preceding discussion that media can be extremely important in interpreting leadership in one arena to people in others. Not only do media provide a gauge of someone's reputation for colleagues in the same arena: they provide a gauge for people elsewhere. Thus media interpret the doings of Cabinet Ministers to Members of Parliament; Members of Parliament to constituency activists; trade union leaders to their members, and so on. In some circumstances, such as the definition of a crisis and the evaluation of leaders' crisis-management, media seem to be especially critical – not least because the aftermath of crisis tends to bring Leaders exaggerated rewards or punishments (Churchill in 1945 is a perverse example).

Put another way, the linkage of arenas by media extends a Leader's grasp. Political advancement generally involves moving from one arena to another, either literally – for instance, by becoming an MP as well as a local councillor – or in terms of one's familiarity and reputation elsewhere. The hierarchy of Figure 1.2 could be viewed somewhat like a game of hopscotch, or perhaps of *Monopoly*, where leaders successively enter arenas which increase their scope for publicity.

In some of the changes media play an open, almost formal part. The party election broadcasts are a clear example, regulated as they are by party agreement, with the electoral law in the background. Ritual press publicity, like the publication in full of the major party manifestos (Question: how much space will minor parties get?) has been a formality over many elections. No one knows precisely what difference media make to general election outcomes.[28] But it is hard to believe they make no difference at all. More indirectly, considerations of candidates' media performance increasingly affect the party electorates' choices of their own Leaders. These electorates have been limited, historically, to comparatively small elite groups. Now they have widened beyond Westminster, quite substantially in the Labour case; and, as one commentator puts it: 'the new electoral "colleges" are bound to prefer the witness of their own eyes and of the TV screen to the nudges and winks of the party Establishment.'[29] Neil Kinnock was a product of this preference. So was David Owen – a very effective broadcaster, chosen (by a system of one member one vote in the SDP) to succeed a political heavyweight, Roy Jenkins, who had shown in the 1983 election that he was not a master of the new media techniques.

Many MPs, too, have based their move into the parliamentary arena directly on their performance in a media arena – not content, as the Days and Burnets have been, purely with a media role. (Day stood as a Liberal candidate before his broadcasting career was launched). Brian Walden of *Weekend World*, and Matthew Parris his successor, as well as Robert Kilroy Silk, made the move in the contrary direction, stepping from a parliamentary career to that of interviewer. Day's colleague as a pioneer ITN newscaster, Chris Chataway, who also had a national reputation in a non-political arena as an Olympic athlete, moved into Parliament and then quickly to government office. More recent examples are Austin Mitchell, who made a name for himself on Yorkshire TV and won Grimsby after Anthony Crosland's death in 1977, and the Liberal MP, Clement Freud.

Since media coverage is part of the environment in which political leaders operate, much of its influence is likely to be indeterminate and long term. But there is also a distinct catapult effect. A burst of publicity in one arena can catapult someone into another. Labour's victory in the GLC elections catapulted Ken Livingstone to national fame and gave him access to arenas such as radio and TV talk programmes. (Within eighteen months he was second only to the Pope in BBC Radio 4's 'Man of the Year' poll.)[30] The miners' strike of 1984 – 85 catapulted Arthur Scargill into the media. The Falklands War made the names of services chiefs like Lord Lewin familiar to the public: Lewin was even trailed as a possible Defence Minister after the event.[31] An earlier conflict in 1967 in Aden, one of the last of Britain's decolonisation emergencies and the first covered prominently by TV, made a public figure out of Colonel 'Mad Mitch' Mitchell. He was catapulted into Parliament on the strength of it and headed a campaign to 'Save the Argyll and Sutherland Highlanders' from disbandment as part of Ministry of Defence economies.

In reverse, the catapult works more like a firing squad. Publicity can destroy a political career overnight. 'The press lives by exposure,' wrote a nineteenth-century editor of *The Times;* and a politician can die by exposure. 'Investigative journalism' helped to procure the resignation of the Conservative Minister Reginald Maudling in 1972. A single indiscretion to a journalist about the contents of the Budget he would be delivering the same afternoon cost Hugh Dalton his position as Chancellor of the Exchequer in 1947.[32] For an example from a by-election, one could not do better than quote the extremely critical media treatment of Peter Tatchell, Labour candidate at the Bermondsey by-election in 1983. This seemed likely to have torpedoed his hopes of a parliamentary career for the indefinite future. Some of the most dramatic political downfalls have involved sexual indiscretion – the resignations of John Profumo (War Minister, 1963), Lord Jellicoe (Lord Privy Seal, 1973), Lord Lambton (Air Force Minister, 1973), Cecil Parkinson (Trade and Industry, 1983), the Liberal Leader Jeremy Thorpe (1976), and most recently Jeffrey Archer (Deputy Chairman of the Conservative Party, 1986). Indeed Archer's downfall was not so much exposed by the press, as engineered by it, as *The News of the World* suggested to a prostitute that she should induce Archer to offer her money. Such downfalls do not necessarily remove people from leadership arenas altogether (Dalton, Maudling and Parkinson remained MPs, for example). It can be a relative decline.

The more arenas a leader occupies, the greater would one expect his publicity to be. Whether this implies a greater scope for *managing* his publicity is less certain. One of the problems of TV in the early days of its expansion of political coverage was that its audience, especially for the news, was fairly undifferentiated in social, economic and educational terms, compared with the daily press. Harold Wilson committed possibly his most memorable gaffe by attempting to make the consequences of sterling devaluation in 1967 comprehensible to the ordinary viewer. It would not mean that 'the pound in the pocket is worth 14 per cent less to us now than it was this morning,' he suggested.[33] Well, yes: in a sense. Tabloid journalists are adept at putting across specialist topics in print to a lay readership. For prime ministers, on TV, it is more chancey.

That is only one type of problem – and one which the diversification of channels and specialist programmes has probably lessened in the 1980s, though it had an echo in the the *Belgrano* row, which for some people was as much an issue of presentation and veracity as of whether the ship should actually have been sunk at all. Access to a range of arenas must provide opportunities for selection, and for targeting the right audience with the right rhetoric. Party conferences typically evoke fraternity and upbeat rhetoric. Labour Leaders parade working-class credentials (inherited or acquired); Conservatives bay after such issues as law and order. Yet neither conference looks quite as comfortable on the TV as in the hall. What seems rousing in the hall may seem rant on the small screen. Well-meant conventions of address ('Comrades...!') may sound spurious. Clothes may look wrong. (Gordon Reece is said to have told Mrs Thatcher to avoid being interviewed on TV wearing a hat.) If media bring different arenas too close together, in other words, the problem of managing publicity to best effect may be worsened. It can be solved sometimes by 'isolating' a passage which is intended particularly for TV consumption in a hustings or conference speech. Party Leaders learned such knacks in the 1960s – and they were one of the reasons why the Commons were so reluctant to risk letting in TV cameras. Sound broadcasting of the Commons has shown in the obtrusiveness of the background noise and the styles of interruption, how communication that is normal in one arena can sound incongruous in another.

Access to multiple arenas, then, brings costs as well as benefits. But surely any Leaders in the 1980s who do not actively try to manage their communication show either a blind-spot about the intrusiveness of media into politics or a blind optimism about their public image.

**Conclusions**

So what does the bulging plastic bag contain? Analysis in terms of arenas and stages of leadership gives us none of the specific answers which we truly want to know. How can Neil Kinnock overcome the bias Labour alleges in a Tory press? How can a complex ideology be put across on TV? Does the 'street politics' of an organisation like the National Front find a natural ally in the TV camera? In general, do modern media make leadership easier or more difficult than when the press was dominant? How far can leaders control their public communication, and how far, rather, are their behaviour and public images shaped by media?

As the introduction suggested, most such questions, including the most specific, lead to intrinsically uncertain answers because of the difficulty of isolating media as a separate variable. Even supposing it could be established to the satisfaction both of the friends and enemies of Tony Benn and Arthur Scargill, for instance, that their treatment by media was at odds with the treatment they would like, it would still remain to be established whether their leadership goals were in fact advanced or hindered by such treatment; and leadership goals are rarely, if ever, so precisely limited that such a question could expect a definite answer. Questions in media research – certainly, one might say, the interesting ones – are subject only to approximate answers.

Such a disclaimer provides a useful excuse to end with some sweeping assertions, clothed for the sake of decency as questions.

Are media (chiefly TV) becoming an increasingly important arena of political leadership (that is, an arena in their own right, in addition to reporting activity in other arenas)? It is a commonplace, for instance, that the presidential election process in the USA, including the key element of candidate evolution, has become dominated by TV. Is TV becoming a prime factor in the evolution of Party Leaders here? If Home was the first Leader indirectly retired by TV, was Kinnock the first indirectly created by TV?

At all levels of leadership, including pressure groups and parliamentary candidacies, are the new arenas of TV accentuating the role of media in the crucial period of the informal emergence of leadership which precedes a move into office (in the same or a new arena)?

Is it true that, with the exception of a firing-squad effect, media have less influence on the unmaking of leaders than on their making? Or is the influence just more difficult to detect?

Do media undervalue the political significance of arenas that do not describe themselves as explicitly political? One does not have to be a Marxist to believe they do. The implications vary with the arena, but it presumably follows that the routes to political leadership are more numerous than might be supposed. Politicians themselves now seem more ready than twenty years ago to appear in non-political arenas such as radio and TV chat shows. Harold Wilson's appearance with (fortunately not in) England's World Cup team on the victory night in 1966 was much noted at the time and may have been something of a landmark.

Are media causing a decline in the political party as anything but an election-fighting machine and parliamentary caucus? In other words, is party a less important leadership arena than in the days before TV and the growth of pressure groups? If parties *are* in decline, the causes are complex, but the ability of leaders to reach people through media arenas and without intermediary organisations seems likely to be one of them.

Is TV, with its emphasis on visual content and its clumsiness at expressing complex ideas in a form that can be digested and retained, turning leadership more and more into a business of symbolic and expressive behaviour, with managerial and policy matters made inconspicuous?

In the same way, do modern media encourage ever more emphasis on the presentation of leadership decisions and goals (by a prime minister or opposition leader, for instance) and less, comparatively, on the substance? The probability of a policy being successfully implemented is presumably always a factor in calculations about whether that policy should be adopted. If implementation depends upon its proper understanding by those responsible for implementing it, then presentation can never be entirely ignored in considerations about substance.[34] The suggestion here is that TV is making these considerations stronger.

Is it too sweeping to claim that the characteristics of some arenas make a better fit than others with the content 'needs' of media? The contrasting suitability of ideological left-wing minor parties to TV with that of the Fascist National Front has been suggested. Here is a longer list, arbitrarily chosen and not exclusively political:

| *Affinity to TV medium* | |
|---|---|
| Positive | Negative |
| Prime Minister and Cabinet | Opposition Leader and Shadow Cabinet |
| Army | Civil Service |
| Police | Crime |
| Personality-based parties and pressure groups | Policy-based parties and groups |
| Defence policy arenas | Economic policy arenas |
| Management and employers | Trade unions |
| Archbishops and bishops | Theological issues |
| Applied sciences, transplant surgry etc. | Theological sciences |
| Snooker, tennis, football | Rifle-shooting, bridge |

Finally, is not political leadership, in general, a constant struggle by leaders against misunderstanding?

A list of such questions could go on interminably, ending this chapter with a gradual fade-out. That would not be inappropriate to the theme. 'Media and political leadership' is a subject of enormous scope. If it is to be tackled at all, it must either be piecemeal, through detailed studies of persons and events, or it must involve some schematic analysis. But the latter, as here, will offer only tentative answers. They must be squashed into a plastic bag: for nothing tidier is practicable.

## Notes

1. Ian Gilmour, *The Body Politic*, London: Hutchinson, 1969, p.78.
2. For general accounts, see James Curran and Jean Seaton, *Power Without Responsibility*, 2nd edn, London: Methuen, 1985; Colin Seymour-Ure, *The Political Impact of Mass Media*, London: Constable, 1974.
3. The housewife's question (about the *Belgrano*) is described in Tam Dalyell, MP, *Thatcher's Torpedo*, London: Cecil Woolf, 1983, p. 79.
4. Jeremy Tunstall, *The Media in Britain*, London: Constable, 1983, contains a variety of data on audiences.
5. On the Lobby correspondent system, see Jeremy Tunstall, *The Westminster Lobby Correspondents*, London: Routledge, 1970; Michael Cockerell *et al.*, *Sources Close to the Prime Minister*, London: Macmillan, 1984; Colin Seymour-Ure, *The Press, Politics and the Public*, London, Methuen, 1968; Marcia Williams, *Inside Number Ten*, London: Weidenfeld and Nicolson, 1972.
6. For the history of Downing Street news operations, see James Margach, *The Abuse of Power*, London: W.H.Allen, 1978; Cockerell, *op.cit.*; Royal Institute of Public Administration, *The Government Explains*, London: Allen and Unwin, 1965.
7. Max Atkinson, *Our Masters' Voices*, London: Methuen, 1984, pp.111-23.
8. Michael Crick, *Scargill and the Miners*, Harmondsworth: Penguin Books, 1985.
9. Michael Foot, *Another Heart and Other Pulses*, London: Collins, 1985; Tony Benn, *The Need for a Free Press*, Nottingham: Institute for Workers' Control,1979.
10. Colin Seymour-Ure, 'The SDP and the Media', *Political Quarterly*, 53.4, 1982, p.433-42; Ian Bradley *Breaking the Mould?*, Oxford: Martin Robertson, 1981.
11. Colin Seymour-Ure, 'The Press and the Party System Between the Wars', in Gillian Peele and Chris Cook (eds), *The Politics of Re-Appraisal 1918 – 39*, London:Macmillan, 1975.
12. Clive Ponting, *The Right to Know*, London, Sphere Books, 1985.
13. An anthropologist might point out here that some societies, such as the Nuer, have had no formal leadership roles and explicit idea of selective political office at all. E.E. Evans-Pritchard, *The Nuer*, London: Oxford University Press, 1940.
14. There is a large literature on leadership. All that is needed for this chapter is a simple working definition. The one chosen is derived from K.Lang, in J.Gould and W.L.Kolb (eds), *Dictionary of the Social Sciences*, London: Tavistock, 1964, p.380.
15. Seymour-Ure, *The Political Impact of Mass Media*, ch.4.
16. Colin Seymour-Ure and Adrian Smith, 'Prophets and Wildernesses', in Robert M.Worcester and Martin Harrop (eds), *Political Communications*, London: Allen and Unwin, 1982.
17. David Butler and Dennis Kavanagh, *The British General Election of 1983*, London: Macmillan, 1984.
18. A useful categorisation of news values is in the much anthologised article by J.Galtung and M.H.Ruge, 'The Structure of Foreign News', *Journal of International Peace Research*, 1, 1965, reprinted in Jeremy Tunstall (ed.), *Media Sociology*, London: Constable, 1970.

19.  Grant Jordan, 'Parliament Under Pressure', *Political Quarterly* 56.2, 1985, pp.174-82.
20.  Christopher Driver, *The Disarmers*, London: Hodder and Stoughton, 1964.
21.  Bruce Headey, *British Cabinet Ministers*, London: Allen and Unwin, 1974, ch.11. He puts Ernest Marples and Tony Benn in this category.
22.  The flourishing 'open government' literature includes, recently, James Michael, *The Politics of Secrecy*, Harmondsworth: Penguin Books, 1983; David Leigh, *The Frontiers of Secrecy*, London: Junction Books, 1980; Ponting, *op.cit.*; K.G.Robertson, *Public Secrets*, London: Macmillan, 1982.
23.  See respectively Stephen Koss, *Fleet Street Radical*, London: Allen Lane, 1973; David Ayerst, *Guardian*, London: Collins, 1971; John Evelyn Wrench, *Geoffrey Dawson and Our Times*, London: Hutchinson, 1962; D.Ayerst, *Garvin of the Observer*, London: Croom Helm, 1984; Kingsley Martin,*Editor*, London: Hutchinson, 1968.
24.  Sir John Hoskyns, 'Conservatism is not Enough', *Political Quarterly*, 55.1, 1984.
25.  Andrew Forrester *et al.*, *Beyond Our Ken*, London: Fourth Estate, 1985, esp.ch.3.
26.  Worcester and Harrop. *op.cit.*
27.  The fullest analysis of Opposition remains R.M.Punnett, *Front-Bench Opposition*, London: Heinemann,1973.
28.  For a useful introductory discussion of the electoral impact of mass media, see the essay by Denis McQuail in James Curran *et al.*, *Mass Communication and Society*, London: Edward Arnold, 1977.
29.  David Watt, *The Times*, 18 February 1983.
30.  Forrester, *op. cit.*
31.  *The Guardian*, 17 November 1982.
32.  Ben Pimlott, *Hugh Dalton*, London: Jonathan Cape, 1985.
33.  Harold Wilson, *The Labour Government 1964 – 70*, Harmondsworth, Penguin Books, 1974, pp.588-9.
34.  It is interesting that in 1984 the same person, Nell Myers, doubled as NUM press officer and as Arthur Scargill's personal assistant, sitting in on some of the negotiations with the Coal Board. Crick, *op.cit.* p.130.

# 2 Class
## *Howard Davis*

The language of class is anything but fashionable. Current political rhetoric assumes that class vocabulary and interests are obsolete. The rise and fall of party fortunes, the spread of new social movements, mass consumption of goods and entertainment are all regularly taken to indicate the erosion of class and class cultures. While class has never ceased to be a fundamental category in social theory, the social analysis of inequality, power and conflict has tended to adopt a narrower focus in recent years. Thus, problems of the labour process and changing division of labour have diverted attention away from some of the macro-level issues of class structure. Interpreters of political trends are also less inclined to explain attitudes or voting patterns in terms of clearly defined class interests. This is equally true in studies of politics and the influence of mass media. Very rarely do researchers find a use for the category of social class except in the most limited and descriptive sense of socio-economic groups. Without denying the problems associated with 'class' analysis in the fuller, structural sense, my purpose in this chapter is to give directions for a possible synthesis of social analysis and media research which would enhance the explanatory potential of the concept. A full reinstatement would, of course, require a much more elaborated theoretical framework and a substantial amount of empirical evidence gathered for the purpose.

To explain the continuing importance of social class relations for the subject of politics and the media in Britain requires two types of argument. The first is about the persistence of class structure and the ways in which the media are implicated in it through patterns of ownership, control, production and consumption. There is no general agreement that class is relevant at all. Some traditions of media research such as those which feed off the image of a 'mass society' have never acknowledged it to be important; but even those which stem from classical Marxism have increasingly concentrated on the production and content of messages to the neglect of their reception by different social groups. Indeed, some perceive that the kind of critical research which does in principle recognise the importance of social structure has allowed the audience to all but disappear from its agenda.[1] Fortunately, however, the case for class analysis of both society and the media has been made elsewhere and need not be repeated here.[2]

The second type of argument, which is developed in this chapter, concerns the mechanism by which class culture and relationships are maintained, reinforced, eroded or transformed by the consumption of media. The techniques of communication analysis which can be applied to this problem have developed to a point where the complex processes of mediation at the individual and family level are to some extent understood. For instance, the relationships between an individual's media use and voting behaviour during an election campaign can be related to past history and to the immediate social context.[3] It does not follow, however, that media influence is bounded by categories such as age, gender and occupation. The more fully these are understood, the more it becomes clear that they are pieces of a social puzzle which can only be reconstructed by means of a theory of society which incorporates a theory of information and communication. While recognising the importance of such a project, the aim of this chapter is far less ambitious: to point to ways in which the question of media and social class might be reinstated by reflecting on the results of studies of class attitudes and awareness on the one hand, and selected audience studies on the other.

The starting assumption is that in a class society such as Britain the media contribute substantially to the maintenance of the class system. It would be strange indeed if the major instruments of social communication did not exist in parallel and interlocking relationships with other institutions. To think of the media as apart from society, as though they were neutral channels conveying messages on behalf of others, is no less simplistic than ascribing neutrality to the education or legal system. The opposite view, that media are merely the instruments of some other agency, be it government, a cultural elite or a 'dominant class', is equally naive and unconvincing. The problems of coordinating such a conspiracy on a day-to-day basis are probably insoluble in any complex society with a substantial amount of public accountability and democracy.

The real problem depends on the character of the media as major social institutions which for economic and cultural reasons have to interpret society to maximum achievable audiences. In doing so, they must communicate with sections of the audience whose views and perceptions are not necessarily congruent with those in the media who interpret social and political phenomena. Some media, notably the press, are highly differentiated in terms of their appeal to particular sections of society and these differences can be minimised, but television and radio are far less so. In these cases, the sharpest issues arise for both media and audiences at significant boundary areas in the class structure, where there is ideological uncertainty (e.g. over the legitimacy of strikes) and where the structure of society itself becomes a matter for media attention (e.g. when the future of welfare or the subject of law and order are under discussion).

To grasp how the media both mediate and contribute to the shaping of social class relations, it is necessary to know some of the factors which contribute to social consciousness and to class identity in particular. Ethnographic studies and survey data have led researchers to conclude that specifically working-class cultural forms have diminished in scope and importance in the decades since the Second World War. 'Class cultures', whether of the working class, bourgeoisie or the elite, are not to be taken as perfect expressions of 'objective class interests' but as specific, lived experience of social structures and relationships in a particular locality. Various of these forms have been documented at some length.[4] The attempts which have been made to map changes in class cultures and life-styles in the post-war period have led to two general conclusions: that class consciousness as such is rarely found, but that there are some consistent variations in social consciousness and imagery between different levels in the social structure; and that the changes which have occurred are closely related to the transformation of the industrial and occupational structure.[5]

The argument has been that the conditions of work and community which were the basis for occupational identity, solidarity, class imagery and other elements of class culture have been steadily undermined by changes in material living conditions. A secondary argument is that the media have come to occupy an increasingly large part of the increasingly 'privatised' space in which personal relationships are structured. One of the key problems in identifying the media's role in this is to relate their extensive, undifferentiated and unselective penetration into the private sphere to the general conditions of social consciousness which make their messages relevant at all.

The most fundamental ingredient of social consciousness is identity. Social identity has been variously conceived as being a sense of self in relation to an 'external' social order, a frame for interpreting personal experiences, or a 'grid' which describes the set of social relationships upon which one has 'drawing rights'. They all refer to the understanding which people have of the fragments of personal and social experience and the ways in which they assemble them into meaningful patterns. Work, or more precisely, the division of labour and relations within the production process, sets fundamental conditions for social identity and the construction of social consciousness. It explains, for example, why there is a close relationship between occupational position and social standing. Yet patterns of working in paid employment are being transformed continuously through the application of new technology, pressures of competition and changes in managerial technique.

In recent years, high rates of unemployment and job dislocation in virtually every industrial sector have removed the prospect of a continuous career in one occupation or locality for most workers. The other side to the continuous evolution of the economic system is the changing pattern of work in the informal and domestic spheres. Formerly, in situations of relative occupational stability, certain aspects of experience and occupational career tended to find spontaneous 'commonplace' and 'clichéd' expression in conversations and interviews. These expressions may be interpreted as indicators of workers' consciousness, occupational ideologies or even class sentiment. For Popitz in the 1950s in Germany, these commonplace 'Topics' as he called them included technological change and unemployment and they were articulated in characteristic metaphors and turns of phrase among the steelworkers he studied.[6] Others subsequently found similar evidence of recurring themes in a range of working-class communities.[7] More recently, there have been attempts to examine possible Topics like the 'fair wage' or the 'right to work'.[8] While some of the findings echo earlier studies, there is evidence of a long-term decline in the extent to which these Topics embrace society-wide issues and judgements. Empirical studies regularly disclose what appears to be the 'inconsistency', the 'inchoateness' or the 'indeterminacy' of working-class images of society. Such studies do not provide sufficient empirical evidence to show whether this can be attributed to the gradual replacement of working-class cultures and consciousness with something less well defined, but the specific implications for social identity are clear: there has been a loss of identity based on work achievement and performance, particularly among those occupations or groups which hitherto involved traditional skills and close-knit social networks.

The counterpoint to this 'fragmentation' and 'disintegration' is the consolidation and strengthening of the means which the organisers of industrial and other kinds of work have at their disposal to ensure discipline and integration of the workforce. As conceived in contemporary analyses of the labour process, this is achieved through the ever more systematic application of scientific, rational methods to the organisation and control of labour. With the current crisis of low profitability it is unlikely that employers will cease to use whatever means are available to motivate their employees. What is significant for workers' identity about this counter-trend is that the aspects of the social division of labour and occupational skill which provide a basis for self-esteem and for making legitimate claims on the rest of society are being continuously replaced by a technical division of labour and nexus of relationships which have far fewer possibilities for identity construction. In short, the world of work and occupations provides increasing evidence of a contrast between diversification in the 'grid' or frame of reference for personal and social identity construction and increasing consolidation of the system of managerial and social control.

However, in a complex society there is no single key to identity. Although ethnicity, religion and class sentiment may sometimes be jointly expressed through work and occupational communities, the individual does not normally find identity with any single institution or set of relationships but with several. Identities can be multiple, involving not just work but the family, politics, religion, ethnicity and so on. The question of whether these other sources of identity have more stability than is currently found in the sphere of work has to be considered. The conjugal family, for example, is an enduring social institution according to the evidence of high rates of marriage and re-marriage, the predictable patterning of roles within the family, the failure of most 'alternative' familial arrangements and the persistence of patriarchal authority. Yet alongside these and other indicators of continuity and stability of the family as a source of sexual and social identity, there is another theme: the state of turbulence in values and popular thinking about the family. The symbols, models and meanings of marriage, sex and family life have become more blurred and conflicting as the processes which are commonly described by the shorthand 'privatisation' have developed. Thus, the family, like work, would appear to have become a less stable and viable model for identity construction.

In broad outline, political and administrative tendencies also bear some resemblance to those in the realm of work and the family. Here the main disjunction is between the symbolic system which defines political interests or the field of political activity, and the powerful institutions of the modern state which ostensibly serve these political objectives. The growth of the modern state has ensured the spread of bureaucratic influence and the incorporation of the public sphere of economic, social and cultural life into a single state bureaucratic system. Moreover, the means of social control available to the state are increasingly effective. On the other hand, there has been a decline in bipartisan politics and relatively predictable patterns of attitudes and voting behaviour which rest on simple distinctions and consistent views on a wide range of issues. This may not be anything as dramatic as the 'crisis of legitimation' which some have diagnosed, but a general dissolution of the motivational structure which until recently provided a secure link between political identity and the political system.[9] The implication is that unless the nation-state itself, or the 'national interest' become objects of collective identification, as they did during the Falk-

lands War and in the Conservative government's strategy to fight in-
flation, the search for political identity is likely to be inconclusive or
essentially individualistic.

In such a world, where community and collectivity carry less weight,
and where the most potent symbols of success are goods, the processes
of private consumption clearly provide materials for the construction of
social as well as personal identity. The world of goods is not simply the
means to satisfy individual needs, be they material or non-material, but
is part of an attempt to identify with, and impose sense on, the environment.[10] However, there is evidence to suggest that the capacity of material objects to signify in direct, unambiguous ways is diminishing.
This is not something to do with the properties of objects as such, but
the properties of the 'information system' of which they are a part. As a
system it has become increasingly complex, certainly, but there are
some signs that the social linkage which goods may provide is becoming
attenuated. Douglas, applying a concept of 'linkage' taken from economics, draws out the contrasts between consumption in the traditional
mining community of Ashton and consumption among the 'affluent
workers' of Luton in the 1960s.[11] In the first of these, the above-average
earnings of the Ashton miners did not lead to increased consumption of
goods. In fact, not all the workers were earning the same high level of
wages: only some (particularly face-workers underground) were in
highly-paid work for a period of their lives. The slightly unexpected
finding was that these years of relatively high wages did not lead to
significantly higher standards of consumption or investment in the
home. Instead the strong group identity of the miners (enhanced no
doubt by the geographical isolation and work experience in the pit) did
not encourage one person to adopt a superior standard of consumption
to others. If a miner had more disposable income, there were prescribed
ways of spending which did not threaten the basic equality within the
group. Thus we find the surplus (over and above the basis 'wage for the
wife') being used for social rather than individual purposes – much of it
being consumed in drink and public conviviality. In this community,
then, there was evidence of a strong 'social linkage' or network of involvement in consumption and relatively weak linkage to the wider information system of consumer goods.

Douglas takes the example of the Luton 'affluent workers' to illustrate the opposite tendency: low dependency on the group and relatively strong linkage of a purely 'technical' kind (i.e. access to a use of
resources without directly involving other groups or individuals). Consumer durables, furnishings and homes themselves are examples of this
type of consumption when it is pursued within the private, domestic
sphere. If the contrast between these two examples illustrates a general
trend from the former context of community where social linkages in

consumption are strong to the latter, privatised situation, there is good reason to suppose that the growth of domestic, unshared consumption coincides with a general decrease in the capacity of goods to provide a coherent social information system. With less direct consumer interaction and cross-referencing, the meaning as well as the consumption of goods will become more private and less usable in the construction of social identity. Advertising will be directed more towards the creation and cultivation of individual, 'unique' identities than to already existing status models.[12]

The origins of social identity are now to be found, therefore, in the combination of these circumstances in the experiences of individuals and communities which tend towards fragmentation. Even a superficial examination, however, shows that there has been at the same time a tendency for the means of cultural and ideological production to become more concentrated and monolithic, notwithstanding the multiplicity and diversity of their products.[13] The point of this for the argument about class and the media is that these tendencies in identity formation are likely to have affected the conditions of receptivity of audiences for the broadcast media. The basic facts are these: the individual is likely to experience a greater number of institutions and role relationships in a lifetime, and to have access to a greater variety of templates or models for the organisation of social and psychological processes. In this situation there seems to be a potential for symbolic confusion, not to mention the dissolution of class cultures. However, this does not necessarily apply. The differentiation of audiences and the multiplicity of experiences of the receivers of mass communications and as constructors of identity is not synonymous with disintegration. Whether or not that occurs must depend to a large extent on what these audiences are receiving in the way of messages. These typically emanate from large-scale, centralised and structured cultural bureaucracies of which broadcasting is by far the most powerful. Thus, the dynamic of the present situation is that the proliferation of identity models coincides with the availability of technical and organisational means to cultural producers which are capable of being used to reintegrate audiences and recreate uniform models of identity.

If this is a correct description, and individual experience is replacing collective experience as the basic resource and reference point for images of the social order and political process, and if these images can no longer provide such a comprehensive and consistent action orientation as in the past, how far do the media simply reflect this variety in their search for audiences and how far do they provide alternative frameworks, deliberately or otherwise?

A great deal of analysis of media content in recent years has focused on television, the dominant medium, and has stressed the consistency

6000

of the frameworks of interpretation used, especially across the spectrum of informational programming. Other studies have analysed the pattern of 'flow' in programme schedules as a whole and have arrived at similar conclusions.[14] Taking news, news magazines, current affairs and documentary programmes, most of the major categories of television content have been studied in some depth including politics, economic and industrial affairs, foreign affairs, crime and deviance, health and social welfare.[15] These categories together normally account for a large proportion of the output of television news bulletins and there are additional thematic studies of portrayals of ethnic minorities or women, for example, which include some of the remainder. What is significant is that a whole range of studies based on a variety of working assumptions about the social impact of the media and offering different interpretations of selectivity, 'bias' and so on, speak with a similar voice about the content as such. Whether the terminology is that of systematic bias or distortion, agenda-setting, frameworks of interpretation, encoding or vocabularies of motive, the conclusion is generally the same: informational content is neither unmediated representation of facts and events nor is it a complex expression of the diversity and contradictoriness of the society it purports to describe. Instead, it is the predictably structured artefact of day-to-day professional practices. The processing of information by these means, which have all the marks of an industrial process, routinely resolves the variety and contradictions of the world into simple distinctions between violent and non-violent behaviour, normal and abnormal motives, law-abiding and criminal actions, good and bad, extreme and reasonable, etc. The positive side of these opposing sets is identified with the interests and perspectives of both the broadcasters and the audience. In general, these distinctions between 'them and us' in broadcast output are far less subtle than the so-called 'dichotomous' image of society found by researchers in some working-class communities.

In other types of informational programming such as documentary, feature and schools programmes, there is a similar tendency to look for the point of equilibrium within difference. By airing 'both sides' of an argument such programmes cancel out differences and secure support for one interpretation or meaning – that represented by the point around which the balance is secured. The centre is the point of reference although it is rarely articulated as such.[16] Where programmes deliberately abandon this equilibrium approach they are likely to encounter difficulties with broadcasting authorities, as examples from time to time show.[17] Programming which comes under the general heading of entertainment is not bound by the same conventions as informational and educational output. Here, processes of identification by members of the audience are crucial to the success of the programme. Whereas the 'need' for news may be assumed to arise in all sections of the audience, the possibilities of 'favourable' identification with fictional characters, personalities and presenters are more limited and have to be more carefully considered. There tends therefore, to be a more elaborated view of the audience among makers of these programmes than among producers of informational programmes. Because there is safety – both for audiences and producers – in simple dramatic structures with predictable outcomes, there is a powerful imperative to avoid complex forms, except in some minority programmes.

In this connection, it may be noted that, while audience ratings seem to matter to most broadcasters, their actual knowledge of the audience, even in terms of simple variables like age, class and sex, is usually very limited and their image of the audience is unsophisticated. It is usually based on formulas which owe more to tradition and professional mythology than to actual audience research.[18]

In the light of studies of both the structure (formal properties) and content of television programming and the patterns of 'flow' as a whole – which show that television viewing is understood by schedule planners to be a type of activity which is continuous and undetermined by the content of individual programmes – it can be concluded that the vicarious experiences which broadcasting provides are rendered far less complex than they might be.[19] While this is true of 'individual' experience depicted in personal relationships, it is even more true of collective experiences. In fact, the pattern of television output is such that in all areas of programming there are very high levels of redundancy, to use the information theory analogy. The range of identity models normally available to the viewer is narrow and their content is unambiguous, however exotic they may appear to be at first sight. One could go so far as to say that the TV channels which appeal to mass audiences have what amounts to a 'personality' which expresses a world-view and which has a consistency of orientation to the totality of programmes, not just to each one individually. This personality which dominates the output is masculine rather than feminine, white, middle-aged, middle-class, metropolitan and liberal pluralist in character.

A paradoxical effect of the amassing of content studies has been to call into question whether broadcasting output can actually be taken as a starting point or datum for other kinds of media analysis. The more that is understood about content, the more questions there are both about the production process and audience reception. Any questions about 'effects', 'ideological impact' and so on have to give an account of the relationships which may pertain between content and other aspects of the communication process. It would be mistaken to assume that evidence of consistency in media output is matched by similar consistency in the process of reception.

At a purely descriptive level, however, one thing does stand out clearly: that is, the stark contrast between the findings of research into social consciousness with their strong indication of the destructuring processes at work, particularly among the working class, on previously integrated social experience and identity, and the finding that the experiences and identity models mediated by broadcasting are highly coherent and consistent. Any attempt to integrate and interpret these discoveries has to take full account of the relevant research in both areas. At the same time, however, it must avoid the pitfalls of much behaviourist audience research, which assumes that the relation between messages and receivers depends on the properties of those two phenomena and that no reference to external factors is needed; and the equally reductionist tendency of some previous research into social consciousness which assumes that the link between experience and ideas can be made without explicit reference to those institutions like education and the media whose specific task is to mediate ideas to a wide public.

The definite progress which has been made in identifying structures, patterns and frameworks of interpretation in the content of contemporary media has not so far been matched by progress in reception studies, for conceptual rather than purely practical reasons, although these are considerable. In order to assert the relevance of the predominant explanatory frameworks, even quite detailed analyses of content have had to make assumptions about the audience which are essentially derived from the head-counting activities of in-house research. For example, the Glasgow Media Group's studies of television news made the reasonable assumption that news is important because of its centrality in the schedules, its high audience ratings, and the high levels of credibility which most audiences believe it has. But very little indeed is known about comprehension, learning, recall and the disposition to hear and see the message as intended by the programme makers. One approach to these questions, which have to be answered before other questions of class and the media can be properly addressed, is to develop a notion of 'receptivity' involving the social conditions which predispose audiences to respond in particular ways. Reception would not be particularly problematic if the conditions of receptivity were known and predictable, i.e. relatively stable over time and across the range of social groups. But if these conditions are inherently variable or unstable as the findings of research on social consciousness and sub-cultures would suggest they are, the problem of reception must loom large.

The limiting cases in a model or receptivity would be (1) the totally transparent message which is received and understood precisely according to the sender's explicit intention, and (2) the message which failed to reach any audience or was totally unintelligible because so poorly conceived and structured. But in between these hypothetical limits there are two further possibilities: (3) the well-conceived message which failed to communicate to some sections of its audience, and (4) the case of a highly receptive audience being fed with scarcely intelligible messages. This last case could be illustrated by many broadcasts from western sources to audiences in the Third World whose recognition, let alone understanding, of what is offered may be determined by quite other cultural assumptions. These hypothetical variations are the possibilities created by the intersection of two sets of circumstances which can be called 'message conditions' and 'conditions of receptivity', each defined according to whether these conditions are conducive to communication. Assuming that conditions are not normally either maximally positive or maximally negative, it is the (independent) variations in (3) and (4) which need to be explored more fully.

The communication and reception of information about one particular set of social relations has probably been studied in more detail than any other except party politics, namely industrial relations and industrial conflict. The sources include empirical studies by Blumler and Ewbank (1970), Hartmann (1975/76; 1979) and Morley (1980). For the purposes of analysis I shall begin by assuming that the 'message conditions' are stable (they are set by routinised procedures in large-scale, inflexible organisations) and are generally conducive to communication with a wide audience (in news reporting they are shaped by procedures which are designed to reduce complexity and minimise ambiguity). Accordingly, there is likely to be a 'preferred reading' of the message built into its linguistic and discourse components.[20] Conditions of receptivity, on the other hand, are assumed to be variable for the reasons given earlier. The extent of this variation is probably at its greatest between audiences for different types of 'minority' programme and least among audiences for the main news bulletins. With news, for example, there are large and apparently credulous audiences. Research indicates that broadcast news is seen by about 60 per cent of the population during the course of an average day; that most of this viewing is unselective; that news viewing varies to some extent by socio-economic position and age, so that older people in higher positions view more of this type of programme; and that the majority of all groups consider broadcast news to be accurate and trustworthy, whether or not they use other sources of news. However, such measures tell us little about the conditions of receptivity except that there is a high propensity to consume news among a large majority of the population. It tells us little about detailed variations through time or across classes – or, for example, why there has been a long-term decline in the BBC's 'trustworthiness' index. Short-term variations also require an explanation. According to IBA research, 73 per cent of viewers in 1984 believed that television in general provided fair and unbiased coverage of news and current affairs programmes. The corresponding figure for 1985 was 63 per cent.[21] How much are such variations influenced by political pressure and campaigns like that of Norman Tebbitt's against the BBC?

Against this background of a general inclination to receive news, Blumler and Ewbank's (1970) finding that trade unionists at all levels apart from the 'officials' are highly dependent on broadcast media for their information is not surprising; nor is Hartmann's (1979) confirmation that working-class audiences derive ideas on industrial relations from the media which run counter to the interpretations which have currency within trade union and working-class traditions. These authors are cautious in their interpretation, but they claim to find some support from these patterns of viewing for the idea that the media function to promote national consensus. Hartmann, however, acknowledged that 'media output may be interpreted or reinterpreted within subculturally derived perspectives' (1979,p.269). He explored the differences in perspectives on industrial relations between working and middle-class groups and related them to studies of industrial news. Views of industrial relations were not polarised along class lines and in fact media and audience perspectives were broadly congruent on many issues. However, he found this to be greatest among middle-class respondents. Working-class respondents were slightly more inclined to explain strikes in terms of economic causes, for instance, but the differences between samples were small. One possible indicator of the direction of media influence was the finding that working-class people who held views of a 'middle-class' kind (e.g. giving 'bad communication' as a cause of strikes) were more reliant on media information than others in the working-class sample.

The question of the relation between working-class culture and the media has been examined in more detail by members of the Birmingham Centre for Contemporary Cultural Studies (including Hall, Morley, Corrigan and Willis). In his influential theoretical paper on this subject, Hall addressed the problem through a discussion of the 'codes' (dominant, professional, negotiated, oppositional) which make the television discourse a complex process of meaning construction and not just a simple behavioural event.[22] This discussion is linked to a theory of class domination which originates in Marx but which in practice relies heavily on Parkin's categories of dominant, subordinate and radical 'meaning systems' or frameworks of social understanding (Parkin, 1972). In subsequent empirical research, Morley (1980; 1983) set out to clarify the processes of 'understanding' and 'misunderstanding' which intervene between content and the audience. He showed video-recordings of two 'Nationwide' news magazine programmes containing industrial and economic news to 29 small groups drawn from a variety of social and cultural backgrounds and initiated discussion of the contents to establish the degree of congruence between the referential frameworks of each group and the broadcasters' frameworks. The technique was to explore the vocabularies and schemata of the programmes and the group discussions. He found certain variations between groups which provide some basis for conjecture about the sources of identification and the symbolic resources they use in making sense of media messages. Morley gives as an example the contrasts in the 'decodings' made by groups of apprentices, trade unionists and shop stewards, and young black students at an FE college. Of the three, the apprentices group were the ones most inclined to accept the programmes at face value. The pattern of their discussion, which Morley describes as 'a form of populist discourse' was compatible with the patterns in the programmes. They described 'Nationwide's questions and interpretations as 'common-sense', 'natural' and 'pretty obvious'. The shop stewards spontaneously produced the most articulate and oppositional interpretation of the programme. They rejected the programme's attempt to construct a national identity ('us'; 'the problems facing the country'). At the same time Morley noted that the trade union officials were much more approving of the programme's stance. Discussion in the group of black students – or rather the relative lack of it – showed that there was little correlation between their concerns and cultural framework and the concerns and framework of the 'Nationwide' programme. Morley says, for instance, that they could find no point of identification within the programme's discourse even about problems as basic as those of families, because 'their particular experience of family structures is simply not accounted for'.

Morley interprets these findings in terms of the 'codes' and discourses which different sections of the audience inhabit, and their relation to the preferred (or dominant) manner in which the messages were initially encoded. He does not explore in depth the social factors which govern the distribution of codes between different sections of the audience although he does suggest that the differences between the shop stewards and trade union officials could be explained by the degree to which they are incorporated in formal organisational structures. While he is right to point out that social class position does not directly correlate with decodings, he found a range of difference between audiences which was not registered in earlier studies. In fact, the findings allow for an interpretation in terms of two class-related factors, namely the degree of involvement in the occupational system and the extent of participation in an organisational hierarchy. Where integration is high on both counts (among trade union officials and apprentices, for example) there is the greatest congruence between programmme and audience perspectives. Where integration is low on both counts (among

black students) one finds an almost total lack of congruence. The intermediate case of a high level of commitment to the occupational system
and low institutional integration may account for the shop stewards'
oppositional interpretation involving what might be called 'negative
identification' rather than complete dismissal. This interpretation finds
further support in the well-known fact that congruence (as measured by
the belief in impartiality and accuracy) is more likely to occur at an
abstract, general level than at a concrete, local level where matters relating to the viewer's immediate experience are under discussion.

There are grounds here for relating specific conditions of class and
social experience to variations in the decoding of media content. This is
not simply to say that there is some 'selectivity' in audience perceptions: that audiences hear or see what they want to hear or see because of a disposition to acquire certain types of knowledge (e.g. about
actors, not the roles they play) or a disposition to attend to the medium
only as a form of entertainment rather than for information or education. Selectivity of this kind is well known and documented in both
audience research and the 'uses and gratifications' approach which examines the psychological and social needs which people bring to the
listening and viewing experience. Rather, the approach through differ-
ential 'decodings' which takes a unit larger than the individual or the
domestic viewing group as the unit of analysis, opens up questions
about the conditions of receptivity in a more sociological than psychological way.

However, this approach, which is well illustrated in Morley's work
and which represents an important step towards an empirical understanding of class and the media, suffers from a major impediment. It
uses an unsophisticated notion of class which is oddly incongruent with
the often detailed and sensitive descriptions of actual milieux which
cultural studies have produced. For instance, Morley claims that the
variety of working-class frameworks of interpretation may be seen as
inflections of Parkin's dominant, subordinate (negotiated) or oppositional meaning systems. But this inhibits the conclusions which can
be drawn from the results. Only the most rudimentary typology of class
positions allows the statement that the three groups referred to above
'can all be said to share a common class position, but their decodings of
a television programme are inflected in different directions by the discourses and institutions in which they are situated'.[23] What Morley has
shown, in fact, is that the different collective experiences of at least
some working-class groups are significant and that they mediate their
reception of broadcast messages no less than the immediate circumstances of viewing. But there is no independent analysis of the 'discourses' and 'institutions' which give rise to these variations of their
class character.

The interpretation of class responses encounters difficulties when it starts from and returns to the 'moment of reception' as the object of analysis. The concept of 'code' (as in encoding and decoding) is partly responsible for this because it encourages an essentially metaphorical analysis of the linkages between culture and class. As Corner (1983) has pointed out, it is a way of linking media content, sub-cultures and class by implication when the method does not allow any stronger form of connection to be made. What is required is an independently derived empirical understanding of class cultures and class imagery. One of the strengths of the empirical study of social consciousness (unlike, say, the study of public opinion or audience research) has been its close attention to context, the relation between social experience and its conscious articulation. There is already in existence, therefore, a way of facilitating the convergence between studies of media imagery and images of society. It suggests that a sociologically-based notion of the conditions of receptivity might be developed in the following way in relation to broadcasting.

First, it needs to be based on the assumption that there is near-equality of access to the medium and that the core output of the medium is directed towards a mass audience and is not specifically targeted towards a great variety of sub-groups. These assumptions are not unreasonable, given the present high levels of TV ownership and use, and the continuous flow pattern of the output. How then do the conditions of receptivity vary? The suggestion was made earlier that much of the variation in Morley's sample can be accounted for by two main factors or types of integration: occupational integration and institutional participation. Without much modification these can stand as the main dimensions along which variation takes place. To give them wider applicability they can be relabelled 'social integration' and 'normative integration'.[24]

*Social integration*
This is a shorthand to refer to the pattern of implication in social relations which follows from membership of a social category or role within the division of labour, the hierarchies of age and sex within the family, etc. – in fact, any position which affords possibilities for social identity construction. These categories are not fixed and models are required of the ways in which they are evolving in order to understand the patterns of implication: for example, the transition from an 'occupational' system of work to a 'technical system' involving deskilling. Taking the example of occupational integration we are likely to see a complex relationship between levels of integration and position in the class hierarchy. Integration does not necessarily increase in the upper levels of the hierarchy but varies according to factors like the level of

occupational training and skills, the presence or absence of a career structure, the predictability of employment, etc. Conditions of high integration along this dimension are likely to include:

– a high level of predictability in social experience,
– the existence of influential occupational identity models,
– cohesive occupational sub-cultures,
– strong awareness of class or status.

The opposite will tend to apply under conditions of low integration.

*Normative integration*
This dimension refers to participation in one or more social institutions (political party, trade union, profession, church, etc.) which provide a relatively complete normative system which regulates action in a given sphere. This is certainly not to presuppose the existence of a general normative system or value consensus from which individuals may diverge in varying degrees but rather a variety of possible normative orders of differing strengths. In the world of work, these would include 'managerialism' and 'trade unionism'.[25] But these normative orders are more directly class-related than some others. Conditions of high integration along this dimension are likely to include:

– comprehensive frameworks of interpretation and social
  discrimination,
– a long tradition of social action,
– access to institutions and bases for collective action,
– legitimate sanction and support for demands on society.

Where normative integration is low, these features are likely to be absent, with more random and individualistic forms taking their place.

Pursuing the example of industrial experience and reporting it is possible to work out the hypothetical location of a number of occupational groups according to these two dimensions, where social integration is defined according to occupations and the world of work and normative integration is defined according to levels of participation in the trade union and labour movement. The same exercise could be repeated with other domains such as politics or the family to yield comparable data. This procedure provides a basis for estimating how far the messages of industrial news are likely to be (a) received, and (b) interpreted in a way which harmonises with the dominant interpretive framework of the broadcasts. Where integration is high on both scores, conditions exist where rates of viewing are likely to be low and where the propensity to accept anti-Labour interpretations will also be low. This is a combination of minimum receptivity with regard to the pre-

ferred frameworks of interpretation. Where social and normative integration are both low, conditions exist where rates of viewing are likely
to be high and where there are few obstacles (i.e. alternative points of
identification, an alternative tradition) to the interpretations handed
down by the media. This is a combination leading to maximum receptivity. The other combinations represent intermediate conditions.

The predicted variations in receptivity correspond quite well with
what is known about the perception of broadcast news items and programmes which deal with 'industrial' matters. For example, trade
union (especially branch) officials are more exposed to informational
programmes and current affairs than shop stewards, and a higher percentage of shop stewards consider that TV is biased against trade
unions than either members or officials (Blumler and Ewbank, 1970).
The same authors and Hartmann (1979) found that those groups least
actively involved in a topic are most likely to hold views which harmon-
ise with media frameworks of interpretation. 'Effects' research has produced evidence that trade union members' views about *strikes* are influenced by media content but not their views on other topics which are
less fully and less consistently reported in industrial news. The 'agenda-
setting' power of the media as well as the power of particular interpretations therefore depends on the social and normative integration of
audiences. At no point is it suggested that audience perceptions of industrial relations are strongly polarised along class lines, only that some
variations exist. They obviously need to be explored more fully. None
of the evidence so far uncovered can be taken unambiguously either to
prove or disprove the proposition that the media have a powerful effect
through the incorporation of subordinate classes. There are obvious
grounds for suspecting this but until the relative movement in message
conditions and conditions of receptivity can be assessed, it remains an
open question. The close scrutiny of the moment of reception has yielded important insights into the social production of meanings but the
horizon needs to be extended to include those traditions, institutions
and milieux which can generate meanings without the direct agency of
the mass media.

The argument of this chapter has been that two strands of empirical
research can contribute to an understanding of how the media are implicated in social class relations. They relate to the conditions under
which messages are produced and the conditions under which they are
received. The surprising fact is that they have rarely been considered
together as two relatively independent sets of conditions which are capable of combining to create a wide range of 'effects'. In this chapter I
have emphasised that the message conditions for broadcasting at least
are such that a dominant view, or restricted range of preferred views,
does prevail in key areas of the output. This, however, is not to be taken

as a constant. The political and commercial environment in which broadcasting operates is changing rapidly and the production system referred to here is highly vulnerable to developments in satellite transmission, cable and other innovations related to intense commercial pressures. The outcome is likely to be a more diversified, decentralised system which creates increased possibilities for co-variation in message and reception conditions, but with what effect is highly uncertain.

On the other side, I have considered the evidence that one of the dominant tendencies as far as the conditions of receptivity are concerned is the decline in social and normative integration. Allowing for the possibility that this conceals a process of polarisation (integration having increased in some sections of society) the likelihood is that receptivity – always high for mainstream broadcasting – has been enhanced. Taken together, these two sets of evidence suggest that the broadcast media have acquired a powerful and independent role in the nexus of class relations, perhaps more by default than design. Yet at the very point where the mass media have fulfilled their potential for creating powerful effects, changes are rapidly occurring which seem set to undermine their position of dominance. Whether these changes will open up more genuine possibilities for the expression of subordinate cultures is a question, not of media analysis, but politics.

## Notes

1. See e.g. Fejes (1984) on the neglect of the audience in critical communications research in America, and Corrigan and Willis (1980) on the limitations of 'discourse theory' in this respect.
2. The literature is vast but for an overview, see Westergaard and Resler (1975), and Hall (1977). See also Chapter 6, 'Mass Media in a Class Society' in Glasgow University Media Group (1982).
3. H.Himmelweit, et al, *How Voters Decide*, (1981).
4. M.Bulmer (ed.) *Working Class Images of Society* (1975) contains a number of such studies. For a list of sociological studies of postwar working-class culture, see Clarke, Critcher and Johnson (eds), *Working-Class Culture* (1979) p.13. Note that middle-class cultures have received less attention.
5. For a fuller account of this, see Davis (1979), ch.1.
6. Popitz *et al.* (1957), and translation in Burns (ed.) (1969).
7. Bulmer (ed.), *op.cit.*
8. Cf. studies by Nichols and Armstrong (1976), and Nichols and Beynon (1977), for example.
9. See e.g. Offe (1984).
10. See Douglas and Isherwood (1979).
11. Dennis *et al.* (1969); Goldthorpe *et al.* (1969).
12. Thus advertising executives typically describe advertising as both 'reflecting' social needs, and as 'creating a market'. See K.Myers 'Understanding Advertisers', in Davis and Walton (1983).
13. T. Burns, in Curran, Gurevitch and Woollacott,(eds) (1977), pp. 67-8.
14. R. Williams (1974).
15. Representative studies include: Halloran *et al.* (1970), Pateman (1975), Tracey (1978) on politics; the Glasgow University Media Group (1976, 1980), Hartmann

(1975/76) and Morley (1977) on industrial news; Davis and Walton (1983), Galtung and Ruge (1973) on foreign news; Chibnall (1977) on crime and deviance; Golding and Middleton (1982) on health and social welfare.

16. Thompson (1979), p.183.
17. E.g. the *Viewpoint* series for schools and other examples discussed by A.Goodman in P.Beharrell and G.Philo (eds.) *Trade Unions and the Media* Macmillan (1977).
18. E.g. T.Burns, M.Tracey.
19. The increasing range and diversity of outlets for broadcasting, narrowcasting and video are likely to change this.
20. For a discussion of this concept, see Corner (1983), pp.278-81.
21. IBA Research Department, *Attitudes to Broadcasting in 1984* (IBA 1985) and *Attitudes to Broadcasting in 1985* (IBA 1986).
22. Hall (1974).
23. Morley (1983) p.117.
24. It might be possible to gereralise these categories even further and see them as referring to 'social integration' and 'system integration'. 'Whereas the problem of social integration focuses attention upon the orderly or conflictual relationship between the *actors*, the problem of system integration focuses on the orderly or conflictual relationships between the *parts*, or a social system.' (D.Lockwood, 'Social Integration and System Integration', in G. Zollschan and W.Hirsch (eds.), *Explorations in Social Change*, Routledge and Kegan Paul, 1964).
25. See Emmison (1985) for an empirical study of conceptions of the economic system held by managers and shop stewards.

# Bibliography

Blumler, J. and Ewbank, A. (1970) 'Trade unionists, the mass media, and unofficial strikes', *Brit. Journal of Industrial Relations*, vol.iii,pp.32-54.

Bulmer, M. (ed.) (1975) *Working Class Images of Society*, London: Routledge and Kegan Paul.

Burns, T. (ed.) (1969) *Industrial Man*, Harmondsworth: Penguin Books.

Burns, T. (1977)'The Organisation of Public Opinion', in J.Curran *et al.* (eds), *Mass Communication and Society*.

Chibnall, S. (1977) *Law-and-Order News*, London: Tavistock.

Clarke, J., Critcher, C., and Johnson, R. (1979). *Working-Class Culture*, London: Hutchinson.

Cohen, S and Young, J. (eds) (1973) *The Manufacture of News*, London: Constable.

Corner, J. (1980) 'Codes and Cultural Analysis', *Media, Culture and Society* vol.2, no.1, pp.73-86.

Corner, J. (1983) 'Textuality, Communication and Media Power', in Davis and Walton (eds).

Corrigan, P. and Willis, P.(1980) 'Cultural Forms and Class Mediations', *Media, Culture and Society*, vol.2, no.3,pp. 297-312.

Curran, J. Gurevitch, M. and Woollacott, J. (eds) (1977) *Mass Communication and Society*, Arnold: London.

Davis, H. (1979) *Beyond Class Images*, Beckenham: Croom Helm.

Davis, H. and Walton, P.(eds)(1983) *Language, Image, Media*, Oxford: Basil Blackwell.

Dennis, N. Henriques, F. and Slaughter, C. (1969) *Coal is Our Life*, London: Tavistock.

Douglas, M. and Isherwood, B. (1979) *The World of Goods*, Harmondsworth: Penguin Books.

Emmison, M. (1985) 'Class images of the economy: an empirical examination of opposition and incorporation within working class consciousness', *Sociology* 19.1, pp. 19-38.

Fejes, F. (1984) 'Critical mass communications research and media effects: the problem of the disappearing audience', *Media, Culture and Society* 6, 219-32.

Galtung, J. and Ruge, M. (1973) 'The Structure of Foreign News', in J. Tunstall (ed), *Media Sociology*, London: Constable.

Glasgow University Media Group (1976) *Bad News*, London: Routledge and Kegan Paul.

Glasgow University Media Group (1980) *More Bad News* London: Routledge and Kegan Paul.

Glasgow University Media Group (1982) *Really Bad News*, London: Writers and Readers.

Golding, P. and Middleton, S. (1982) *Images of Welfare*, Oxford: Martin Robertson.

Goldthorpe, J. *et al.* (1969) *The Affluent Worker in the Class Structure*, Cambridge: Cambridge University Press.

Hall, S. (1974) 'Encoding and Decoding Television Discourse', CCCS, mimeo.

Hall, S. (1974) 'Culture, the Media and the "Ideological Effect"' in Curran *et al.* (eds) *Mass Communication and Society*.

Halloran, J. *et al.* (1970) *Demonstrations and Communications*, Harmondsworth: Penguin Books.

Hartmann, P. (1975/76) 'Industrial Relations in the News Media', *Industrial Relations Journal*, vol. 6, no. 4, Winter.

Hartmann, P. (1979) 'News and Public Perceptions of Industrial Relations', *Media, Culture and Society*, vol.1, no.3, pp.255-70.

Himmelweit, H., Humphreys P., Katz, M., Jaeger, M. (1981) *How Voters Decide*, Academic Press: London.

Morley, D. (1980) *The Nationwide Audience*, London: BFI.

Morley, D. (1983) 'Cultural Transformations: the politics of resistance', in H. Davis and P.Walton, (eds), *Language, Image, Media*, Oxford: Basil Blackwell.

Nichols, T. and Armstrong, P. (1976) *Workers Divided*, London: Fontana.

Nichols, T. and Beynon, H. (1977) *Living with Capitalism*, London: Routledge and Kegan Paul.

Offe, C. (1984) *Contradictions of the Welfare State*, London: Hutchinson.

Parkin, F. (1971) *Class Inequality and Political Order*, London: Paladin.

Pateman, T. (1975) *Television and the February 1974 General Election*, London: BFI.

Piepe, A. *et al.* (1978) *Mass Media and Cultural Relationships*, Saxon House.

Popitz, H. *et al.* (1957) *Das Gesellschaftsbild des Arbeiters*, Tubingen: Mohr.

Thompson, G. (1979) 'Television as Text', in M.Barrett *et al.* (eds) *Ideology and Cultural Production*, Beckenham: Croom Helm.

Westergaard, J. and Resler, H. (1975) *Class in a Capitalist Society*, London: Heinemann.

Williams, R. (1974) *Television: technology and cultural form*,London: Fontana.

# 3 Voters
## *Martin Harrop*

'Reinforcement, not change. Reinforcement, not change'.
In dusty lecture rooms throughout the land this dubious cliché of media impotence is still presented to students of political behaviour. The undergraduates are sceptical, indeed increasingly so, but they do not protest too much. For they know that their role in the academic masque is also to reinforce, rather than to change, the received wisdom.

The reinforcement thesis maintains that the mass media conserve but do not change the political attitudes and behaviour of the electorate. It is a proposition which has long been moribund; the purpose of this chapter is to kill it off altogether.

In the 1940s, the reinforcement thesis provided a valuable counterpoint to assertions of media omnipotence which had characterised much discussion of propaganda in Nazi Germany. The thesis has long been rejected by media specialists but remains influential in mainstream political science in Britain. Why? Essentially, it seems, because the idea of reinforcement is simple, counter-intuitive and well marketed. Simple, because the proposition can be reduced to a slogan: 're-inforcement, not change'. Selective exposure, interpretation and recall of information also provide a catchy summary of the mechanisms underlying the notion. Counter-intuitive, because the thesis gave social scientists a 'finding' which could be presented as a valid but non-obvious product of empirical research. Well-marketed, because Joseph Klapper's *The Effects of Mass Communication* (1960!) provided a clear statement of the proposition after a careful review of the evidence then available.[1]

Yet as a guide to media effects, the reinforcement thesis has long been more of a hindrance than a help. It poses an over-simple question to which it gives an over-general answer. Underlying the reinforcement thesis is the query, What are the effects of the media on electors? But reality is more complicated than this question allows. As Berelson, Lazarsfeld and McPhee pointed out forty years ago: 'the familiar question as to whether the mass media "influence" elections is, on the surface, an absurd question. It is dubious whether any decisions at all would be possible without some mass device for enabling the leaders to present their proposals to the electorate'.[2]

Imagine, for a moment, British elections without the mass media – no television, no newspapers, no radio, no magazines, no cinema. The consequences would be dramatic. Stale information, limited in both quantity and quality, would be served up on the doorstep by party hacks. Local parties would be rejuvenated and party loyalties would re-emerge in the electorate. The site of the election would shift from the living-room to the doorstep and the village hall. Party leaders would become less important. The qualities required in leaders would change from the capacity to be friendly on television to the ability to convey passion from the podium. David Steel would be out; Michael Foot would be back. Personal communication would become a major in- gredient of electoral choice, allowing social groups to exert greater sway over the voting behaviour of their members. National events would ap- pear more remote; local issues would come into sharper focus. At the very least, things would be different. Communication has always been central to politics; the mass media are now central to political communi- cation. In elections especially, the media do not cover the campaign; they *are* the campaign. We must ask how, not whether, the media mat- ter.

Just as the reinforcement thesis is based on a naive question, so too does it provide an over-general answer. The empirical base, such as it is, was a survey conducted by Lazarsfeld, Berelson and Gaudet of about 3000 electors in Erie County, Ohio, during the 1940 presidential cam- paign.[3] Whether these 3000 respondents were representative of any wider population is in a sense to miss the point; their mission for the next forty years was to *define* normality. In Erie County in 1940, only a quarter of those interviewed made their electoral decision during the campaign; those who did so paid less attention to the media than did stable voters. I should stress that there is no reason to doubt the accu- racy of these figures; criticism centres solely on how they have been generalised – from an era of radio and newspapers to one of television, from the United States to Britain, from an era of partisanship to one of dealignment, from voting behaviour to political attitudes and, above all, from the short-term focus of an election campaign to the longer perspective of the inter-election period. Generalising from a brief cam- paign is as unjustified as exonerating cigarettes because no one gets lung cancer over the course of a three-month study.

In different ways, each section of this chapter represents a criticism of the reinforcement thesis. The next part considers the conditions of media influence, an issue barely touched on in the traditional literature. This is followed by a section examining how the importance of the media has grown in Britain since the war. The trends here serve to undermine whatever force the reinforcement thesis once had. I then review the literature on the role of the media in British election campaigns, suggesting that the media are now a vital link in the chain of electoral change. The conclusion suggests that a deeper understanding of media impact presupposes a more careful analysis of interpersonal communication.

Throughout the chapter, I adopt a broad definition of media 'effects'. In particular, I do not distinguish between the impact of the media as a transmitter of communication, from effects resulting from the manner – tone, emphases, style – of media coverage. Both count as 'effects'. Although the distinction is theoretically and politically important, it is still too subtle for the blunt instruments used in research. No empirical studies have been able to separate these aspects.

## When the media matter most

The reinforcement thesis has survived for so long because academics prefer even a leaking boat to drowning. This chapter is not a rescue service, providing the new idea which enables everyone to abandon the sinking ship. None the less I can at least provide some material with which to supplement the ageing lecture in praise of reinforcement. Table 3.1 sets out some conditions under which the media are most influential. Based largely on American research,[4] these general conditions are probably also applicable to Britain. The table suggests that media impact depends on the nature of (1) the elector, (2) the society, (3) the message, and (4) the type of effect.

### Electors

The media will have most impact on people who rarely discuss politics, who have limited prior knowledge of the issue concerned, who have moderate exposure to the media and whose motive for exposure is general surveillance of the political environment. The intriguing point here is that media effects do not increase in direct proportion to exposure. In fact, heavy media use often reflects prior interest and knowledge, variables which soften the impact of new information. This explains why studies used to justify the reinforcement thesis found that the media had limited effects; by concentrating on heavy users, they were looking in the wrong place. It is among the middle majority – people who neither switch on nor switch off political programmes – that the media exert most sway.

### Society

The media will be most influential when loyalties to parties and social groups are weak. In Britain, for example, partisan dealignment has

*Table 3.1 Conditions of media influence*

|  | Media have high impact | Media have low impact |
| --- | --- | --- |
| *Electors* | | |
| Media exposure | Moderate | Great or none |
| Discusses politics | Rarely | Often |
| Prior knowledge | Limited | Extensive |
| Motives for exposure | Surveillance | Reinforcement |
| *Society* | | |
| Group and party loyalties | Weak | Strong |
| *Message* | | |
| Age of issue | New | Old |
| *Effect* | | |
| Timescale | Long-term | Short-term |
| Impact on | Information | Attitudes and especially behaviour |
| Nature | Crystallisation and reinforcement | Conversion |

created more room for the media (and indeed anything else) to affect the electorate. The relative neutrality of TV news has probably contributed to the very process of dealignment which has in turn allowed the media's influence to increase still further. But where political and social loyalties run deep, both the organisation of and exposure to the media are structured on partisan lines. Paul Arthur's chapter on Northern Ireland illustrates the point that in divided societies reinforcement does indeed provide a useful guide to media 'effects'. But Ulster is exceptional.

*Message*
'Whoever says the first word to the world is right,' said Goebbels. Undoubtedly media coverage will influence attitudes to the new more than to the familiar. For example, the image of the SDP is less securely anchored in history than is the perception of older, better-established parties. But the page is never wholly blank. In appraising the SDP, the public brings preconceptions based on the category of object to which the SDP belongs – namely, a political party. If this outline is not filled

in promptly, the clarity of the resulting image will be permanently impaired. Thus the media can help to crystallise attitudes to new issues, events and actors even if the subsequent role of the media is confined to reinforcement. In fact, I shall show later that television was particularly important to the success of the SDP/Liberal Alliance in the 1983 election.

*Effect*
Media impact depends on the type of effect under review. For example, the long-term cumulative impact of the media is almost certainly greater than short-term effects measured over a brief period such as an election campaign. A single episode of *Coronation Street* may not matter, but twenty years' worth is a different proposition. Certainly short-term studies provide no basis for denying long-term effects.

It is equally important to distinguish effects on information (largest), opinions (middling) and behaviour (smallest). Media effects on information are limited only by the recipient's desire to obtain, and ability to retain, data. As evaluations and interpretations of facts, opinions carry more emotional current and show greater resistance to change. Behaviour is even more habitual; change in behaviour is more often provoked by the demands of an immediate social situation than by remote, impersonal media images. Hence, by concentrating on electoral behaviour, the early studies adopted an excessively narrow perspective on media effects. As I shall show, recent studies have demonstrated a clear relationship between media exposure and information gain, even over the short span of an election campaign.

**Why the media have become more important**
Changes in the nature and context of media use over the postwar period point to a growing role for the media in shaping the electorate's information and concerns (certainly), opinions (probably) and behaviour (possibly). This section reviews these developments in paragraphs covering television, video-recorders, newspapers, the overall flow of political communication and political change itself.

Television is of course the crucial development. The proportion of households with television grew rapidly from 10 per cent in 1950 to 90 per cent in 1964. Today only 5 per cent of households lack television: a small but intriguing group. Helped by extended broadcasting hours, viewing has continued to increase long after access to a set reached saturation point. The average number of hours per week spent watching television rose steadily from 16 in the winter of 1967 to 20 in the winter of 1979 (viewing drops in summer, on average by about 5 per cent for each 2 per cent rise in average monthly temperature). Since 1979 viewing figures have appeared to oscillate, partly as a result of the measurement problems posed by televisions connected to home computers and video recorders. The heaviest users of television are groups with the least interest in politics – the retired, the unemployed, the working class and children. Lack of prior knowledge and low self-esteem means these groups are particularly susceptible to influence by television coverage of politics.

Most viewing is low-key. Cameras mounted on televisions in American living rooms show that all indoor activities can be performed with the TV on as well as off. Though we are more discreet about allowing a wide-angle lens into our sitting rooms it is no doubt equally true that British television is something 'to be chatted over, knitted by, read through, eaten and drunk by'.[5] For many Britons television functions as a time-sink, disposing of time not spent on more active and fulfilling pursuits. In considering the effects of television, it is important to bear in mind the superficial quality of most viewing. The crucial point about television is its reach rather than the intensity of the viewing experience.

Of the 20 hours a week spent in front of the set, only a few involve explicitly political material. News broadcasts and some magazine programmes come near the top of the ratings; most current affairs programmes are nearer the bottom.[6] But the unselective nature of TV viewing means that even current affairs programmes are more than broadcasting ghettoes for the political *cognoscente*. And exposure to political programmes does cumulate, even over the brief period of an election. In the 1983 campaign, for example, the average audience for ITN's *News at 5.45*, the most popular news programme, was 7.3 million, less than half the figure for *Coronation Street*. Yet over the course of the campaign, a typical viewer saw something like five editions of the *News at 5.45*, four of the *Nine O'clock News*, five of *Nationwide*, several party election broadcasts and one *Panorama*.[7] In and out of campaigns, most people will not view any one news broadcast; but just under half will watch at least one such broadcast on a single day. As with television generally, so with political television specifically: reach is what matters.

Domestic video-recorders have probably produced a very small reduction in exposure to politics on television. By early 1985, almost one in three households had a video recorder. Of these, three-quarters recorded at least one programme a week and 40 per cent rented a cassette at least once a week. Entertainment is, of course, the dominant motive here. Who watches yesterday's news? Thus, access to a video reduces exposure to broadcast television; news and current affairs programmes doubtless suffer their fair share of this loss. But the effect of video-recorders on the electorate's viewing of politics on television is less than that caused by other factors such as the arrival of Channel 4 and general trends in viewing time. Broadcast television is and will long remain the dominant medium of mass communication about politics in Britain.

Against all expectations, national morning newspapers have survived the onslaught from television. The circulation of national dailies eased from 16.6 million in 1951 to 14.4 million in 1974 but has held firm since. Against the general trend, the qualities, led by *The Guardian*, have increased their circulation. And many more people read newspapers than buy them. About three in every four adults read a national morning paper, a figure only exceeded by the industrious Japanese. Each day at least as many Britons read a paper as watch TV news – and they claim to spend longer with their paper than with the news bulletin.[8]

The reason for the continued vitality of newspapers is that they have learned to complement rather than compete with broadcasting. The press is strongest where television is weakest – among men and the young. The *à la carte* opportunities of a newspaper contrast with the *table d'hôte* menu of television news. (As yet, few have adopted the *nouvelle cuisine* of Channel 4.) Television news is regarded as a source of accurate, current but essentially superficial information, but readers of the quality press prefer the range, depth and interpretation offered by their paper. Even readers of the tabloids seem to appreciate the way press opinion complements television's 'facts'. Television is preferred for personalities; quality papers for issues. Among the electorate as a whole, newspapers run a strong second to television in terms of their rated usefulness in following election campaigns.[9] In short, although television has become the main source of headline news, the quality papers still provide background information, while the tabloids continue to mix in prejudices all of their own.

Media coverage of politics generally and election campaigns in particular has sharpened up over the postwar period. In television, news values have gradually become more important in determining coverage though artificial criteria of balance still limit television's room for manoeuvre.[10] In the quality press, the calibre of election coverage has undoubtedly improved. In the tabloids, news coverage may have declined in quantity but full-blooded press partisanship has returned with a vengeance since February 1974. As media coverage of politics becomes less insipid, so the likelihood grows that voters will take note of what they see, hear and read.

The most dramatic effect of television has been on radio rather than the national press. Gone are the days in 1945 when party political broadcasts on radio reached an average of 45 per cent of the population, and exchanges between Churchill and Attlee set the tone for the whole campaign. By 1979, half the population said they spent no time at all following the election campaign on radio; in 1983, only 14 per cent said they listened to any party election broadcasts on the radio. Older middle-class respondents are most likely to rely on radio coverage of elections, but even these voters prefer television and the press. Still, it is important not to ignore radio completely. People spend an average of nine hours a week listening to the radio; much longer if background listening is included. And exposure to the radio has grown since the mid-1970s as local radio has developed and the national networks have expanded their air-time. Radio remains a mass medium of communication even though it now operates in the long shadows of television.

The use which people make of individual media has been carefully researched. However, less is known about how these streams of television, press and radio merge into the overall flow of political communication reaching the elector. I suggest that people can be divided into three main categories of media use: the apathetic, the accessible and the addicted:

The *apathetics* employ the media exclusively for entertainment. They avoid television news and read a tabloid paper. Exposure to political communication is inadvertent; equally, politics rarely intrudes into conversation. The apathetics are the ten per cent of the population who say they switch off election coverage on television. They are a difficult group for campaigners to reach.

The *accessibles* use the media mainly for entertainment but also to keep abreast of major political developments. Television news is the primary vehicle for this. Political conversation is not routine; the media are thus the principal source of information for the accessibles. They are the largest group, represented by half the population who say they are willing to watch some election coverage if they encounter it unintentionally. Reaching this group depends crucially on getting coverage on television news.

The *addicted*, by contrast, are the smallest group. They use the media primarily for information, not entertainment. They follow politics not just through television news but also through the radio, a quality paper and current affairs programmes on television. Politics is a common topic of conversation among the addicted. Disproportionately middle-class, this group is drawn from the quarter of the population who say they make a point of watching as much election coverage as they can.[11] Campaigners have no difficulty in reaching this group.

The electorate's own ratings over the postwar period of the importance of media channels are shown in Table 3.2. This confirms that the mass media have long been dominant sources of political information. As early as 1950, newspapers and radio were more significant than meetings and conversation. By 1964, television had supplanted the other media as the major purveyor of information, resulting in voters receiving more powerful and credible messages from the media than ever before.

*Table 3.2 Electors' ratings of the most important source of political information, 1950 – 83.*

|  | *1950* (Greenwich) | *1955* (Bristol NE) | *1964* (Britain) | *1983* Britain) |
|---|---|---|---|---|
| Television | – | 2 | 1 | 1 |
| Newspapers | 1 | 1 | 2= | 2 |
| Radio | 2 | 3= | 4 | 3= |
| Conversation | 3 | 3= | 2= | 3= |
| Meetings | 4 | – | – | – |

*Sources:* see note 12.

Since 1945, three political changes have lowered the electorate's resistance to these messages. The first of these is the decay of local party organisation. As Figure 3.1 shows, most electors are no longer canvassed personally during campaigns; even fewer attend meetings. This is notwithstanding the fact that elections are the peak period of party activity. Increasingly people are left in peace to watch the campaign on television; indeed they have been known to resent the interruption to election viewing which canvassing presents! (However, research on local elections suggests that what little canvassing still takes place does stimulate turnout.)[13]

A second, more fundamental development has been the weakening of party loyalties among the electorate. Now that 40 per cent of people can be expected to change their voting behaviour from one election to the next, reinforcement is certainly an inadequate account of media effects. Undecided electors cannot be reinforced; they are much more likely to use the media positively to help them reach a decision. It is worth noting here that many social psychologists believe avoidance of discrepant information only begins *after* a decision has been reached; in the pre-decision phase, competing viewpoints are welcomed. In 1973, Seymour-Ure could still claim that 'teeming shoals of voters do not lie ready to be trawled by press magnates'. Well, they do now – though television has the best nets.

The third development is the increase in both political conflict and change in Britain during the 1970s and 1980s. When more happens, the media matter more.

It is often argued that television has itself contributed to these changes, first accelerating the shift from community-centred to home-

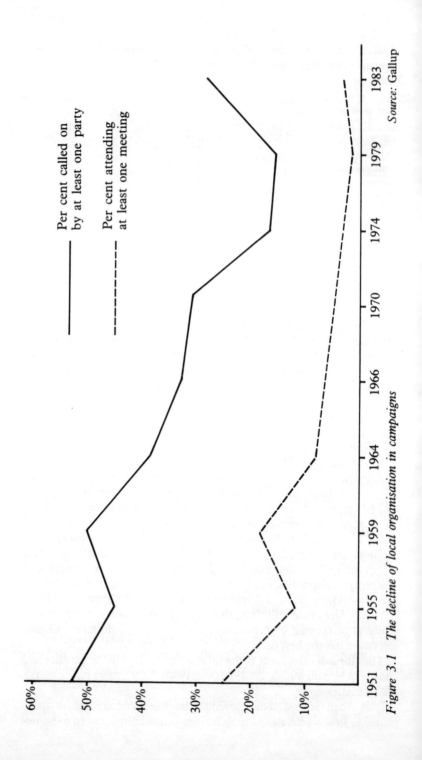

Per cent called on
by at least one party

Per cent attending
at least one meeting

60%

50%

40%

30%

20%

10%

1951    1955    1959    1964    1966    1970    1974    1979    1983

*Figure 3.1  The decline of local organisation in campaigns*

*Source:* Gallup

centred activities, before emerging itself as a major influence on mass attitudes, and behaviour. As a Tyneside woman put it (speaking, ironically, in a TV documentary): 'In the old days we all used to go down to the Town Hall to hear the results. We all knew we were Labour then but now we stay at home watching TV and we don't know what to think.' For this woman, the main effect of television has been to shield her from the reinforcement traditionally provided by her local working-class community. Unfortunately, the counterfactuals here are extremely murky. What would people be doing if they were not watching television? What political effects would such activities have? We do not know for sure although surveys do suggest the home was the main site of leisure activities long before television.[14] Whatever the explanation, voting clearly has become less securely anchored in the social structure, with the result that electoral behaviour is now more responsive to the ebbs and flows of the political tide, as documented on television and evaluated by the press.

**Why the media matter in election campaigns**
An election campaign is an unfavourable laboratory for discovering media effects. It is a brief, frenetic affair during which most people talk about politics. Conversation provides a mechanism through which the values of a specific class or community can influence the individual. Outside campaigns, the political pulse runs at a lower rate and most people do not regularly talk about current affairs.[15] Between campaigns, opinions are more superficial, more volatile and more susceptible to media influence. In an era of the instant opinion poll, such opinions are not necessarily unimportant. Yet, for better or worse, the campaign is the context in which most studies of media effects have been conducted. In this section, we review these findings, beginning with television and then turning to the impact of the press. I argue that despite the unfavourable setting, the media are a crucial mechanism of electoral change within campaigns.

The best documented proposition about the media and voters in election campaigns is that television enlarges knowledge. Trenaman and McQuail's finding in Leeds in 1959 has been replicated several times since: 'Here is a very significant association between the amount of political news and propaganda an elector received through television and his better understanding of the policies the parties were putting forward'.[16] Similar results from other countries led Katz to describe election campaigns as 'the major learning experience of democratic polities'.[17] Later research added a gloss to these findings. Blumler and McQuail noted in 1964 that information gains tailed off among television 'junkies' whose heavy exposure to campaign broadcasts did not reflect real interest in the election.[18]

Given that the press is rated as particularly helpful in understanding party policies, it is anomalous that newspapers do not increase actual knowledge of policies as much as television. This may simply reflect a failure of the studies to distinguish between the quality press (whose readers probably show large gains) and the tabloids (where increments will be smaller). Generally, however, these results on *actual* information gain confirm what people themselves report: television is the main source of campaign information.

Changes in opinions are less common than changes in information. None the less, when such changes do take place the media generally and television in particular are heavily implicated. Again, the early studies illustrate this point. In 1959, Trenaman and McQuail discovered that 'attitudes were extremely stable, even over a period of intense propaganda like an election campaign'.[19] They concluded that electors' attitudes were far more resistant to media effects than their cognitions. Yet the next election (in 1964) did see substantial changes in attitudes during the campaign. The fortunes of the Liberal Party were transformed by the campaign and, hey presto, increased sympathy for the Liberals proved to be strongly related to TV viewing of the election, especially through news bulletins.[20] Exposure to election television does not guarantee changes in attitudes and behaviour but it does seem to be a vital mechanism through which any such changes take place. The implication of this is that we should cease asking, 'Are heavy users of the media more volatile than light users?' Instead, we should ask, 'What are the effects of the media on those electors who *do* change their views during a campaign?'

Television's influence is easiest to spot when it is associated with net changes in support for a party during a campaign. The Liberal rise in 1964 is one example; Labour's decline in 1983 is probably another. But it is, of course, possible for the same programme to influence people in different ways. Watching the same interview, one viewer may decide to vote for Mrs Thatcher because of her determination while another decides to vote against her because of her obduracy. Overall support for the Conservatives remains the same, thus concealing television's impact. It is therefore still useful to ask electors the direct question: 'Did television influence your vote?' Though not without difficulties of its own, this question should pick up the gross effect of televison.

The replies to such a question asked after the 1983 election are shown in Table 3.3 Overall, almost one in five electors said television helped them decide which party to vote for. The medium was regarded as particularly important by Alliance supporters, new electors and those whose vote differed from the 1979 contest. As many as 43 per cent (N = 60) of those who switched to the Alliance said television contributed to their move. These findings confirm a pattern first noted in 1951:

'floaters' are more likely than 'loyalists' to cite the media as an important influence even though 'floaters' are below average in their exposure to mass communication. And this in turn strengthens the claim that the media are an essential link in the chain of electoral change.

*Table 3.3 Influence of television on voting behaviour, 1983 election.*

| | All | Conservative | Labour | Alliance | Same as 1979 | Different from 1979 | New Voters |
|---|---|---|---|---|---|---|---|
| | | Vote | | | Stability of vote | | |
| | % | % | % | % | % | % | % |
| Has television coverage helped you decide who to vote for? | | | | | | | |
| Yes | 18 | 17 | 19 | 30 | 13 | 25 | 31 |
| No | 79 | 81 | 79 | 67 | 85 | 73 | 63 |
| Don't Know | 3 | 2 | 2 | 3 | 1 | 2 | 6 |

*Note:* All numbers exceed 100, except last column (N = 46). Voting behaviour in 1979 is subject to recall errors.
*Source:* BBC/IBA survey. See note 7.

The influence of television on electoral change during campaigns is, therefore, well established. But what of the national press, a more partisan if less credible medium than television? Here, we must adopt a longer time perspective since most studies have examined the impact of newspapers on voting behaviour over a period of years rather than weeks. Roosevelt once remarked that he would give the editorial columns to the opposition during the campaign if he could continue to fill the news columns between campaigns. Thus, this focus on change between rather than within campaigns may help to identify any effect the press may have.

The general conclusion here is that the press is the one medium where the reinforcement thesis has worked well. Newspapers exert at most a small direct influence on changes in voting behaviour among their readers. In the most elegant study to date, Miller *et al.* concluded from a panel survey of Scottish *Daily Express* readers that the power of the press, to the extent that it exists at all, is the power to conserve rather than convert.[21] Using less sophisticated designs on national samples, other studies have produced slightly larger estimates of press impact, though the magnitude of these effects is still small by comparison with television. For example, Butler and Stokes showed that in the 1960s readers who agreed with their paper's partisanship were more stable in their electoral choice than readers whose choice of party differed from their paper's.[22] And at that time most readers *did* agree with the political line of their paper; cross-reading, especially of a conscious kind, was a minority sport. Butler and Stokes also showed that newspapers could crystallise a party preference among initially uncommitted electors. I have obtained similar evidence of reinforcement and crystallisation from panel surveys taken in the 1970s. Given the greater readership of Conservative papers, I have estimated that this 'press effect' is worth a swing of about one per cent from Labour to Conservative between two elections.[23] This is equivalent to approximately ten seats – not to be sniffed at but hardly decisive either. Larger estimates have been obtained from cross-sectional surveys but these are far less convincing than the evidence from panel studies.[24]

There is nothing immutable about the impact of the press. In fact, there are several reasons for supposing that the electoral significance of national newspapers is waxing rather than waning. These are:

– the re-emergence of press partisanship since 1974;
– the declining circulation of Labour newspapers and the consequent increase in cross-reading;
– the increasing recognition by readers of their paper's partisanship;[25]
– the growing readership of the more influential quality papers;
– the backdrop of increasing electoral volatility;
– the increasingly important indirect role of the press in shaping the agenda of television news.

The argument for the declining impact of newspapers is much simpler:
– television.
But there is no direct evidence either way. My judgement is that the electoral impact of the press in the 1980s is unlikely to differ by an order of magnitude from the 1960s and 1970s, when the effect was small.

Is the decision to vote influenced by media coverage of campaigns? Turnout is certainly correlated with exposure to the media. Between 1964 and October 1974, turnout was on average 21 per cent higher among heavy users of the media than among those with very light exposure.[26] The problem here, of course, is that turnout and exposure both reflect political interest; evidence of a cause-and-effect relationship between the media and voting rates is much harder to come by. In a study conducted before and after the 1970 election, Blumler and

McLeod found that communication exposure only affected turnout among young voters.[27] A cross-section survey taken after the European election in 1979 showed a particularly large effect of exposure on turnout among electors with little or no interest in the campaign. (Television, incidentally, again proved to be a more persuasive channel than newspapers.)[28] Together, these studies suggest that the media do influence turnout but that the effect is largely confined to electors for whom, or elections in which, voting has not become an ingrained habit.

Overall, there is no doubt that the reinforcement thesis is an inadequate guide to the effects of the media in election campaigns. The media can change information, attitudes and behaviour. Indeed, the evidence that the media change attitudes is in one way more convincing than the evidence for reinforcement. In the early studies, reinforcement was often just inferred from the absence of change; few investigations captured the mechanism at work. Now that television news has become the most important channel of communication, reinforcement has declined in significance. Rightly or wrongly, television news is perceived by viewers as an unbiased medium which offers few opportunities for explicit reinforcement. Certainly, viewers themselves do not regard reinforcement as a primary motive for watching election television. General surveillance of the political environment ('I want to see what they would do if they get in') is rated more highly.[29] Over the short span of a campaign, television is best regarded as a vital mechanism of electoral change. But the extent of change still depends more on 'external' factors: on how many voters are undecided at the outset and on what actually happens in the campaign itself. Over the longer term, however, television probably contributes to the weakening of party loyalties which in turn makes campaigns (and television's coverage of them) more decisive.

**Conclusion**
Always simplistic, now also wrong. That, in short, is the indictment which this chapter has offered against the reinforcement thesis. There is an important connection between these two criticisms. By adopting an over-general account of media impact, advocates of the reinforcement notion became insensitive to postwar changes in how people use the media. Yet these developments indicate that the media are now full members of the family of significant influences on voters' political attitudes and behaviour. This point has been made in several ways in this chapter:

1. The media are more important when party loyalties are weak – and party loyalties have diminished in Britain since the 1960s.
2. The media are more important when there are new subjects to

cover – and British politics has seen major developments since the 1960s.

3. The media are more important when coverage is credible – and the arrival of television has strengthened the credibility of the media.

4. The media are more important when people rarely discuss politics – and television has supplanted conversation as a major channel of political communication.

So what next? How can the expanding territory of media effects be explored further? One negative point here is that there is little point in substituting blanket assertions of media omnipotence for bland assumptions of media impotence. As an influence on the electorate, the media are just one member of a large and growing family. An obvious caution perhaps, but one which is ignored by media critics, on both the Left and the Right. In their eagerness to condemn the content of the media's coverage of politics, these commentators often presuppose a narrow, one-dimensional interpretation of the voter. Yet this is precisely the intellectual straightjacket from which research on the effects of the media has struggled to escape over the past twenty years.

A more positive approach is to locate the media in the context of personal communication. Unravelling the relationship between talk and television is the key to understanding both channels. This requires an emphasis on receivers rather than messages and on qualitative observation rather than quantitative surveys.

In the influential studies of American elections in the 1940s, the media were presented as playing second fiddle to primary groups. A higher proportion of voters were reported to discuss politics than to follow the election through the media. Radio and newspapers were only invoked to explain the electoral choice of those voters who were isolated from social relationships or who did not discuss politics within these relationships. Yet for three reasons this emphasis was exaggerated. First, the authors of these studies were reviving primary groups from the battering they were receiving from the emerging literature on mass society; as a result, they over-played their hand. Second, the evidence for the electoral homogeneity of primary groups was based entirely on respondents' perceptions. This led to exaggerated estimates of how many voters knew the political affiliations of their family and friends; it also overestimated the extent of political agreement within such groups. Third, the social changes reviewed in this chapter point to a decline in the importance of primary groups. Television has supplanted discussion as the main channel of election communication.[30] The increased proportion of the electorate in mixed class locations means primary groups have become electorally heterogeneous. And dealignment means that social pressures to reactivate traditional allegiances during a campaign have become less intense. For example, after the

1983 election in Britain, only 55 per cent of married people said their spouse was going to vote for the same party; the remainder either did not know (36 per cent) or said the spouse supported a different party (10 per cent).[31] Personal influence on electoral choice should certainly not be ignored but it urgently needs reassessment.

In the early studies, the 'two-step flow of communication' served as the theoretical link between the mass media and personal communication. According to this notion 'ideas often flow *from* radio and print *to* the opinion leaders and *from* them to the rest of the population'.[32] Opinion leaders were the bridge over which media traffic travelled. Whatever the value of this idea in the 1940s, it is not applicable to the 1980s. The traffic now reaches the electorate directly through television and opinion leaders have been reduced to *post facto* interpreters of the broadcast material. Much of this interpretation is itself on television, often producing an odd situation where television interprets itself. For example, it is noticeable how many Americans change their own snap judgement of which candidate won a presidential debate after the commentators have had their say.

The content of political discussion, then, is now actively influenced by television. As Howard Davis puts it in Chapter 2: 'Conversations which once looked like improvisations on the themes of direct personal experience are now more likely to be improvisations on last night's TV programmes'. The discussion may still be more salient than the programme but television none the less sets the agenda. It influences what people think about, if not what they think. Walter Lippman's view of the press is applicable to the media generally: 'It is like a beam of a searchlight that moves restlessly about, bringing one episode and then another out of the darkness and into vision.'[33] This agenda-setting role of the media has proved to be a fruitful line of enquiry in the United States; there is an urgent need for similar studies in Britain.[34]

Noelle-Neumann's theory of the spiral of silence is a European formulation of the agenda-setting idea. She argues that opinions expressed in the media induce people with opposing views to keep mum. This powers a bandwagon which rolls on until the media view predominates. This is an appealing idea but one which turns out to be virtually impossible to test. Such evidence as is available for Britain does not point to a general spiral of party popularity (or unpopularity).[35] However, the Bermondsey by-election suggests the spiral of silence (or invective) may apply in specific circumstances.[36]

All these ideas – the two-step flow, agenda-setting, the spiral of silence – are operating in the right neck of the woods. They all address the central issue of the relationship between interpersonal communication and mass communication, between talk and TV. Enough has been said in this chapter to show that the impact of the media on the electorate can no longer be dismissed with vague references to re-inforcement in Erie County in 1940. At the same time, a deeper under-standing of the what, when and how of media effects presupposes a more precise model of how opinions in general are formed. We need a theory of communication before we can have a theory of the mass me-dia.

### Notes

1.  New York: Free Press. My thanks to Hugh Berrington and the editors for their helpful comments on a draft of this chapter.
2.  B. Berelson, P. Lazarsfeld and W. McPhee, *Voting*, Chicago: University Press, 1954, p.234.
3.  P. Lazarsfeld, B. Berelson and H. Gaudet, *The People's Choice*, New York: Columbia University Press, 1944. The 1948 survey in Elmira County, reported in *Voting*, adopted a similar perspective on the media – often word for word!
4.  G. Eyal, 'The Role of Newspapers and Television in Agenda-Setting', in *Mass Communications Review Yearbook: Volume II*, ed. G.Wilhoit and H. de Bock, London: Sage, 1981, pp.225-34; and D. Weaver and J. Buddenbaum, 'Newspapers and Television: A Review of Research on Uses and Effects', in *Mass Communications Review Yearbook: Volume I*, ed. G. Wilhoit and H. de Bock, London: Sage, 1980, pp. 371-80
5.  David Littlejohn, quoted in A. Ranney, *Channels of Power*,New York: Basic Books, 1983. On the relationship between self-esteem and persuadability, see E. Aronson, *The Social Animal*, San Francisco: Freeman, 1980, p.87.
6.  A useful source on this and other aspects of the media is J. Tunstall, *The Media in Britain*, London: Constable, 1983.
7.  This is a mild extrapolation from figures obtained by a BBC/IBA survey. See B. Gunter, M. Svennevig and M. Wober, *Television Coverage of the 1983 General Election*, London: BBC/IBA, 1984.
8.  In 1977, 62 per cent of readers *said* they spent more than 30 minutes perusing their paper.
9.  P. Kellner and R. Worcester, 'Electoral Perceptions of Media Stance', in *Political Communications: The General Election Campaign of 1979*, ed. R. Worcester and M. Harrop, London: Allen & Unwin, 1982, pp.57-67.
10. On this, see the contributions by M. Even and M. Pilsworth to *Political Communications: The General Election Campaign of 1983*, ed. I. Crewe and M. Harrop, Cambridge: Cambridge University Press, 1986.
11. Figures on attitudes to election coverage are taken from the BBC/IBA survey of 1983. See note 7.
12. The sources are 1950 – M. Benney, A. Gray and R. Pear, *How People Vote*, London: Routledge & Kegan Paul, 1956, Table 31; 1955 – R. Milne and H. Mackenzie, *Marginal Seat*, London: Hansard Society, 1958, p.105; 1964 – D. Butler and D. Stokes, *Political Change in Britain*, 1st edition, London: Penguin Books, 1971, p. 271; 1983 – *Television Coverage of the 1983 General Election*, Table 9. Neither the population sampled nor the question wording is constant so the data have been reduced to a rank order. Equal positions have been given where the difference between two media is 5 per cent or less.
13. See, for example, J. Bochel and P. Denver, 'Canvassing, Turnout and Party Support: An Experiment', *British Journal of Political Science*, vol. 1, 1971, pp. 257-69.
14. In 1957, when television penetration was far from complete, the leisure activities most frequently mentioned in a Gallup poll were all home-centred. They were, in order of mention, knitting, gardening, needlework, reading and manual hobbies; 'communal activities' came a poor sixth. See G. Gallup, *The Gallup International*

*Public Opinion Polls: Great Britain 1937 – 75*, vol. 1, New York, Random House, 1976, p. 416.

15. After the 1964 election, 60 per cent of Butler and Stokes' sample said they had followed the campaign through conversation. A year earlier, outside the context of an election, only 27 per cent said they followed politics through conversation. See *Political Change in Britain*, 1st edition, p. 271.

16. J. Trenaman and D. McQuail, *Television and the Political Image*, London: Methuen, 1961, p. 233.

17. E. Katz, 'Platforms and Windows: Broadcasting's Role in Election Campaigns', *Journalism Quarterly*, vol. 38, 1971, pp. 304-14.

18. J. Blumler and D. McQuail, *Television in Politics*, London: Faber and Faber, 1968, p. 165.

19. *Television and the Political Image*, p. 231.

20. *Televison in Politics*, Ch.13.

21. W. Miller, J. Brand and M. Jordan, 'On the Power or Vulnerability of the British Press: A Dynamic Analysis', *British Journal of Political Science*, Vol.12, 1982, pp. 357-73.

22. *Political Change in Britain*, 1st edition, Ch.10.

23. 'Press Coverage of Post-war British Elections', in *Political Communications: The General Election Campaign of 1983*, ed. I. Crewe and M. Harrop, Cambridge: Cambridge University Press, 1986.

24. For example, Dunleavy's claim that only the combination of class and sector can match the importance of the press-dominated media is based solely on cross-sectional data and ignores the more convincing (and more modest) results of panel analysis. See P. Dunleavy, 'Fleet Street: Its Bite on the Ballot'. *New Socialist*, January 1985.

25. For example, recognition of the *Sun*'s Conservative support rose from 33 per cent in a survey taken a week before the 1979 election to 64 per cent in a survey taken a week after the 1983 election. See D. Butler and D. Kavanagh, *The British General Election of 1983*, London: Macmillan, 1984, Table 9.9.

26. I. Crewe, T. Fox and J. Alt, 'Non-voting in British General Elections 1966 – October 1974', in *British Political Sociology Yearbook*, Volume 3, ed. C. Crouch, London: Croom Helm, 1977, pp. 38-109, Table 27.

27. J. Blumler and J. McLeod, 'Communication and Voter Turnout in Britain', in *Sociological Theory and Survey Research*, ed. T. Leggatt, London: Sage, 1977, pp.265-312.

28. J. Blumler, 'Communication and Turnout', in *Communicating to Voters*, ed. J. Blumler, London: Sage, 1983, pp. 181-213, Table 7.

29. *Television in Politics*, Ch. 4.

30. In 1983, more than twice as many people cited party election broadcasts as personal discussion as a reason for their vote choice. Among late deciders, the ratio was far greater. See Ivor Crewe, 'How to Win a Landslide Without Really Trying: Why the Conservatives Won in 1983', in *Britain at the Polls, 1983*, ed. H. Penniman and A. Ranney, Washington, DC: American Enterprise Institute, 1985, Table 3.

31. *British Public Opinion: General Election 1983*, London: MORI, 1983, p.44.

32. *The People's Choice*, p. 151.

33. W. Lippman, *Public Opinion*, New York: Harcourt, Brace.

34. For a review of these studies, see D. Weaver *et al.*, *Media Agenda-Setting in a Presidential Election*,New York: Praeger, 1981; and the articles cited in note 4 above.

35. E. Noelle-Neumann, 'The Spiral of Silence: A Theory of Public Opinion', *Journal of Communication*, Vol. 24, 1974, pp. 43-51. For a useful review, see D. McQuail and S. Windahl, *Communication Models for the Study of Mass Communications*,London: Longman, 1981, pp. 68-9. On Britain, see R. Wybrow, 'The Spiral of Silence: A British Perspective', in *Political Communications: The General Election Campaign of 1983*, Ch.21.

36. P. Tatchell, *Battle for Bermondsey*, London: Heretic Books, 1983.

# 4   Elections
## *Jenny Craik*

### Introduction: not a conspiracy but a social force.

> A survey following the 1970 General Election suggested that voters generally found interviews and debates between politicians more informative than party broadcasts. . . . Perhaps the electorate would be more receptive to being treated as 'would-be problem-solvers'. We took Dr Blumler to be implying by this that it was time the political sophistication of the electorate was recognised by party political broadcasts. Those of the electorate who watch party political broadcasts approach politics as adults and expect to be treated as such.[1]

This quotation from the *Annan Report* pinpoints the dilemma of the relationship between elections and the media. On the one hand, election material in the media is deemed to be largely unpopular and perhaps misdirected, while on the other hand, the electorate is recognised as having changed from habitual, passive voters to sophisticated and informed media audiences who may choose to engage with political information and in political behaviour. Annan, like other analysts, has become bound up with the dilemma and unsure of how to address the consequences of those changes within the representation of politics and within electoral space.

   This chapter examines the changes in those arenas in order to complement the perspectives already offered. In previous chapters, questions about the role of the media in relation to electoral behaviour (class and volatility) and leadership have been discussed. As Seymour-Ure's conclusion illustrates, discussion tends to generate more questions than it answers. None the less, contributors agree that there have been significant changes in three areas:

1. The relationship between media and politics is an important social interface rather than a tool of individual persuasion.
2. There has been a profound shift from early media research which looked for 'effects' to recent work which seeks the conditions and forms of influence.

3. There have been considerable changes to the demarcation and conduct of political space, reflected especially in the decline of the class vote, and in emergent patterns of leadership.

Analysis of elections and the media must take account of such changes not as a backdrop to politics 'elsewhere', but in the demarcation of the space of media and elections. Much work on elections (e.g. the Nuffield studies on postwar Britain) has only belatedly and grudgingly addressed the role of the media as more than self-evident reportage. Even now, however, the number of works *specifically* devoted to the relationship between media and elections are few, with reference continually made to the few milestones – the Chicago 'effects' studies (e.g. Berelson; Lazarsfeld), the uses and gratifications approaches (e.g. Blumler; McQuail), and the consumer choice models (e.g. Crewe; Robertson).[2] The situation has been partially redeemed by the collections of Worcester and Harrop, and of Crewe and Harrop.[3] Perhaps the strongest single contribution has been that of Seymour-Ure.[4] Taken together, however, this list is marked by its brevity and this has brought about a tendency to treat the texts synchronically and not as archival traces; each relates to a particular historical stage of the valuation of 'the media', the state of the art of media research, and to particular sociopolitical conditions.

Even now, research on media and politics is seen as not quite respectable in certain academic circles. Curiously, however, it is now becoming acceptable within the media such that academics regularly contribute work about the media to the media, e.g. in *The Guardian*'s weekly 'Media Page' and, conversely, journalists contribute to academic works. Equally, politicians and party workers have joined the debate. These developments are an index of the pervasiveness of the role that the media have acquired and how intertwined the media and politics have become. Indeed, the media have become a decisive force in political contestation, a role that has a particular demonstration and a crucial outcome during election campaigns. The argument makes two central assumptions: first, that 'media' and 'politics' cannot be seen as separate entities – the former a reflection of the latter; but rather, the media now constitute a political force where 'politics' is seen as sets of practices, institutional arrangements and conventions of behaviour that cross-cut various arenas; second, that the significance of the media is less the capacity to change attitudes and behaviours than to form knowledges and conventions that ultimately feed into attitudes and decision-making. Under these assumptions, the media cannot be seen as having precise effects but instead are seen as a formative terrain of social practices.

This approach dispenses with conceptual frameworks that either seek measurable effects or assume that politics is a separate and dominant entity, visible in its institutions, procedures and outcomes. Despite the tenacious retention of such assumptions, studies have repeatedly indicated their inadequacies and inappropriations to deal with the phenomenon (as suggested by Harrop in his review of the effects tradition; and by Hindess in the case of politics.[5] This chapter will examine the emergent relationship between elections and the media through the concept of arenas and the metaphor of representation,[6] terms which coalesce with empirical referents during election campaigns.

Why elections? Harrop argues that 'an election campaign is a poor laboratory for studying media effects. It is a brief, frenetic affair during which most people talk about politics.'[7] Yet this is precisely their value. Elections constitute a bounded space – both temporally by the duration of the campaign, and spatially by the rules of campaign conduct and the mechanics of electoral practice – which necessarily produces, through consolidation and compromise, political positions. The party manifesto is an interesting exemplification of this. Between elections, it is notoriously difficult to gauge where a party stands except in either the broadest terms or on particular critical issues. Factional conflict, party tussles (especially constituency versus national), leadership challenges and changeovers, and so on, undermine such attempts. Thus, although party manifestos are, by definition, documents of compromise vying with unrealisable promises, and as such have a problematic place in party, media and public deliberations during a campaign, these documents provide rare archival traces in the long run.[8]

Similarly, the differences between the prioritising of issues by a party and the agendas developed by the media and the public provide important data not available between elections. The act of voting at the end of the campaign often produces patterns and outcomes that are contrary to opinion poll predictions and/or canvassing indications, despite the enormous investment in those predictive endeavours.

Most important, however, is the nature of political opinions during and between elections. Harrop argues that 'Between campaigns, opinions are more superficial, more volatile and more susceptible to media influence . . . . the media are a crucial mechanism of electoral change within campaigns.'[9] This assumes that (1) political opinions correspond to the answers given to poll questions; (2) political opinions are different types of things in election and non-election times; and (3) an opinion or stated intention will correspond to a subsequent voting choice. All assumptions are questionable. Political opinions may not correspond to the easily retrievable multiple-choice replies to pollsters, and frequently do not map into a voting choice. Opinions are far less the assessment of who would make the best government than an opposition, say, to nuclear arms, a belief in preserving soil or rain forests, a belief in educational opportunity, or wanting more advantageous conditions for those in small business. Such opinion sets do not map easily into party promises and even less so into government deliveries.[10] One might even argue that voting choice frequently and increasingly bears minimal relation to a voter's political knowledges and personal priorities.

Consequently, just as 'television enlarges knowledge'[11] so the media have enlarged political knowledge that is simply not reducible to polling choices (opinion or voting). The field is much richer than a vote or a campaign can express, thus the concern about recent elections as to whether a particular campaign was *dull* or not, see the Butler series, or Pateman on the British February 1974 election campaign:

> I did not find the three weeks of extensive viewing generally entertaining or educative, and that had the information I undoubtedly received been more relevant to my own, not particularly idiosyncratic, political concerns, it would have been more easily assimilable.[12]

If analysts tend to find campaigns dull, how, we might ask, does the general public find them? But perhaps there is hope and from the media itself: take Goot on the 1980 Australian Federal Election:

> In the space of two weeks, a 'dull' contest became a 'cliffhanger'. Central to this transformation were, of course, the polls. They dominated the press coverage and the television news; caused the Liberal Party to revamp its campaign and redouble its advertising; and both directly and indirectly affected the vote. The polls symbolised the campaign as contest in its purest form.[13]

How, then, might we view elections as a political practice? Election campaigns have a decisive outcome in the production of a government. They are not just another event on the political calendar, yet, equally, the campaign does not 'produce' the outcome in any simple way. Rather elections entail a distinctive relationship between the contesting arenas of political practice emanating from the notation of *representation* in which the media have a peculiarly privileged position. This derives from the double sense in which the term representation is employed – both as a metaphor for the techniques of representation (the codes and conventions by which the media produce texts) and as the outcome of electoral voting (as the mechanism of the popular vote in selecting political representatives).

The double movement of the concept of representation necessarily entails ambiguities and conceptual slippages, and it is this slipperiness which enables the media to occupy several roles concomitantly (if not tongue in cheek) – as the faithful scribe of certain political events, as *agent provocateur*, as the watchdog of the people, and as players in various events and arenas (from broadcasting Parliament to exposing scandals in private life).

The complexity of media activities guarantee media institutions a prime role in the social formation. Correspondingly, the roles of the media in the lives of the electorate are complex and pervasive, and are not confined to measurable or unmeasurable 'effects' on voting behaviour. The media have contributed in large part to the formation of knowledges about politics, that is to say, in forming the rhetorics that are available for public discussion and assessment of political practices, rhetorics which turn on the concepts of representation and accountability. Elections are a specific monitor of the shifting terrain of political knowledges. In this process, the media contribute in two ways:

*As spaces of representation*

The media constitute spaces for representing political practices in which the character of those representations derive from certain conditions of representation. Such conditions are determined neither exclusively by the ideals of democracy nor by the practices of recording (textual production). Centrally, the arena of media representations – and indeed the very acts of representation – constitute a form of political practice within the institutions of media as a political force.

*As transforming political practices*

Through the development of the media as a political force, the terrain of politics has been significantly transformed – most clearly evident in the reordering and articulating of constituent arenas of contestation. Such changes can be summarised by the interpolation of the media into campaign strategies, by intervention into, undermining of, existing practices, and their subsequent reconstitution. Rather than dwelling on the disappearance of traditional campaign procedures, closer attention needs to be given to the rearticulation of the campaigning arena.

**Media interpolation of the political terrain**

> The advantages [of televising Parliament] could be enormous. Politicians would gain in stature and their responsibilities be emphasised by their being seen in the historic surroundings of the Palace of Westminster: constituents would be less dependent upon the invitations for their television appearances; informed commentaries could illuminate the issues and the procedures just as they have done, and continue to do, when television presents the results of a General Election. Above all, viewers would be able to see for themselves what was happening; their experience, as in a dozen other spheres, would be first-hand: they would no longer have to depend upon the printed or verbal reports of others.[14]

Goldie's hopes for the televising of Parliament may not fully have been realised by the experimental televising of the House of Lords, for although the broadcasts have undoubtedly contributed to political knowledges, those knowledges do not take that idealised form of seeing democracy in action.[15] Yet her work on television and politics is illuminating in making explicit the assumption that politics is a privileged domain and one which is accorded both a kind of transparency and direct correlation among its players, and which therefore can be 'seen' through the media of representation. It is a conception common to most work in political analyses, and one which for Goldie, as the doyen of BBC political broadcasting, has had profound effects on the form of that tradition.

Pateman also adopts this view:

> Here is a true ideology of knowledge: liberal democracy permits us not only to vote but to know. It gives us not only power, but also access (if we wish it) to the truth necessary for the rational exercise of that power.[16]

Moreover, this assumption underpins most official stances on broadcasting, such that the media are positioned as a conduit – a channel for the transmission of messages – but also almost as an extension of the electoral system. Fundamentally, it assumes that liberal democracy is composed of a set of tenets that can be automatically and unproblematically actualised in the various games of politics.

> We are in no doubt that the major political parties should have direct access to radio and television time. The parties are there to provide the statesmen and the policies which will govern the country. They are at the heart of democracy and it is they who formulate the economic and social policies on which depends the prosperity of everyone. The nation's media should give them the opportunity to address people in the terms and manner they see fit and particularly through broadcasting which reaches almost every elector in the country.[17]

Hindess has argued that parliamentary democracy has been analysed 'in terms of a relation between the supposed natural sovereignty of the individual and the sovereignty of the parliamentary state'.[18] This tends to be elaborated either as the aggregation of that natural sovereignty of individuals into an elected body, or in terms of 'mechanisms' whereby 'citizens can control that effective sovereignty'. Both of these conceptions are at work in the above quotations.

The alternative 'radical view' still assumes that relation between citizens and elected bodies but explores 'the inevitable discrepancy between the representative machinery of parliamentary democracy and the democratic ideal in which the people, or their interests or desires, are truly represented revealing the inadequacy of the machinery in question'.[19] Hindess points out that ideals of democracy can vary enormously and are scarcely evident in the mechanisms of organisation, procedure and decision-making that compose the diverse institutional arrangements of a parliamentary democracy.

In the case of electoral politics, analysts assume that parties and electoral outcomes reflect or represent the 'desires' of the electorate, but this assumes 'first, that the votes of the electorate reflect interests and/or desires that are formed independently of the practices of parties and other agencies, and second, that these are effectively aggregated through elections'.[20] In refuting this, Hindess emphasises the complexity of electoral practice – constituency allocation, vote aggregation, seat distribution, party organisation and conflict within and between parties, influences of diverse state apparatuses, and so on, which militate against a view that elections can in some magical way encapsulate the popular mood (interests and desires):

> That idea has only to be stated for its absurdity to become apparent: it requires either a realm of constitutive subjects endowed with free will and an autonomous capacity for rational calculation and decision, the unmoved movers of society and history, or else, … it requires that class interests determined ultimately by the structure of the economy are able to override the distorting effects of these other agencies and their practices.[21]

The consquences of this is that elections cannot be seen as the apex of parliamentary democracy, as the articulation of citizenry into Parliament, but are the outcome of diverse practices – the specific electoral machinery, the choices and issues that are adopted by parties, relative strengths of and differences between parties – factors which have effects which cannot be supposed to automatically be derived from a unitary set of interests of the bourgeoisie.[22]

So what has become of parliamentary democracy? Once we discard a general principle of democracy which determines, and is reducible to, all political agencies, we can explore the differences between agencies and their various (sometimes contradictory) workings. To this end, Hindess has developed the notion of arena to refer to the diverse fields of contestation within political practice, a definition which is more radical than Seymour-Ure's 'places, events, groups and offices . . . which may attract the attention of media'.[23] Under this usage of arena, the media are not just another place for political fallout, but a force of contestation.

Primarily the notion of arena is working to depose the segmentation of the social formation into separate spheres composed of certain institutions, agents, agencies and codes of conduct (by legislation and convention). In the case of 'politics' as a separate sphere, links with 'the people' occur conventionally through political party membership, parliamentary activities and electoral practices, that is, via three conduits between the spheres of politics and people. In this account, the media are constrained to constitute merely, at most, an additional conduit.

In undoing this account, Hindess has, in the case of parliamentary and extra-parliamentary practices, dismantled the neat boundaries (and the assumptions of 'democracy' on which that turns) in order to argue that analysis cannot simply be reduced to the visible mechanisms of the democratic state, but rather must examine 'what the scope of democratic modernisms is and how it is determined':[24]

> It is the relationships between what falls within the scope of democratic mechanisms and what does not, that provides the space for the intervention of other determinants of the practices of the state apparatuses.[25]

In the case of elections, Hindess argues that:

> Different electoral arrangements have different effects, and we may wish to argue that some are preferable to others. But what those effects are will depend on the character of the parties and other forces at work in the electoral arena. They are never simply a product of electoral arrangements as such.[26]

By rejecting explanations of politics in terms of democratic ideals or notions of sovereignty, a space is created for radically shifting the terms of debate about elections and the media whereby diverse media representations and contestations concerning political questions can be given the status of legitimate contestation, that is, as vital agencies within the actualisation of parliamentary democracy.

As such we are arguing against claims of reflection, reinforcement or change and instead emphasising the transformative consequences of the media by employing the term interpolation to refer to the mechanism by which the electoral arena has been transformed. Interpolation refers to a range of effects – intervention, interposition, incorporation and reconstitution.

This approach is designed to get beyond the polarity reflected in, for example, Blumler's alarm about the dramatic 'intervention of television into politics':

> The implications of these environmental trends for communication roles in politics are tolerably clear. First, as traditional party ties lose their salience for people, and as their social situations become politically less homogeneous, the potential for mass communication to exert an influence correspondingly widens. Secondly, the enlarged body of float-

ing voters can no longer be regarded as consisting mainly of people who
have opted out of the political communication market.[27]

Rather, there is a need to pose a more general and pervasive con-
ceptualisation of the media as a force within the political terrain whose
activities are characterised as interpolation; media representations constitute the increasingly dominant form of articulating notions of representation and accountability. As such, the media are a contesting
force both as a space of representation and as a means of transformation.

## The consolidation of the media as a force of contestation

> [Aneurin] Bevan was not a successful radio broadcaster, largely because
> he had a stutter. . . . Silences, or impediments in speech, are of the
> utmost importance in sound radio. If a pause is longer than usual, while,
> for instance a speaker is trying to consider how to answer a question, the
> listener is apt to think that something has gone wrong and begins to
> fiddle with the controls of his set. But on television nothing is more
> fascinating than to look at a person who is thinking, who is revolving a
> question in his mind and trying to decide how to answer it. This is a
> genuine situation, real and immediate; and the message of the act of
> thinking is conveyed visually by the expressions on the face of the man
> who is answering.[28]

The possibilities offered by the advent of television for the representation of politics and of election campaign activities have been well documented. The concern with television *per se* has, however, blinkered an
appreciation of how television has fitted into the broader terrain.
Although television-related 'facts' are important – like the saturation of
homes with television sets, the greater credibility accorded to television
news and current affairs by viewers, and the trend to citing TV as the
dominant source of news and of political information – there are limitations to the surveys which seek viewers' stated preferences and beliefs
about their viewing practices. The limited data about recall by viewers
suggest that the index of credibility in particular is somewhat suspect.
Self-assessment of credibility and source of information fails to account
for significantly lower retention of information from that medium. A
study in Melbourne looked at patterns of recall of TV news across channels by varying groups (age and sex) of viewers . This found that 25 per
cent of viewers could not recall *any* news item, let alone the lead stories.
News-viewing appeared to be habitual (viewers watched only one
channel) and involved a strong belief (despite any 'comparative' viewing) that the chosen channel gave a good summary of the day's events,
and that its content were very similar to the news on other channels.
Moreover, news-viewing was fraught with many other distractions (in-

cluding sleeping!), suggesting that, at best, TV news was 'half-watched'. They concluded that although viewers showed strong channel loyalty, they were not viewing:

> with alertness and concentration . . . If pressed, she/he will usually remember, after some initial difficulty, a 'story' (or news item) which has been prominently featured both in terms of time and the position in the ordering of items in the newscast.[29]

These results have been complemented elsewhere; recently, a study by the IBA used hidden cameras to observe viewers viewing and found that rather than being 'diverted, entertained and informed': 'that television rarely gets the viewer's undivided attention. People are reading, eating, squabbling, knitting, or kissing and cuddling at the same time'.[30] The study undercut the reliance on traditional techniques of ratings surveys – in Britain, generally by self-completed diary; and in America, by an electronic device in the set.[31] These techniques rely on equating what channel/programme was apparently switched on with the fact of watching. Television programmers have been especially shaken by the findings of large-scale and consistent *inattention* to what fills the screen.

The significance of these results for election campaign representations is that there is a huge discrepancy between campaigners' and producers' tendency to see the TV screen as an extension of the hustings space into the living-room – that is, to capture the attention of potential voters – and the use of TV by viewers, not as a pedagogic device but as a backdrop for other activities. Proselytising, policy statements and soft-sell may therefore be radically misplaced. At best, politics on television may feed into political orientations and knowledges; it is unlikely to be the key to determining voting behaviour.

This is not to say that television is not an important medium for the representation of politics, but it does question the basis of almost all research on the subject. Against the change/reinforcement shift in theories of the media, arguments about political television have been in terms of (1) mere coverage, a window on the world; (2) trivialisation of politics into entertainment; and (3) television elections (replacing 'politics'). Yet television must be seen in relation to other media, particularly the press and radio. Television has profoundly inflected those inter-media relations, although television has not eclipsed other media. None the less, television is frequently seen as *the* troublesome development, as a recent and potentially powerful agent of change, whose effects are sought in a way very similar to the moral concerns raised about early radio and early cinema. Television continues to attract moral outrage on its behalf, despite the lack of evidence yielded by vast amounts of research.

Moreover, the anticipated death of the press has not come about; rather, the press has maintained, if not enhanced, its capacity to present fuller accounts, opinions, editorials, and so on, and to be consumed in diverse ways, and at leisure. Television and press have reluctantly developed a complementary relationship, each characterised by spending considerable text/broadcasting time dwelling on the other! This process of feedback and cross-referencing is a vital part of the network of media texts operating as a set of signs by which people traverse that network. The intensity of traversing cannot be enhanced at the will of election campaigners: indeed, it is those people who are already interested in politics who enhance their activities; those who are not – Harrop's apathetic group; the vast majority according to studies cited by Spence[32] – show no signs of rushing out to become involved. Consequently, we might query the argument that this group is the most likely to be influenced by campaign material. If levels of interest and knowledge are very low, any 'influence' will look a lot, but it may not be enough to persuade people to go out to vote (where voting is voluntary) nor carefully ('rationally'?) consider that vote. Thus there may be a threshold level of interest and knowledge below which media-attributed 'influence' hardly matters.

Of the analyses listed above, none appropriately characterises the situation: the considerable flux and uncertainty in voting patterns (and marked decline of party membership) go against either notions of change or reinforcement. Patterns of actual media usage go against notions of coverage (a window on the campaign) and trivialisation, and considered alongside cross-media patterns, against notions of 'a television election'. Television may be 'switched on' more than other media sources for most voters but television:

1. viewing exhibits low attention and recall;
2. functions as one source among others for those interested in politics;
3. has the dual character of being highly fragmented (into programme types) yet 'appears' and is viewed as a flow;[33]
4. is viewed in patterns which are mostly distracted by other activities, and are increasingly selective (particularly with the advent of remote control and VCRs).

As a consquence television can be seen neither as the bogey of politics nor as the usurper of the terrain of politics. Stuart Hall has cast the role of television as the representation of politics, as a sort of parallel contest, in which TV representations reproduce the conditions and struggles of the parliamentary struggle, but skewed in favour of the status quo. He compares terms of a television debate with a parliamentary debate – each involving opposing speakers and a neutral anchorperson/Speaker proceeding by certain rules of debate and censure. By this parallel adoption of parliamentary procedure, Hall argues that television representations 'mirror' and favour the parliamentary system in a way that is patently open and obvious. As support, Hall quotes a Director-General of the BBC who said: 'Yes, we are biased – biased in favour of parliamentary democracy'.[34]

This account conflates rules of procedure with outcomes of procedure, assuming a uniformity across arenas into what Hall terms a 'structure of dominance': 'It is in politics and the state, not in the media, that power is *skewed*.'[35]

In this account, the media (and current affairs in particular) are constrained to only reproduce power relations articulated elsewhere: 'to try to *hold the ring*, to sustain an arena of "relative independence", in order that this reproduction of conditions of political power can take place'.[36] That is, television reproduces, though imperfectly, the class struggle on television. This argument remains within the consensual model with television '*both* autonomous and dependent',[37] constrained to the mere reflection of struggles located elsewhere.

Several assumptions are at work here: first, that struggles do indeed occur elsewhere in the mysterious land of politics; second that these struggles determine, outweigh and are identical to 'struggles' elsewhere; third, that political struggles can be identified as some unitary theme whose outcome can be known, guaranteed and recognised; and fourth, that the conditions and outcomes of political struggle are somehow already given and beyond the influence of specific struggles.

While Hall argues that television constitutes the ultimate reflection of politics elsewhere, Pateman has made an even more confusing move, arguing that the political field as a distinct domain has dissolved into a form of *televisual practices*. He says that there is no longer a campaign that has an independent existence: 'We do not have television coverage *of* an election; we have *a television election* '.[38]

For Pateman, an election campaign has become a field of political actors and TV superstars playing the 'games' of TV programming[39] for a more sophisticated version of this in terms of notions of conflict as dual and televisual 'presence'. Politics has become the televisual.

Both positions have limited usefulness for understanding media and politics – either politics becomes some pallid reflection in the media, or it has become embodied in media tinsel and determined by the logics of TV programming. The relationship is rather more intriguing just like the viewers/voters:

– political practices have changed significantly, attributable in large measure to the interpolation of media into the traditional arenas of politics;

– as a result, election activities exhibit an intertwining of media and political arenas;

– this proceeds against a backdrop of a general belief (still!) in ideals of democracy that can be both expressed and realised in unproblematic forms; the variants and complexities of 'democracies' and mechanisms by which they may be articulated are largely ignored.

Media representations of election campaigning involve:

1. *The mobilisation of public relations machinery* – 'managing' the images of candidates; organising media entourages; organising campaign activities to suit media priorities and agendas; maximising exposure in the media.

2. *The structuring of the campaign around opinion polls* – both within and across media and in terms of party strategies.

3. *The consolidation by the press as central monitor* – the terms of press coverage have not changed much in postwar elections (even under the impact of television) yet the press has consolidated its pivotal role – through the use of opinion polls, editorials, cartoons and extended analyses.

4. *The emergence of televisual approaches and programmes* – demoting conventions like party political broadcasts and advertisements and favouring interviews, panels and analyst-based formats.

5. *Maximising talk-back, meet-the-people and walkabout activities* – in opposition to the 'media packaging' of campaigns or the visibility of campaigns through media channels, direct access of potential voters to candidates has been recognised as vital. It confirms the belief that rather than television having made morons of voters, that the living-room immediacy of political practices has engendered a demand for face-to-face confrontations. Although the talk-back and walkabout should not be idealised as 'democracy in action', the mechanism of 'putting politicians on the spot' and seeing citizens through their idiosyncracies has itself become much of the importance of those encounters, frequently where the awfulness is the very pleasure of the format!

6. *The emphasis on leaders and qualities of leadership* – while not accepting the thesis of the 'presidentialisation' of politics, the nature, particularly of television, requires familiar, instantly recognisable inhabitants on the screen, hence leaders are increasingly groomed 'for the set'. Other candidates rely on press coverage, though the minor stars and highly articulate also contribute to the requirements of television. The presidential thesis ultimately assumes a correlation between leader visibility and voting patterns: British election outcomes militate against that reductionist hypothesis (particularly the personal unpopularity of Mrs Thatcher).

Overall, the media as a whole can no longer simply 'cover' a campaign – partly because so many media personnel accompany the campaigners! The British press has reverted to partisan advocacy, which is in a way easier to 'read' since it is now predominantly of Conservative sympathies. As television has become the dominant source of 'news', the press has largely abandoned its own distinction between news ('objective reporting') and comment (in editorials and by commentators). The 1979 election was the turning-point in this trend, as straight news virtually vanished from the press to be replaced by accounts that explicitly contained impressions and opinions. The interests of different sectors of the press were more directly acknowledged, both in terms of those which were explicitly advocated and those which were 'merely' being 'represented'. This trend in newspapers has provided a theme for weeklies in commentaries on press coverage, for example, by the *New Statesman*, as a new form of journalism, in which the editorial position adopted by papers can be related to the agenda and style of coverage.

These shifts in press coverage have enabled television to consolidate its dominant position in the media arena and to represent the press as an 'object' for scrutiny in the election contest. To this end, numerous television programmes have become devoted to addressing questions of press bias and political influence, assessing press coverage, the style of campaigning, television images of leaders and the role of opinion polls. These types of interpretative television suggest a shift from the strictly factual and balanced programming conveyed in broadcasting charters to a format of critique and auto-critique. Apart from 'special' programmes such as *Campaign 'X'* or *Hustings*, television has more generally extended news programmes into a 'magazine' format that goes beyond 'news' to emphasise both the issues and styles of campaigns.

Directly engineered formats of election television, especially staged interviews with leaders and party political broadcasts (PPBs) have fallen casualty to televisual requirements, reflected in low ratings and hostile reviews,[40] barely tolerated as 'television' or as 'politics'.

In all, television has succeeded in divorcing itself from press representations, although feedback between the two is a staple part of their respective activities. Television has achieved a viable and respected role in campaigning while the press appears outdated, unable to respond to the dictates of the *visual*, of *immediacy* and of the *documentary*, nor to the reconstitution of the contemporary campaign. The 1979 campaign saw the emergence of television as the dominant form of campaigning – not merely as a means of transmission, a channel for exposure, but as a force within the campaign arena itself.

Evidence about the changing nature of campaigning and of potential voters has been confirmed in a study at ITN:

In addition to asking our respondents *which* issues should be covered on television, we also asked *how* the campaign could best be covered. We wanted to find out which of several ways of covering an election on television was most attractive to people...At the top of the list came phone-in programmes..., and a televised debate between the leaders of the two main parties... The second level contained: comparison of policies on various issues; studio discussions between politicians; and interviews with party leaders. The third level contained the least-popular forms of coverage; party political broadcasts; film extracts of politicians' speeches; reports from different regions of the country; reports from individual constituencies; reports of opinion polls; and reports of the parties' daily press conferences.[41]

This list essentially reverses the order of priority accorded to media activities that is used by parties. People simply do not like political prosletysing. None the less, even the media resist the implications of the stated preferences; McKee, citing the 'difficulty' of organising phone-ins and the Leaders' rejection of a debate suggesting that perhaps 'we should pull our socks up and make our presentation in these [unpopular] areas more attractive and interesting.[42] There seems to be an extraordinary reluctance to accept that viewers/voters do not like traditional forms of political television and that this can hardly predispose potential voters to favouring those agencies who continue to produce such programmes.

## Opinion polls and their role in campaigning

In the 1960s things changed a great deal. First, competition came to the polls – NOP started in 1957, Louis Harris and ORC came in the mid-1960s, and Marplan and other firms offered their services to the press. Almost all the national newspapers carried polls, but they came to realise that it was an extremely expensive way of filling 20 column-inches. They . . . therefore . . . let them be quoted by the other papers . . . and re-lease[d] them to the broadcasting authorities . . . [reaching] a far wider audience . . .

Opinion polls came to dominate the election . . . it meant that the horse-race, the betting, element of the election was coming to dominate the coverage.[43]

Polls have become part and parcel of election campaigns. They might be seen as a prototype of the emergent form of electoral politics in which the media are an integral force. It is this status rather more than the ability to predict electoral outcomes for which they should be studied.

Polls are intended as indications of 'self-assessed' opinions; that is, they are the answers respondents give (often reluctantly) to pre-determined questions but by pollsters. Although those concerned with polls concentrate on the accuracy of techniques and on the distinctions between opinion, intentions and behaviour,[44] much more attention needs to be directed to the very notion of 'a poll' as a 'measure' of 'public opinion' – individual views constantly resist neat categorisation and are quite distinct from those aggregations of 'opinion' that are cast as 'the public voice': indeed, the very idea of 'public opinion' as a knowable entity is problematic.

Despite improvements in the predictive accuracy of polls and the growth of the industry of political polling, the significance of polling is rather more their pivotal role in the organisation of the media-electoral space both within the media and in relation to campaign strategies. Polls function as the weather report of a campaign for both the press and television: 'Mori calculates that 4 per cent of the front-page news coverage in the 1983 general election was directed to opinion polls';[45] even in 1970 Butler calculated that *The Times* ran 'front-page stories about polls on 16 days – and main lead stories on 8 days'.[46] Television news and current affairs devotes even more space and time to polls, since it reports all polls and, unlike the press, compares results across poll companies and over time.

The purpose of the polls is to assess opinion and to try to anticipate voting intentions. As polling techniques have become more sophisticated and responded to electoral changes, both a greater predictive success has been achieved, and the results of different companies have tended to converge during the course of the campaign.[47] None the less, the manner in which polls might influence voting behaviour, canvassed by terms such as bandwagon, underdog, and self-falsification, have been equivocal:

> A senior Labour figure observed that he did not have any idea about what happened during the election in terms of any movement of opinion; no one offered him solid evidence on whether they were succeeding in moving the argument on the tax cuts issue, or on the personalities of readers. Some of these things can be found in the later paragraphs of the poll reports during the election but they are not presented in the systematic way that is possible, as one can see from the private poll reports that were available after the 1974 elections.[48]

In the press, polls are presented as a percentage gain or loss over previous polls, a figure which is frequently presented as if it were an election outcome. Statistical riders about such figures are ignored in describing changes as 'substantial' or 'dramatic'; rather 'journalists will tend to build a story out of *any* change in the figures regardless of confidence limits'.[49] As a result, poll results appear like the photo-finish at the racecourse. More significantly, they structure other election coverage, through headlines, editorials and features, across to TV news and they considerably influence the course of party campaign strategies. Moreover, as Marsh notes: 'It is ironic that the most unreliable poll results are not only the most likely to be picked up by the press but they are possibly the most influential'.[50]

Headlines perhaps are most misleading since one or two percentage points can suggest a good headline,[51] for example, from the 1979 election:

'Maggie to win by 110'.
'Maggie more popular than ever before'.
'Poll shock for Maggie boosts Jim'.

The issue is not whether readers believe such headlines or poll results – readers are used to headlines and their elusive sensations – indeed, headlines may be largely ignored since across papers and over time they are so contradictory. Newspapers do not present their poll results in carefully tabulated forms (as a series of results over time or between polling companies) making it difficult for a reader to follow the poll trends during the campaign.[52] However, headlines aside, the polls do structure the selection and 'slant' of editorials and features. Often, 'interpretations' of poll results seem almost arbitrary, being represented in four ways:

1. along partisan lines where issues that are 'popular' in a poll are treated as testimony to a party's position and as an omen of electoral victory;
2. but dismissed, where the caricature of polling is emphasised, for example, in this statement by Jon Akass of the *Sun* during the 1979 campaign:

> According to the polls we are lurching from side to side, left to right, like drunks. ... . The sensible thing to do is to tell outrageous lies to any pollster who accosts you. It is not nice to be thought average, or typical, or worst of all, predictable.[53]

3. inaccurately, or at best, out of context, where certain results are accorded a greater importance than the results warrant. For example, an article by Richard Rose during the 1979 campaign which was discussing the traditional pattern of women's votes as more conservative, was headlined: 'Women's vote could clinch it for Mrs T.';[54]
4. such that support for a leader is directly equated with support for a party – an assumption which is especially vulnerable to the mechanisms of translating votes into seats and seats into parties.

As indicated, polls fare better in TV news where the medium suits the full presentation of results due to the visual possibilities. With access to all poll results, polls often form the basis of election programmes on television. McKee emphasises the rules by which ITN covers opinion polls: putting poll results in the context of other stories; covering all available poll results (to achieve 'balance'); giving the poll source; and only using reliable polls.[55] As a result, opinion polls can organise the structure of programmes and be used to relate different programmes and issues most effectively:

> The basic voting-intention figures are put in the context of previous surveys and a brief reference to levels and trends in leadership ratings is followed by the results of a question on a televised debate between the party leaders, an issue which was particularly current at that point in the campaign.[56]

ITN also initiated featuring poll trends over the week on a Sunday in order to:

> demonstrate trends and to highlight the results of marginal polls and Scottish surveys, thus pointing to the possibility of regional divergence from national figures . ... so the Sunday broadcast was used to put the polls into perspective and point out some of their implications.[57]

On the whole, then, television has been able to incorporate opinion poll results across its programming with a comparative basis and within an interpretative framework which much more accurately accords with the weather report status of polling.

And finally, polls increasingly influence party strategies[58] – rather than following a pre-planned campaign, parties are coming to make continual adjustments in terms of mobilising and deploying party workers and politicians; how issues are formed into a hierarchy of importance; which party policies should be emphasised or played down; and how to manage press conferences, including which candidates should speak and about what.

Overall, then, whether the polls are treated as snapshots of a race or as predictive indicators, they are represented as the organising framework of coverage and campaigning. While the press use polls to consolidate a partisan position, television and weeklies construct a pluralist discourse. An additional aspect of the polls is the way in which they feed into press cartooning, since the summary format of polls appeals to the technique of caricature – party leaders are represented as gnomic encapsulations of party policies, leadership qualifications and personality quirks; or, as Ralph Steadman has remarked, how politicians can be 'hung, drawn and quartered.'

## Media and the changing face of the campaign

> Television is also the one information source which invariably receives
> more mentions than does any other when people are asked . ... which
> medium they depend on most for following an election. Its massive pres-
> ence has stimulated a host of party publicity adaptations – in rhetorical
> manner in the length, content and style of messages, and in the organis-
> ation and tactical conduct of campaigning.[59]

It is clear by now that media interpolation has transformed the terms
of election campaigning. Seymour-Ure has argued, with reference to
Leaders, that as the management of image and style becomes a preoccupation of the way politics is practised, so qualities of leadership have
shifted away from executive and ideological functions towards symbolic or expressive ones. Rather than this being a replacement, however, the symbolic/expressive might be seen as a necessary though not
sufficient condition for leadership (and electoral success): consider, for
example, Shirley Williams' losing her seat in 1979 despite her enormous popularity, visibility and 'suitability' to the media, and especially
television. Campaigning has moved away from the whistle-stop tour by
family car, the pound in your pocket, and the exhortations of 'Honest
Jim', but this has not necessarily entailed simple adoption of the
wrapping-paper and ribbon of publicity and media machines, as Mrs
Thatcher's image-creation has indicated. Populism has had a whole
new lease of life but that populism has involved a multifaceted ren-
dition, for the primarily elusive and transformative nature of the medium of television (in particular) precisely encourages a schizoid image,
eloquently demonstrated in Thatcher's definition of herself on television as the Iron Lady, the Instinctive Woman, and the Homemaker.
The apparent incompatibility of these three roles has been consistently
challenged by the success of television performances and leadership
style of combining strident rhetoric with an increasingly 'fluffy' image.
One commentator cast the qualities of strength and passion as a form of
political magic, terms in which female national leaders are familiarly
represented (cf. Mrs Gandhi, Golda Meir); where political strength is
seen to emanate from gender: 'What Mrs Thatcher indeed is, is La Pas-
sionara of modern British politics. She is passionate about her politics,
and men are frightened by passionate women'.[60]

The political calculation has paid off as Mrs Thatcher has developed
a style of politics characterised as 'personal' in which perceived qualities of strength and courage have been seen to work – witness the Falklands campaign and the 1983 election. It is a style which Cosgrove has
characterised as the *warrior* form of politics,[61] in which every encounter
must have a winner and a loser, a style which derives from 'a single-

issue temperament, a profit-and-loss shopkeeper's mind'.[62] The significance is that creation of a highly personalised style which has been the basis of Thatcher populism, as opposed to a party image or set of policies; Thatcher's successor will not be able simply to assume the mantle but will need to engage in an equally purposive moulding.

While the Conservatives have in recent years embraced the new style of campaigning, Labour has been more reluctant.[63] While Wilson capitalised on a down-to-earth appeal which was adopted in part by Callaghan, the changed circumstances of politics by 1979 made that style which shunned media staging and publicity gimmicks seem anachronistic.

The lack-lustre campaign of the Labour Party was further undermined by widespread disillusionment with the lack of direction and change which Callaghan's pragmatic approach to politics, that is, the absence of ideological commitment of philosophical basis: 'the public mood no longer had much time for Mr. Callaghan's "steady as she goes" style of pragmatism. What the voters wanted was not just a warrior but a crusader'.[64]

The Thatcher premiership has consistently projected an image of the crusade and has clearly rejuvenated the leadership game, probably irrevocably. Aitken has commented that:

> The lesson of all this for Mr.Callaghan's successor should be clear: young Mr Kinnock has no alternative but to match Mrs Thatcher's ideology with a more convincing ideology of his own, even if were tempted to do otherwise. Indeed it would be almost impossible for him to attempt the Sunny Jim style of electioneering.[65]

Seymour-Ure has argued that Kinnock may be a leader created by the media and certainly the representation of Kinnock's performance at the 1985 Labour Party Conference has adopted this line, heralding an aggressive, uncompromising style, relishing verbal contest. Hugo Young commented: 'If leadership consists of rallying the warriors and putting heart into those who feel they've lived for years with their backs against the wall, the Labour Party has a leader'.[66] Within campaigns, activities and strategies have changed, modified in part by the public opinion polls and even more so by the jealously guarded internal party polls, and geared increasingly to the agendas within the media. One particular change has been the shift away from the big evening speech which traditionally would be covered next day, to daytime activities that would capture the early evening news and short speeches to catch the mid-evening news. Activities balance constituency canvassing and prosletysing with 'human interest' activities – meeting shoppers or workers, or engaging in talkback programmes.

An index of how campaigning has changed is the daily press conference of each party leader. After the 1964 campaign, the daily press conferences had developed into the key campaign element through which
parties could assert and defend their policies, attack the opponents, and
subsequently modify policies, issues and tactics depending on the reception. As each party held its press conference at a different time, the
media would progress from one to another, revelling in stirring up
party conflict, attack and counterattack. Conferences were widely reported and televised and were generally regarded as an important arena
of public debate. The format seemed to fulfil the promise that media
intervention into political campaigning could make the contest immediate, tangible and active. Equally, the verbatim proceedings of the
conferences were devoured by party strategists in determining each
campaign move.

In the 1979 election, however, this new form of campaigning was
nipped in the bud by Mrs Thatcher's refusal to follow the convention
that the Opposition went first. She chose to hold conferences simultaneously with the Labour Party. Although a tactical move (attributed
to her advisers), the decision had the effect of delaying feedback between parties to the next day which, from the point of view of the media, was beyond 'newsworthiness' and immediacy. Hence although the
conferences were attended in huge numbers by the media, they formed
only a small part of press texts and television broadcasts: that is, they
became a media sport but lost the attention of the electorate. As a result,
this new hope of campaigning was marginalised, although the staggered
format was revived in the 1983 campaign, thus reinstating the tactical
advantages:

> Prime Minister Thatcher's authoritative handling of the daily press con-
> ferences and her effective use of briefing materials enabled her to explain
> and dismiss the leaked economic documents [of the NADC disputing
> the government's claim of economic recovery]. Fortunately for the Con-
> servatives, the press was distracted by a blazing row within the Labour
> Party [over nuclear disarmament].[67]

The Labour Party's management of the daily press conference illustrated that, despite its new headquarters, the Party had not taken account of the importance of a sizeable media room, an extraordinary
omission for a contemporary political party. It was obliged to use its
former home, Transport House, for press conferences, an arrangement
that had numerous disadvantages.[68] Moreover, Foot's unpopularity
obliged the Labour Party 'to project Labour's other leading spokes-
people – Healey, Shore and Hattersley in particular'.[69]

At first the strategy seemed to have some success. The main purpose of the morning press conference was to obtain favourable coverage in television news bulletins between lunchtime and the early evening. During the first week of the campaign, when Shore usually had the lead role, Labour achieved its highest poll ratings of the election campaign. As the campaign progressed, however, Labour's press conferences became ordeals to be endured with minimum harm, rather than opportunities to gain support.[70]

The physical problems, the lack of one clear leader and internal party dissensions were aggravated by the continuing inability of the Labour Party to engage effectively in political communication as reflected in the styles with which they were chaired:

Thatcher controlled the Tory conferences with an air of an effective teacher marshalling a group of schoolchildren on a day outing, while Mortimer ran the Labour conferences like a union official trying to control members he did not like and whose loyalty he doubted.[71]

The case of the daily press conferences illustrates the degree to which the representation of politics has become part of the contestation, and how vital the management of representations are to the tactical success of a campaign. After the fiasco of 1979, Thatcher has recognised the role of the conferences and their priority in the campaign.

Finally, perhaps the oddest feature of the emergent campaign format is the election night coverage. This is regarded on the one hand, as the climax of media campaign practices as that which can make sense of all that has gone before:

The Television Election builds up dramatically, with the days being ticked off, not to the Election but to the all-night programme of Election Results (*The Nation Decides* on ITV), when all the technology and personnel used in the previous three weeks are employed together in both the competitive race between the two television organisations and as a sort of celebration of television and its power.[72]

From the point of view of the media, the election night special is the closest to political 'behaviour' that they can engage in, by participating in the counting, the progress reports, the victories and the losses. On the other hand, the significance of the election night special has been given a rather more grandiose purpose, as the figure of democracy in action:

The Results programme demonstrated that television could present to the nation the compelling drama of a great national political occasion in which every voter had participated by putting his [sic] cross on the ballot paper. They did not have to wait for others to tell them what would be decided and what their next government would be. They could see for themselves.[73]

Once again, both views see politics as something that is obvious (a definition of democracy shared by all and actualised quite unproblematically) and in which the media is a reflective plane of the 'real politics'. The incoherence of this argument is especially clear in the case of the election night special, since until the majority of votes has been counted, the special proceeds by treating progress reports as predictive indicators which must be continually revised. Above all, the special is inherently divorced from political activity since it has no ability to alter the outcome. It might be said, then, to be supremely irrelevant to the practice of politics though it may constitute a new spectator sport.

## Conclusion: dealignment or reconstitution

The election night special is an indication of how political practices have been reconsituted by the interpolation of the media such that traditional political activities have either disappeared, been marginalised, revamped into popular formats, or been succeeded by new forms. Correspondingly, the contents of political promises and packages have also responded to popular appeals and formats, upturning many of the conventions of political science. 'Populism' is less a description of a position than the organising principle of diverse political-media practices, centrally marked by *visibility* and *accountability*, both terms functioning as metaphors, since the referents and articulations of each term shift radically over time.

Politics is no longer partisan in the Left/Right sense (if indeed it ever was) but is a much more complex terrain which is traversed by many political knowledges and forms. In this reconstitution, the media have become the symbol not only as watchdog but as an active process of scrutiny and accountability: both a space of representation and an arena of political contestation.

The issue is not dealignment (a term which functions as the marker of an end) nor the floating voter (as the deviant of electoral politics engaging in undisciplined disruption of political certainties) but rather it entails grasping the reconstituted idea of politics as a terrain of contestation which is made up of numerous arenas – some overlapping, some contradictory, each essentially organised around specific rules, mechanisms and strategies. While elections produce a government, the sum of political practices involves a mottled assortment of agencies and produces a range of outcomes. In this process, the media, especially during election campaigns, contribute to the formation of political knowledges as a prime element in that political terrain: they are not, however, the movers of the unmoved.

## Acknowledgements
Thanks are due to Barry Hindess, Beverley Brown and Jeffrey Minson for comments on earlier versions; to Kim Hillier for library assistance; and especially to Robyn Pratten.

## Notes
1. Annan, Lord (Chairman), *Report of the Committee on the Future of Broadcasting*,Cmnd. 6753, London: HMSO, 1977, p.297.
2. cf. Harrop (Ch.3 this volume).
3. Worcester, R. and Harrop, M. (eds), *Political Communications: The General Election Campaign of 1979*, London: Allen and Unwin, 1982; Crewe, I. and Harrop M. (eds) *Political Communications: The General Election Campaign of 1983*, Cambridge: Cambridge University Press, 1985).
4. Seymour-Ure, C., *The Political Impact of Mass Media*, London: Constable, 1974), especially Chapter 8.
5. Hindess, B., *Parliamentary Democracy and Socialist Politics* (London: Routledge & Kegan Paul, 1983); cf. Cutler, A., Hindess, B., Hirst, P., and Hussain, A., *Marx's 'Capital' and Capitalism Today*, volume 1, London: Routledge & Kegan Paul, 1977, especially Chapters 11, 12, 13.
6. Craik, J., *The Transformation of Election Campaigning Through the Media in Britain since 1945*, PhD thesis, University of Cambridge, 1980.
7. Harrop, M., 'Voters' (Ch.3 this volume) p.55.
8. cf. Robertson, D., *A Theory of Party Competition*, London: John Wiley, 1976, Chapter 4 and p.208.
9. Harrop, p.55.
10. For example, see Robertson, *A Theory of Party Competition*, pp. 71-2, for his analysis of the votes of MPs on the social Reform Bills on divorce, abortion and homosexual behaviour. These do not illustrate a clear cluster of variables that one might anticipate are associated with 'a dimension of pure "social liberalism"'; rather 'a sanctity of life dimension . .. could interfere with our stereotypes of either social liberalism or conservatism'.
11. Harrop, p.55.
12. Pateman, T., *Television and the February 1974 General Election*, London: BFI Television Monograph no.3, 1974, p.1.
13. Goot, M., 'The Media and the Campaign', in H. Penniman (ed.), *Australia at the Polls. The National Elections of 1980 and 1983*, Sydney: Allen and Unwin, 1983, p.140.
14. Goldie, G.W., *Facing the Nation. Television and Politics 1936 – 1976*, London: The Bodley Head, 1977, p. 334.
15. The impact of the broadcasting of Parliament is less as the actualisation of parliamentary struggle 'before our very eyes' and rather more the widespread denigration of the antics of parliamentarians; this has long been documented in Australia where verbatim radio broadcasting of both Houses of Parliament was introduced in 1946; for one account, see Inglis, K., *This is the ABC. The Australian Broadcasting Commission 1932 – 1983*, Melbourne: Melbourne University Press, 1983, pp. 128-32, 144-6, 421-2.
16. Pateman, p.27.
17. Annan, p.298.
18. Hindess, pp.49-50.
19. Ibid., p.50.
20. Ibid., p.72.
21. Ibid., pp.72-3.
22. Ibid., p.76.

23. Seymour-Ure, 'Leaders' (Chapter 1 this volume), p.6.
24. Hindess, p.51.
25. Ibid., p.52.
26. Ibid., p.77.
27. Blumler, J., 'the Intervention of Television in British Politics', *Report of the Committee on the Future of Broadcasting* (Annan), Appendix E, Cmnd.6753-1, London: HMSO, 1977,p. 1.
28. Goldie, p.120.
29. Powell, B., Cunningham, A., Hughes, P., Keating, G. and Smith, M., 'The forgettable news: two studies on the recall of TV news', in P. Edgar (ed.), *The News in Focus. The Journalism of Exception*,Melbourne: Macmillan, 1980, p.199.
30. Long, A., 'Stop it, George! . . . someone's watching', *The Sunday Mail* (Brisbane), 13 October 1985.
31. The US Neilsen company has been experimenting with 'people metres', an instrument like a remote-control channel changer into which viewers record their viewing selections, absences from the room, etc., thus improving demographic information about the viewing habits of all family members as well as tapping patterns of channel-hopping and advertisement-avoidance. The device is already being used by Roy Morgan Research in Australia in the hope of winning networks and advertisers away from the ratings provided by McNair-Anderson which are diary-based. (Kaplan, P., Price, J., 'A new toy in the TV ratings game', *The Sydney Morning Herald*, 19 October 1985).
32. Spence, J., 'Trends in political participation in Britain since 1945', in T. Leggatt (ed.), *Sociological Theory and Survey Research*, London: Sage, 1977, pp.313-34.
33. cf. Williams, R., *Television: Technology and Cultural Form*, London: Fontana, 1974.
34. Hall, S., Connell, I. and Curti, L., 'The "unity" of current affairs television', *Working Papers in Cultural Studies* (Centre for Contemporary Cultural Studies, University of Birmingham), no.9, 1976, p.92.
35. Ibid., p.92.
36. Ibid.
37. Ibid., p.53.
38. Pateman, p.2.
39. cf. Group Lu Hsun, ' "On Equal Terms": analysis of a televison programme', in J. Caughie (ed.), *Television: Ideology and Exchange*, London: BFI Television Monograph no.9, 1978, pp.13-34.
40. cf. Blumer
41. McKee, D., 'ITN's use of opinion polls', in Worcester and Harrop, p.135.
42. Ibid., p.135.
43. Butler, D., in A. Stuart, N. Webb and D. Butler, 'Public Opinion Polls'. *Journal of the Royal Statistical Society*, A, 142, Part 4, 1979, p.453.
44. cf. Worcester, R., 'Pollsters, the press, and political polling in Britain', *Political Opinion Quarterly*, 44(4), 1980, pp.548-66.
45. Marsh, C., 'Back on the bandwagon: the effect of opinion polls on public opinion', *British Journal of Political Sociology*, 15, no.1, 1984, p.72.
46. Butler, p.453.
47. cf. Craik; Butler.
48. Butler, p.455.
49. Jowell, R., in Stuart *et al.*, p.457.
50. Marsh, p.73 fn.
51. cf. Crespi, I., 'Polls as journalism', *Public Opinion Quarterly*, 44, 1980, p.473.
52. During my study of the 1979 election campaign, despite access to almost complete press and television coverage, there was considerable difficulty in obtaining essential details of the various polls from media accounts alone; cf. Barter, J., 'Newspaper coverage of the polls', in Worcester and Harrop, pp. 126-31.
53. 9 April 1979.

54. *The Daily Telegraph,* 11 April 1979.
55. McKee, pp.132-3.
56. Ibid., p.136.
57. Ibid.
58. See Kavanagh, D., 'Political parties and private polls', in Worcester and Harrop, pp.141-51.
59. Blumler, J., *The Challenge of Election Broadcasting* Leeds: Leeds University Press, 1978, p.67.
60. Gale, G., *The Daily Express,* 23 April 1979.
61. Aitken, I., 'Lucky Jim exists, still travelling light', *The Guardian Weekly,* 3 November 1985, p.18.
62. Young, H., 'The shopkeeper's eye view of the world', *The Guardian Weekly,* 3 November 1985, p.4.
63. Despite the media attention which the SDP has attracted, the Party strategy of not concentrating leadership in any one figure and associating the image of the Party with those leadership qualities undoubtedly undermines much of the force of the visibility of the SDP in the media (and thereby interferes with electoral chances).
64. Aitken, p.18.
65. Ibid.
66. Young, H., Kinnock's passion flowers, but the harvest is still to come', *The Guardian Weekly,* 13 October 1985, p.4.
67. Pinto-Duschinsky, M., 'The Conservative Campaign', in H. Penniman and A. Ranney (eds), *Britain at the Polls 1983,* Washington, D.C.: American Enterprise Institute, 1985, pp.51, 56, 58.
68. Kellner, P., 'The Labour Campaign', in Penniman and Ranney, pp. 73-5.
69. Ibid., p.74.
70. Ibid.
71. Ibid.
72. Pateman, p.26.
73. Goldie, p.67.

# 5 Local press
## David Murphy

In looking at the press in local politics I wish to examine not only how the local press treat the particulars of political activity but how in their manufacture of news they help to define the agenda of issues which are regarded as 'normal' or respectable politics in a 'liberal' democracy. I hope to show how this definition of reality is the outcome of a negotiated order of work routines, technology, markets for labour and products, and forms of ownership and control in the newspaper industry.

In approaching an analysis of the local press it would be an error to regard it as a quaint and antique sideshow in the context of the mass media industries. In the structure of ownership and of journalistic occupations there is a profound interpenetration between the local and national press. The pattern of ownership in the British press means that the industrial conglomerates which own regional and national newspapers often also own chains of local newspapers and have interests in commercial broadcasting companies. Over the period between the Second World War and the present this tendency has accelerated, and has been accelerated by, the progressive and ultimately total elimination of competition in the markets for local evening newspapers.

One of the traditional career patterns for Fleet Street journalists has been to commence as a junior reporter on a local weekly and progress via the local and regional evening and/or daily newspaper to a staff job in a national paper. Graduate training schemes in the big newspaper combines also use the local weeklies and evenings as initial training grounds for their trainees. The structure of the freelance news market also means that reporters working for local newspapers and to a lesser extent staff reporters on local newspapers are accustomed to sending more news stories and 'tip-offs' in a form which meets the requirements of the national press. There is thus a common journalistic culture and one of the aspects of this common culture is the form of knowledge of what constitutes 'news' or a 'good story'. Implicit in this definition of versions of events as worth including or excluding from the columns of the press is the identification of certain issues as legitimate or illegitimate for inclusion in the agenda of political debate. The coverage of local authority politics, of parliamentary elections, of party politics; the inclusion of readers' letters about local issues or about such national issues as civil defence or nuclear disarmament delineate politics as a form of life as much as the national press, 'Any Questions?' or 'Question Time'.

But the local press is important in another way. In general it has been more able to accommodate technological and social innovation than the national press. Fleet Street was the source of the Northcliffe revolution in the change in the presentation of newspapers and in their content to meet the market potential of the more or less universal spread of near-literacy since 1872. But this did not occur until the turn of the twentieth century: the upsurge of new local newspapers in the late nineteenth century was hardly less remarkable and had taken place forty years earlier. These papers were generally based on a new 'professionalism' which eschewed the Liberal or Conservative partnership of their libellous predecessors and promulgated the notion of the neutral and unbiased publication of political news.

Local newspapers have recently also initiated technological change such as photosetting and colour printing in a way which has not been possible in Fleet Street where patterns of industrial relations and ownership generate rigidities. The *Shropshire Star* for instance, was able to print with the new technology from the early 1960s. The fact that it was a new newspaper meant that instead of generating redundancies, the new technology created jobs. Local papers in Wolverhampton, Wigan, Portsmouth and Nottingham have taken up the 'new' technology. Only now is Fleet Street coming to terms with a technology already widely established in the provinces.

The 20 million copies of local newspapers which circulate regularly in this country are thus an important part of the process by which members of society define the nature of politics. This definition includes the role of the press which has often been established first by newspaper owners, editors and journalists.[1] They have tended to identify their function as a combination of providing information (preferably 'official' information according to one writer)[2]; a forum of differing views,[3] and a watchdog over the doings of local government politicians and officials.[4] This paradigm of their functions in the local political arena, however, ignores the fact that newspapers exist in the world of economics which limits their political scope. Politics is one of the commodities that the newspaper enterprise sells. The selling takes place in the market, and the market defines the situation for the journalist.

In order to understand news manufacture, it is therefore necessary to see how the operation of the markets in which newspapers operate affects the way in which news is made. In examining the relationship between the press and local politics in the mid-1970s I argued[5] that the market in which the newspaper operated resulted in a constant downward pressure on costs. This meant that a reporter's time became a commodity, representing a production cost and that commercial newspaper production demanded the maximum output of news for the minimum input of reporter's time purchased. It also meant that the news produced should have the maximum earning power, by attracting more readers and advertising combined with least consequent costs arising from such undesired outcomes as libel suits.

I argued that the consequence of this state of affairs in the political sphere was to push the journalist into the production of anodyne replications of readily available and non-contentious official versions of events, and routine descriptions of debates, rituals, celebrations and other formalities designed by political authority figures as public events. I later argued that this acceptance by newspapermen of the agenda set out by established groups exercising power amounted to a form of self-censorship.[6]

What was excluded was precisely the sort of journalistic endeavour in which the newspaper spoke with its own voice, having investigated versions of events and having drawn its own conclusions about the factual accuracy of such versions. Yet such would be the necessary precondition of the exercise of the role of watchdog over public affairs. I was not concerned with mere expressions of opinion about ideology or party politics but with making statements of fact about the nature of some aspect of the political or social or economic world under the scrutiny of the newspaper.

This is not to make the claim that newspapers are biased to the right or left, nor that they do not tell 'the truth'. The ideas of bias or truth as something which can be readily identified, often by numerical techniques, is both widespread in academic literature and simpleminded. It does not necessarily follow that academics who employ such notions are also simpleminded. It is merely that such techniques as content analysis provide ready means to provide 'proof' of what their commonsense notions already tell them. The fact such 'proofs' can lead to opposite conclusions about the same data should give pause for thought.[7] At a more basic level it must be clear that 'bias' implies that there is some central, neutral position about issues which is unbiased. Such a proposition assumes that it is possible empirically or analytically to establish the superiority of some views over others: it argues from an 'ought' to an 'is'. Equally, the idea that there is some objective truth about the nature of social life is a form of essentialism which implies that one accurate statement – a given number of people are out of work, say – is more 'true' in what it reveals about a given society than another equally accurate factual statement – that there are more video-recorders per head of population in Britain than any other European state.

Let me illustrate the point by an example in the field of journalistic coverage of local politics. While collecting data for my Masters thesis in the early 1970s, I went with a reporter to a rates tribunal. Three cases were heard and in each case the householder was successful in obtaining a reduction in rates. In two cases this was because of disturbance to amenities due to the activity of a local building firm and a local transport contractor. In the third case a view had been ruined by the erection of a factory after the ratepayer had bought from the same building firm.

The editor published these cases as three separate stories. But what interested me at the time was that the chairman of the rates tribunal was also the owner of both the building firm and the transport contractors. No attempt was made to hide these facts, but equally the chairman did not declare his interest. When I asked the editor why he did not do a story pointing out this state of affairs, he replied that everyone in the town knew that the man concerned owned the town anyway.[8]

Now both my version of the stories and the editor's were factually accurate. But which one was 'true'? Mine clearly imposed an interpretation on the events which was contentious and implied a value judgement. The editor's version, however, while it was non-contentious within the existing political and social context, was still implicitly dependent on a value judgement.

What we may be able to establish, rather than truth or bias, however, is what versions of events are reproduced in the production of news; who promulgates these versions; how the work practices of journalists affect this process and how the context of the news production industry affects the nature and development of work processes.

In all of these areas the past decade has witnessed fundamental changes in the potential for journalistic scrutiny of the political system. The new print technology which has become available is relatively cheap to buy and its use easily learned, has provided new opportunities to change the context in which journalistic work practices take place; it has provided the potential to liberate the journalist to adopt new work processes and it has created the possibility of widening the scope of differing versions of events processed into news. It has created the potential of change from a monolithic business-oriented press in which the major sources of news are different parts of the political establishment, to one in which such newspapers exist alongside other, different organs of news, radically oriented with cooperatively organised workforces and offering a voice to sections of society with views of politics previously excluded from the agenda of public debate in the local press. This is not to subscribe to the notion that such developments will automatically follow from the technological change, as some seem to have suggested.[9] But the change in technology may enable the social changes arising from social forces to take place in a way which was previously excluded by the unequal distribution of power and wealth, and the methods of organisation of news manufacture given appropriate conditions.

While the possibilities for change seem to encourage the birth of news outlets, however, other factors in the nature of the market context of the news idustry and its domination by local corporate monopolies noted repeatedly elsewhere [10] seem generally to ensure their demise.

Let us examine how the traditional commercial press covers political events as a solution to an organisational problem in an economic process of production and compare this with the organisation of news production in the alternative press. We may then examine how the two types of news organisation have coped with economic and technological change and how this has affected the relationship of the press to local politics.

In the production of news, journalists have to solve two fundamental organisational problems at the conceptual and practical levels; those of signification and validation. By signification I mean that they have to show that a news story is relevant to a perceived audience, at the social or communal level. By validation, I mean the means by which a story is deemed accurate according to some socially sanctioned canon of proof. The solution to both of these problems does not primarily inhere in the implicit nature of the story but in its sociological context. The construction of a viable news story is a social accomplishment, in the context of rule-governed activities.

For the editor of the traditional local newspaper engaged in political news production, both of the problems are solved by the choice of news sources. By selecting to write about events generated by 'officials' of organisations defined by those taking part as communal and by accepting 'official' versions of events both problems are solved. A reporter has an authoritative source for the accuracy of his or her news; the relevance to the community is established by the fact that the events depicted concern those institutions by which journalists and politicians define the community. Thus, sources of news are headmasters, vicars, councillors, town hall officials, police officers. Directly observed events such as court cases, mayoral inaugurations, council meetings are also the routine raw material of traditional local political news. That such events and individuals are the manifest embodiments of the communal life of local society is one of the taken-for-granted assumptions of journalistic work. It is not only an implicit assumption, however. When discussing the viability of areas as newspaper markets and the existence of communal life and vigour, editors regard the existence and activities of such institutions as the major indicators determining whether a district is 'a good area for news'. Similarly, a story is seen as accurate for all practical purposes if it accurately reflects what is said by appropriate contacts, or is an accurate account of something said or occurring at an 'official' occasion such as a court case or a council meeting.

This does not mean that newspapermen necessarily believe in such institutions as the metaphysical embodiments of local society. They may or may not. It does mean that such contacts and institutions are the means by which journalists are able to solve two crucial problems of organising conceptually the world into news and non-news on the basis of the social position of the sources, and the implicit functionalist perspective from which society is viewed by such journalism. And this selection of such contacts by journalists for their purposes of news production because they are seen as giving access to circulation market, is what makes such contexts 'gatekeepers'[11] – not the fact that they occupy some actual position in an objectively identifiable system of social relations.

An incident from my own career as reporter will illustrate the general point. In 1964 I wrote a story in a local weekly paper stating that Stretford (a town near Manchester) would 'go comprehensive' by 1966. This caused a local furore. The Borough Education Officer wrote to all head teachers in the borough saying that this was 'irresponsible journalism' and that no such decision had been taken. My editor called me to his office and asked what basis I had for the story. I replied that the Chairman of the Education Committee had told me. He asked if I had a note of the conversation and I said I had. He said, 'O.K.' The issue was at an end. The editor said he did not care whether or not the story was true, so long as we were only reporting accurately what was said by the Committee Chairman; if he and the Education Officer were at loggerheads that was their fault. A few days later the Chairman wrote a letter to the paper acknowledging the error as his own*.

Official news contacts provide access to news which is seen as relevant to target audiences; their news does not require checking because they are 'spokesmen' (authoritative sources) in the areas defined by their institutional roles, and this indicates the communal significances of the stories they tell. In this they have an implicit source of social control over the newspaper. The withdrawal of their cooperation would render the paper unable to gain access to its audience and would pose the problem of how easily and quickly to obtain news ready validated and significant at the level of the community.

When faced with the question of causing offence to such contacts, editors I have worked for as a journalist and observed as a sociologist, offer a version of the motto: 'We have to go back to these people'. And

* As it transpired this story did not presage a great career in journalism. One of the few distinguishing characteristics of Stretford, other than its connection with Manchester United, is that it is one of the few areas in the country to have retained intact its local authority grammar schools right up until the present.

this is a valid inference from the premises of the need to sell papers to raise revenue directly and to attract advertisers by means of this readership – and given that they subscribe to a sociological analysis which is functionalist authoritarian and institutional.[12]

Contacts who tell stories disruptive of such a Panglossian vision are treated as cranks and pose only problems for the journalists in the political area. Two cases illustrate this point. A local 'character' told a reporter that Tory worthies were at war over claims by one that the other was unfit for office in the local Masonic lodge by virtue (or the lack of it) of his keeping a 'fancy woman' in furs and a Rover motor car in a luxury flat in Altrincham. While this became a story among journalists it was never considered for publication. No attempt was made to check out the woman or even to interview either of the warring parties. But when one of the principals voluntarily entered a nearby private lunatic asylum and an inquiry was instituted by the Regional Office of the Conservative Party, the issue became a newspaper story. The inquiry verified that something was happening at the societal level. Journalists therefore could report the events by simply obtaining quotations from the officials, from the parties to the dispute or from their lawyers. The problems of validation and signification were solved at a stroke by the fact that the raw materials of news production were being generated by the political institutions, and the newspapers could adopt their role of 'reporters of events' by which they mean recorders of versions of events promulgated by spokesmen legitimated by the political system which they, (the journalists) are depicting. When the story came only from a low status individual, outside the circle of normal political contacts, it was not considered even worth investigating, let alone publishing.

The second case illustrates the cost element in the social control over newspaper reporters' activities. A group of householders in a Manchester suburb were much disturbed by a councillor's husband's purchase of a house and land on which planning applications had been refused over the years and its subsequent resale at a profit of 250 per cent, after the council had changed its mind and had given planning permission for redevelopment. The municipal reporter on the local evening paper to whom they reported the affair apparently did nothing. I interviewed him and he described the group (who were all over 40), as 'cranks', and added that there were 'extremists' working in the area to oppose a nearby redevelopment scheme undertaken by the council and a property development company. He had been to the Planning Department in the Town Hall and the officials there had told him there was no truth in the rumours. He worked from the press office in the Town Hall for most of the time, and expressed the view to me that the idea that local politicians were corrupt was inaccurate: they were well-intentioned if stupid people. Local government officers were by and large both decent and efficient and he was not inclined to believe accusations of corruption in general, and regarded them as inspired by a sort of conspiracy theory.

The 'cranks' gave him photocopies of letters, planning applications, the appropriate refusals and acceptances of these, he never returned. This, the 'cranks' interpreted as inculpating the reporter into the conspiracy. The far more likely explanation is that the reporter never returned them because he lost them and could not be bothered to look for them. Local newspapers, like the nationals, work to deadlines, and when a current deadline is past, the next one is the dominating consideration. The maintenance of regular news contacts facilitates this process; keeping in with the 'cranks' does not. They have no contribution to make to the normal regular functioning of news coverage. Therefore, annoying them involves no cost to the newpaper's capacity to meet its deadlines.

All but one of the traditional commercial local newspaper editors to whom I have spoken, expressed the view that stories involving weeks of investigation were not worth doing because at the end they still only filled a limited amount of space which could as well be filled by a story or picture obtained through normal processes taking perhaps half an afternoon's work and selling just as many or more papers. And perhaps a libel action might follow with massive legal costs even if the case never got to court. Alan Doig,[13] in his analysis of the press treatment of corruption, refers to the case of the editor of the *Lancashire Evening Post* who exposed the corrupt practices of the former Chief Constable of Lancashire resulting in his dismissal. This resulted in the editor being awarded the Press Award for 1977. The North West Newspaper Editor's Guild in a citation for his work, declared it was 'remarkable that he did this at a time when he could have done nothing'.

The aftermath, however, was interesting. The local government reporter who worked on the story reported loss of cooperation among his official contacts. Alan Askew, the editor, reported no increase whatever in newspaper sales. And two neighbouring papers, *The Morecambe Guardian* and *The Lancashire Gazette* both attacked the *Post* for its campaign and claimed that they had known all along about the story but did not act because of the advice they received from their lawyers. Another case from my own experience concerns a councillor who bought a bulldozer as scrap from the council for £50 and subsequently sold it for £500 having used it for six months. When I put this to an editor of an evening newspaper as the sort of story not investigated by the local press, he dismissed it as gossip. But when later the same councillor was in court for receiving stolen earth-moving equipment removed on a low loader, his trial and imprisonment were a front-page lead in one of the weekly papers under the general editorship of the same editor.

The commercial gains from the active scrutiny of local authority figures are invisible to the naked eye. Editors offer two different sorts of explanation for their own unwillingness to tackle such stories. Whenever I inquired whether an editor would publish an embarrassing story about local worthies or powerful businessmen each one answered in the affirmative if such a story cropped up and were proved. On each occasion when such a story cropped up, however, the story was rejected because it was in some sense held not to be a story (e.g. it was 'merely gossip' or 'something everybody knows already') or it could not be proved and would therefore incur the full horror of the libel laws (which, for most journalists, are feared but never experienced). The other explanation put forward when the general lack of such news was raised, rather than individual instances, was the issue of the economic and organisational difficulties of doing such work – shortage of staff; the pressure of deadlines; the need to 'go back' to contacts in the normal cooperative process of news-gathering.

### 'Alternative news'

The fundamental proposition underlying this last argument is that news stories in the end are obtained by going to official spokesmen. They both validate and make significant the versions of events which journalists process into news stories. Thus, the work routines of traditional local newspaper journalists lead to implicit value judgements about their depiction of the truth about the nature of society, politics etc. The approach to news of the 'alternative' local newspapers, however, is based on a diametrically opposed proposition: that the purpose of news is to tell the truth which the official spokesman wishes to hide; is to discredit those spokesmen and so expose the wrongs endemic to the system. The alternative press is a phenomenon of the last fifteen years, and is not particular to this country. In the United States such papers exist across the country and revel in such titles as the Californian *Mo Jo* (Mother Jones). They are transitory in their nature and generally have literally meteoric careers in as much as they suddenly appear, glow briefly and then crash to the ground in darkness and oblivion. If we include among them all of the news publications which are not capitalist and establishment, then the net would include a variety of community newspapers, regional and local arts periodicals, CND publications such as *Sanity* or *Radioactive Times*, or other papers published to promulgate a particular party or sectional view of news such as, say, *Spare Rib*, or the *Socialist Worker*.

I would argue that these papers and magazines do provide alternative sources of views and news to the established agenda for political debate and that they do attempt to promulgate sectional versions of news, otherwise denied circulation. But they do not attempt as a central purpose the reformulation of what constitutes legitimate political news. If they do this, it is as a by-product of some other political purpose.

The news magazines *cum* newspapers that I wish to concentrate on in this chapter are those which attempt to widen and refocus the nature of political debate by altering what is regarded as a legitimate depiction of reality. Traditional establishment newspapers and political magazines have always seen it as their purpose to conduct the debates and provide the information implied in the constitutional forms of liberal democracy, and to rely on these forms as unquestioned bedrock assumptions. Submissions by the NUJ, the Editors Guild as well as the newspaper proprietors to successive Royal Commissions, all rely on such a position. In this sense the *Daily Herald* of thirty years ago was the same as the *Daily Mail* or the *Manchester Guardian*. *The New Statesman* was the same as *The Spectator*: they were both journals of opinion in which the great and the good or not so good gave voice to their views of politics, morality, philosophy, ethics, literature, music, films and broadcasting.

The alternative version of news promulgated by alternative coverage of news does two things which its conventional rivals do not do. The first is that they concentrate on one aspect of the traditional routine justification of the press in a liberal democracy – the 'watchdog' function. They take this task literally and examine with a sceptical eye the doings of politicians, civil servants, the police, big business, trades union leaders. Secondly, they attempt to use the news they reveal about individuals in the system, to divulge the inadequacies of the system.

I am interested in such developments as they affect the local press, partly because I was already interested in the local press but more because these developments have primarily occurred locally. Locally, also, there is a sharp clash between the aggressive irreverent version of news put out by such news outlets and the bovine quiescence of the traditional commercial newspapers. This journalistic quietude is sometimes held up against the apparent abrasiveness of the Fleet Street papers manned apparently by literate skinheads dedicated to the exposé and cheque-book journalism. I would argue however, that this abrasiveness is skin deep, and that the Fleet Street press is fundamentally as free from the taint of offering any real challenge to the assumptions of the British Constitution, as is the *Congleton Chronicle*, the *Coventry Evening Telegraph* or the *Newcastle Journal*. The evidence for this can be seen in such studies as Jeremy Tunstall's devastating analysis of the Lobby correspondents who are 'on licence'[14] from the government on grounds of good behaviour, or Liz Curtis's study of the media coverage of Northern Ireland.[15] Indeed, the Fleet Street papers themselves are at times opposed to freedom which questions such notions as patriotism or the national interest. At the time of the Falklands crisis, we saw the symbiotic relationship between the Conservative War Cabinet and the Fleet Street editorial writers as they vied with one another, the harder to denounce the cowardly and scurrilous BBC for referring to 'us' by the insultingly disinterested phrase 'the British'. The *Guardian* and the *Daily Mirror*, also apparently short on patriotism, were lacerated by their fellows.

In the same vein the Fleet Street dailies are often willing to draw their own line about what is acceptable and what is not, *in their coverage of news* i.e. there are some facts which must not be stated. As Liz Curtis states:

> The supposed effects of television coverage of the war in Vietnam on the American Public, were fresh in the establishment minds. A *Sunday Express* commentator, heavily critical of television for showing the British Army in a 'bad light' noted: 'It is only now that we in Britain are running up against this problem. It is one that has assailed the United States for nearly a decade.
>
> There can be little doubt that television coverage of the Vietnam War was largely responsible for sapping the moral fibre of the American people to continue the struggle'. [16]

It is important that we are not discussing *opinions* but *news*. Some versions of events are replicated as factual news; others are not. Normally, this is an implicit characteristic of news-gathering routines: sometimes, as we have seen, the choice becomes explicit. The reason for the exclusion of some versions of events from public debate is fear of the consequences on the political system of certain sorts of news because of its supposed effects on the consciousness of the readers, viewers or listeners. Among the writers of the alternative press there is the same analysis of the process, but the conclusions drawn are the opposite.

The analysis takes the form: 'News affects readers' loyalty to the political system; "Bad news" for the system erodes this loyalty'. The inference drawn by the established news media including most of Fleet Street is where such versions of events present themselves they are to be ignored or excluded. The inference for the writers of the alternative press is to seek out such versions and publicise them. The relationship of alternative journalism to the political system is therefore that it aims to change the scope of legitimate political debate towards a consideration of the basis of political legitimacy and towards a discussion of the nature of ideology. Gunter Walraff, the author of a collection of such journalism *The Undesirable Journalist* is described in the Introduction by Mervyn Jones as:

> a practical man; his theoretical reflections on literature are intermittent and are limited to the form in which certain facts can be spread as widely

as possible. He seeks to 'spread the truth about this system of anarchy, disorder, and personal enrichment at the expense of others! When he speaks of 'truth about the system', he means 'capitalism, a system of chaos without guiding principle, generally called "the free market economy"'.[17]

And again:

> by his activity, Walraff rouses public opinion. . . . . As an individual he sets himself against continually intensifying trend towards press monopoly, against the manipulation of the people by the papers of the Springer group (Bild) which is planned . . . to the last detail.[18]

The relationship in the UK between the alternative press and the established media, is complex. The first truly 'alternative' modern news 'organ' was *Private Eye*. This has sometimes generated news coverage notably of the dealings of the late Reginald Maudling which have eventually emerged in Fleet Street. Paul Foot who was a prominent, active reporter in the early development of *Private Eye* news coverage now has an 'alternative page' in the most radical of the Fleet Street pop dailies *The Mirror*. *Private Eye* has become more and more successful and favourite reading for stockbrokers, while its leading writers also 'moonlight' for the super-respectable *Spectator*. *Time Out* and later *City Limits* have at times spawned reporters who have gone on to write in Fleet Street or to work for the broadcast media. The nature of the old Hampstead leftist *New Statesman* was radically altered with the advent of Bruce Page who encouraged a new investigative approach to journalism and brought in reporters such as Rob Rohrer and Duncan Campbell to do it. They were concerned with revelation of the 'real' nature of the system and had trained themselves in radical journalism in the alternative press in Liverpool and on the south coast.

In the provinces there are now numerous fortnightly or more rarely weekly radical magazines, owned, managed and produced cooperatively, based on a common format: investigative news and news features, entertainment and arts pages. Their news coverage does not require the cooperation of the official spokesman because any 'news' he might be interested in would be of no interest. The sources of this news are the very cranks and subversives whom the traditional journalist busily turns away in order diligently to pursue official (and therefore safe) sources of information.

In the process of using the claims of contacts as the raw material of stories the journalist attempts to stand up factual claims about the world. The processes and routines for accomplishing this are the taken-for-granted work of the alternative journalist. The traditional journalist stands up a story by leaning it against the concrete wall of authority, convention and order; the investigative reporter has to make the story stand on its own feet, and the journalist first has to make the feet. First, he or she has to demonstrate that the story says something about the society he or she is depicting, (i.e. that it is significant); secondly, it has to be shown to be accurate. Both of these are practical, socially-defined achievements.

There are two modes of investigating a system of political authority which achieve this purpose by making the system speak against itself. The first is to force those vested with authority to acknowledge the significance of what is at issue by themselves taking action as office holders, and in doing so admit both that some degree of factual credibility attaches to the story, and that it is an issue which is significant to the social order. A typical action of this type might be the issuing of a statement or the institution of an official inquiry. The second method which is much harder work, is to collect documents produced by officials, which 'prove' the story. Crucial to this process are journalistic and legal notions of proof, although there is not sufficient scope here to deal with this issue in detail.

For such journalism then the day-to-day assumptions of local political life are made problematic. Councillors, officials, heads of universities, are all regarded as potential deviants who are able to hide their deviance behind the mask of their authority. The means by which journalists prove stories factually and in terms of their societal relevance, are both integral to the conceptual 'technology' of radical news manufacture.

In the case of the councillor's husband's property speculation, (see earlier) a television reporter who also worked in his spare time for the radical *Manchester Free Press* did take up the story, and after a three-month investigation, he and I had accumulated a file of photocopies of documents showing the correspondence, planning permissions and refusals, contracts of sale of land, and a signed letter from the former owner. We put this before the Chairman of the Planning Committee who initiated a Town Hall inquiry. This was undertaken by the Town Clerk who interviewed the husband, Harold Tucker, who was by then also a councillor, after a year's absence from the Town Hall. The Town Clerk reported back to the Council in a confidential document which was leaked to the TV reporter. Granada screened a ten-minute film on their regional news programme, which was based on the Town Clerk's report and which used the 'serious questions remain to be answered' formula to raise the issue of the conflict of interest between the public figure and the private speculator.

Tucker issued a writ for libel and silenced any further coverage of the issue. Six years later in 1979 a reporter on a radical newspaper, *The New Manchester Review* who was investigating another part of the councillor's business activities, referred again to this affair. He had made a contact with a Housing Corporation in London who was able to enlarge some of the details of the deal, since the land had been sold by Tucker to a housing association of which he was Secretary. Subsequently Paul Foot in the *Daily Mirror* referred to the story when Tucker became leader of the Manchester Tory group. By this time the libel writ against Granada and against the Planning Committee Chairman, Ken Eastham, now a Labour MP who appeared on the film, had lapsed. Paul Foot obtained his information from the original TV reporter and from a news agency run as a workers' cooperative operating in Manchester. By 1984, twelve years after the land deal, and ten years after the film appeared, the story was aired again. First it was published in a third radical news magazine *City Life*, with some new information obtained for the 1979 instalment but not then used. The public event giving rise to this new assault on Tucker was his election as Mayor. The story described the issuing of writs against Granada and against Councillor Eastham and contrasted the present peaceful cooperation between Tory and Labour groups, allowing for Tucker as leader of the minority Tory to be Mayor with a time when 'writs flew across the council chambers'.

A week later, by chance, the story made its first appearance in the *Manchester Evening News* with the news that Eastham's lawyers were claiming costs of up to £10,000 against Tucker.

The following week the fornightly *City Life* ran yet another story with the standfirst:

> Manchester Lord Mayor, Harold Tucker's activities as a property speculator were reported in CITY LIFE 16 which described an early seventies housing deal. Mr.Tucker privately bought land; gained a change in its planning use, and sold it at a large profit to the Housing Society of which he was secretary. The money from this last transaction came from the public purse. Readers of Harry Crawley's story will be interested in the latest facts to emerge.

These 'latest facts' were first, Tucker's wife's non-declaration of an interest in the property in question when decisions on its planning status were taken, and her failure to declare it in the statutory register of councillors' interests; and secondly, Eastham's lawyers' claim for costs. The first came from the reporter's assiduous searches at the Town Hall. The second were merely following up the *Manchester Evening News* court story.

This case illustrates that for the radical journalist the 'fact' the purchase of the property in itself is neither interesting or otherwise in determining whether or not it is 'news'. Nor is its newness. What qualifies it as news is that some event is generated in the arena of public affairs which makes the mere 'fact' of the property deal an issue of the legitimacy of authority. In the first airing on television, the 'cranks" protests were examined by checking the council minutes, interviewing witnesses, obtaining copies of contracts. But it was the Town Clerk's report which was the 'event' which was the peg on which the story was hung. The second airing related to an inquiry into other matters by officials of the Housing Corporation. Paul Foot's entry into the fray celebrated Tucker's elevation to the leadership of the Manchester Tory Group and the efforts of *City Life* were occasioned by his election as Mayor. The final event, the claim for costs in the courts, brought the traditional local press into the arena for the first time, since this now satisfied the criteria for their definition of news. The decade-long history of the story is a nice illustration also of the point that news is the product of newspaper workers' routines.

An interesting sidelight on the operations of the journalist in depicting reality is exemplified in the case of the unfortunate Mr.Tucker. There is an old saw among press folk that 'one good picture is worth a thousand words'. It is Mr Tucker's particular misfortune that he is fat and reminds journalists of the stereotype Mafia gangster of early Hollywood films. On every occasion therefore, appropriate or not, a photograph accompanies the story, and these are generally chosen to make him look as spotty, fat and unappetising as possible. Generally, when I have been present at the time of choice, there has been an embarrassment of riches. In addition to the picture, graphic words are used, generally coming under the heading of 'fat toad jokes'. The words 'corpulent', 'bulky', 'ample', 'weighing in', 'larger than life', are tried for size. It is what might be called the Leon Brittan factor.

Thus, ridicule, vulgar abuse and unnecessarily accurate descriptions are used further to deflate the credibility of authority which is often symbolised in the traditional press and in the public rituals of authority by eulogising and deferential accounts of the good deeds, charity work, visits to children's homes, etc. of the incumbents of public office.

A further example of radical journalism illustrates again how validation and signification are effected in the course of generating news which is intended to demonstrate the endemic corruption of the system and rule of authority of the government structure. The deed again was itself the mere raw material out of which the journalist used his craft to manufacture a news story.

In the early part of 1979 a police contact informed a journalist whom I was observing as part of the fieldwork for my PhD thesis that the Iranian chargé d'affaires in Manchester had sent two crates of very expensive Crawfords deluxe whisky to named high-ranking Manchester police officers. The informant said that the legation Daimler, complete with CD plates, had drawn up outside the police headquarters and a lackey had carried the gifts into the building. The parcels bore the names of individual officers: all were above the rank of Inspector, and while the normal gift was a bottle per head, the Chief Constable, James Anderton, had been given a crate all to himself, the informant claimed.

The incident was simple but three factors made it a story for the journalist concerned:

1. the police disciplinary code bans the receipt by serving officers of gifts from the general public and is operated rigorously in Manchester on lower-ranking officers;
2. the police had previously been called to the Iranian legation to remove students protesting against the Shah, and this along with the whisky could be used to imply a chummy relationship between James Anderton and the Shah's man in Manchester;
3. Anderton was and is a furious public advocate of driven snow-type morals and therefore any blot on his escutcheon would be magnified by the application of his own publicly iterated standards.

In order to make the delivery of the whisky into news, the reporter's job was first to prove that it had happened and secondly that it mattered. This he did first by interviewing the Consul on the pretence that he was interested in the plight of Iranians in the North West of England at the time of their nation's agony, (the interview took place at the time of the Shah's fall). During the course of the interview he managed to steer the conversation around to the topic of Christmas gifts and the Consul mentioned that he had sent five bottles to the police.

The journalist rang up the police PRO and said that during an interview, the Iranian consul had 'mentioned' the gift of whisky. He asked if this was a breach of the police disciplinary code banning the receipt of gifts from the public. The PRO said he would look into it and the day after rang back with the following statement:

> It appears that, unknown to the Chief Constable of Manchester, a parcel containing intoxicating liquor from the Iranian consulate in Manchester may have been delivered to a Manchester police station before Christmas. The matter is now being investigated. A further parcel addressed to the Chief Constable and Mrs Anderton from the Consul General of Iran in Manchester and his wife, was delivered at the same time to the Chief Constable's office. The benefit of this gift was passed on to the Northern Police Convalescent Home at Harrogate, since it is the Chief Constable's policy that personal gifts should not be retained.

Despite its transparent circumlocutory devices the statement fulfilled exactly the requirements of the story. First it admitted that the facts were at least partly as the journalist had believed, and secondly, in announcing that there was to be an internal police inquiry, the statement acknowledged that the facts, if true, raised issues of the legitimacy of actions of senior officers in relation to the normative order on which their authority rested.

The story appeared in the *New Manchester Review* under the provocative strapline 'Corruption' and the headline 'Police Probe a Case for the Prosecution'. Like the headline the story was two 'nosed' on the inquiry. This 'official' action then drew the commercial news media into the fray, again reporting simply the action taken by legitimate authority. *The Daily Mirror, The Observer* and the *Manchester Evening News* all followed up with stories based on the GMP statement, and anodyne quotes from police sources.

It is not difficult to see that the different political stance of the investigative radical journalist results in an intellectual armoury for processing the world of events into stories fit to be told, which is different from that of the traditional local journalist. As is indicated by Gunther Walraff's *Undesirable Journalist*,[19] he sees himself as a revolutionary, forcing the engines of the state and business to reveal their own contradictions. The two sorts of journalism mirror the differences between functionalist and radical social science.

Much of the work of the undesirable journalist involves finding suitable contacts, checking their stories, and generating the circumstances in which the spokesmen of officialdom are made to acknowledge weaknesses in the system which sustains them. Their skill in writing stories involves both a demonstration that what they are saying does all of this but is, at the same time, not libellous. Their output in terms of column inches of news is, therefore, slight by comparison with the traditional functionalist hack in the local commercial press. It is also restricted to one or two particular issues at a time.

This has consequences for the styles and structure of the alternative local press. The news content tends to be limited to a relatively small section of a fortnightly or weekly magazine, the rest being made up of the arts, sport, general features and 'What's On' sections. Alternative news organs are thus not simply the same sort of item as a 'straight' newspaper, but filled with different contents. Their organisation – usually workers' cooperatives, – and their style of writing, are radically different from the mainstream press. The threat to their survival is that they compete in the same markets.

This new form of magazine operates on a high degree of specialisation. The rock, film, art and features work, tends to be done by correspondents, while the news layout, subbing, advertising and listings are normally done by staff or co-op members. Thus there exists a division between the inner circle of workers who decide on policy, deal with the bank, the landlord, the printer, the Cooperative Development Agency and the advertisers, and the outer circle who simply deliver their contributions, usually unpaid, and perhaps attend contributors' meetings. But within the inner circle there is likely to be an exclusive division of labour. The one or two news specialists live in an alien world from that of the listings or the advertisements.

The context of these ventures generates a contradiction between the 'socialism in one cooperative' of the magazine and the savage market conditions in which they operate. The audience for such ventures is seen by the staff and advertisers as predominantly in the 20 – 30 years age group. They are not regarded as an affluent section of the age group, and the advertising is generally aimed at rock-oriented leisure activities, as well as alternative bookshops, flat agencies, wholefood restaurants, and the like. Advertising therefore has to be sold at cheap rates. (One of the difficulties for advertising staff is to avoid revealing how small the circulation is without actually lying). At the same time, the new cheap technology which reduces printing costs for the radical press has also created the conditions for the growth of competitors for the advertisers' business.

There has been a rapid growth in the advertising freesheet business, based mainly on advertisements and delivered free to the home. Editorially they are the apotheosis of the commercial press, the minimum of news along with features based heavily on advertisement backing. The response of many existing commercial newspaper empires has been three-pronged: to close down the least profitable papers while buying up competitors; to reduce staff wherever possible, and to buy into the freesheet market. This creates a constant downward pressure on advertising rates and cover prices, since the only way to keep up advertising rates is by increasing the number of readers.

In this situation a number of solutions are available to the cooperatives. First, they can pay themselves low wages, which they generally do. In this event members put with the relative deprivation for a short period while they are young. The market economy provides an individualistic solution, however. The successful reporters and features writers attract offers of freelance work in the national press and broadcasting media. They then tend to gravitate towards full-time staff jobs or successful freelance careers in London. Similarly, clever advertising agents receive offers of better-paid work elsewhere, or make the contacts they need to go into business on their own account.

Where magazines equip themselves with typesetting machines, darkroom and layout facilities, the staff who develop expertise are able to go into business as typesetting and origination studios. Two of the Manchester co-ops ceased funtioning as magazines and went into the layout business because while publishing a magazine accumulated debts, the studio work was profitable. In the case of the *New Manchester Review*, this ceased publication with a burden of debt, which the type-setting business paid off.

The market economy creates conditions fissiparous for the journal-istic cooperative, and the new cheap technology provides an attractive outlet for the energies of workers exhausted by years of hard work at low wages with a large debt as a reward. There is thus no automatic technological panacea creating an egalitarian access to the competition of ideas and ideology.

In effect, new alternative newspapers and magazines are founded with a life-expectancy of a few years, and the variety of news styles available relies on a constant process of the formation of new ventures to replace those which have demised. Ironically, for the members of these cooperatives they may constitute a way into entrepreneurship or an en-trée into the career structure of the national newspapers and broadcast-ing corporations, and thus have a Mertonian 'latent function' in the successful adaptation of the commercial news media.

Whether or not they also widen the scope of the political debate in British society is another question. The alternative papers are not read by large sections of the total newspaper readership. Therefore the only ways in which the stories they promulgate and the stance they adopt towards the nature of political 'fact' are spread, is either by some ver-sion of 'two-step' communication process, or by their having an effect on the professional practices of journalists generally. They may particu-larly influence those in the broadcast media, where the influence of monopoly ownership is less pervasive and there are some limited re-courses for resistance to government control. At present, the best guess must surely be that they are likely to be assumed into the very system they attack, by a sort of 'repressive tolerance'.[20]

### References and notes

1. See Ian Jackson, *The Provincial Press and the Community*, Manchester: Manchester University Press, 1971, p.59.
2. Dylis Hill, *Participating in Local Affairs*, London: Penguin Books, 1970. In one revealing section the author demonstrates an extraordinary example of social sci-ence taking for granted the assumptions of professionals in which she lauds the reporting of 'official facts' by journalists as a desirable end in view, (p.116-31).
3. See Norfolk News Co.Ltd, evidence to Royal Commission in the Press, 1947-49, quoted by Jackson op.cit., p.59.
4. Jackson *op.cit.*, pp. 94-6; 132-44.
5. D. Murphy, *The Silent Watchdog*, London: Constable, 1976.
6. D. Murphy, 'Control Without Censorship', in James Curran (ed.), *The British Press: a Manifesto*, London: Macmillan, 1978, pp.171-92.
7. For example, the conclusions drawn by the research on the press treatment of industrial relations. Dennis McQuail's work for the 1977 Royal Commission on the press is quite different in its generally more optimistic account of the press coverage of disputes than, say, the work of the Glasgow Media Group.

8. That afternoon, the reporter who was new to the area was to meet the same council tribunal chairman (the appointment was made by the editor) in yet another incarnation, that of the chairman of the Urban District Council. The purpose of the meeting was that the same *grand fromage* should provide the hack with a list of contacts to get to know what was happening in the area.

9. Bruce Page, 'New Print Technology and Newspaper Culture', in Curran (1978), *op.cit.*, pp. 271-82.

10. See Graham Murdock, 'Large Corporations and the Control of the Communications Industries', in Michael Gurevitch, Tony Bennett, James Curran and Janet Woollacott (eds.), *Culture, Society and the Media*, London: Methuen, 1982, pp.118-50, both for such an analysis and references to other similar accounts.

11. The gatekeeper studies of the 1950s were based on the idea that some individuals' roles enable them to control communication flows in social systems. My objection to this form of analysis is that it accepts organisational structures as the source of power and control while ignoring the way in which the ideologies, practices and beliefs of individuals and the distribution of resources give rise to such organisations. See, for example, David Manning White, 'The Gatekeeper: A Case Study in the Selection of News', *Journalism Quarterly*, 27(4), 1950, pp.383-90; Walter Gieber, 'Across the Desk: A Study of 16 Telegraph Editors', *Journalism Quarterly*, 33, 1956, pp.423-32.

12. In my doctorate I attempt to show how journalists base their accounts of the world on journalistic sociological theories, and that social science models of society are reflected in the 'commonsense' assumptions made by journalists as the basis for their descriptions of the social world. D. Murphy, PhD thesis, University of Manchester, 1981, Chapter 2.

13. Alan Doig *Corruption and Misconduct in Contemporary British Politics*, London: Penguin, 1984, pp.291-6.

14. Jeremy Trustall, *The Westminster Lobby Correspondents*, London: Routledge & Kegan Paul, 1970.

15. Liz Curtis, *Ireland: The Propaganda War*. London: Pluto 1985.

16. Ibid., p.9.

17. Wallraff, *The Undesirable Journalist*, Steve Gooch and Paul Knight trans. p.9.

18. Ibid., p.7.

19. Op. cit.,p.9.

20. Quoted from Herbert Marcuse, 'Repressive Tolerance', in Paul Connerton (ed.), *Critical Sociology*, London: Penguin, 1976, pp.301-29.

# 6 The Lobby
*Peter Hennessy and David Walker*

Michael Macdonagh, a turn-of-the-century reporter in the gallery of the House of Commons, once described the work of the corps of the daily papers' Westminster correspondents. Their task was 'gathering the political gossip of Members, the official communications of the Government and the Opposition', in order to serve them at breakfast the next day 'in brief crisp paragraphs, often with spicy personal comments'.[1] The formula has changed little since.

The business of the Lobby, as that corps had become known well before the end of the nineteenth century, is political ephemera. Indeed, the single newspaper or broadcast 'story' is rarely significant in itself; rarely counts as a political event. Yet the quotidian flow does leave a residue. The agenda of politics is constructed daily. Single reports cumulate. Eventually they shape the contours of policy and personality in politics. A succession of stories about ministerial opponents of Mrs Thatcher during her first administration (1979-83) made the characterisation 'wet' stick.

The press mediates in the careers of politicians. The Lobby was, during the summer of 1985, a conduit for unattributed reports of the impending exclusion from the Cabinet of the Secretary of State for the Environment, Mr Patrick Jenkin. The stories served to soften up the victim while testing the opposition to such a move within the Conservative Party. Anticipatory character assassination is a minor political process at which the Lobby excels: an interesting feature of Mr Jenkin's fate was that the usual source of prime ministerial intention, the Chief Press Secretary, Mr Bernard Ingham, was comparatively silent out of a respect for Mr Jenkin, gained when they worked together at the Department of Energy.

The way the press story is put together deserves attention as a term in the equation. Just as what the papers never said is an essential element in political history and explanation, so is some description of what the papers did say – for example, after tendentious briefing of the corps of specialist political correspondents in the parliamentary Lobby.

The Lobby is a formal association of newspaper and broadcast journalists who work out of the Palace of Westminster and who are the primary source of the political news published. Lord Hill of Luton, *de facto* Minister of Information in the government led by Harold Macmillan, called the Lobby 'the most important group of journalists in the political arena'.[2] Political in these sentences means the activities of the legislature and the parties; it covers, but much more problematically, the executive and judicial functions of the state.

In his memoirs, Lord Hill reflected that 'the relationship between government and press can be compared with that between husband and wife', developing a sexual metaphor that the clandestine nature of the Lobby has suggested to other prurient British writers.

> The husband – the Government – is older and heavier than his wife, serious-minded, a bit pompous, rather humourless and slow of speech, altogether a worthy character and wanting only a quiet life. The wife – the Press – is livelier, shrewder and more perceptive, wise to the ways of the world, quick of tongue and addicted to gossip. Of course, husband and wife bicker: she often drives him to distraction. But he cannot do without her and he knows it.

The channel for consummation of the relationship is the Lobby.

Hill used the word 'government'. He intended the conventional synonym Cabinet, Prime Minister, ministers at the top of the Executive. The Lobby specialises in reports about and emanating from these power-holders; over its century of existence, the Lobby's reportage has stopped short at the boundaries of the Executive-in-Parliament. Government – what happens in Cabinet committees, the life of officialdom – is covered only sporadically, and then through the single conduit of briefings by the personal representative of the Minister of the Civil Service, the First Lord of the Treasury, the Prime Minister. As for the rest of government, in local authorities, the National Health Service and the quasi-autonomous bodies, it generally escapes not only the attention of the Lobby, but also of specialist journalists of any kind. During 1985, a novel sight was seen. Members of the Lobby were writing stories about a local authority, the City of Liverpool. Liverpool's fiscal 'crisis' was by that point of long standing; rule by adherents of the *Militant* line was two years old. The Lobby's interest stemmed entirely from the involvement in Liverpool of national politicians.

Mr Ian Aitken, veteran political correspondent of the *Guardian*, has said:

> we are really general reporters in dirty raincoats. We come in here every day and hang our dirty raincoats on the hook outside our offices, and we just have a ticket to get us downstairs into the lobby or into some of the bars or corridors.[3]

It is a charming disclaimer. The most suspect word in it is 'general'.

For the Lobby journalists are specialists, specialists in the public face of central government power, assessors of reputation, students of party dynamics, critics of ministerial performance in Parliament, Cabinet and the wider arenas. Over its century the Lobby has come to fulfil a specialised function in the British polity: the construction of political personality, especially the personality of the Prime Minister.

The Lobby has never, even in its nineteenth-century origins, been short of critics. In recent times, the Lobby has been called a conspiracy and worse. Lord Hill's sexual metaphor for press–government relations has been used to indicate a kind of carnal passivity on the Lobby's part. Writing in the days when politicians' indiscretions with (female) prostitutes were news, Anthony Howard reported:

> It's almost like Piccadilly before the Wolfenden Report. There stand the Lobby correspondents waiting, soliciting, for the politicians to come out. They treat them as if they were their clients and, you know, in some ways I think the fact has to be faced that Lobby correspondents do become instruments for a politician's gratification.[4]

This theme of pliant hacks, readily duped by prime ministers and press officers, was taken up in our own book, *Sources Close to the Prime Minister*.[5]

Such criticism, when applied to individuals and their newspapers, may be well deserved, though it tends to be based on the rather shakey foundations of a liberal free-market model of information flows which has never had much explanatory power in British history. Such criticism is not fairly applied to the Lobby as an institution.

The fairest criticism of the Lobby is that it has remained a parliamentary institution, one which like Members of Parliament, their committees and rituals fails to check and balance other organs of the state. This is most noticeable in parliamentary supervision of the Executive and in reporting of the 'presidential' prime ministership. The Lobby, we shall argue here, has failed to adapt in a dual sense. Its political reportage, which often amounts to the totality of political reporting in both newspapers and the broadcast media, has remained Parliament-bound; it fails to report government in the broad sense, as it takes place day by day in Whitehall, the Cabinet and its committees. Or rather, its reportage of government is filtered because of the Lobby's dependence on a single source of executive information – the Prime Minister's office.

The second sense of failure to modernise concerns the organisation and dynamics of the mass media themselves. Until the 1950s, the electric/electronic media were merely complementary to press reporting:

political reputations were not won or lost because of performance on the radio. Broadcasting was, generally, a one-way flow of ministerial voices; newspapers alone tackled the issues and controversies. The advent of television in British politics dates precisely from the creation of Independent Television News (with its subsequent effects on BBC coverage). Here was a channel for ministers and prime ministers to engage directly with the populace, and to be engaged without the obvious intermediation of reporters and story-lines. How should the Lobby, a cartel for the provision of political news and information, respond?

The predictable response was to re-emphasise the kind of reporting which newspaper reporters alone can do: tell of third parties. 'Off the record' is a process for written media. Mr John Cole, the BBC's Political Editor, telling of unseen and unheard sources is immediately less convincing than a written presentation of the source's words. Now the Lobby and British political journalism might in the years since the mid-1950s have concentrated on genuine 'off the record' reporting – to locate and chase power and decision-making through the recesses of executive government where in the nature of things non-attribution is the price that has to be paid for information. Instead – we shall develop this theme later – the Lobby chose a soft option. It emphasised 'off the record' without stirring from the parliamentary aerie. It talked to ministers off the record, the Prime Minister off the record, and all manner of departmental spokesmen unattributably. It laid itself open to misinformation, and the quality of political journalism suffered.

The mid-nineteenth-century Whig politician Lord Granville was once accused of intimacy with the editor of *The Times*, the celebrated Delane. Granville replied:

> Public men have three ways of communicating with writers in the Press. First, showing them social civilities; second, furnishing them with facts and arguments which need not be kept secret, and which may be useful in determining public opinion; and third, imparting to them official secrets which ought not to be divulged.[6]

It is in a real sense under the first category that the relationship of politicians and the Lobby falls. Lobby journalists are privileged guests in an antique club.

The Lobby, practically speaking, is only the 150-strong list of names of journalists issued with passes allowing access to parts of the Palace of Westminster otherwise restricted to MPs, peers and their staff. The list is lodged with the Sergeant-at-Arms. Its form is entirely traditional. A limited number of newspapers, magazines and broadcasting organisations have 'tickets': they allocate one of their staff to a Lobby place and he (there are few women) receives a pass automatically. *Notes*

*on the Practice of Lobby Journalism* issued to Lobby members in July
1982 (and not intended for wider readership) states:

> There is no 'association' of Lobby journalists, but in our common inter-
> ests we act collectively as the Parliamentary Lobby Journalists. It has
> been found convenient to have an organisation consisting of chairman,
> officers and committee for that purpose.[7]

And for that purpose there are rules of conduct and a mechanism for
disciplining recalcitrants. The Lobby journalist, says the *Notes*, has
'complete freedom to get his own stories in his own way. But he also
owes a duty to the Lobby as a whole, in that he should do nothing to
prejudice the communal life of the Lobby or its relations with the two
Houses and the authorities'. This includes a measure of voluntary
myopia. Lobbymen are supposed not to see anything that takes place
outside the Chambers of the Lords and Commons – for example,
drunkenness or, occasionally, assault. They are not supposed to use
their notebooks in the Lobby – a breach of etiquette which may indeed
impair reportorial accuracy. Lobbymen may not sit on the leather ban-
quets that line the Lobby (i.e. the ante-chamber to the Commons). The
privilege of Lobby membership is physical access to politicians, and to
state papers – the named members of the Lobby can wander the Ways
and Means corridor and approach the Vote Office to pick up parliamentary papers ahead of most other people, including the bulk of backbench MPs. They roam the Lobby-antechamber, 'the scene', in one
journalist's idealised version, 'of the greatest activity, as Members and
Ministers rush to and from the Chamber, gossip with each other or
meet the political correspondents.'[8]

The Lobby's prize, in the words of Ian Aitken of *The Guardian*, is:

> being able to get down there and talk to all those MPs and ministers who
> on the whole, during the week, are barricaded behind ranks and ranks of
> civil servants who are absolutely dedicated to not letting you get at them.
> ... When they come down here for divisions they are absolutely defence-
> less and you can trap them, you can lure them downstairs and tank them
> up with whisky.[9]

Alcohol is by tradition the essential lubricant for such institutionalised
intercourse: there are thirteen drinking places at Westminster and the
Lobby correspondents even have their own bar, 'Annie's'. These, then,
are Lord Granville's social civilities.

Sociologically, Lobby journalists do not differ markedly from their
colleagues. Since Jeremy Tunstall's fieldwork for his book *The Westminster Lobby Correspondents*, the educational background of journalists

has changed, with a higher proportion now likely to be graduates. The Lobby was then, and is still dominated by representatives of the 'provincial press', newspapers published outside London – a preponderance unjustified by circulation or quality of reportage. Lobbymen from the provincial papers have undoubtedly in recent years acted as a block to reform and modernisation of procedure; their role, however, has parliamentary significance in so far as they serve as a useful local conduit for those backbench Members unlikely ever to make the pages of the national papers or even Radio 4's 'Yesterday in Parliament'.

The Lobby is a group of journalistic specialists: experts in political parties and politicking, experts in parliamentary procedure and Commons lore. They are based at Westminster, away from their newspapers' offices, which gives them both a collegiate spirit lacked by other specialists, and a degree of autonomy from newspaper/media imperatives. The lobbymen will, for example, command an area of editorial space far greater than their colleagues; as important, they will, because of their proximity to the flow of political news used by most papers as the axis for daily news coverage, be able to determine the salience of items in the running order. In a sense all other journalistic specialists are second-order in their coverage of news from and about government. The agriculture correspondents, for example, may understand price regimes under the Common Agricultural Policy, but it is the lobbymen who are first told the breaking story about British payments into European Community funds and who may, in their relative ignorance, write the vital first account.

The term 'Lobby' thus aptly describes not only the association of political correspondents at Westminster but also the culture and organisation of much of British journalism. Only the so-called quality newspapers, the BBC and ITN/IRN have subject specialists. The areas of specialisation in newspapers are limited; there are large gaps, for example, in coverage of the law as an institution, Britain's participation in Europe as evidenced from London rather than Brussels, and most tellingly of Whitehall. What specialist coverage of Executive process and argument there is takes second place, generally, to the coverage of Executive personality politics. The most notable exception is reporting economics, where the specialists have access directly to the Chancellor of the Exchequer and his officials; economics news tends, on most papers, to be organised separately in a 'business section'.

The nature of the Lobby can be illustrated from its history. Its century divides into an era roughly ending with the Second World War in which, despite far-reaching changes in the organisation of the press, the Lobby remained a loose association of journalistic competitors. Since the war, the Lobby, acquiring greater collective discipline, has become an accomplice of Big Government and an amanuensis of successive prime ministers as the conventions of Cabinet government have slipped.

The Lobby had its birth in the decade from 1875, a momentous phase in the development of the British state. As the products of the Northcote–Trevelyan reforms flowed into jobs, so the Civil Service became professionalised. In February 1875 a Treasury Minute stated that no official information might be communicated to public journals without internal sanction – the first Official Secrets Act was only 14 years away. Government became private business.

The state was under attack – the decade saw a series of dynamite outrages by Fenians. In 1884 physical access to the Lobby was restricted for security reasons: entry was to be be given only to Members, staff, and to journalists and political agents whose names had been entered on the Serjeant-at-Arms's list. Thereby the Lobby acquired its power of cartel.

There had previously been a journalistic bifurcation. Partly because of newspaper competititon, in the 1870s a new specialism had grown up – the embellishment of verbatim reports of parliamentary debates by means of descriptive summaries and spicy personalised accounts of individuals and parliamentary manners. This was the beginning of the parliamentary 'sketch'. The conduits for political news were up to this point various: John Delane of *The Times* had wined and dined with members of the Cabinet and needed no informant in the Lobby. But as Parliament's salience in the national life grew, along with the metropolitan pull of London, so parliamentary reporting became the focus of political news-gathering.

Michael Macdonagh tells an amusing anecdote about the new thirst for parliamentary tittle-tattle, which gave the Lobby its late nineteenth-century impetus.[10] When there was little news to be had, Macdonagh reported, journalists had to resort to invention. One night a provincial journalist was sitting on the stairs leading from the Lobby to the Peers' Gallery, ruminating on the lack of news. Gladstone, then Prime Minister, came up and asked to be allowed past. Up jumped the 'Lobbyist' and stood aside – then headed straight to the telegraph office and sent a message to his paper: 'Meeting Mr Gladstone this evening in the lobby, I had a brief but interesting conversation with him. . .'

The man's half-column story contained nothing new, says Macdonagh. It was mainly a rehash of recent public speeches by the Grand Old Man; but such is the shortness of memory it passed muster.

Lord Granville, in describing three forms of press–politician contact, had carefully distinguished providing journalists with 'facts and options' that would be useful in selling, say, an administration's case, and 'secrets', the publication of which was morally or legally wrong. The institutionalisation of the Lobby coincided (especially in the period of

Anglo–German naval competition in the early twentieth century) with the build-up of an apparatus of law and procedure defining first some, then all Executive information as secret. The bridge between the two was built, wittingly, by ministers prepared to engage in what in the 1880s were charmingly known as 'leakages'. Gladstone in that decade developed a keen nose for ministerial conspiracy involving the press, though he himself was not above occasional passage of material helpful to his cause. Joseph Chamberlain, Gladstone's chief suspect, later admitted there was considerable contact, citing a meeting in November 1880.[11]

> At one of these Cabinets there was a warm discussion on the subject of communication between Cabinet ministers and the press, and this question was revived from time to time afterwards. The fact was that several of the ministers were in intimate connection with Editors of newspapers. Thus, Forster was continually communicating with Chenery of *The Times* and I believe Mudford of the *Standard*. Dilke was intimate with Hill of the *Daily News* and I was in constant intercourse with Morley, Editor of the *Pall Mall Gazette*. . . .
>
> It was pointed out that without special intercourse it was impossible to secure in the press an adequate defence of the decisions and policy of the Government. Whether the confidence made in any case overstepped what was right must be a matter of opinion, but as far as myself I know nothing underhand or unfair was done by any member of the Government.

These remarks, of course, apply to a small circulation press, one, as Hamilton Fyfe put it, written by men with top hats for men with top hats.[12] Yet it is intriguing how early some of the Lobby's modern habits were built in. For one thing, the free and easy commerce between newspapers and ministers which Delane had characterised was becoming less and less common; more important, the access to civil servants had stopped thanks to restrictions imposed by Gladstone. By the mid-1890s even Delane's paper, *The Times*, had its own Lobby correspondent.[13] Lobby correspondents who earlier had to fight for office space were equipped by the end of the century with what Sir Alexander Mackintosh[14] called a score of rooms (providing for the reporters of the Press Gallery as well) and 'the comforts and conveniences of a well-equipped club'. The habit of non-attribution was well-established. Labouchere, a Radical MP was scathing: '"I am enabled on undoubted authority to state." "I am in a position to inform". "I learn from a private but official source." "The Government thinks". All this sort of inventive trash, although disgusting to persons of good taste, has its effect with millions'.[15]

Indeed that was the Lobby's ticket to a new era of mass circulation papers whose readers were deemed uninterested in lengthy reports of parliamentary debate and speech-making. The Press Gallery atrophied; the survival of daily parliamentary reports even in *The Times, Telegraph* and *Guardian* is now questionable.

The Lobby passed into the twentieth century an established but far from well-known organ of political life. Spencer Leigh Hughes, a journalist and MP, recorded its aping of parliamentary ritual.[16] It became, he said, a 'select club. The Secretary of the Gallery and Chairman of the Lobby are positions unknown to the outside world. The Committee insisted on phraseology [e.g. of address] that would be regarded as excessively official even on the Treasury bench'. Such an attitude of veneration meant that the Lobby and its reportage were indifferent to the changing mechanics of government. The formalisation of Cabinet meetings, especially through the agency of Maurice Hankey and the Edwardian Cabinet secretariat, went unnoticed.

The Lobby's history in the twentieth century can be illuminated by two vignettes. The first shows the first new building to take place at 10 Downing Street since the mansion was built by Sir George Downing in the seventeenth century: an annex was built in 1932 to accommodate an important new officer of state, the Prime Minister's press liaison officer. One of his central functions was to maintain a link with the Lobby. In subsequent years it became clear that such liaison was on behalf of the Prime Minister personally, rather than the Cabinet or government collectively.

The second features an event which took place in September 1964. This was the first organised press conference given by the Labour Party in that year's general election campaign. This account comes from Anthony Howard and Richard West's book, *The Making of the Prime Minister*[17]

> A little group of 'lobby' correspondents objected to the television cameras, not only because of the whirring noise they made, but because they, the correspondents, did not want to appear on television.
>
> The *Evening Standard's* Robert Carvel and *The Times'* David Wood were particularly adamant on the last point. 'This involves an issue of principle for some of us', said Wood a few days later. With some papers the issue is one of commerce rather than principle. The proprietors do not want the public to see the press conference on television before they read about it in the newspaper. Most of the lobby correspondents were merely jealous of having to share their traditional top talks with a whole lot of outside journalists. As the left-wing *Tribune* rightly sneered: 'They wanted to hold the election off the record'.

What we are considering here are major changes in the life of the Lobby over fifty years. One has been its *collectivisation* – the sense of the

Lobby as a ready-made press conference, most often for government news, rather than a disorganised set of competitive individuals. Second has been its *appropriation* as an instrument for the dissemination of government information. Government growth, especially during the Second World War, established a demand for reliable conduits for official information. News of *Operation Overlord*, the invasion of Normandy, was entrusted to the Lobby in advance (after some lobbying on the Lobby's behalf by journalist Guy Eden and others). The Lobby's discretion was afterwards held up as proof of its trustworthy discipline. A third process has been the *codification* of a set of rules enforcing non-attribution of news sources while at the same time, encouraging lobby-men to rely on a single source, most often the Prime Minister or his or her spokesman. The Lobby reacted to the advent of television in the late 1950s and early 1960s by going down the path of 'inside dopeste-rism', asserting the supremacy of print by relying more on non-attribution, non-recorded conversations. By coincidence a set of Lobby rules was promulgated in 1956 just as television's competitive strength was dawning. Those rules, not made public until 1969, stated firmly: 'members of the lobby are under an obligation to keep secret the fact that [collective Lobby] meetings are held'.

These processes of collectivisation and appropriation took place in three stages. The first was the organisational work done, on the one hand, by lobbymen Guy Eden and, on the other, by Fife Clark, the Number 10 PRO under Churchill from 1952 to 1955. They established a routine of government briefing. This process had its consummation in the first three years of the Wilson premiership when – it is widely admitted – there was a three-year 'love affair' between the Lobby and Number 10. Harold Wilson was shameless in his manipulation of a system that he once described as a 'golden thread' in the skein of British parliamentary democracy. When the love affair ended in tears in 1967 the Lobby did not vow to avoid all future compromising with prime ministerial power and put its dealings with Number 10 on the record. No, until 1984 subsequent efforts at reform came from outside: from Edward Heath who had an admirably acute sense of the corruption of the Lobby system on both sides, and from Joe Haines, Number 10 PRO under the second Wilson premiership. Beneath a bank of self-serving rhetoric, Haines mounted a forceful critique of the Lobby's operation and eventually took the obvious step of suspending Lobby briefings altogether. Under Jim Callaghan and Margaret Thatcher the system revived. Bernard Ingham, number 10 PRO from 1981, is comparable with Macmillan's man, Sir Harold Evans.

Guy Eden, working first for the Beaverbrook papers, later for the defunct *Star*, had a sharp sense of the Lobby's responsibility – meaning, in the last analysis, withholding official information from the pub-

lic. In a symposium of – this is significant – House of Commons func-
tionaries published in 1948 Eden desribed his work as watching 'political events to keep you [the public] informed about them, and in general
be the eyes and ears of people who may never have seen the inside of the
House of Commons'.[18] This is a statement of the old parliamentary theory of the Lobby's role and fine as far as it went. But in more modern
vein Eden continued: 'He has to be able to tell everybody what a
government proposal means, sometimes more clearly than the government itself'. Because of their 'special personal relationship' Lobby correspondents 'have also to know when not to write as well as what and
when and how to write'.

Eden's version of collective Lobby discretion towards official information became one of the postwar hallmarks of political reporting. The
Lobby was the institution towards which, in the later 1940s and 1950s,
the newly-established Government Information Service gravitated: the
Lobby could be trusted. This discretion did not of course rule out
scoops, but they were of a different kind. Thus in 1948 the Lobby had a
*coup* with the Budget revelation that led to Hugh Dalton's resignation
from the Chancellorship. But the information did not come from bur-
rowing in the Treasury. On his way into the Chamber to deliver the
Budget speech, Hugh Dalton gave John Carvel of the London *Evening
Standard* some hints. This is classic Lobby stuff: an individual contact
in the ante-chamber makes a story. Nowadays Budget 'leaks' tend to
come in predigested form through the briefings arranged for the Lobby
collectively.

Churchill, as a Great Parliamentary Personality, held the nineteenth-
century idea that ministers of the Crown should keep their distance
from grubby political reporters. Editors and proprietors, Max Beaverbrook or Brendan Bracken, were better conduits for necessary political
messages. When he returned to power in 1951, Churchill resolutely
refused to have anything to do with either of those war-time creations,
the collectivised Lobby or the Government Information Service. He
instructed the Number 10 PRO inherited from Attlee, a civil servant
named Reginald Bacon, to desist from Lobby contacts and then effectively sacked the man. It was only some months later, when the Tory
grandees became alarmed about press coverage, that a link between
Number 10 and the Lobby was re-established under the political guard-
ianship of the Earl of Swinton, Lord President of the Council.[19]
Churchill was to be the last prime minister to treat the Lobby with such
insouciance.

Yet it was under Churchill that the previous rather irregular pattern
of meetings between the Lobby as a group and 'government spokesmen' became a habit; the agent was the astute PRO brought in by
Swinton to liaise between Number 10 and the press, Fife Clark. Within

a week of the restoration of 'normal' Lobby contacts in 1952, Churchill agreed to see Clark from time to time to prime him for what became a regular sequence of morning and afternoon briefing sessions for the Lobby, taken either by Clark or his deputy. Other ministers were in time encouraged to attend Lobby conferences and have their departmental information officers make use of the 'facility': perhaps once a fortnight a minister would come to the afternoon briefing to deliver an off-the-record speech. The pattern is similar today.

Fife Clark's reward was a period of successful news management. The story of Churchill's illness and stroke, in 1953, was effectively suppressed by the collective reluctance of the Lobby to probe behind the bland briefings. The Lobby cannot alone be held responsible for a high degree of public ignorance of the government's doings. Editors were unwilling to rock the boat. 'Any attempt', opined *The Observer* on 28 March 1954, 'to give revelations of divergent opinions at Cabinet meetings would be wrong, for it would undermine the principle of joint responsibility on which the whole Cabinet system depends' – thus, no inkling of the acute worries among Churchill's ministers about his capacity to lead. The upshot, according to Anthony Seldon, was that:

> the press failed to provide details of the most politically sensitive issues during 1951–55 such as Churchill's health and retirement plans and the struggles to induce him to retire, or those most disputed in Cabinet such as the de-nationalisation of steel, the future of commercial television, or policy towards a summit meeting with the Soviet Union.[20]

Two caveats should be entered here. Lobby journalists, as noted above, are employees of newspaper organisations whose goals are not always disclosure of information and the discomfiture of those in power; journalists may propose but it is editors and proprietors who dispose. Second, Lobby journalists did some things well in this period, especially when it came to party political squabbles in the Labour Party. Richard Crossman's voluminous backbench diaries are full of the anguish of Labour's National Executive Committee about press leaks – so much so that at one point Harold Wilson, neither then nor later a lover of open government, moved that the NEC take a collective vow of secrecy.

During the 1950s, broadly speaking, the Lobby trusted government. Successive *Times* lobbymen could move without much apparent heart-searching from reporting Executive power to, in the cases of Max Mason and John Groves, flakking for it. This trust helps explain some of the bitterness felt in the aftermath of Suez. As a former Foreign Secretary, Anthony Eden, who succeeded Churchill as Prime Minister in 1955, was an accomplished briefer of the press and, the Lobby thought, a good friend. Twenty years after Suez, old Lobby types could still shed a tear at the recollection of Eden's generosity in inviting not them alone, but also their wives for hospitality at Number 10. (Jeremy Tunstall's sociological study of the Lobby pinpointed the fact that its members, generally, led a suburban domestic life.) The political correspondents came to fall in easily with a sequence of off-the-record briefings given to them and their editors by Eden and his entourage as the crisis over Suez broke. During these the press were deliberately encouraged to threaten Nasser with war. What shocked was not just the duplicity underlying the Suez operations but Eden's subsequent denial that any briefings had been given nor any suggestions of bellicosity made. But, like all the lessons about the dangers of unattributable briefings and single-source stories ever given to the Lobby, the Suez lesson was not learnt.

Under the emollient influence of Charles Hill and Macmillan's amiable Number 10 PRO, Harold Evans, relations were quickly restored. Evans' diary of his years at Downing Street (1957 – 63) are full of an easy camaraderie – chaps all playing the game.[21] Amusingly, he notes a lunch in July 1961 with Guy Eden, then retired, who moans about the decline in Lobby discipline and the relaxing of secrecy about its doings. Evans' reward for his cultivation of the Lobby was when during the Profumo scandal the Lobby followed the official line with what seems in retrospect surprising docility.

Regular briefing of the Lobby on what happened in Cabinet, more or less, was an innovation of the Macmillan era, thanks to Charles Hill. In his memoirs Hill described the extent of the contact: 'Soon after I took on the responsibility for coordination of the Government Information Services, the Lobby extended to me an invitation to attend a meeting in their room regularly every week. . .'[22] From then on one of the central prime ministerial preoccupations has been 'how the Lobby would react'; later, under Wilson, the content and methodology of Lobby briefing may have taken up as many hours at Number 10 as subjects of state. The Lobby's 'invitation' became for it the high point of the week – on Thursdays.

Consequently Fridays were never again to be the same for the unsuspecting newspaper reader. An entire political history (albeit incomplete) could be written on the basis of one day's newspapers each week. Reports in all papers acquired a strange sameness that morning. By the early 1960s Richard Crossman, then a columnist for *The Guardian*, could claim (in the recollection of editor, Alistair Hetherington) 'to provide an almost verbatim account of what Rab Butler as Leader of the House was saying to the Lobby at his Thursday meetings with them simply by putting together the reports in the *Times*, *Guardian* and *Telegraph*'.[23]

Harold Wilson is, the Thatcher media campaign notwithstanding, the most 'media-conscious' of the postwar premiers. In his case, an ob-

sessive desire successfully to sell himself and his policies to the newspapers and television married with a strong suspicion of the media's
manipulative tendencies (which he showed long before he became
Prime Minister) and a personal agenda of slights and favourites.

In retrospect his early intimacy with the parliamentary Lobby is an
odd episode. Ever since his election to the leadership of the Labour
Party in 1962 he had cultivated political correspondents. Wilson gave
out tid-bits; he gave access to himself, all at a time when the Prime
Minister, Sir Alec Douglas-Home, adopted a rather Churchillian distance from the press. With Wilson there was a mutual admiration society. When he arrived at Number 10 in 1964 up to three separate
Lobby briefings were given a day, many by him personally. His first act
as premier was to appoint a favoured lobbyman as Prime Ministerial
press secretary. This was Trevor Lloyd-Hughes, political correspondent of the *Liverpool Daily Post,* who as a provincial would not upset the
*prima donnas* of Fleet Street. Wilson showed off his knowledge of how
the press worked, of deadlines and editorial pressures; he was affable
and always good copy. This he gave; and in return there was a build-up
both before and during the 1964 election of Wilson as a new man, even a
British Kennedy.

Yet it was in keeping with Wilson's character that on an intellectual
plane he was fully aware of the iniquities of the Lobby system and the
opportunities it gave, on both sides, for manipulation. In a speech in
1963 he had complained about the restriction of information from
government to journalists who were critical. On vital issues, Parliament
was being told less and less, Wilson said, and press comment was increasingly laundered through official press conferences. He used the
example of the Foreign Office:

> Nothing is said to Parliament by the Foreign Office, and diplomatic
> correspondents are reduced to utter dependence on a daily briefing at
> the FO. If the press exercises its undoubted right to criticise, then facili-
> ties dry up. Correspondents are demoted from the inner ring to the outer
> ring, and are denied information altogether in a system of administrative
> blackballing.

Wilson's strictures could hardly have been a more accurate guide to
how he behaved in office, with the creation of a celebrated 'White Commonwealth' – an inner ring of trusted Lobby correspondents.

That came later, after a honeymoon that lasted till after the 1966 election. This period was the heyday of Prime Ministerial 'steers' and selective briefing. The essence was planting a story in the press – a scoop for
some favoured journalist or paper (for example, Walter Terry of the
*Daily Mail*) – without any of the responsibility or political discredit
attaching to Wilson personally. Once 'a story', its import could be em-

bellished, turned around, even attacked, certainly *used* as a political fact. It is a subtle process.

An example, from Wilson's second term of office, comes from *Daily Telegraph* lobbyman, Harry Boyne:

> It was the eve of the final day of this Commonwealth conference and there was a big garden party given in, I suppose it would be, the Governor's residence. Joe Haines, who was then the press secretary at Number Ten, made an arrangement to see me at a certain time on the steps of the mansion. I turned up and Joe ushered me up to an upstairs room in the place. Harold came in and told me it was his intention to change Tony Benn's position in the government, move him from Industry to Energy. He then explained that he was intending to move some amendments to the Industry Bill and explained to me in some detail what these were.
>
> He did so with permission for me to write a story about it, which I duly did. I said 'Of course I won't put any by-line on this story. I think I'll just send it as *Daily Telegraph* reporter'. Well no, he says, you can make it 'By Our Political Staff'. This was typical of his knowledge, his quite intimate knowledge of how things worked in Fleet Street and in the Lobby, too.
>
> I felt I was being used as a means of giving information which was very interesting and useful to the public and to the political world in general and if it came as a surprise to other members of the Cabinet and to the gentleman minister concerned, well that was just too bad.[24]

In a speech to the Institute of Journalists in 1968, Edward Heath made the point that the *ignorance* of Lobby journalists laid them open to manipulation. Trouble came when they were used 'to put across technical information which the average Lobby correspondent is not equipped to test and question searchingly'. This was a charge that inevitably arose after four years of Wilsonian news management, especially on devaluation, the trade balance and other economic subjects. It is not necessarily to the discredit of the Lobby as a group of political specialists that they were (still are) ignorant of macroeconomics; but it is an indictment of the Lobby as a reliable means of reporting government. In his 1968 speech Heath gave an example:

> When the Vote on Account was published earlier this year it showed – just over two months after the Government's so-called expenditure cuts – a £1000 million increase in Government spending. The government spokesman – if one reads correctly between the lines – explained to the Lobby that the Vote on Account was of no importance and this year was largely meaningless. One Lobby correspondent – but one only – refused to accept this bland assertion, and it was largely due to him that this deliberate attempt to mislead the public failed.

The Heath critique resulted, when he became Prime Minister, in an unsuccessful but important experiment in communications. The attempt was in two parts. The first was to put messages from Number 10 fully on the record by means of televised press conferences staged at Lancaster House. Only two were eventually held but here was a useful reminder of an alternative model. At the same time efforts were made by Heath to boost the position of subject specialists outside the Lobby, on the grounds that the Lobby was lacking in 'intelligent background appreciation' of the issues. Even Margaret Thatcher as Secretary of State for Education made determined stabs at wooing the nascent Education Correspondents group.

The Lobby, needless to say, was none too happy with such innovations and it was counted a triumph for the older ways when, as the Heath government slid into crisis, 'regular' Lobby relations were restored. Yet it was at this time that Harold Wilson, in Opposition, vowed to eschew Lobby briefings and (pious note this) reserve the scoops for Labour's own paper, *Labour Weekly*.[25] After some delay the first part of the pledge was carried out: 'In June 1975', says Joe Haines, 'in what I believe were the best interests of journalists and government alike, I abolished [Lobby briefings] altogether, amid cries of anguish from those who did not object to being spoon-fed'.[26]

But, typical of Wilson, this was as much the product of animus against the press especially in the matter of Marcia Williams as critique of the Lobby system. In retrospect, Haines has amended his criticism: 'I think a certain part of the system is necessary', he now says:

> You cannot have a situation where Ministers or MPs cannot talk to journalists on a confidential basis. What I'm against is the institutionalised conspiracy of the Lobby whereby ministers and press secretaries can go along and speak to journalists, maybe one hundred, 120 of them in what is basically a large press conference and give news which is inevitably slanted.
>
> I did not go out of my way to give anti-government news. I might give pro-government news, often did because the source of the news is suppressed. I think that the readers are not fully aware of the value of the news. They cannot themselves value it unless they know that the particular item of news which is common in all the newspapers is not an official statement of fact, but it is what is said to be fact by a prejudiced or biased or interested person, i.e. a member of the Cabinet.

Haines' suspension of the Lobby briefings had no lasting effect. On Wilson's resignation the machine cranked back into gear with a complaisant Prime Minister in James Callaghan and a willing briefer in Sir Tom McCaffrey, his press secretary. The closeness of relations in the Callaghan years is seen at its worst in such incidents as the transfer of the British Ambassador in Washington. On Thursday, 12 May 1977, the front-page headline in the London *Evening Standard* said 'SNOB ENVOY HAD TO GO'. The same afternoon, the headline on the front page of the London *Evening News* said: SNOB ENVOY HAD TO GO'. The similarity might have been coincidence. In fact the message in the headlines had been given to the Lobby in a collective briefing earlier that day. Sir Tom McCaffrey briefed a Lobby meeting about the impending departure from Washington of the Ambassador there, and his replacement by the journalist, Mr Peter Jay, who was Callaghan's son-in-law. Nothing so crude as 'snob envoy' had been said during the briefing; the next day's papers reported, rather, the need for a modern approach in Britain's Embassy to the Carter administration, and the need for young blood. Apparently on the spiral staircase that leads from the room where the Lobby holds its briefings the respective correspondents of the *Standard* and the *News* had had extra words with Sir Tom, giving them their 'steer'.

During Mrs Thatcher's tenure of office, the practical arrangements for the Lobby have been these. Each weekday morning (special time-tables govern the parliamentary recess periods) a small group of lobby-men arrive at Downing Street for a briefing in the offices of the Prime Minister's press secretaries. This is generally routine, and services primarily the evening regional newspapers. More important is the briefing given at just after 4p.m. in the House of Commons. It is a briefing the existence of which is not officially acknowledged; it takes place in the Lobby's own briefing room – a location which until the cameras of *Panorama* found their way in four years ago had never been photographed nor indeed publicised in any way. (This 'turret' room is at the top of a rather dangerous spiral staircase leading off the Upper Committee Corridor in the House of Commons.) The main briefing of the week takes place on Thursdays after the Cabinet meets. In some circumstances the Prime Minister's Chief Press Secretary simply 'makes himself available' – i.e. he hangs about the Lobby to guide correspondents. More usually, there is a formal meeting addressed by the Press Secretary, then by the Leader of the House and, an hour later, by the Leader of the Opposition. According to Mr Francis Pym, Leader of the House in Mrs Thatcher's first government, 'We first of all would start with questions about next week's business. Then we go on to wider matters, anything really in the whole realm of government. I was available to guide them, make comments and give them a steer'.[27]

Steered the Lobby has been – during the miners' strike, against Mr Pym (sacked after the 1983 election), against the Ministry of Defence during the Falklands War, against the Wets: it has, in short, been in recent years an invaluable tool of news management. Most of the steering has been in the Prime Minister's favour and effected by Mr Bernard

Ingham, her Chief Press Secretary, a career civil servant who on her behalf has not shrunk from political controversy.

The system of 'approved' leaks through the Lobby was tested to destruction in January 1986 in the Westland Affair. An 'authorised' leaker, Miss Colette Bowe, the director of information at the Department of Trade, thought she had the approval of the ultimate official leaker, Mr Ingham, to use the Lobby for an operation to discredit a Cabinet minister for the sake of another minister and/or the Prime Minister. Pulling the cloak of Lobby confidentiality around them, the Department of Trade and Number Ten gave to the Lobby Correspondent of the Press Association selected snippets from a privileged and protected document, an opinion to fellow ministers from the Solicitor General Sir Patrick Mayhew. The leak turned out to be an instrument not only for vanquishing Mr Michael Heseltine, the intended victim, but also Mr Leon Brittan the Trade Secretary. The Lobby rules – non attribution of sources, perfect discretion – were if anything reinforced by the episode.

Mr Ingham has been adept at the business of ventriloquism. It was said of Mr Trevor Lloyd Hughes, Press Secretary to Lord Wilson from 1964: 'if you disagreed with Trevor, you were almost certainly disagreeing with the Prime Minister himself'. Mr Henry James, Mr Ingham's predecessor at Number 10, said the same:

> I've always seen myself as the *alter ego* of the Prime Minister.
>     You have to develop a knowledge of the style and the way of thinking of the person you're dealing with. It's not a Svengali role, but frequently without even consulting with the Prime Minister I have been able to reflect to the media what she subsequently said when I told her what the question was.[28]

The power inherent in the Number 10 Press Secretary's job is contingent on journalists believing that his voice is that of his master/mistress, and this is Ingham's great strength. When he told the Lobby[29] that remarks by Labour MP Mr Peter Shore were 'bunkum', it was indeed Mrs Thatcher speaking through him; likewise when he disparaged Mr Pym or Mr Clive Ponting. The ventriloquism can go wrong.

An amusing example of ventriloquist's error comes from early 1982 when Mr Pym, still Leader of the House, was being non-attributably berated for gloom over the economy. The Press Association reported: 'Colleagues maintain that the undeniable difference between Mrs Thatcher and Mr Pym arose from his natural pessimism. Whitehall sources compared him to the war-time comedy figure, Mrs Mopp, and her catch-cry 'It's being so cheerful that keeps me going'. The joke of course, was made by the Prime Minister's Press Secretary at a Lobby briefing. But, in being faithfully, and non-attributably, reported, the Press Secretary's error had been repeated: it was not Mrs Mopp who coined the lugubrious phrase but Mona Lott.

If the ratio of stories favourable to Mrs Thatcher relative to her Cabinet colleagues has buttressed her supremacy and assisted in her demotion of the Cabinet as an instrument of government, some credit must go to Mr Ingham and the flow he has channelled through the Lobby. Yet in this he is largely unknown. The Lobby reports the words of 'sources'. The source is known to initiates but not the public. Sir Angus Maude, for a time Mrs Thatcher's ministerial coordinator of information, argued:

> if a newspaper comes out and says – Mr Bernard Ingham, the press secretary at Number 10, says X and X turns out to have been a wrong steer not through any fault of Mr Ingham's then he looks stupid and anything he says in future is compromised.
>
> Where it says 'sources close to the government suggested that' or 'it was implied from Number 10 that' then it is no skin off anybody's nose if it turns out to be wrong. [30]

That is the Lobby's credo.

Yet if Friday morning's newspapers contained accounts of the previous day's Cabinet attributed to a named individual or even a Cabinet spokesman instead of stories from anonymous sources, such stories might (a) better reflect the Cabinet's conclusions than the Prime Minister's rendering of those conclusions; (b) prevent prime ministers so easily setting the tone or mood of political discussion; and (c) possibly eliminate distortion and untruth.

The Lobby makes journalists, their newspapers and their readers – likewise broadcasters – parties to the management of news by the government. The timing, novelty and interpretation of 'news' are decided by ministers and their officials: the Lobby provides a conduit. Worse, it is often an uncritical conduit. Lobby journalists are political specialists, meaning that in the subject matters of government they are generalists. In the presentation of economic or technical news, the government has the Lobby at severe disadvantage. In newspapers and broadcasting organisations where – this is usually the case – there is minimal contact between the Lobby staff and other specialists, the government wins. What matters often is first impression. The first gloss put upon a set of figures in, say, trade or macroeconomic policy is the one that sets the tone of subsequent discussion and reportage. Newspapers apply to themselves norms of speed and competitiveness in the coverage of events (norms which available marketing data show the public by no means accept) which force Lobby journalists into hasty and half-digested accounts: the result is good news for the government or, rather, better news than it deserves.

## Notes

1. Michael Macdonagh, *The Reporters' Gallery* London: Hodder & Stoughton n.d.
2. Lord Hill of Luton, *Both Sides of the Hill*, London: Heinemann, 1964.
3. Michael Cockerell, Peter Hennessy and David Walker, *Sources Close to the Prime Minister*, London: Macmillan, 1984.
4. Anthony Howard, in Anthony King and Anne Sloman (eds) *Westminster and Beyond*, London: Macmillan, 1973.
5. Ibid.
6. Sir Edward Cook, *Delane of the Times*, London: Constable & Co., 1915.
7. Reproduced in Cockerell, Hennessy and Walker, op.cit.
8. James Margach, *How Parliament Works*, London: Tom Stacey, 1972
9. Cockerell, Hennessy and Walker, op.cit.
10. Macdonagh, op.cit.
11. Alan J. Lee, *The Origins of the Popular Press 1855 – 1914*, London: Croom Helm, 1976.
12. Hamilton Fyfe, *Sixty Years of Fleet Street*, London: W.H.Allen, 1949.
13. *The History of The Times: The Twentieth Century Test 1884 – 1912*, London: *The Times*, 1947.
14. Sir Alexander Mackintosh, *Echoes of Big Ben. A Journalist's Parliamentary Diary 1881 – 1940*, London: Jarrolds, n.d.
15. Lord Burnham, *Peterborough Court, The Story of the Daily Telegraph*, London: Cassell, 1955.
16. Spencer Leigh Hughes MP, *Press, Platform and Parliament* London: Nisbet and Co., 1918.
17. Anthony Howard and Richard West, *The Making of the Prime Minister* The Quality Book Club, 1965.
18. Guy Eden, 'Lobby Correspondents' in *Parliamentary Affairs*, Winter 1948, Vol II No.1.
19. J. A. Cross *Lord Swinton*, Oxford: Clarendon Press, 1982.
20. Anthony Seldon, *Churchill's Indian Summer: the Conservative Government 1951-55* London: Hodder & Stoughton, 1981.
21. Harold Evans, *Downing Street Diary. The Macmillan Years*, London: Hodder & Stoughton, 1981.
22. Lord Hill of Luton, op.cit.
23. Alastair Hetherington, *Guardian Years*, London: Chatto & Windus, 1981.
24. Sir Harry Boyne, unpublished conversation with Michael Cockerell, 1984.
25. Barbara Castle, *The Castle Diaries 1974 – 76*, London: Weidenfeld & Nicolson.
26. Joe Haines *The Politics of Power*, London: Jonathan Cape, 1977.
27. Francis Pym, unpublished conversation with Michael Cockerell
28. Henry James, unpublished conversation with Michael Cockerell.
29. Cockerell, Hennessy and Walker, op.cit.
30. Sir Angus Maude unpublished conversation with Michael Cockerell.

**Addendum**

In the summer of 1986, in its 102nd year, the Westminster Lobby faced its first serious breakaway. Appropriately enough, it was the first quality newspaper to be founded in Britain for 131 years, *The Independent*, which dislodged the masonry put into place in Gladstone's time. The new paper made it plain it would have nothing to do with the Lobby, it would operate outside the club from the start. The editor, Andreas Whittam Smith recruited his team of Westminster and Whitehall specialists on that understanding. As a result, Peter Preston, (editor of *The Guardian*) with the unanimous backing of his political journalists and commentators, decided, though he did not acknowledge this when announcing it in his paper, to break the cardinal Lobby convention of non-attribution. In future, briefings by the No.10 Press Secretary would be attributed to 'a Downing Street Spokesman'.[1]

Preston had tried at a breakfast meeting in the late summer of 1986 to persuade Charles Wilson of *The Times* and Max Hastings of *The Daily Telegraph* to join him. Wilson showed scant interest in reform. Hastings, though an open critic of the Lobby, decided to delay a decision until he saw what effect *The Guardian*'s initiative would have.[2] At the time of writing (early October 1986), the most likely outcome of the actions of *The Independent* and *The Guardian* are the short-term survival of the Lobby while the Ingham–Thatcher partnership continues in Downing Street (Bernard Ingham has refused in the past to brief attributably, so the Lobby will probably regroup itself with *The Guardian* excluded); and its long-term dismantling after a change of government. The developments of the summer and early autumn of 1986 became historic rather than merely historical, to borrow a distinction used by Professor Sammy Finer, when, prompted by Preston, the three leaders of the opposition parties, Neil Kinnock, David Owen and David Steel, wrote to *The Guardian* pledging an end to non-attributable Downing Street briefings should the electorate propel them into Number 10.[3]

On 29 October the Lobby journalists voted in a strict ballot to maintain the Lobby system; and at the same time voted to set up an inquiry into how 'the Lobby operates'.[4]

**Notes**

1.    Exchange of letters between Peter Preston and Bernard Ingham, *The Guardian*, 25 September 1986.
2.    Peter Hennessy, 'The case of the visible spokesman: the Lobby reforms itself', *New Statesman*, 3 October 1986.
3.    *The Guardian*, 2 October 1986.
4.    *The Guardian*, 29 October 1986.

# PART II
# Media Revolution and Political Change

# 7   The struggle for 'balance'*
## *Jean Seaton and Ben Pimlott*

'Balance' in broadcasting is a strange concept, with no equivalent for the press. The assumption in the case of newspapers is of imbalance, with each paper reflecting a particular editorial or proprietorial point of view. Broadcasting 'balance' is beset with philosophical and practical difficulties. At best, it can prevent the complete domination of the ether by one party or set of opinions. At worst, it pretends to impartiality while choosing carefully where the fulcrum should be placed. In multi-party conditions, the problem becomes even greater – or, perhaps, simply more evident. Nevertheless, the idea exists and is taken seriously. Indeed so integral has it become to the workings of all radio and television in Britain that one has to go abroad to appreciate its peculiarity.

Why is the spoken word in this country supposed to be governed by Queensberry rules, while the written word is not? Like other aspects of broadcasting, 'balance' was not suddenly invented. It evolved. This chapter will consider the first and most critical phase of its evolution, up to the Second World War. It will look at attempts by the labour movement (especially the TUC) to gain recognition and acceptance from the BBC. Finally, it will examine a strange, significant incident during the last days of peace, which brought the struggle to a climax.

### Outside the arena

'Balance' is the child of 'public service'. The decision to finance broadcasting by a licence fee, and the establishment of the BBC in 1926 as a public corporation with a Royal Charter which deemed it desirable 'that the Service should be developed and exploited to the best advantage and in the national interest', imposed duties of a public nature.[1] How these duties were to be interpreted, depended partly on an earlier broadcasting heritage, partly on the personal dictatorship of the first

*The authors wish to thank the British Academy for a grant which helped to finance the research for this chapter.

Director-General, and partly on political buffetings which became rougher as the importance of the new medium was made apparent.

Incorporated into the state, it was natural that the new organisation should adopt Establishment values. From the beginning, broadcasting managers showed themselves unsurprisingly susceptible to a form of the aristocratic embrace: displaying an eager desire to please those in authority as a passport to respectability. The inter-war period was the heyday of the one-party system. Conservative-based governments held office for more than 17 years out of 21. There was little incentive, therefore, to present an alternative point of view. Hence, despite a strong and in some ways paradoxical instinct towards independence within the Corporation, the political aspect of 'public service' meant the respectful projection of official attitudes. Liberals, and liberal views broadly defined, were permitted some expression; the fledgling Labour Party, except during its brief moments of electoral success, almost none.

At first the Labour Party, whose growth in significance paralleled radio's own, shrugged off the BBC's partiality as an irrelevance. It was the General Strike, occurring in the year of the BBC's Charter, that provided a turning-point. The BBC saw the strike as something 'which is to broadcasting what the Great War was to flying . . . it put it on the map'.[2] For the first time, dependence on broadcasting became universal, and the perceptions of the average citizen (in the words of Beatrice Webb) 'centred round the headphones of the wireless set'.[3] In Cabinet, Churchill pressed for the commandeering of this newly discovered weapon of industrial war. John Reith, not yet nationalised, resisted. At first, news bulletins were dispassionate. There was a need, however, to tread delicately. Reith believed that the BBC might act as a conciliator, yet was desperately concerned not to give the government grounds for interference. Hence the choice of speakers was tightly restricted. A Catholic bishop was encouraged to broadcast a declaration that striking might be sinful; but the Archbishop of Canterbury was not allowed to make an appeal for negotiations, which might have appeared too sympathetic to the union point of view. Government ministers were given ample air-time; but the Leader of the Opposition, Ramsay MacDonald, was excluded on the grounds that he might 'incite' the strikers. Who was to blame? When labour movement leaders complained to the BBC, they were told that the government was responsible; when they complained to the government, they were assured that the broadcasting authorities had imposed the bans themselves. The strikers called the BBC 'the British Falsehood Company', and regarded it as an instrument of government power. Resentment over this episode of injustice provided the idiom of trade union rhetoric and complaints in quite different situations later.

But the General Strike was not the only cause of bitterness between the wars. Anger at obvious bias was powerfully reinforced during the 1931 election, which ended in Labour's catastrophic defeat. If the exploitation of the fraudulent Zinoviev letter by the press was often blamed for Labour's loss of office in 1924, a broadcast allegation by the turncoat Chancellor, Philip Snowden, that Labour's programme was 'Bolshevism run mad', was widely taken as a cause of the 1931 calamity. Clement Attlee, one of the few survivors, later described the 1931 election as 'the most unscrupulous in my recollection'.[4] The complaint against the BBC was that Labour had been denied a right of reply. It seemed that in this most one-sided of contests, the Corporation abandoned all pretence at neutrality, arbitrarily weighting the scales to the benefit of the 'National' coalition.

One issue concerned an interpretation of the rules: the BBC decision to treat each of the three elements in the government – Conservative, 'National' Liberal and 'National' Labour – as if they were separate and independent bodies, when, in reality, all were dependent on the National ticket and did not compete electorally among themselves. On this basis, eight out of eleven pre-election broadcasts went to government speakers, and only three to the official Labour Party.[5] A second grievance, after the campaign, concerned the broadcast of speeches by the Prime Minister and Chancellor during the gold crisis which preceded the election. 'Under the guise of national appeals and statements on the financial emergency,' protested the Labour Executive, 'Ministers and their supporters had a complete monopoly of broadcasts.'[6] A third accusation was that the BBC presented National Government slogans as though they were the Corporation's own moralisms. 'On your action or failure to act', the BBC had admonished listeners just before polling began, 'may depend your own and your children's future and the security and prosperity of the country.' These were almost precisely the terms in which the 'National' parties had pushed their 'national unity' platform.[7]

'It was really quite thrilling', Reith wrote privately, when the result was known, 'a tremendous sweep . . . every member of the late Cabinet turned out.'[8] Attlee, the new Deputy Leader, made Labour's feelings clear to MPs when Parliament reassembled. Following up a NEC report that the Party had been denied 'anything approaching equality of opportunity in respect of political broadcasts', he told the Commons in December 1931 that if broadcasting were allowed to become a tool of government, 'anyone who is temporarily or permanently against the government will be in a position of grave inferiority'.[9] Thus the newfangled medium might become a Frankenstein monster, undermining the conventions of political justice.

At the 1932 Party Conference (in some ways the most radical between the wars) a resolution deploring Labour's exclusion from the airwaves was carried unanimously. The railwaymen's leader, C.T. Cramp, voiced the widespread frustration, which contained elements of Luddite bewilderment and hostility towards technical innovation:

> The publicity which we had prior to the discovery of wireless was the newspapers and ordinary meetings and we were always at a disadvantage in those days because the pennies of the workers were so few that we could not have a daily paper to get our point of view across, and now that we have a daily paper to put our case, this new invention comes into our very homes and is reaching people who would otherwise neither read nor listen to any matters of public importance; and these matters are now sandwiched between entertainment programmes.[10]

It was left to Walter Citrine, General Secretary of the TUC, to make the most intelligent case for the trade unions, and to lead a highly effective campaign for better treatment. A superficial 'survey' of the year of the General Strike, broadcast in 1932, was one of the earliest provocations. Everything about the programme, Citrine wrote, was wrong. The union arguments were simply not presented at all: 'How many trade unionists have been invited to give talks?' he demanded. 'I broadcast twice, once with five employers, and the second time with ten employers. How many attempts have been made to get the trade union point across?'[11] The BBC response became its standard defence – expressing its own, internally unquestioned, definition of 'balance'. The Corporation, declared Reith, was frequently charged by people on the Right with showing a leftward bias. If the trade unions now accused it of being biased to the Right, balance had evidently been achieved.

The following year the TUC set up a sub-committee to monitor broadcasting, and in 1934 the TUC Conference urged its General Council to take the necessary steps to secure that the policy of the working-class movement be broadcast under all circumstances.[12] One delegate noted a pro-German, anti-Soviet slant at the BBC, another suggested using foreign commercial stations to 'put forward the working-class idea'. Each year in the mid-1930s, the TUC agenda contained a range of anti-BBC resolutions.

One persistent objection, repeatedly voiced by Citrine as by the Labour Party leaders, was the unfairness of the Corporation in its choice of speakers. When, rarely, trade unionists were permitted to broadcast, they did so strictly on the BBC's own terms; scripts were prepared in advance, and carefully vetted. Uproar was caused (and the Corporation's worst fears were apparently vindicated) when a union speaker tricked his producer by departing from his approved speech while at the microphone, in order to denounce the BBC's censorship. Invitations to trade unionists were, however, infrequent. As the General Council caustically observed, mine owners and industrialists were regarded as acceptable, but union leaders were considered 'partisan'. The Board of Governors, which included businessmen, contained no labour representative.

In 1934, conscious of trade union bad feeling, the BBC tried to make amends. A series on the history of British trade unionism was proposed. Members of the General Council were lunched at the Athenaeum, to prepare the ground. Once again, however, the possibility of trade unionists actually speaking in the programmes was excluded. Citrine complained: but the Head of Talks remained adamant.[13]

The TUC saw the BBC attitude as simple prejudice against the working class, which was a reasonable assessment. But there was also a quite sophisticated justification, reflecting BBC philosophy. If the TUC was a proud exponent of collectivism, the BBC was an equally determined upholder of liberal individualism. Repeated clashes between the organisations reflected this difference.

Citrine spoke always for his General Council and often (in a style characteristic of union officials) took refuge behind Council or TUC pronouncements, or the lack of them. Reith, by contrast, saw his own resistance to TUC 'pressure' as part of a personal crusade against organisational pressures in general. The ethic of hostility to organisations pervaded his staff as well. In broad cultural terms, the BBC was far from conservative. Even in the field of economic or social ideas (when detached from immediate events) the accusation of rightward bias could scarcely be sustained. Maynard Keynes, still officially out of favour, was a frequent speaker; so was William Beveridge. Indeed, the list of pre-war broadcasters, which included many of the most fertile and imaginative speakers of the day, has led some historians to suggest that the spirit of reform of the 1940s had been nurtured by radio during the previous decade. Party or organisational politics, on the other hand, were another matter. The BBC would only countenance reform in the terms of which it approved: 'non-partisan', advocated by speakers talking in an individual capacity, who had been invited on the basis of their particular achievement or of personal friendship with somebody at the BBC. 'Contacts' was a key word in Corporation circles. Trade unionists did not count as 'contacts'.

Citrine fought on behalf of his General Council. After 1931, the demands of the General Council and those of the Labour Party were frequently combined, because of the close involvement of the Council in Party affairs, through the strengthened National Joint Council (from 1934 called the National Council of Labour). The TUC and Labour Party viewed broadcasting from significantly different perspectives. Both, however, had to contend with the unusual character and conscience of the BBC's Director-General.

A major complaint from the Left was that Reith acted as judge and jury on what was 'national' and therefore required Opposition comment on the air, and what was mere 'politics' and therefore precluded it. This highly personal power, as Labour's most prominent lawyer, Sir Stafford Cripps, pointed out, enabled the Corporation 'to determine the lines on which the public are to be invited to make up their minds'. In elections, in particular, the BBC was able to decide the nature of the issues to be discussed.[14]

Here then was power without responsibility, with a vengeance. More than half a century later, agenda-setting remains one of the most important roles of radio and television. In the 1980s, the justification for choices in current affairs broadcasting is often made in terms of supposed 'news value', an undefined and self-generating concept. The direct ancestor of news value was the Reithan idea of 'the national good' – autocratically, rather than bureaucratically, determined.

One problem with 'the national good' was that it tended to follow fashion. Thus, when official Labour was out of public favour following the break-up of the second Labour Government in 1931, 'national good' was equated with the pronouncements of the National Government. When George Lansbury, as Party Leader, complained in 1932 at the exclusive presentation of the MacDonaldite point of view through a series of broadcast speeches by members of the first National Government, Reith haughtily replied that 'no question of controversy could possibly arise'.[15] Yet the subject matter ranged from gold to disarmament – the gamut of the hotly debated topics of the day. 1932 was a year in which unemployment reached its pre-war peak, close to three million. Was this a matter for a debate that might involve the Opposition? Apparently not. Lansbury's request for a broadcast retort to the Prime Minister on the subject was flatly refused. 'I object', Lansbury told the Commons, 'to this elevation of the British Broadcasting Corporation into a kind of God to choose who shall speak and who shall not speak'.[16] In vain he wrote to the Director-General: 'What you do not appear to realise is that politics could not be kept out of broadcasting. Housing, unemployment, these *are* political issues'.[17] Sir Stafford Cripps wanted the House of Commons to replace the Director-General as arbiter, and pressed for a select committee, arguing against 'the continual outpouring of ministerial statements over the ether, without any reply'. No committee was set up.

One reason was the overwhelming domination of Parliament by Conservatives, who found less cause for complaint. Another was the time-lag in appreciating the political influence, actual and potential, of the new medium. The Labour Party, because adversely affected, was jolted into an acute awareness of the truth by the 1931 campaign. Cripps was able to see clearly the capacity of radio 'to make a politician overnight by giving him an audience of 5,000,000 or 6,000,000'.[18] Others were slower to make the same calculation. By the 1930s, mass cinema audiences had created the phenomenon of the film star, and the power of the cinema newsreel was perceived. Radio stars were only just beginning, and it was not until late in the decade that radio became fully confident – even arrogant – about its ability to bestow fame on any individual of its choosing.

Meanwhile, the power of the medium was better appreciated by those outside the Establishment who sought legitimation, than by those within. The clamour for air-time from axe-grinders and would-be celebrities of all kinds was becoming part of the daily life of broadcasting officials. 'At first I approached celebrities with caution', recalled one producer, describing the change, 'usually through some mutual friend, but as broadcasting developed it became possible to write to every celebrity suggesting a broadcast. The offer was seldom refused'.[19] The offer, it might have been added, was seldom extended to those who might cause offence. 'How can I or my movement reach the mass of the people', asked Marie Stopes, the birth control campaigner, 'indeed . . . be taken as an authority with serious views . . . if you continue to deny me the ether?'[20] The view of the BBC as a legitimiser received only gradual acknowledgement, earlier and more painfully by the Left than by the Right.

There was a double standard: an appreciation of power in the would of entertainment, more evident as the decade progressed, which was not applied or accepted for public affairs. Thus the BBC made ruthless use of its monopoly to extract highly favourable contracts from comedians and singers, knowing that they would be accepted in return for publicity provided by radio. Theatrical agents 'became cooperative almost to an embarrassing degree',[21] and there was wide agreement that radio was responsible for the decline of the music hall. But the power to make some famous while leaving others in obscurity was not considered relevant to broadcasts by politicians.

Instead, the BBC saw itself as above the fray – on the one hand, a populariser, reducing 'the yawning gulf between expert and citizen', on the other, able to sort out the bogus from the sincere. Here was a new, super-human attribute, which placed the airwaves apart from mortal agencies. The microphone, claimed Hilda Matheson, Head of Talks, 'has a curious knack of showing what is real and what is unreal . . . what is sincere and what is an appeal to the gallery'. Broadcasting could be presented, not as an instrument in the hands of powerful people wielded on behalf of other members of the elect, but as a 'technology of truth'.[22] Four decades later Grace Wyndham-Goldie, another pioneer, justified television political coverage in similar terms. Television, she claimed authoritatively, 'reveals people as they really are'.[23] This myth of the 'revealing intimacy' of radio and then television, based on the beguiling notion that to meet somebody is to know them, became part of broadcasting lore. It enabled producers, without need of further explanation, to select the articulate, the moderate, the relaxed, the well-spoken, the well-known, the all-round plausible, and to dismiss the rest. If the aim was to choose 'good broadcasters', whose sincerity was transparent, what credence could be given to accusations of bias?

Labour persisted in its complaint. Apart from the regrettable non-respectability of its views, too many of its spokesmen or supporters lacked the necessary qualifications as potential performers. 'You are getting really into a Hitlerite position,' Attlee warned in 1933.[24] But the allegations of slanted comment came also from the Right. It was the sense of being attacked from both extremes that made it possible for the Director-General to believe that he was maintaining 'balance'.

Newspapers, generally on the side of reaction, maintained a steady attack on the BBC on the grounds of its excessive interest in progress. The *Daily Mail* and *Daily Express* campaigned with particular vigour against what they called the 'Menace of Red Bias in Radio' which was undermining social order, family life, morals and 'national consciousness'. 'Innocent Minds Barbarised by War Monger', shouted a *Mail* headline, following a broadcast during Children's Hour by the Berlin correspondent of the *Manchester Guardian*.[25] Catholic Tory MPs backed up the *Mail*'s assault on the Corporation's supposed pinkness in its attitude to 'red murderers' in Spain.[26] The effect was to bolster Reith's sense of his own independence. For the point was made (and still is) that if both sides were annoyed and suspicious, fairness was being achieved.

Such a claim might have been reasonable in a perfectly pluralist world. In the 1930s however, it was by no means the case that one side counterbalanced the other. Not only was the 'political' Right, outside the government, able to exercise a greater influence. The government itself, informally and behind the scenes, ensured that its own requirements received attention.

Unlike some of his staff, who argued that the best way to counter attempts at government manipulation was to publicise them, Reith believed that independence would only be further undermined by confessions of subservience. He was also much more sensitive to criticisms from Central Office than from Transport House: a 1935 minute from the Director of Talks which argued that Conservative criticisms could best be met by 'series of a constructive character, all of which help to consolidate the accepted institutions and traditions', echoed the opinions of the Director-General.[27]

Yet the much neglected Labour Party was the BBC's strongest advocate in one respect, at least. From the outset, Labour had been a keen supporter of the BBC's status as a public corporation. Its constitution had been a model, during the 1929–31 administration, for the London Transport Board and, subsequently, for other Morrisonian blueprints for nationalised industries. In the 1930s the BBC faced capitalist competition: from privately-owned relay stations that pirated BBC programmes and broadcast selections from them, and from foreign commercial stations, which provided a superior reception.[28] Hence Labour had its own double standard, as the Party's evidence to the Ullswater Committee on Broadcasting, which reported in 1936, showed.[29] It was able to combine virulent criticism of BBC behaviour with ardent backing for its aspirations.

Labour perceived, rightly, that Sir John Reith, a public employee, took his public responsibilities seriously. The quarrel was over their interpretation. We have drawn attention to the 'individualist' attitude of the Corporation in its treatment of competing organisations – favouring persons over collectivities – and to its mechanistic view of broadcasting, as a tester, rather than a projector, of opinions. In addition, the BBC saw its educational role – at the heart of 'public service' – in strangely idealised terms, as though education could be divorced from argument. The aim of better news was better information and hence better equipped citizens in a well-functioning democracy. Hilda Matheson liked to imagine that radio's vast listening public was 'more aware of the world and what it contains than any public at any previous moment'.[30]

Before sophisticated opinion surveys, it was hard to argue against this optimistic (even megalomaniac) view of the relationship between broadcasting networks and their audience. Practical politicians, however, especially those who sought power, were becoming conscious of the malleable nature of public opinion in a newly enfranchised electorate. What was 'public opinion'? Politicians had an organic view of it, as something which took shape and could, in its broad contours, be influenced. Once the range and influence of broadcasting began to be appreciated, radio was increasingly seen as a 'mind controller', exceedingly dangerous if allowed to fall into the wrong hands.

The BBC, on the other hand, merely counted. Claiming to see the population as composed of equally intelligent, open-minded and attentive beings, its main method of assessing public response was by examining the letters it received, of praise or complaint. Here, indeed, the 'balance' mentality was seen at its most basic. The calculus was crudely arithmetic, and the Corporation was happiest when expressions of one view exactly cancelled out the other.[31]

### The struggle for balance and the struggle for peace
'Balance', as it came to be accepted after the Second World War, owed much to the reassertion of the two-party system, and the swing of the

electoral pendulum. It was also influenced by a furious row over recognition of the labour movement and a labour movement point of view by the BBC, just before war was declared. This dispute brought to a head all the complaints of the Labour Party and TUC of the preceding decade and a half, and ended with a *de facto* acknowledgement of an Opposition right to be heard.

In the 1930s, foreign policy did not separate the political parties; it split them. Within each party, there were major tensions on the subject of armaments and deterrence. This was as much true on the Left as on the Right. At first Labour, bewildered by German resurgence, presented a variety of conflicting opinions, some pacifist, others against 'capitalist' arms, others advocating collective security. Increasingly, it was the last approach, based on what one historian called the Dalton – Bevin – Citrine block,[32] which prevailed. By 1938 the dominant labour movement view, backed by an alliance of key parliamentary leaders and the union establishment, was against appeasement and in favour of a strong response to threatened aggression.

The new labour attitude owed much to direct contact with European socialists and trade unionists. Hugh Dalton, strongest advocate of rearmament on the NEC and in the PLP, had been deeply affected by a visit to Germany in 1933. Citrine, too, had close German contacts, and had watched with concern the annihilation of union networks in Germany. Citrine was critical of tactical errors on the part of German unionists. But he continued to believe that sections of the German working class might, in the right conditions, be prepared to resist Fascism. This faith, based on a belief that the German masses could be distinguished from their rulers, played an important part in BBC – labour movement relations as war approached.

The labour movement leaders believed that, if properly approached, ordinary Germans might be persuaded to overthrow their oppressors. The direct concern of the BBC in the approaching crisis, on the other hand, was not to undermine the government's diplomatic initiatives. This meant, in effect, a pro-appeasement stance. Where Labour hoped to influence German public opinion, the BBC hierarchy, reflecting Foreign Office and Downing Street anxieties, became obsessively concerned not to offend the Nazi leaders. Thus, in February 1938, the robustly patriotic Labour MP Josiah Wedgwood was removed from a planned programme, and replaced by the Chamberlainite editor of *The Times* Wickham Steed, on the grounds that 'the BBC could not allow dictators to be personally criticised'.[33] Vernon Bartlett was banned from Children's Hour on similar grounds,[34] and a positive effort was made (in the words of the Midlands Programming Board) to 'help counter the resurgent fears and antagonisms which so threaten attempts at appeasement'.[35]

Such an approach was powerfully reinforced in 1937, on the appointment of Reith's successor as Director-General, W.F. Ogilvie – a man far less capable of standing up to government pressure even if he had wished to do so, which on the whole he did not. Ogilvie, a man of limited abilities and no knowledge of broadcasting, would scarcely have found it easy to steer a course through the competing pressures upon the Corporation in more stable times. At a moment of acute national crisis, he proved incapable of perceiving that the Corporation had a duty to maintain political independence.

This became evident in a rumbling row with labour movement leaders, which erupted in the final days of peace, on the issue of direct broadcasting to the German people. At first, the BBC had shown itself sympathetic to a modest NCL request. In the summer of 1938, the first of a series of messages was broadcast. Written by Herbert Morrison, it urged the Germans to speak out 'against the use of force and violence in the settlement of international disputes'.[36] In June 1939, another message was broadcast, this time warning that British workers, though anxious to avoid war, were prepared to fight. Returning from a foreign visit shortly afterwards, Citrine reported to the NCL that this had had, in his opinion, a considerable effect, both in encouraging anti-Fascist movements abroad and in convincing ordinary German citizens of the seriousness of British intentions.[37]

Such a view was, no doubt, wildly optimistic. Nevertheless, it had an importance for the British labour movement. For in the desperate weeks before the invasion of Poland, Labour and union leaders were made humiliatingly conscious of their absolute inability to affect the course of policy. Meeting for days in continuous session after the announcement of the Russo-German pact in August, the NEC, NCL and General Council were eager to assist the government. Chamberlain contemptuously ignored them.

Thus, it happened that on 25 August, Hugh Dalton, Labour's foreign affairs spokesman, suggested a 'final message of friendship and warning' to be broadcast to the German people. The idea receiving enthusiastic support, he and Harold Laski were asked to write it. 'War is very near,' began the message. 'You must understand that Britain and France both stand firmly by their pledges to Poland ... British Labour tells you with all solemnity that the pledges of the British Government, with the full approval of British Labour, will stand completely unaffected.' The message was apparently addressed at some notional average worker, supposedly capable of urging restraint. It continued in a style derived from the writings of E.D. Morel and H.N. Brailsford: 'Remember that it is not you who want war. It is a small handful only of your rulers. Remember that it is you who will pay heavily for the war – all war, with its tragic burden, falls most heavily upon the common people of all lands.'[38]

Copies of this scarcely momentous message were sent to the BBC, and also to the Foreign Office, the French and Polish embassies, and to Sir Robert Vansittart, the government's Chief Diplomatic Adviser. In order to ensure its speedy transmission, Dalton rang up Ogilvie's secretary. An hour later, he rang again. It became clear that consent to broadcast would be far from automatic. A decision on the possible use of the message, the Labour leader was informed, had not been reached.

A meeting was demanded and arranged. Facing Dalton and Citrine, the Director-General hedged. The suggestion was made that Citrine might read the message on the air. In the BBC's experience, Ogilvie replied, messages were less effective when delivered personally. 'Very well,' said Dalton. 'I take it that you will put over our message as news.' Ogilvie was evasive. The meeting ended tensely.[39] The Director-General noted afterwards that his visitors 'became apoplectic with fury at our refusal'.[40] The existence of the Labour 'message' was briefly mentioned on the News, but without any indication of what it was about.[41]

There were a number of elements: on the one hand, government fear lest the remaining possibility of peace might be disturbed by a minor irritant; on the other, Labour suspicions (partly justified) that the government was considering another sell-out. At the same time, there was the government's assumption that the BBC would do what it was told; and Labour's rage at its exclusion from deliberations, combined with accumulated resentment at its partisan exclusion by the BBC. Thus there existed, during this high emergency, a primary concern at the very top of the Labour Party and TUC, not with conscription, evacuation or bombs, but with an anodyne moral entreaty which, even if broadcast, few Germans would hear, and those who did hear would undoubtedly ignore.

That Labour and union leaders continued to focus on this trivial issue for several days, would have mattered little had not the government had a secondary interest: maintaining an appearance of national unity. Hence, while unwilling to have the message broadcast, there was also concern not to antagonise Labour into public criticism. The labour movement leaders were able to use this political card to ensure that Foreign Office officials and ministers, and even briefly the Prime Minister, were brought into the controversy.

Because of the need to appease not only Hitler but Labour as well, the government attempted to explain its position. Just before the existence of the message received brief attention on the News on 25 August, R.A. Butler, the Parliamentary Under-Secretary for Foreign Affairs, telephoned Dalton and told him that its contents were felt to be too dangerous to broadcast. The Foreign Office was waiting for the deciphered copy of a long telegram from the British Ambassador in Berlin,

Nevile Henderson, and, in any case, the message did not accord with government information about German public opinion. Labour fury, however, could not be so easily assuaged. 'I do not think the matter can be allowed to rest here,' noted Dalton.[42] Neither did Citrine, who wrote immediately to the Foreign Secretary, Lord Halifax. The Foreign Office, he declared, had been trying to censor Labour. 'We have endeavoured to avoid any impression of disunity during the present critical times,' he stated, 'but we are not prepared to allow the legitimate viewpoint of the labour movement, representing nearly 5,000,000, to be stifled.'[43] It was a familiar grievance.

Butler now did his best to make amends. Taking Dalton into his private room at the House on 29 August, he apologised for the mishandling of the affair, and declared in a conciliatory manner that he and Halifax 'were most anxious to create some machinery – none now existed – to prevent any repetition of such an incident'. Dalton gathered Citrine and Philip Noel-Baker, another Labour MP and member of the NEC, and the same night they met the three Foreign Office ministers, Lord Halifax and his two juniors, Butler and Lord Perth. Citrine poured out the feelings of the trade union movement, of anger and humiliation and injustice, which had been mounting since the General Strike. Ogilvie, he said, was not fit for his job. 'Our people are getting pretty fed up with being expected to shout with the Government one day and being treated like a lot of children or nobodies the next.' Halifax replied that it had been felt that appeals of the kind proposed by the NCL were ineffective, as were attempts, in general, to divide Hitler from the German people. He admitted, however, that the decision to block the Labour message had been taken without his knowledge, 'on the judgement of his officials, for whom, of course, he must accept responsibility'. 'These are most superficial and trivial considerations, . . .' snapped Dalton, '[Y]ou have been ill-served.' Halifax tried to defend Ogilvie, declaring him to be 'a first-rate man'. Dalton brushed this aside, and returned to the message. 'Would it not be helpful now that, perhaps with a few modifications, it should be broadcast after all?'[44]

Next day, 30 August, Lord Perth, speaking for his chief, gave way. He agreed to recommend that the message should be broadcast the same night on the BBC's German News. Perth added: 'Of course, Ogilvie is the final arbiter.' Dalton countered by threatening to go public if, at this stage, the request was refused.[45] The Labour message, virtually as it had originally been written, was broadcast across Europe that evening and repeated next day, 31 August. Early in the morning of 1 September, German troops crossed the Polish frontier, precipitating British and French ultimatums.

Despite the utter irrelevance of the issue at such an historic moment, Dalton counted it a personal and labour movement victory, and in a way he was right. What is significant is not the pressure put on the BBC by the government at this time, which was to be expected, but the willingness of frantically busy ministers to give up time to the Labour complaint. Their amenability is the more interesting because (unknown to the Labour leaders) the censorship decision had not been taken, as Halifax claimed, by one of his own officials. Ogilvie had contacted 10 Downing Street directly. Scribbled on the BBC memorandum recording Dalton's request of 25 August for the message to be broadcast is a sentence, in the hand of a Corporation official, which reveals all: 'Rucker [the Prime Minister's secretary] rang and confirmed that the PM particularly did not want anything of this kind broadcast tonight.' The time given was 5.15 p.m.[46]

It is not hard to work out why. Events had been moving fast. That morning, Hitler had summoned Henderson in Berlin. The same afternoon, the Ambassador telephoned Sir Alexander Cadogan, Permanent Under-Secretary at the Foreign Office, to pass on the news that 'Hitler had made him a communication and had suggested he should fly back to London.'[47] Round about the time that the Labour request to broadcast reached Downing Street, Chamberlain, Halifax and Cadogan were studying the German Chancellor's final proposals (the 'long telegram' mentioned by Butler). It was not until 11.30 p.m. that Halifax telegrammed the British refusal. In this context, Labour's ambition to assert its broadcasting rights must have received only a passing, dismissive consideration.

By 30 August, on the other hand, different counsels prevailed. Last-minute hopes for a compromise over Danzig faded. Attention now shifted, fleetingly, to the possibility that Hitler might after all be restrained. On 28 August, Cadogan noted in his diary intelligence reports of 'trouble with reservists in Germany'; and two days later, again, 'rumours of trouble in Germany'.[48] Possibly this was wishful thinking, but it may have contributed to a feeling that Labour's message would no longer be harmful. Most important, however, was a new feeling that in the war that now seemed almost certain to come, dealing with the Labour Party and the trade unions in a cooperative spirit would be a high priority. In particular, the government was concerned to involve the TUC and the NCL directly in a new Ministry of Information.

Thus the emergency increased the labour movement's potential influence, and the message incident was the first indication of the change of status. What Dalton called 'attempts to pour gallons of oil upon troubled waters',[49] were stimulated by a new *esprit de conciliation* which was to take the form, a few months later, of a general belief in the necessity for a Coalition and, eventually, Chamberlain's resignation because Labour refused to serve in a government of which he was head. Hence we find Butler, during three critical days, scrupulously keeping

Dalton informed about the countries in which the now widely dis-seminated message could be heard, and Lord Halifax writing a ful-some, mollifying letter of apology to the General Council. The official line was that an unfortunate error had occurred, which would not be repeated. The Home Office emphasised that nothing of the kind could possibly happen again, as long as Labour collaborated with the Minis-try of Information; and the BBC undertook that any future message would receive 'priority treatment'.

Suspicion of the Corporation did not cease. Nevertheless, the hands of Labour and the unions had been greatly strengthened. Public powers over the BBC, formerly held by the Postmaster-General, were trans-ferred to MOI, and the number of Governors was cut from seven to two. At the end of September, Attlee voiced a fear that the Corporation had 'now become part of the Government's bureaucratic machinery, at a time when it should be most closely in touch with public opinion'.[50] There was unhappiness about Labour's relations with MOI, seen on the Labour side as little more than formal. Even after the Coalition had been formed, the TUC alleged that Conservatives were represented at key points in the Ministry, 'while contacts with and advice from the labour movement were unwelcome or, at most, grudgingly accepted'.[51] Citrine had earlier suggested that a TUC/MOI liaison committee set up at the outbreak of war was a government bluff, designed to provide the name without the substance of involvement.[52] Yet the name was im-portant to the government, and so gave the labour movement leverage.

This was illustrated by the tail-end of the message affair, which had begun with the government leaning on the BBC not to broadcast on behalf of Labour, and concluded with the precise opposite. 'A very dif-ficult situation would arise,' Lord Perth wrote, almost threateningly, to Ogilvie on 1 October, if the BBC continued to refuse the labour move-ment permission to broadcast.[53] Meanwhile Citrine made the most of his new strength. After refusing several invitations to give a talk on trade unions, he was persuaded to meet Ogilvie in December, at the initiative of the Minister of Information, Lord Macmillan. During a three-hour interview, the Director-General noted afterwards, Citrine was at times 'thoroughly vituperative'. The superficial reason: the message incident of three months before. Citrine accused Ogilvie of being 'crooked, weak, dictatorial', and, unlike the Foreign Office, fail-ing to apologise afterwards.[54] 'I appreciate that if the BBC has become a mere government organ and that you are subject to political censoring, it is not your fault,' Citrine wrote acidly before the meeting. 'But if that be so, I think it should be publicly stated.'[55] Before the interview took place, Ogilvie warned the Lord Privy Seal, Sir Samuel Hoare, of a 'storm brewing on the Opposition side about their share of the air'.[56]

Increasingly, in the new conditions, Labour was finding that attack was the best means of defence and that, moreover, resistance was much less than in peacetime. Having issued an invitation to Attlee to broadcast in mid-December 1939, the Director of Talks noted to a colleague: 'Labour is so touchy at the moment I have left the question of subject open.'[57] It was a significant retreat. Another symptom of the BBC's newfound need for political appeasement was a memorandum, drawn up on Ogilvie's instruction, listing talks and news bulletin references in the second half of the year, in order to demonstrate the Corporation's fairmindedness.[58] Labour, however, was not appeased. When the NCL considered a complaint about censorship to the Prime Minister,[59] Halifax again intervened and a new TUC/BBC summit was arranged.[60]

It took place early in the New Year. This time the meeting was large and formal. The TUC delegation stressed its independent status: not a section of the Labour Party, but representative of an organisation that required separate treatment. Urging that the BBC should grasp the importance of the TUC contribution to the war effort, delegates complained about BBC foreign propaganda that used speakers who (in Citrine's words) 'were mostly of the professional classes'. Where, asked the General Secretary, were the working men to speak to fellow working men, at home and abroad?

It was an acrimonious discussion, and the air soon filled with 'bad feeling, hot temper and extravagant language'. A central controversy – one which had been at the core of the message affair – was how far and in what way broadcasting should address itself to ordinary people. When a BBC official argued that German refugees broadcasting on BBC radio would be treated as traitors by their own compatriots, Citrine retorted: '. . . [T]he German people were being identified with their government, and the principle now being advocated was – smash Germans.'[61]

But the real issue was the TUC right to be heard. Faced with a threatened union boycott, the BBC made proposals which would never have been envisaged in peacetime. Would the TUC, the Chairman of the Governors suggested, care to present a series 'to illustrate the great part which the trade union movement is playing in the prosecution of the war?' Would the TUC care to provide a list of German refugees whose 'manner of speech would be acceptable to German working-class listeners?'[62] The General Council agreed. Privately, BBC staff sneered. The trade union scripts, painstakingly prepared, 'by our standards' (wrote one producer), 'were all, I think, unusually dull'.[63] Nevertheless, the TUC series was broadcast and attracted a huge correspondence.

It was the start of a new arrangement. Liaison committees between the BBC, MOI and TUC were established; a broadcaster, Wilfrid Pickles, and a socialist don, Patrick Gordon Walker, were specially appointed to foster good relations. Through a 'display of power politics', as one BBC official put it three years later, the TUC had scored a notable triumph. The trade unions had discovered new muscles. The General Council 'had made it clear to us as they did to the Cabinet that without their support the war would stop'.[64]

If the declaration of war imposed on the government a need for friendly relations with erstwhile political opponents, the fall of Chamberlain and the establishment of a Coalition involving Labour created a much stronger imperative. Having contracted a marriage of convenience, there was a persistent fear on the Tory side of a divorce. Labour, moreover, was well placed within the new administration, especially on the home front, and well able to press its point of view. An added factor was the appointment in the summer of 1940 of Hugh Dalton, the new Minister of Economic Warfare, to head the new Special Operations Executive (SOE) whose responsibilities included 'subversive' broadcasting to enemy countries.

A sign of the radically changed climate was provided in August 1940, when the BBC approached Citrine for a contribution to a proposed series on trade unions for broadcast to the USA. The response was explosive. Refusing to broadcast, he attacked the Corporation for failing to consult the TUC sooner, for proposing unsuitable speakers and for being 'a collection of anarchists who do not understand team spirit'.[65] Instead, he turned to the new Prime Minister. Within two days, Broadcasting House had been bombarded with an emphatic reaffirmation by Churchill of his predecessor's request that all departments should cooperate with unions, followed by demands from Whitehall about the steps the Corporation had taken to comply.

Gone were the days when trade union complaints could be cavalierly tossed aside. When, in early 1941, Citrine himself was subject to Air Ministry censorship (for referring in a talk to the USA to landmines as evidence of indiscriminate German attacks) there was a row that echoed publicly. 'Sir Walter rang up most indignantly . . . ' noted a BBC official. 'He was *very* angry.'[66] 'Now it is a short step,' the pro-Labour *Daily Herald* dutifully fulminated, 'from the muzzling of harmless fact to the muzzling of opinion.'[67] The *Manchester Guardian* called for an investigation of BBC bias, and even the *Daily Telegraph* expressed bewilderment.[68]

In the old days, the BBC would have dismissed the complaint, which in this case did not involve their direct responsibility, with a lofty shrug. Now they felt compelled to convene a joint committee to consider how best to beard the General Council lion in its den. Urged to make a direct approach, envoys were dispatched. In vain they told Citrine that the cuts in his talk were not the BBC's fault. 'It isn't the slightest use talking to me,' he said. 'You are wasting my time.' The BBC, he went on, was and always had been biased against him personally, and against the labour movement. Even if the order were revoked, he would never broadcast again.[69] To the intense embarrassment of the Corporation, Ed Murrow, star American reporter and keen Anglophile, devoted an entire broadcast to his fellow countrymen to the notorious case of the BBC censoring the British workers.

As before, the row was defused, by making further concessions to the union point of view. Once again, Churchill intervened and met a TUC delegation.[70] A Labour MP, Ernest Thurtle, was appointed Parliamentary Secretary to the new Minister of Information, Brendan Bracken. Two extra talks on the role of trade unions were arranged. The TUC General Secretary was, eventually, persuaded by Bracken to broadcast.

## Conclusion

Developments in BBC–labour movement relations during the remaining years of the war make another story. By 1941, however, a quite different set of rules, tacit and explicit, had been established, from those that prevailed before the invasion of Poland. From the end of 1941, the BBC was regularly consulting the TUC and Labour Party about programming. There was also a new, fast-developing populism, which ran ahead of immediate political concerns, and was partly based on a sense in all parts of the Coalition of the need to offer the public a better postwar world. Meanwhile, the BBC was fighting its own battles for truth and accuracy, against Service Ministry constraint. Ogilvie departed, and with him many of the old assumptions. By the time that Labour fought, and won, the 1945 election – in which the BBC, broadcasting to servicemen all over the world, had a wholly unprecedented importance – the 'struggle for balance' had by no means been won. But the concept of political fairness in broadcasting had changed out of recognition. The election of a majority Labour government reinforced the new relationship with the BBC, and made harder any return to the *status quo ante bellum*. Meanwhile, the medium developed. The arrival of television, the extension of news and current affairs coverage, the introduction of commercial broadcasting, all added their own complications. Yet the essence of the modern idea is still firmly based on the wartime understanding. Partly this was the product of increased labour movement strength, and effective pressure. Partly, it was because the BBC acquired during the war an activist, campaigning view of its own role, which fitted labour movement objectives better than the unreformed paternalism of the 1930s.

The Labour Party and TUC attitudes were not, however, identical. As we have seen, Labour's view of the Corporation was ambivalent, containing an element of approval, because of the BBC's state-owned, corporate structure. At the least, Labour greatly preferred the BBC to most of the capitalist-owned press, and its leaders pressed for fair treatment, not revolution. In the 1940s in particular, the public service puritanism of the Labour establishment had echoes in Broadcasting House.

The TUC attitude, on the other hand, was more hostile. Unlike the Labour Party, the TUC had no intellectuals. It saw the BBC as an organ of government, and of the employers. This view was strengthened by the BBC's refusal to regard the TUC as anything other than a pressure group, whose claims should be resisted. Hence the TUC fight was a fight for organisational recognition. It was a fight which, by 1945, was largely won. Undoubtedly, a major factor was the 'incorporation' of trade unions in wartime, and the need to pay a price for their involvement in the war effort. The demand needed to be made, however, for it to be met: and the record of trade union relations with the BBC shows that the latter yielded only with the greatest reluctance. Against this background, it may be seen that the German message protest was not accidentally timed. Coming at a moment of great national peril, it was a declaration that a new season had begun.

# Notes

1. A. Briggs, *The History of Broadcasting in the United Kingdom.* Vol. 1, *The Birth of Broadcasting*, London: Oxford University Press, 1961, pp.357-8
2. BBC, 'Retrospect', 1932, BBC Written Archives, programme files.
3. Beatrice Webb's unpublished diary, 3 May 1926.
4. C.R. Attlee, *As it Happened*, London: Odhams, 1956, p.91.
5. NEC Report on the Election, 27 August 1931, p.257, NEC minutes.
6. NEC minutes, 10 November 1931, p.237.
7. See C. Stuart (ed.), *The Reith Diaries*, London: Collins, 1975, p.109. Entry for 26 October 1931.
8. Ibid., 27 October 1931, p.109.
9. HC Debs [260] col. 2313, 11 December 1931.
10. 1932 Labour Party Annual Conference Report, p.227.
11. BBC Written Archives, R51/600/1/1A, p.15.
12. 1932 TUC Conference Report, p.217.
13. W. Citrine – C.A. Siepmann correspondence, February 1932. Citrine file, 910; BBC Written Archives.
14. National Joint Council (NJC) minutes, 22 November 1932, p.89.
15. NJC memorandum No.5, NJC minutes, 22 November 1932.
16. HC Debs [274] col. 1844, 22 February 1933.
17. 22 December 1932, File R34/534/2, BBC Written Archives.
18. HC Debs [274] col. 1829, 22 February 1933.
19. L. Fielden, *The Natural Bent*, London: André Deutsch, 1960, p.104.
20. M. Stopes to J. Reith, 23 April 1932, File 910, BBC Written Archives.
21. E. Maschwitz, *No Chip on My Shoulder*, London: Herbert Jenkins, 1957, p.73.
22. Hilda Matheson, *Broadcasting*, London: Butterworth, 1933, pp.97-9.
23. G. Wyndham-Goldie, *Facing the Nation: Television and Politics 1936 – 76*, London: Bodley Head, 1977, p.97.
24. HC Debs [280] col. 2264, 24 July 1933.
25. *Daily Mail*, 15 July 1937. See also 'Complaint from Conservative and Unionist Central Office', 2 April 1938. R34/323, BBC Written Archives.
26. 'The BBC and Left-Wing Bias', Internal Report, R34/323, BBC Written Archives. See also *Conservative Weekly*, 12 October 1931.

## 152   The Media in British Politics

27. Director of Talks memorandum to the Director-General, 25 April 1935, R34/523, BBC Written Archives.
28. See R.H. Coase, *British Broadcasting. A Study in Monopoly*, Longham, Green and Co., 1950.
29. See *Report of the Broadcasting Committee* (Chairman Lord Ullswater), London: HMSO, 1936, Cmd.5091.
30. Matheson, *Broadcasting*, p.108.
31. See 'The BBC and Left-Wing Bias'.
32. J.F. Naylor, *Labour's International Policy: the Labour Party in the 1930s*, London: Weidenfeld and Nicolson, 1969, p.135.
33. BBC internal memorandum, 15 February 1938, R34/512, BBC Written Archives.
34. Record of a Foreign Office telephone call, 1936, R34/416, BBC Written Archives.
35. Midland Programme Board, ll October 1937, R34/512, BBC Written Archives.
36. 'Message to the German People', 27 September 1938, National Council of Labour (NCL) Minutes, pp. 77a-c.
37. NCL minutes, 25 July 1939, pp.129-30.
38. 'British Labour's Message to the German People', 25 August 1939, NCL minutes, 25 August 1939, pp.23-4.
39. Hugh Dalton's unpublished diary (HDD), 25 August 1939.
40. R51/600/1, BBC Written Archives, 25 August 1939.
41. See Dalton to Citrine, 26 August 1939, Dalton Papers.
42. HDD, 25 August 1939.
43. Citrine to Halifax, 28 August 1939, TUC Correspondence.
44. HDD, 29 August 1939.
45. Ibid., 30 August 1939.
46. Record of telephone conversation, 25 August 1939, 5.15 p.m., R51/600/1/1A, BBC Written Archives.
47. D. Dilks (ed.), *The Diary of Sir Alexander Cadogan 1939 – 43*, London: Cassell, 1971, p.201.
48. Ibid., pp.203-5.
49. HDD, 29 August 1939.
50. HC Debs [351] col.1491, 28 September 1939.
51. Memorandum on Ministry of Information (MOI), NCL minutes, 11 March 1941, p.2.
52. NCL minutes, 21 November 1939, p.43.
53. R34/107, BBC Written Archives.
54. Report (by Ogilvie) of Meeting, 24 November 1939, R34/600/1/1A, BBC Written Archives.
55. Citrine to Ogilvie, 30 November 1939, R51/600/1/1A. BBC Written Archives.
56. Record of Telephone Conversation, 1 December 1939, R51/205/1, BBC Written Archives.
57. Director of Talks correspondence, 16 December 1939, Attlee File, 910/1, BBC Written Archives.
58. List of Talks, December 1939, R51/600/1, BBC Written Archives.
59. See 'Labour Charges against Ministry', news report in *Daily Herald*,21 December 1939.
60. Ogilvie to Halifax, 24 December 1939, PRO, FO 800, 322/XCIA/2297.
61. Report of the TUC Delegation Meeting, 16 January 1940, R34/897, II, BBC Written Archives.
62. Sir Allen Powell (Chairman of the Governors) to Citrine, 17 January 1940, R51/600/1/1A, BBC written Archives.
63. Memorandum to Controller of Talks, 25 April 1940, R51/600/2/1b, BBC Written Archives.
64. A. Stewart to Scottish Director, 13 December 1943, R51/600/2/1b, BBC Written Archives.

65. Memorandum by Miss Wace to Director of Talks and Director-General, 16 August 1940, R51/600/1b, BBC Written Archives.
66. Report of telephone conversation, 6 March 1941, Citrine File I, 910. BBC Written Archives.
67. *Daily Herald,* 8 March 1941.
68. *Manchester Guardian,* 8 March; *Daily Telegraph,* 6 March 1941.
69. Memorandum, N. Collins to W. McAlpine, 19 March 1941, Citrine File II, 910, BBC Written Archives.
70. NCL minutes, 22 July 1941, p.41.

# 8 Reporting atrocities: the BBC and the holocaust*
*Jean Seaton*

Atrocities may often be unbelievable. How do we come to believe them? How do we come to do anything about them?

A society may be judged not only by the conditions that prevail within it, but also by its sensitivity to what is happening elsewhere. Not appreciating or acting on the horrors abroad may make our society more susceptible to the perpetration of horror at home. The way in which we expect to be alerted to such events is through the media. The role of the press and broadcasting is at least in part to alert us, warn us, inform us and make us aware of our responsibilities. Thus when considering what was known and not known, done and not done about what happened to the Jews of Europe under Nazism, one of the problems has always been, why didn't the Allies do more? Why weren't the public better informed? The press and broadcasting are always seen as central to this question.

In this chapter, the problems of information and action are considered. In particular, what did the BBC know and broadcast? The Corporation was broadcasting throughout the war to occupied Europe, it was staffed with many foreign nationals, it processed and deciphered German news material. Above all, in a variety of ways, it represented an official collective 'voice of Britain'.

The 'holocaust' – a name only invented by historians in the 1950s – is the exemplary twentieth century atrocity in the sense that the attempt to destroy a race has been retrospectively identified and analysed as a discrete, intended and exceptional event. It is the atrocity that is the model, of what should never happen again. It demonstrated the irrational barbarity of a particular regime, suggesting the horrible example of a civilised nation's civilian compliance with acts of extraordinary inhumanity, and the failure of the rest of the world to act at any of the points when the calamity could have been averted or at least mitigated. It is in this sense that the holocaust has become a symbol of

*The author wishes to thank the British Academy for a grant which helped to finance the research for this chapter.

the patterns of reaction to such horror. A new crime – crimes against humanity[1] – involving a novel legal principle, was one response to the horror. Thus, quite apart from the particular events, reactions to and explanations of the events surrounding the reaction to the holocaust have also become, at least in part, mythologised as the typical problem and response to such events. Indeed, as William Shawcross in his book on Cambodia *The Quality of Mercy*, has pointed out, many contemporary events are often refracted through the imagery of the holocaust.[2]

There have been two main arguments advanced for why more was not done, and why public opinion was not more roused. The first is that the explanation lies in British and American anti-Semitism. This is the conclusion of Bernard Wasserstein. He identified the refusal to single out for special attention the specific nature of the German atrocities against the Jews as founded partly on principle and partly on political calculation: the former in that it was often felt that to emphasise the fate of the Jews would involve a spiritual surrender to German racialism; the latter, in that attention given to the German treatment of Jews might give a handle to the German propaganda theme that stressed 'The Jewish war'. More important, he suggests that recognising that the German treatment of the Jews fell into a 'special category' would have involved the 'embarrassing corollary' that the problem required a 'special solution' in Palestine.[3] Anti-Semitism is identified particularly with the British Foreign Office, but is also seen as endemic in British institutions and society. Indeed, *fear* of public anti-Semitism seemed to play a large part in official reluctance to run public opinion campaigns about the fate of Jews in Europe.

The other explanation advanced is that of ignorance. Many accounts of why more was not done depend on information as a key factor. The World Jewish Congress papers on the holocaust are catalogued under the heading 'Breaking the Silence'. Martin Gilbert's book, *Auschwitz and the Allies*, although concerned with how eye-witness accounts of what was happening in Auschwitz were available, centres on the problem of 'what was known about the final solution and how it was known'.[4] Walter Lacqueur and Anton Sharf have written books whose purpose is to chart how much was known, by whom, where and when about the fate of Jews in Europe.[5] Sharf's sophisticated book represents a modification of the information thesis. It is concerned not so much with whether information was available or suppressed, but rather with how it was presented: 'Although events were fully reported in the British Press,' he argues, 'one is left with the feeling that the open abandonment of legality by the Nazi regime was not fully appreciated'.[6] Walter Lacqueur's book, which raises a variety of important general problems about knowledge and facts, modifies the thesis to suggest the problem was one of belief.

Thus the problem for many commentators seems to be to explain why more was not known or understood about the terrible fate of Jews, particularly in the period immediately preceding and after the implementation of the 'final solution' programme at the Wansee Conference in 1942. By implication it is assumed that had more information been available, accepted or recognised, then more would have been done by the Allies to alleviate the situation. In this view, information is the key to political action. Should this analysis be correct, the independent role of the BBC as a source of information would have been crucial in any political mobilisation over the holocaust.

**Eye-witnesses and the camps**
Contemporary eye-witness accounts of the liberation of the camps in 1945 are all convincingly couched in terms of the horror that the writers had not known about. Thus Richard Crossman only went to see Buchenwald because of the intervention of a young American officer who told him he had to go. Crossman, who had spent the war debriefing German prisoners and putting out propaganda to Germany, wrote:

> Though we had heard and reported many stories of Nazi massacres of Jews and Slavs we had never believed in the possibility of 'genocide'. We had interrogated countless SS men; we had reported their brutality and corruption; we had known in theory that they were in favour of extermination, but until we saw the concentration camps and the gas chambers we only believed with our brain.[7]

Crossman then went on to give a vivid description of the camp not only in terms of the appalling physical horror but also emphasising the grotesque disorganisation and surreal world even after liberation; amidst starvation, Angora rabbits continued to be better looked after than people. 'Even the most sensitive and intelligent men and women we met seemed to accept the camps as the only reality, and to think of the outside world as a mirage'.[8] Hugh Greene, Director of BBC Propaganda to Germany during the war, and later Director-General of the BBC, recalls his first sight of German schoolgirls walking, apparently unseeingly, beside train-loads of bodies in the sun, and realising as he approached Dachau that more was to come when he saw the roadside full of Americans being sick. He too, commented on his total unpreparedness for what he saw.[9]

Ed Murrow, broadcasting from Belsen, asked his American audience: 'I pray you to believe what I have told you about this place. I only reported what I saw and heard, but only a part of it. For most of it I have no words'.[10] One correspondent, having broadcast about what he had seen in the camps, was refused an interview by a prominent Allied prisoner of war because of the 'lies he'd told about the Germans'.

The 'unimaginable' horror, and its unexpectedness, was how the news was broken to the public. Richard Dimbleby was the first British correspondent to reach a camp. He broadcast a report 'The Cesspit Beneath' from Belsen, on 19 April 1945. Belsen, he wrote, was 'the first of these places to be opened up'. He had only gone to Belsen with the advance team of medical services to follow up a story of an outbreak of typhoid. But they expected nothing different from the many POW camps they had already been through. He described the horrific conditions that he saw and, like Crossman, the surreal otherworldly nature of life in the camps, where apparently all order and all rules had broken down. Dimbleby emphasised the appalling shock: 'No one could have imagined a scene like this, no one even hinted at what I was to see.' He broke down five times while he was recording the broadcast. But when the recording was received at the BBC, he wrote, it was queried. The broadcast was delayed by over a day,[11] 'and the BBC kept coming back to him to check the authenticity of the account'. Apparently the Corporation was anxious. 'When they heard it some people wondered if Dimbleby had gone off his head or something. I think it was only the fact that I'd been fairly reliable up to then that made them believe the story'.[12] Dimbleby, who was to return to Belsen several times later, emphasised that he had no idea of the role of the camps and that he had been totally unprepared for what he saw. No briefing had dealt with it.

It has been suggested that Dimbleby was utterly changed by his experience at Belsen, and never recovered from it. Indeed, Leonard Mial argues that Dimbleby's subsequent handling of royal and public occasions was given a depth by the respect for order and tradition that the experience of seeing the disorder of Belsen had heightened almost unbearably. Within seven days of Dimbleby's broadcast, a parliamentary delegation was sent to report on conditions in the camps, and within two weeks a film crew was sent to produce a film, directed by Alfred Hitchcock. The enormity of what had been happening to Jews began to be revealed.

Thus the dominant theme in eye-witness accounts of the opening of the camps was one of shock and unpreparedness. This was obviously an attempt to deal with the appalling things they saw. Almost unanimously the eye-witnesses claimed that they had not known what they were going to see. In the spring of 1945 when the full horror of the camps was revealed, the problem crystallised into one of why more was not known.

## Atrocities: belief and numbness

Part of the explanation lay in the resistance to atrocity stories, which had been built up in the inter-war period. Indeed, there is a general problem about what is regarded as an atrocity. As the rules of engage-

ment change, so does the definition of what is unacceptable. In the
period before the war there was a distinction between machine-imposed
death (by bombers and tanks) which was regarded as an atrocity, and
man-imposed death which was not. Since 1945 this definition seems to
have been reversed, and the involvement of individuals in, for example,
terrorist affairs, now seems to be the 'atrocity', not the death meted out
by machine. 'The bombing of civilian targets, by aircraft, although it is
to be expected in any forthcoming engagement, does raise new problems for news,' ran a 1936 BBC memorandum on the handling of news
in war, 'being a quite new dimension of the horrors of war. One which
all civilised people must oppose.'[13]

But beyond this, when the Corporation came to news of what was
happening to the Jews of Europe, what were the traditions in which it
was likely to at least attempt to understand the news? One interpretation of the BBC (and indeed of other European broadcasting authorities) advanced by Anthony Smith is that they were all founded on the
rejection of the false propaganda of the First World War. The very institutional arrangements of the Corporation were intended to make
impossible the extremism of the propaganda of the First World War.[14]
Thus, as an institution with a domestic broadcasting philosophy of political balance and neutrality, the Corporation was ill-suited to deal with
the extreme case of systematic atrocities.

Indeed, by the time news about what was happening to European
Jews began to filter through, there was already a profound and widespread scepticism about atrocity stories. This was partly based on a
reaction to the First World War. Then both sides had based their
propaganda on the other side's atrocities. Stories about buckets full of
eyes (a feature of war horror stories since the Crusades), rope made of
human hair, soap made from human bodies, had all featured in Allied
propaganda in the First World War. Of course, as several commentators had pointed out, the reaction against propaganda had come
to obscure the reality – that awful atrocities had indeed been committed
in the First War. More significantly, propaganda about atrocities con-
cealed the truth about the terrible scale of casualties in the War. By the
late 1930s, progressive and liberal thinkers thought that stories about
German behaviour had been improperly exaggerated. So, by 1942, at a
crucial time when the stories, not merely of the harassment, but of the
attempt to exterminate the Jews became known, Robert Fraser, head of
the Production Division at the Ministry of Information, issued a warning against the use of atrocity material to the BBC: 'It must be remembered,' he argued, 'that some people are contra-suggestible to atrocity
propaganda. I do not know whether there was a corpse factory or not.
But most people believe that there was not.'[15]

Indeed, one of the problems is that acts which had been faked and lied about in the First War were real in the Second. And this may have added a mythical element that distanced accounts from reality. Thus, a commonly known 'Hun' atrocity of the First War was the gassing of 700,000 Armenians. (Many did, indeed, suffer this fate, though scarcely on such a scale). In the Second World War, the figure '700,000' became a symbol of limitless evil. Early in 1942, Cardinal Hinsley, speaking at the first large meeting about the fate of Jews in Europe, in the Albert Hall, referred to the 700,000 Jews who had already been gassed to death in Poland alone. He subsequently repeated this figure in a BBC broadcast.[16] In reality, it was an underestimate. Yet it could easily be seen as part of a vague and general condemnation, rather than a specific indictment. Repetition of First War accusations, indeed, impeded an appreciation of the scale of Second World War atrocities. In September 1942 the President of the World Orthodox Organisation told the Americans and British of the news he had received of the evacuation of the Warsaw Ghetto and the extermination of its inhabitants. It was alleged that soap and fertilisers were being made from the corpses. A Foreign Office official remarked that 'until corroborative evidence is forthcoming I think it should be treated with the greatest reserve.'[17] Similar points 'had been quoted in books written about the last war'.

This view provides at least part of the explanation of why more was not believed, broadcast and done about the holocaust. But it may require modification. The period between the wars had also been characterised by a series of atrocity campaigns. For an atrocity is not merely an act of unprecedented violence but is also one that involves political mobilisation. Harold Nicolson, reviewing a book by Israel Cohen in the *Telegraph* as early as 1933, wrote:

> Many and various have been the propaganda leaflets which I have read in the last 20 years. I can recall Italian publicity accounts of Arab atrocity in Cyrenia, and Arab broadsides blaming the Italians for any incidents which may have occurred. The Macedonian and the Albanian quarrel produced a whole library of propaganda, illustrated by generous photographs. During the Great War we had Belgian atrocities and American atrocities, and we shall shortly be receiving bright little books upon the Chaldecon and Assyrian atrocities.

Nicolson went on to argue that as all of the cases depended on general and wild claims, rather than concentrating on a few typical cases; 'languor rather than indignation', he said, was the result.[18]

In particular, public attitudes towards the Spanish Civil War and the Italian invasion of Abyssinia were influenced by stories of atrocities. The Spanish Civil War was a brutal conflict in which the civilian population suffered greatly. It was a war in which, as Raymond Carr commented, 'atrocities were the pornography of revolution'.[19] Koestler's

*Spanish Testament*[20] which went into harrowing detail, about the behaviour of the Nationalists, was an important document that influenced many who went to fight in the International Brigade. Yet in 1954 he said that he had lied about many incidents. Similarly, Claud Cockburn later admitted to making up a lively account of a battle in which the Nationalists were hard pressed but particularly brutal, with the assistance of little more than a street map of the town to give authenticity to his account. George Orwell, early in the war, wrote that there were accounts of events in Spain in the newspapers which 'did not bear any relation to the facts; not even the relation which is implied in an ordinary lie.'[21] Thus during the Spanish Civil War both sides, and different factions within them, invented atrocities. Of course, there were atrocities on both sides, and Spanish history since has been affected by the grim reality of the war. Yet as Carr points out: 'There was a way in which Spain had become what antiquity was to classicists and the Middle Ages to the Romantics; a symbolic land of the mind to which the conflicts of the writer's own society were transported and formalized.'[22] The Spanish Civil War, and the behaviour of the antagonists, were objects of political manipulation, but, more than that, their political manipulation was as much about the domestic policy of the other nations as it was about Spain. The BBC's response to the news on Spain was to develop a policy of 'even handed and balanced reporting'.[23] In particular, it dealt with what were seen as the 'more extreme acts' by developing a system of referral. Reports of atrocities required greater verification than other kinds of news.

The second great cause of the 1930s, the Abyssinian war, also involved the reality and the manipulation of atrocity stories. Haile Selassie recognised that he had little chance of winning any confrontation with the Italian forces, and saw that his only opportunity lay in the ability to get the Allies on his side. Daniel Waley in a book on public opinion and the Abyssinian crisis, points out that the Emperor used a variety of sophisticated techniques, and that he was well aware of the effects that the imagery of the battles might have on Allied public opinion. Waley documents what was seen at the time and retrospectively as an important moment when public opinion about the Fascist regimes seemed to turn decisively towards hostility, and demonstrates how limited official and political perceptions of public opinion still were in 1937. When MPs talked of the 'avalanches' of mail they received over the issue, they meant between 12 and 53 letters.[24]

The cases of Spain and Abyssinia certainly did not show any necessary *disbelief* in atrocities. But they did produce an official scepticism about stories of this kind. This was to be an important element in official reaction to news of Jews in Europe.

There was an additional problem. Jews too had been campaigning in the inter-war period. As Nazi persecution intensified there were many pleas and campaigns for Allied intervention and Allied visas. The British government however, tended to interpret such approaches as thinly disguised agitation over access to Palestine, where the problems of the British Mandate had become intense. 'Another call for a programme on Jewish life,' went one 1939 BBC memo, 'I think it's really to do with Palestine again and should be refused, tactfully.'[25]

Although the pre-war campaigns over Spain, Abyssinia and Jewish persecution did not mean that the atrocities were not believed, it meant that they were seen as likely to be stories with, as it were, a point. Such stories had usually, in the past, been part of campaigns involved with controlling domestic political action. It was such political action that the BBC felt particularly concerned to resist.

## The tone of the war

Another factor influencing the handling of atrocity news throughout the war was derived from the stance, style and tone that broadcasting adopted about the war. In this sense the BBC's content, and arguments about how the issues of the war should be presented to the public, were, in an important sense, establishing how the war was perceived and experienced. The dominant style that evolved of the British at war was one of level-headed, stubborn endeavour. The emphasis was on 'humble, everyday heroism'.[26] It was this vision of the war that was portrayed by Priestley in his popular broadcasts. This was self-consciously pitched against Teutonic images of romantic heroism. Such a style was singularly unsuited to the transmission of knowledge about the kind of horrors that were taking place in the ghettoes. If the war was not exactly a game of cricket, too much accusation of beastliness on the other side seemed to offend against decent, wholesome, British good taste. Crossman, who had characterised the aim of broadcasting to Germany as 'to get inside of the skin and feelings of ordinary Germans', complained that in 1940 the BBC domestic service was about to 'indulge in a positive orgy of War Guilt programmes'.[27] He complained of its likely inefficiency.

In a paper written about the same time, B.E. Nichols argued that propaganda in broadcast programmes had in fact become far too prominent. The problem was not merely that people were naturally resistant to it, but that, in addition, 'We keep on telling them that the Germans have tons of it. Yet nearly half our output seems to me to now have a propaganda element'.[28] Early on in the war 'propaganda' had meant exhortation of the domestic population and defamation of the enemy. As Ian McLaine and Michael Balfour show,[29] the first was found to be counterproductive and abandoned. In its place there began to emerge an image of the British which was heroically mundane. The corollary of this was that anything 'extreme' began to be seen as 'propaganda'. Precisely because, one BBC memo argued, 'Nazi methods are so iniquitous, our own good nation, an easy-going, unmethodical, decent, untheoretical people simply *cannot* credit the existence in large masses of their fellow human beings of ideas, methods and an iniquity so extreme.'[30] An MOI directive argued that in order to make the Nazi threat 'credible' to the British people, it should not be characterised as 'too extreme'. Horror had to be used sparingly, 'and must always deal with indisputably innocent people. Not with political opponents. And not with Jews.'[31] The point is not whether the British were, as a nation, phlegmatically decent, but that this became at least the positive model which broadcasters adopted of them. The systematic extermination of a people lay outside such a world.

Partly, the 'tone' of the war was established in terms of the options, which as the war developed were rejected. Throughout the war the BBC was under pressure to exploit every available theme that could be used against the Germans. Within the German Service there was a split between those like Hugh Greene who believed that moral condemnation of the Germans was likely merely to lose the service listeners, and those like Tangye Lean who believed that it was immoral and opportunistic not to make the Germans aware of moral judgement. The 'criteria should be success or failure rather than right or wrong', went one Greene memorandum.[32] The Greene view of expedient propaganda was successful.[33] This battle was an extension of similar conflicts on the Home Service front. The theme was the subject of a number of papers prepared by Francis Williams for the Ministry of Information during 1940 – 42 which emphasised that any moral approach 'should take into account the distrust of the British for what seems to them "high falutin". It must not fall into the error of trying to make them take themselves too seriously.'[34] Nevertheless, the theme emphasised Christian and altruistic elements of the battle against the Germans. But the most important reaction to the theme for propaganda was that as it was, it was in any case a ridiculous and absurd exercise; it was, wrote the Director of Programmes, too abstract, and entirely impractical. 'We might as well ask producers to keep it in the back of their minds as we would ask them to bear in mind the Epistle to the Corinthians or the 1st Book of *Paradise Lost*.'[35] In addition, it was felt likely to be inefficient, and indeed improper, to make 'upon German listeners an irritating impression of self-righteousness in our morals'.[36] In particular, to seek to appeal to the Germans by 'Eloquence and Emotions'[37] was seen to be meeting them on their own terms. This argument for expediency in the Foreign Service reflected and helped shape views in the Home Service.

The 'tone' of the war, was in part a product of fears about civilian morale, in part of the initially somewhat surprised reaction to the apparent steadiness of civilian morale. It was also involved with the characterisation of the kind of war the British were fighting, and in reaction to the kind of war the Germans were fighting. 'The key to morale,' according to one BBC paper, 'is to remember that it's an everyday matter. It's not about what people *would* do if they were called to, but how they act, think and talk about all the small details of everyday life.' Such a view was antithetical to what were seen as 'grand' views of the conflict. Thus, typically, in 1941 a 'revival in the abuse and persecution of the Jews' recorded by the BBC monitoring service was interpreted as evidence, not of yet another onslaught against the Jews, but as 'a sure sign that Goebbels thinks German morale needs stiffening'.[38]

## The BBC's record: How much did the Corporation tell the public?

Before any judgement can be made about why more was not known or done about German policy towards the Jews, some attempt has to be made to assess what *was* said. Although the technical details of how the extermination was to be carried out, how Jews in friendly but not occupied countries were to be dealt with, were not decided until the Wansee Conference in January 1942, the broad outlines of the final solution had been made clear in *Mein Kampf*. Here, Hitler (who had himself suffered severely from an Allied gas attack during the First World War) wrote:

> At the beginning of the war or even during the war, if twelve or fifteen thousand of those Jews who were corrupting the nation had been forced to submit to poison gas, just as hundreds of thousands of our best German workers from every social stratum and from every trade and calling had to face it in the field, then the millions of sacrifices on the front would not have been in vain.[39]

Pre-war German behaviour towards the Jews provided ample additional evidence that ideas about the extermination of the Jews in Hitler's work were likely to be put into practice.

In the 1930s the British political elite certainly knew about the development of Hitler's plans, but perceived this as a less important problem than the threat to international peace. Certainly the BBC, largely because of the way in which it defined its political role, as arriving at a balance between the political parties, found few ways of dealing with bipartisan anti-appeasement. The problem also owed something to the characters involved: John Reith hated Churchill, and found Labour politicians difficult to take seriously. There were, however, a series of talks in 1938 including one by John Strachey, dealing with 'Herr Hitler's plans', with a detailed analysis of *Mein Kampf*. Hitler's 'racial politics' and anti-Semitism were, Strachey argued, the basis of everything totalitarian.[40]

Where, during the war, did the BBC take its news about the developments in Europe? The problem divides into three periods: the time up to the Wansee Conference in 1942, the time between it and the Allied Declaration on the fate of Jewry of 17 December 1942, and the period after the Declaration. As Yehuda Bauer has pointed out, after the Declaration, the Allies 'now officially admitted the information to have been correct'.[41] Theoretically at least, after December 1942 the problem becomes one not of 'knowledge' or 'belief' but of the impediments to action. In practice, however, the problem remains who knew and believed what, and to what effect.

The BBC's sources of information were wide. The Corporation officially took propaganda directives from the Political Warfare Executive (PWE), but the atmosphere at Bush House, where all the foreign broadcasting services were based, was rebellious and independent. The papers for this German service have been unaccountably lost at the BBC, but Hugh Greene's recollection is that, from 1940, the Service, quite apart from its debriefing of prisoners and analysis of newspapers, received information of a quite unequivocal kind about the destruction of the ghettoes. It is also Greene's recollection that all such information was immediately broadcast back to Germany. Gregor MacDonald was the head of the Polish Service. This received, in addition to the more regular sources of news, at least two postcards (as Walter Lacqueur has pointed out, the post still operated in Europe throughout the War) indirectly from the camps themselves, sent by Jews who in Yiddish made it quite clear that they had arrived at death camps.[42] On 5 February 1941 the Director-General wrote to the Head of Polish and German Services, and sent a copy to the Director of Home Programmes, asking for a 'constant reiteration of atrocity stories in Poland, without exaggeration and with full statistics'.[43]

The BBC treated the postcards as direct evidence of the fate of European Jewry, and as far as can be seen did not doubt their authenticity. 'These awful messages are too poignant,' wrote Gregory MacDonald, circulating the translated contents of two of these cards. The Polish Service was one of the main sources of news about the destruction of Jews, and indeed one of the main and important areas of foreign broadcasting. Right from the start of the Service, the Poles were anxious about Nazi encouragement of Polish anti-Semitism,[44] and constantly emphasised the need for the Service broadcasts to be short, and full of news. In June 1940, there were a series of programmes dealing with the persecution of different groups in Poland and throughout 1940 – 41 a variety of programmes which dealt unequivocally with 'extermination' and 'murder camps'.[45] In 1945, when the personnel of the Polish Section were about to be disbanded, Count Balinsky, the Head of Foreign News section, wrote that he was grateful to the BBC 'for pointing out in connection with German atrocity stories that these were not new and that reports on conditions in Germany had been published, broadcast and emphasised throughout the war.'[46]

Yet even here, after the programmes on the Warsaw Ghetto, there remains an ambiguity which it is hard to understand, for in 1944 and early 1945 the Polish Service was still busily proposing (and getting rejected for reasons which will be clear later) programmes directed specifically at the Jewish community in Poland – long after that community had been exterminated, and long after, if they had completely believed or absorbed the news they were putting out, they knew that community to have been destroyed. There were also problems about liaison with the Home Service. Yet, despite these reservations it is clear that daily digests of bulletins from the Polish Service were distributed widely throughout the BBC.

The BBC, apart from all its other sources of news, also was the first official organisation regularly to buy information from the Weiner Library. Starting in Amsterdam in 1938, Dr Weiner, its founder, at first operated like a door-to-door salesman, carrying a suitcase full of news from customer to customer. Trying to interest them in his stories, Weiner collected a huge archive of information on the widest possible range of topics about Germany and was the source of many of the *Jewish Chronicle's* stories. Vernon Bartlett from the Home Service was the first to buy Weiner's goods in 1939, but he was quickly followed by staff from the German and Polish services. Indeed, the BBC's patronage was directly responsible for the MOI taking up the library as a major source of information.[47]

Finally the BBC took specifically Jewish news from the *Jewish Chronicle*. Indeed, measured against the *Jewish Chronicle* as a sympathetic and pro-Jewish source, on a crude headline count the BBC seems to stand up well. In the period between January 1942 and December 1943, of the 46 front-page lead stories in the *Jewish Chronicle* dealing explicitly with the fate of Jews in Europe, 42 were taken up by the BBC, 21 on home news as well as foreign broadcasts though they were not given great prominence.'[48]

Yet an examination of *Jewish Chronicle*-originated stories shows some of the problems of the weight and kind of belief and knowledge these stories would hold. Harold Nicolson, writing in the 1930s, had argued that much interwar atrocity propaganda was difficult to believe because it was too large-scale, too general. What was needed for the real register of effect were eye-witness and individualised accounts. The BBC took a different view. One of the problems with the way in which news of the fate of Jews in Eastern and then Western Europe became known was precisely that it took the form, necessarily, of eye-witness accounts. 'The Last Jew in Kiev', 'The Borisov Pogrom', 'I was in a Slave Gang', 'The Terror in Denmark',[49] and nearly all the accounts of the extinction of Jewish communities took the form of eye-witness, personal accounts by people who had managed to escape. But although the 'eye-witness' may be more affecting, more moving, it was not necessarily the more convincing. 'Are these accounts authenticated? Who is the informant? What kind of person?', enquired one BBC memorandum. As Martin Gilbert points out, the existence and purpose of Auschwitz were only generally accepted following the accounts of two exceptionally articulate escapees, who had trained themselves to remember precise details of the daily workings of the camp, where the transports had come from, the tattoo serial numbers of groups of victims etc.[50] Yet the problem even with the most plausible eye-witness account was that it remained, in the end, circumstantial. For a bureaucracy such as the BBC, bureaucratic news, less personal, less immediate, more 'representative' or 'authoritative', was more acceptable.

There was of course another problem. The stories seemed too extreme. A BBC official, reading the latest reports at the Weiner Library, remarked that they read like Fox's *Book of Martyrs*.[51] The crimes were so harrowing they seemed to be part of the mythology of the victim, symbolic rather than real.

Yet in addition there seems to be even in the *Chronicle* reports, a reservation or misinterpretation about what was happening at the key points in accounts. Perhaps this was inevitable – the distinct role of Auschwitz as an extermination rather than slave camp was not clear until 1944. But the nuances in description may have been a further impediment to action. Thus, many early stories emphasised 'deportation' as the real horror; the planned 'mass expulsion' of Hungarian Jews was discussed as early as 1942. 'In many places, Jews were deported to an unknown destination. Subsequently it was learned that they had been killed in a neighbouring wood' (3 July 1942). The Warsaw Ghetto was discussed in terms of the 'expulsion of Jews'. On 7 August 1942, the *Chronicle* referred to 'the deportation of Jews from Holland, Belgium, France, Germany and Austria'. There were reports of Jews, 'deported to the East ... where they will be useful' (21 August 1942). Reports of 'Death train' (15 July 1941) and 'Destination horror' (11 May 1942) seemed to emphasise the horror of the *journey*, not its end.

It is really not until after the Bund report on the fate of Polish Jews in December 1942, that something of the systematic nature of the fate of the Jews deported became clearer. Yet even after this, Dutch Jews are reported as being despatched to 'special' camps (January 1943) with the crucial ambiguity left in. Some reports were quite clear: 'The rate of extermination was such,' wrote a Polish witness, 'that no means of rescue or relief on however large a scale could be commensurate with the problem' (7 May 1943). But others wrote of the 'Few Jews surviving in Vitemsk' (22 October 1943) in a way that misdirected attention. On 1 August 1942 it was reported that 'The Jewish Nation in Poland is being ruthlessly exterminated'. In the very next sentence the report continued: 'life continues behind the Ghetto walls'.[52]

In particular, the *Jewish Chronicle*, the Foreign Office and the BBC were reluctant to accept that the extermination of Jews was part of an intended programme, rather than an accidental by-product of official hostility to Jews. On 27 November 1942 Derek Law at the Foreign Office wrote: 'It is of course undeniable that large scale persecutions are taking place, but whether they are the result of a plan is more questionable.' In the same period both the Foreign and the Home News Board discussed the reports of the fate of Eastern European Jews: 'we are considering the question as to whether there is a "plan" of murder', went one memo. 'In the meantime it seems desirable to soft pedal the whole thing.'[53] The notion of a rational plan to carry out the irrational, was apparently hard to accept.

Yet in the case of the *Jewish Chronicle* stories nearly all of the reports were accepted by the BBC. Some were given considerable prominence. Others, curiously in view of the scale of horror they represented, were relegated to minor positions. Yet the evidence of systematic deportation and systematic murder was clearly present. As Lacqueur argues 'often events appeared in the press or were broadcast by the BBC long before there was any official recognition of them'.[54] The BBC took news and made news from an immensely wide range of sources. There was clear evidence, all through 1942, perhaps the most crucial period, of what was going on under Nazi rule in Europe, and much of this was publicly disseminated. Yet there remained an uncertainty, reflecting an element of incredulity in even the most detailed, accurate and first-hand reports, that undermined impact and horror of what was happening.

Apart from news, what other kinds of material did the BBC broadcast? When Crossman went into the camps he said that the British should have sent poets. When Tom Driberg went, as part of the British parliamentary delegation, he said that none of its members ever recovered from what they had seen, partly because 'They lacked the words, the images, the ability to tell anyone properly.'[55] In reponse to an enquiry from the British Board of Deputies on 15 November 1942 about programmes dealing with the 'Jewish problem', the Director-General replied with a list of 17 'talks and other programmes' that had been broadcast, including three by Sidney Silverman, a prominent Jewish MP and representative of the Board, as well as others by the Chief Rabbi, Maurice Edelman MP, and other prominent English and

Polish Jews. But these were mainly news commentaries. A suggestion in August 1942 by Louis MacNeice for three programmes starting with a trial of the Jewish race by the Nazis and of the Nazis as anti-Semites by the British and culminating in a dramatisation of the journey to a camp,[56] was rejected as 'too emotional: a difficult subject'.[57] A programme by Koestler on life in a death camp was also rejected. The poets, it seems, were prepared to write. The BBC was not, for various reasons, prepared to listen, or provide listeners.

Nevertheless the BBC was acquiring a wide range of information, much of it from sympathetic sources. But it was also a major producer of news, with its teams of expert translators and propagandists dealing in information about Europe. What factors within the BBC impeded the public awareness or mobilisation behind the news of how Jews were being systematically exterminated?

As we have seen, many commentators – Wasserstein, Sharf, Feingold and Moise, – argue that more was not done because of anti-Semitism. To what extent were the BBC's decisions in practice determined by anti-Semitism? It is important to locate the BBC's practice within the conventions of the period. This is not to condone practices, but at least to locate their significance. Thus, social anti-Semitism was routinely acceptable in pre-war Britain. It remained so among an older generation afterwards: Harold Nicolson was able in 1945 to ascribe the Labour victory to a Jewish Conspiracy in the *Daily Mirror*, and to write: 'The Jewish capacity for destruction is really illimitable. Although I loathe anti-Semites I do dislike Jews'.[58] A more illuminating and complex example is that of Hugh Dalton, a Labour minister in the wartime coalition. A fervent anti-appeaser, he sheltered a number of Jewish refugees in his own home, and spoke at all the public meetings agitating for action to save Jewry. He hated Germans. He was an active supporter of Jewish claims in Palestine. Yet he cheerfully cracked anti-Semitic jokes in the middle of the war.[59]

## The BBC and anti-Semitism

It is not surprising, therefore, to find attitudes that today would be regarded as evidently anti-Semitic within the BBC. One splenetic letter in 1933, attacking the Corporation for allowing Jews to dominate BBC variety programmes, was sent straight to Reith, the Director-General, who replied that he was 'giving it close attention'.[60] Correspondents who complained of jokes about Jews were told that nothing offensive was intended, and that in any case there were Scottish and Welsh jokes as well.

In a developing relationship between Sidney Salomen at the Board of Deputies and various officials in the BBC that began in the 1930s over music hall programmes, the BBC displayed its worst, elitist tone. All the elements of stereotyping were there. 'In our experience', went one memo about programmes on Children's Hour in 1943, 'if Jewish broadcasts are given an inch they come back clamouring for an ell'.[61]

Once the war started, complaints that the effectiveness of the Rumanian, Hungarian and Polish Services were undermined by Jewish accent were accepted.[62] The Polish Service appointed an 'assessor', 'primarily for the purpose of detecting traces of the Jewish accent and manner'.[63] (Although the Overseas Board had commented earlier that it felt that many of these complaints 'were entirely a racket'.)[64]

One of the problems, indeed, was the politics of Jewishness. Partly it was because Jews were associated with the Left. 'Anxiety over Jewish communist bias',[65] was pencilled on one paper. Worst of all, within the organisation anti-Semitism was still seen by some as a political issue. One programme suggestion was rejected because of the 'political implication', but the memo went on, 'we shall be glad to consider a talk or talks on the moral and religious principles.'[66] As concern over developments in Palestine grew, this became more clearly the case. In as far as it was a political issue, it was not a subject on which the BBC could 'take sides'. A series of attempts to get 'pro-Jewish' talks on the BBC throughout 1943 from both individuals and organisations were all politely received and deferred. But the BBC quite clearly had no intention of broadcasting any of them.

In June 1943, in one of the more bizarre examples of the Corporation's balancing acts, an official wrote an internal paper arguing that the Corporation did not want to accept any 'pro-Semite' programmes, because then 'anti-Semites would demand the right to reply and it would be difficult to refuse'.[67]

Thus, there was anti-Semitism within the BBC, and anti-Semitism was occasionally perceived as a legitimate political position. Yet, paradoxically, a far more serious impediment to *agitation* was the more dominant opposition to anti-Semitism within the Corporation.

It is important to distinguish between two distinct kinds of decisions that were made in what was seen as the battle against anti-Semitism. The first were based on the BBC's (and the MOI's) anxiety about the growth of anti-Semitism within the British public. Other decisions were based on an argument about the moral impropriety of considering the Jews as a special race.

While the elite seemed to think that they could go on making anti-Jewish jokes with impunity, the fear was that the German claim that it was a 'war over Jews' would stick, and undermine the public will to go on fighting. Robert Bruce Lockhart, an influential propagandist, wrote in 1942 'Max [Aitken] got going on the Jewish problem after we listened in to young Julian Amery who did a pro-Nazi broadcast from Berlin. The theme being that we were being "deceived by the Jews". Max

thinks that anti-Semites will be a big problem here'.[68] At the beginning
of the war there were MOI reports from London and Merseyside of
'scapegoating of Jews', and anxieties about 'developing anti-
Semitism'.[69] After the Allied Declaration in December 1942, home intelligence reports apparently demonstrated that all of the news about
the German persecution of Jews was simply making people 'more conscious of the Jews they don't like here'.[70] In February, the Director of
Talks, G.R. Barnes, wrote about another request for 'pro'-Jewish talks:
'this is not the moment to talk about anti-Semitism because of the
danger of crypto-Fascisms at home. Personally I don't want to touch
the subject except by implication... It will do more harm than good'.[71]
By the end of 1943, this view had become high policy. The Director-
General, Hayley, wrote in a memo:

> that we should not promote ourselves, or accept any propaganda in the
> way of talks, discussions, features with the object of trying to correct the
> undoubted anti-Semitism which is held very largely throughout the
> country: but that we should confine ourselves to reporting, and indeed
> giving prominence to the facts of Jewish persecution...as well as any
> notable achievements by Jews, particularly in connection with the war
> effort.[72]

Thus, at the time, it was the strongly held view of even passionate
opponents of anti-Semitism that 'any pro-Jewish propaganda, anything
by way of exhortation'[73] would reinforce rather than dissipate endemic
potential anti-Semitism at home. The most important consideration
was the effect of any agitation on the British public's determination to
fight the war. Winning the war was seen as the priority, and indeed the
solution to a problem which was perceived as practical rather than
moral. Relieving suffering came far lower down the agenda.

However, the BBC was a rapidly growing bureaucracy, and its decisions also developed bureaucratic inertia. Thus, anxiety about public
anti-Semitism became the standard reply to all demands for action
overseas, throughout 1943, 1944 and 1945. The policy, once formulated, was never reassessed. None of the subsequent grounds for innovation, for instance around the specific attempts to save the Hungarian
Jews in 1944, was really considered.

There was, however, another basis for the BBC's rejection of many
attempts to broadcast 'pro'-Jewish programmes. To do so, it was believed, was to fall into a Fascist trap: 'We do not recognise the German
theory of a Jewish nation and we maintain that Jews are citizens of the
country to which they belong'.[74] This attitude, that the war was being
fought against theories of racial discrimination, and that any evidence
that supported such theories was therefore dangerous, was most clearly
developed in the handling of a series of programmes by Sir Robert Vansittart called 'The Black Record'.

Vansittart had been a prominent anti-appeaser and as Permanent Under-Secretary at the Foreign Office during the 1930s, an influential one. In his broadcasts, he execrated Germans in a style and with a violence of language that reminded the BBC's liberals of Germany. He was, they thought, a Fascist anti-Fascist. Vansittart's programmes argued for the inexorable, essentially hereditary nature of German evil. 'The German,' he said, 'is often a moral creature: the *Germans* never.' 'German women' and 'German professors' were particularly nasty. His theme was that since Roman times the Germans had been aggressive, corrupt and brutal. 'The deliberate racial extermination, as systematic, as thorough as an ancient scourge',[75] of Jews and Poles was merely the last symptom of their disease.

The programmes may have been what the public wanted to hear – or at least they may have expressed a view the public was interested in. But within the Corporation they were not greeted with acclaim. 'I feel extremely unhappy about the contents',[76] wrote the producer. His superior, the Director of Talks, wrote when another series was proposed: 'Surely it is the negation of art to overload. What is the point of piling atrocities on atrocities? To me they cease to have any meaning'.[77] Vansittart was even hounded for what, as a Foreign Office employee, he did with the Broadcast fee. (Yet this was just before the Allied Declaration about German treatment of Jews in 1942.) Vansittart's programmes were thought 'too insulting to broadcast to North America'.

A general memorandum on policy suggested that 'many people now adopt a sort of racialist theory that the Germans are wicked by nature'.[78] This, it suggested, was not only proto-Fascist in its implications but also inefficient. If Germans were congenitally evil, they could hardly be held responsible for what they did. The object of broadcast propaganda was to change and undermine German attitudes.

Thus, at a time when 'atrocity' was actually being piled on 'atrocity', Vansittart's attack on the Germans produced within some sections of the BBC a view that this was too 'extreme', and that by implication to claim such things was to give space to precisely the kinds of view which fostered anti-Semitism. It has been argued that the broadcasts were accepted as accurate, but seen as 'non British and in the worst of taste'.[79] Nevertheless, the public found Vansittart's views appealing. The programmes received some of the highest ratings for wartime talks, and when published as a book, sold out three reprints in six months.

Another of the difficulties was the way in which 'anti-Semitism' was constituted within the BBC as a problem. It was not seen as an economically or politically explicable phenomenon. Rather, it was seen as an inexplicable fact; an accidental and irrational mistake. The hostility to modernism, commerce, cities and the celebration of heroic vitality that were associated with the ideology in Germany[80] were incompatible with

the mildly progressive beliefs in reason, routine and planning that prevailed within the Corporation. Therefore, anti-Semitism was not taken
seriously and seen almost as an historical anachronism in the modern
world. Because of this, in discussions of 'anti-Semitism' and its effects
at home, abroad and in Nazi actions, there is almost no consideration at
all of the origin of the views, or indeed any explanation for its apparent
success as an ideology. Indeed, this acceptance of anti-Semitism, characterised all thought about the issue, an unspoken assumption which
acted as an impediment to counterattack. It was felt within the BBC
that to single out 'Jews' for special mention, was in itself uncivilised.

The distance between the BBC's principles and the reality of the
camps is particularly clear in the argument about whether the names of
SS bureaucrats and individuals who were known to be responsible for
acts of savagery against Jews should be broadcast. The problem was
raised as a general issue and as a specific problem repeatedly. In 1940
the European News Director worried whether 'we should condemn the
German people universally or talk as though they were the agents of
oppression'. He went on to argue that although it should be stressed
that nothing could save the German people, nothing should be mentioned about 'what will happen to individual Germans on defeat'.[81] The
Polish Embassy often argued that the BBC could, by naming names,
help to mitigate German excesses. 'Publicity', wrote Count Raczynsky,
'happens to be the only way in which you can help our suffering people
in their most cruel ordeal. It is needed, not in order to give Polish em-
igrés abroad a vain satisfaction, but for a very real purpose'.[82] The
pressure mounted as the war progressed. The British Board of Deputies, and the British Section of the World Jewish Congress, frequently
demanded that individual names that were known should be broadcast:
'We believe that great and concentrated effort is vital to prevent the
further deportation of Jews from such countries as Italy and Romania.
Individuals responsible should be named. We enclose a list of the
names, well known', wrote the Congress Officials to Brendan Bracken
in 1942.[83] In particular, as the war progressed there were many
attempts to persuade the BBC to broadcast lists of known names of
guards and officials in the extermination and labour camps.[84] These
appeals were based on a direct and urgent sense that something might
change by so doing.

For the BBC the problem was one of responsibility. The Corporation
was anxious that if individuals were named, others, equally culpable,
would believe they were safe and so continue in their excesses, while
those named, knowing that their behaviour was known, would have no
reason to change it. The Corporation also argued that classes of offend-
er should be indicted, not individuals. Thus the Corporation broadcast
clear warnings that Germans guilty of offences in camps would, after

the war, be returned for trial to the nation in which the offences had been committed. Only very exceptionally did it broadcast names.[85] Yet Joseph Garlinsky, in his book on Auschwitz, wrote that when in 1944 the BBC announced a list of names of guards and added that they were likely to be condemned to death, 'the behaviour of several SS men changed and there were even some who volunteered for the front'.[86]

### Anti-Semitism and the Establishment

One of the arguments has been that anti-Semitism was the reason why more was not done about the fate of European Jews. As we have seen, anti-Semitism was endemic and deeply engrained in the British social structure. The BBC was routinely 'socially' anti-Semitic in some parts of the organisation, while at the same time being progressively anti-Semitic in other parts. As it turns out both views were in different ways impediments to the free transmission of news about the holocaust.

Yet anti-Semitism did not always have *political* effects. Thus Martin Gilbert's biography emphasises Churchill's concern for Jews and the Jewish plight.In contrast, Anthony Eden was far more concerned, in the Foreign Office tradition, with the desire not to offend the Arabs. He was also personally unsympathetic to Jews: 'Let me murmur in your ear', he said at an Allied meeting in Washington in 1941, 'I prefer Arabs to Jews'.[87] Thus, at the highest level, Eden and Churchill had very different *attitudes* towards Jews, but during the war they pursued the same *policy*: that the Jews would be best helped by an Allied victory, and that Britain was in no position to put supplies at risk to effect any assistance. These views may well have been wrong, but they were shared by men whose attitudes were very different.

### Jews and religious programmes

Within the BBC there were other problems facing Jewish attempts to mobilise opinion. As we have seen, the 'Jewish issue' was seen by the BBC as a 'political' problem. Sidney Silverman, the prominent Jewish MP, was advised to pursue his case in moral and religious terms, because the BBC could be more sympathetic to this kind of appeal.

Indeed, various Jewish organisations, by the beginning of 1942, had begun to make approaches to the Religious Broadcasting Section of the Corporation, and for the next three years religious broadcasting was one of the main focuses of Jewish pressure. There were proposals for religious programmes in Yiddish, for programmes on the role of religion in Jewish life, and a well-organised series of letters from bishops asking for the inclusion of suitable Jewish prayers in Sunday services.[88]

It was consequently particularly unfortunate that just as they started to exert pressure, the Religious Broadcasting Section came under attack. From 1938 the proportion of talks programmes on the service had risen from 7.4 to 23per cent of all programmes. But the proportion of talks programmes that originated from the Religious Department had risen from 8 to over 30per cent. In addition, a memorandum talked about a 'religious pincer movement to capture the remaining free areas'.[89] '"Have you lost your railway ticket"? is the kind of opening which is becoming increasingly fashionable in religious broadcasting', complained one critic.[90] For its opponents the imperialist expansion of religious broadcasting under the command of the redoubtable Reverend Weeks, represented the growth of covert propaganda. From early in 1943, the Director of Talks decided to restrict religious broadcasting. In particular in February 1943, it was decided that these religious programmes should not be allowed to discuss political matters.

Thus successful Jewish attempts to organise neutral Christian dignitaries to bring pressure on the Corporation, and the energy expended on a religious approach were wasted. Maximum pressure was applied between 1942 – 44 in an increasingly ineffective area.

But the relationship to religion was also complex. Machonochie, Director of Talks, together with other critics of the growth of religious broadcasting, had seen it as representing the growth of covert propaganda. But more than that, liberal progressive thought was in some sense opposed in general to religion. Religion seemed to be a superstitious, irrational and supersedable system of thought: 'All this religious sentimentality does not help people face up to the reality of the war one bit',[91] wrote Machonochie. Another critic added, on the subject of another programme suggestion for material on Jewish religious life, 'Surely this kind of thing won't really help their cause? It's playing into fascist hands really'.[92] As one Jewish broadcaster wrote: 'The Nazis are always claiming to "get on well with the churches" – and the BBC always attempts to repudiate this as if Jews were not "a church".'[93]

But the anti-Semitic consequences of liberalism were a fairly subtle influence. Until 1938 the Reithian legacy had meant that there had been no programmes on Jewish religious matters at all, because the BBC regarded itself as specifically Christian.[94]

But there may have been other problems, a product of both anti-Semitism and the nature of the media. By the end of 1943 the British Division of the World Jewish Congress was working to appeal to everyone it could within the BBC (and within government and elsewhere). Yet all of these approaches tended to be made individually. This allowed them to be dismissed. 'Jews' and 'the Jewish issue' were seen by the Corporation as an abstract and generalised problem, yet conversely, individual Jews appealing to the BBC were often seen as 'no more' than individuals with interests. Sidney Salomon, who from the Board of Deputies since the 1930s had been trying to influence the BBC's policy, was in one memorandum referred to in dismissive terms: 'Mr. Salomon

had come back again. What real interest does he represent?' He was
hardly perceived as a representative of a group.

If less discrete promotion of the issues could have been made, then
the BBC would probably have been more responsive. It is as if maximum pressure was not only unknowingly applied in the wrong place,
but also that it was unknowingly applied in the wrong way. This was in
part, recognised by Jewish organisations; an internal memorandum by
Ernest Frischer for the World Jewish Congress argued that 'more running after Ministers and "conferring" with outstanding personalities is
not politic'.[95] But Jewish organisations were in a double-bind. If they
appealed on the grounds of their 'Jewishness' this was seen as political,
difficult, and in any case likely to be dangerously inefficient. Whether
for home or foreign consumption, if they appealed in their individual
capacity, they were likely to be taken less seriously as individuals rather
than interests.

Another problem was the psychological distance of the worst atrocities. There is a definite increase in concern when the matter at issue is
the fate of the Jews nearer home. 'Have we had', declared one memo
from a Policy Director to the Director of Talks,

> and if not, do we want something authoritative on the excesses against
> the Jews in France? As you know the barbarities differ in kind from
> others to which we have now got used to. They are the first of the sort to
> be perpetrated in Western Europe, and the tolerant social relationship
> between the French Jews and the rest of the French people makes them
> peculiarly horrible.[96]

This attitude, that if it is French Jews it is really serious, but that Nazi
brutality was in some sense more acceptable, either if the local population were anti-Semitic, or if it occurred in the barbaric mythic lands of
the East, was widespread. Indeed one of the problems during 1942/43
was that the worst excesses were occurring so deep in enemy-held territory.

As it became clear that French and Dutch Jews were also being deported 'and sytematically murdered',[97] the Director-General, Ogilvie,
suggested that some programmes should be made, particularly highlighting Nazi brutality towards children, 'although in the case of Jewish
children it would be better not to refer to their race'.[98]

## Conclusion

It is now evident that there was plenty of knowledge available and indeed disseminated by the BBC, both at home and abroad, about the
extermination of the Jews between 1940 and 1945. The BBC, though
not focusing attention on the extermination, and despite the linguistic
ambiguity that has been noted, remained surprisingly close in its news

surveys to Jewish sources. The facts from debriefings of escapees from Auschwitz appeared on the BBC before they appeared elsewhere or were officially accepted.

Of course, to say that information was available, is not to say that it was registered. There are a number of problems here. The knowledge was not available, understood or recognised uniformly. In all the 'Sibs',(deliberately falsified rumours to be circulated in order to demoralise the Germans) there is no mention of the systematic extermination of any group.[99] Many refugees have described how the British simply did not seem to want to know about the atrocities Jews were subjected to in Germany, and how even the propaganda organisation at Woburn seemed resistant to and unconvinced by stories of brutality supplied by its own employees.[100]

In his book *The Terrible Secret*, Walter Lacqueur distinguishes between knowledge and belief. The book is concerned with the riddle of why what was known was not believed. His distinction depends on the more general problem of the processes by which there is a 'denial of reality, and the psychological rejection of information which for one reason or another is not acceptable'.[101] There was, he concludes, despite deliberate Nazi attempts to confuse and mislead, knowledge of the holocaust, but for various reasons it could not be accepted, either by those in the next doomed ghetto, or by those who might have done more to prevent it.

But perhaps Lacqueur's definitions need further elaboration. In 1942, when after the Wansee Conference the plans for the 'final solution' were put into action, the Allies and the public did recognise and 'know' what was happening. The Allied Declaration of December 1942 makes that quite clear. Details of the fate of Jews of different nations were abundant in internal BBC news summaries and digests for use both in foreign and domestic services. The public was often told. Perhaps the really difficult problem, and one that was found in 1945 to be retrospectively acutely unacceptable, was that in 1942 and 1943, the politicians and the public felt that there was little they could do, and that anything they might do would be a diversion from winning the war. Martin Gilbert makes Churchill's concern over the extermination camps and appalled sympathy for Jews, central to his book. Churchill, Gilbert argues, actually ordered that something be done, in particular, that the camps should be bombed. What Gilbert fails to explain is why the Prime Minister did not follow his order through. This was not, as Lacqueur suggests, that people did not or could not 'believe' what they were told ('More precise details, very vivid, about means of exterminating Jews,'[102] summarised a BBC European News Digest in 1943): but that, rather more grimly, even those that 'knew' and 'believed', could do nothing with this in the period of war when Britain's survival was so uncertain. Atrocities however awful, in faraway places were distant from the concerns of the public and politicians.

By 1944, when there was more tactical space, bureaucratic inertia had set in. As the strategic anxieties about Palestine loomed, but more crucially as we have seen, within bureaucracies like the BBC, as policy was merely reiterated not reconsidered in the light of changing opportunities, then more wasn't said or done because the answers seem fixed. Throughout, the BBC took its political line from the government.

The failure to mobilise public opinion in England, it has to be noted, is far less significant than a similar failure in America. There Jews were a prominent group, with immediate access to the President, and of some interest to him as an influential voting bloc. On the whole the American public was as quiescent during the war, and as shocked at the end of it, as the British. One campaigner in America had some, though limited, success in changing American policy. Peter Bergson, although an ardent Zionist, attempted to divorce all references to a Jewish nation from his rescue attempts. He campaigned for temporary visa rights, and campaigned in a largely public style: taking huge posters in Time Square, proclaiming 'This is a Race Against Death', 'How Well are you Sleeping?' and 'Driven to Death Daily'.[103] His campaign aim was narrow: he wanted to get the Jews out of Europe. It was this focus that gave his campaign power. But it mobilised the knowledge he knew the public already had.

Within the BBC any prominent official could have known about the Nazi plans and actions against Jews from information that was regularly circulated within the organisation. Indeed, so could any member of the public. They were told as much as readers of the *Jewish Chronicle*. Partly more was not done, and public opinion not more aroused because 'doing' something about it seemed impossible, and it was a low priority on the political agenda.

More focused attention, more mobilisation of outrage, also did not occur within the BBC because of a variety of policy decisions, about the role of religion, about the definition of politics, about the status of Jews, which had the effect of limiting access to the microphone of some of those who might have sought to alert the British public to the terrible events in Europe.

Clearly, then, information was not the key in itself to more action. Indeed, it perhaps needs to be explained why the universal reaction to the news coming out of the camps was one of stunned surprise. The answer is complex, partly because many people had not registered what was there to be known. Yet Lacqueur's definition needs to be elaborated. For him there is a distinction between knowledge and belief. But although knowledgeable and expert officials, like Hugh Greene or

Crossman, could know what was happening and believe it, imagining the scale and nature of the horror in the camps was another matter. For many of the eye-witnesses – all of whom were profoundly and irrevocably marked by the experience – when they said they had not 'known' or 'believed' what they were to see, this was true in an emotional and moral, rather than intellectual sense. What had been happening in the camps was so beyond normal experience that it had to be seen to be properly accepted. Men who had been filing reports about Auschwitz still felt that when the camp was opened they had barely begun to understand what was happening there.

Richard Dimbleby, breaking the news to the British, could admit 'nothing had prepared me for what I saw'. Yet if he had read, or read and absorbed or accepted, one of the briefing documents that was sent to him that talked of 'camps, quite different from POW camps, where Jews and other groups are systematically exterminated', [104] this would not have been true except in the sense that nothing, including full knowledge, *could* prepare anybody for a sight so gruesome.

All those who opened the camps commented on the otherworldly nature of life there. George Steiner, in his book *Language and Silence*, wonders about the 'true relation' of events. While Jews were being murdered in Treblinka, he wrote,

> the overwhelming plurality of human beings, two miles away on Polish farms, 5000 miles away in New York, were sleeping or eating or going to a film or making love or worrying about the dentist. This is where my imagination balks. The two orders of simultaneous experience are so different, so irreconcilable to any common norm of human values, their coexistence is so hideous a paradox – Treblinka is both because some men have built it, and almost all other men have let it be – that I puzzle over time. Are there, as science fiction and Gnostic speculation imply, different species of time in the same world, 'good times' and enveloping folds of inhuman time in which men fall into the slow hands of living damnation?[105]

It was, at least in part the irreconcilability of worlds that those who saw the camps had to face.

When the camps were discovered and opened, the surviving inmates finally reduced to the last extremity by the chaos of the closing weeks of the war, during which even Berliners were starving, seemed to those who dealt with them, and in the pictures that came out to the world, moving in such passive awful suffering. This like the passivity of starving Ethiopians, was the result not of political acceptance but of starvation. But, in a way, the image of life in the camps was inaccurate. Life in the camps had in fact included countless acts of heroism. People had been brave and resourceful. They had been human in the face of inhumanity, yet this was not how they appeared to the appalled liberators.

The holocaust is in its way the 'model' atrocity partly because we have pictures of it. Life in Stalin's camps, death in Stalin's purges, life in Cambodia under Pol Pot, are all visually unrecorded. The media tell stories which have particular unrefutable impact if supported by photographs or film. The role of the holocaust in public memory is fixed by indisputable images.

Some people had knowledge, other people did not. Knowledge was not uniformly available. Some people believed what they knew. Others did not. Many perhaps could not. The disbelief was subtly structured. It was as if the most accurate and vivid accounts were often undercut by a refusal to focus on the consequences if the accounts were real. That information about what was happening to Jews was widely available and widely broadcast is clear. But its focus did not encourage campaigning or action. More was not done because, rightly or wrongly, it was felt that nothing could be done except win the war. The BBC might have taken independent action – but it saw the world with government eyes in the war. When the camps were opened, it seemed like the unveiling of an obscene evil, of which nothing had been known, yet one which proved a final, irrefutable justification for the anti-German war. Yet our conclusion must be in some way, grimmer than the secret that was disclosed. It was a secret known by some, understood at least by some, but over which there was no political will to act.

## Notes

1.  J.I.P. Fox, 'The Jewish Factor in British War Crimes Policy', *The English Historical Review*, Vol. XXII, No. 362, January 1977, pp.82-106.
2.  W. Shawcross, *The Quality of Mercy: Cambodia the Holocaust and Modern Conscience*, London: Deutsch, 1984.
3.  B. Wasserstein, *Britain and the Jews of Europe 1939-45*, Oxford: Clarendon Press, 1979, p. 163.
4.  M. Gilbert, *Auschwitz and the Allies*, Michael Joseph, London, 1981, p.12.
5.  Walter Lacqueur, *The Terrible Secret: An investigation into the suppression of information about Hitler's Final Solutions*, London: Weidenfeld & Nicolson, 1980; A. Sharf, *The British Press and Jews Under Nazi Rule*, London: The Institute of Race Relations & Oxford University Press, 1964.
6.  Sharf, op.cit., p.69.
7.  R. Crossman, *Palestine Mission: A Personal Record*, London: Hamish Hamilton, 1947, p.18.
8.  Crossman, op.cit., p.22.
9.  Interview with the author, 1983.
10. Ed Murrow, *War Record*, London: Hill and Lane, 1946.
11. Jonathan Dimbleby, *Richard Dimbleby*, London: Quartet, 1976, p.142.
12. R. Dimbleby, 'Belsen', in L. Mial,(ed.) *Richard Dimbleby: Broadcaster*, London: BBC, 1966, p.47.

13. BBC Written Archives, R34/106, 'In the Event of War', July 1936.
14. Anthony Smith, *The Shadow in the Cave*, London: Allen and Unwin, 1973.
15. Robert Fraser, MOI, INF 36/129, 1942.
16. BBC Written Archives, Scripts, 'Cardinal Hinsley' 8 July, 1942, 6 p.m., Home Service.
17. PRO, FOG8789/55, 31097.
18. Harold Nicolson in *The Daily Telegraph* 25 August 1933.
19. Raymond Carr, *The Spanish Tragedy*, London: Weidenfeld & Nicolson, 1979, p.95.
20. A. Koestler, *Spanish Testament*, London: Gollancz, 1937.
21. G. Orwell, 'Spain and the Newspapers', *Collected Essays and Journalism*, (ed.) S. Orwell, Harmondsworth: Penguin Books, 1975, Vol. I, p.118.
22. Carr, op.cit., p.23.
23. BBC Written Archives, 'Spanish Civil War', R34/178, 15 May 1935.
24. D. Waley, *British Public Opinion and the Abyssinian War 1935-6*, London: Temple Smith and the LSE, 1975, p.37.
25. BBC Written Archives, R34/952, 'Yiddish Programmes' 1934-39, September 1938.
26. G. Dyson, (ed.),*Heroes of the House*, London: BBC Publications, 1942, p.43.
27. BBC Written Archives, R34/702/2, Richard Crossman, memo on proposed programmes on Riom trials.
28. BBC Written Archives, R34/702/2. B. Nichols, 'Propaganda in Broadcast Programmes', 12 December 1940.
29. I. McLaine, *Ministry of Morale, Home Front Morale and the Ministry of Information in World War II*, London: Allen and Unwin, 1979, Michael Balfour, *Propaganda in War*, London: Routledge, 1980.
30. BBC Written Archives, R34/702/2, Robert Nichols to R. Machonochie, 28 November 1940.
31. Ministry of Information Papers INF/1/251. 'Plan to Combat the Apathetic Outlook', 25 July 1941.
32. BBC Written Archives, R34/639/3, Electra House to DG, Political Propaganda, 25 February 1940.
33. See Michael Tracey, *A Variety of Lives: The Biography of Sir Hugh Greene*, London: Bodley Head 1983, Ch.7.
34. BBC Written Archives, R34/5702/5, Ministry of Information, 'Theme for Propaganda', 13 September 1941.
35. BBC Written Archives, R34/702/5. Director of Programmes to Controller, 22 March 1941.
36. BBC Written Archives, R34/639/3, Political Propaganda 1940, 25 February 1940.
37. Ibid., 13 January 1941.
38. BBC Written Archives, R34/696, 'Propaganda and News Talks',23 November 1941.
39. Adolf Hitler, *Mein Kampf*, Vol. II 'The National Socialist Movement', p.553.
40. BBC Written Archives, John Strachey, File 2a, November 1936– 40.
41. Tehuda Bauer, *The Holocaust in Historical Perspective*, Sheldon Press, 1979, p.24.
42. BBC Written Archives, E1/1148/2, 1942.
43. BBC Written Archives, D.G. to Director of Home Programmes,R34/702/3, 5 February 1941.
44. See BBC Written Archives, E1/114812, Polish Service, File A, November 1940 – December 1941.
45. BBC Written Archives, E1/11481, Polish Service, File B/C.
46. BBC Written Archives, E1/1148/4, Paper 1247, 25 April 1945.
47. Author's Interview with Dr Aronsfeld at The World Jewish Congress, 1983.
48. *Jewish Cronicle* 1942 – December 1943; and BBCWritten Archives, Home News Digest, R42/117/a and Polish and German Digests.
49. *Jewish Chronicle*, 26 November 1943, 6 April 1942, 16 January 1942.

50. See Martin Gilbert, *Auschwitz and the Allies*, London: Michael Joseph, 1981, pp.190-9.
51. Author's interview with Dr Aronsfeld at the World Jewish Congress.
52. *Jewish Chronicle*, 1 August 1942.
53. BBC Written Archives, R34/178, Foreign Adviser News,2 November 1942.
54. Lacqueur, *The Terrible Secret* op.cit., p.35.
55. Tom Driberg, *Private Passions*, London: Quartet,1979, p.74; and *Colonnade 1937-47*, Pilot Press, 1949.
56. BBC Written Archives, Proposals for Programme on the Jews, Louis MacNeice (in Louis MacNeice file).
57. BBC Written Archives, R34/277, 12 December 1942.
58. Harold Nicholson, *Diaries and Letters 1939-45*, London: Collins, 1967, 13 June 1945, p.203.
59. See Ben Pimlott, *Hugh Dalton*, London: Jonathan Cape, 1985.
60. BBC Written Archives, R34/178, 1930-36.
61. BBC Written Archives, R34/277, 11 August 1943.
62. BBC Written Archives, The Romanian Service, R13/194, 1942,The Hungarian Service, R3/19/1, File 1.
63. BBC Written Archives, Polish Service, R13/192, 11 April 1941.
64. BBC Written Archives, Overseas Board, R34/277, R3/19/2.14 December 1939.
65. BBC Written Archives, R34/179/2. 15 February 1942.
66. BBC Written Archives, Policy Censorship, R34/277, 9 July 1941.
67. BBC Written Archives, R34/277, 'Anti-Semitism', 7 June 1943.
68. K. Young (ed.) *The Diaries of Robert Bruce Lockhart*, London: Macmillan, 1980, 17 October 1942, p.231.
69. Home Intelligence Daily Report, INFI/264, 11 September1940.
70. Home Intelligence Report, recorded in BBC Written Archive,R34/277, 7 January 1943.
71. BBC Written Archives, R34/277, 4 February 1943.
72. BBC Written Archives, R34/277, Director-General's Memoranda, 19 November 1943.
73. BBC Written Archive, R34/952, 15 August 1941. Indeed, even foreign broadcasts were limited in this way: 'Any specific pleading, in our experience, increases persecution instead of reducing it', explained one paper. BBC Written Archive,E1/1149/2 Poland, 19 February 1943.
74. BBC Written Archives, R34/952, 'Yiddish Programmes',Comptroller Europe, 3 July 1943.
75. Robert Vansittart, *Black Record*, London: Hamish Hamilton, 1941, pp.19, 47.
76. BBC Written Archives, Talks File, 810-1939, 13 November 1940.
77. Ibid., Barnes to Controller of Home, 10 August 1942.
78. BBC Written Archives, R341/639/5, July 1941.
79. D.C. Watt, *Personalities and Political Studies in the formulation of British Foreign Policy in the 20th Century*, London: Longmans, 1965.
80. See Fritz Stern, *The Politics of Cultural Despair: A Study in the Rise of German Ideology*, University of California Press, 1961.
81. BBC Written Archives, European News Directive, R34/655, 25 May 1940.
82. BBC Written Archives, The Polish Ambassador to Sir Ivone Kirkpatrick, E1/1149/2, 9 January 1943.
83. World Jewish Congress Papers, British Section, 27 November 1942.
84. The World Jewish Congress Papers show at least seven appeals made to the BBC between 1943 and 1945.
85. BBC Written Archives, E1/1149/1, Polish Service.
86. J. Garlinsky, *Fighting Auschwitz: The Resistance Movement in the Concentration Camps*, Julian Freeman,1974, p.231.
87. David Carlton, *Anthony Eden*, London: Allen Lane,1981, p.240.

88.  See BBC Written Archives, 'Yiddish Broadcasting', R34/952.
89.  BBC Written Archives, R34/715, Propaganda Talks, 1942-43.
90.  BBC Written Archives, Policy Propaganda, R34/715, December,1942.
91.  BBC Written Archives, Religious Programming, R34/712,25 January 1943.
92.  BBC Written Archives, Jewish Programmes, R34/405, 2 March 1942.
93.  BBC Written Archives, Nathaniel Mickler, Talks scripts, Friday, 29 December 1940. A letter in preparation for a talk.
94.  BBC Written Archives, Religious Programme Proposals, R34/710, 1926-36.
95.  World Jewish Congress, 'Breaking the Silence' III, Internal Paper, Ernest Frischer, 8 December 1943.
96.  BBC Written Archives, R34/686, Policy Propaganda, Mr Pringle to Director of Talks, 25 September 1942.
97.  BBC Written Archives, R34/686. P.G. Ogilvie to Machonochie,5 September 1942.
98.  BBC Written Archives, R34/686, Policy Propaganda, G.E. Barnes, Director of Talks, 26 September 1942.
99.  See Sibs, PRO, FO 898/101, 898/72, 898/62.
100. Author's interviews.
101. Lacqueur, *The Terrible Secret*, op.cit., p.13.
102. BBC Written Archives, R34/1079, 5 June 1941.
103. S.E. Peck, 'The Campaign for an American Response to the Holocaust 1943-45', *Journal of Contemporary History*, Vol.15, No.2, April 1980, p.367-89.
104. R. Dimbleby, 'Belsen' in L. Mial, (ed) op.cit.
105. George Steiner, quoted in W. Shawcross, op.cit.

# 9 News management and counter-insurgency: The case of Oman
*Fred Halliday*

> I was one of those who, being only intermittently distressed by the political conditions of Oman, rather liked him. I liked his wary doe eyes and his gentle voice . . . . His face was a stylised face, with its fringed beard and its calculating mouth, and his supple but portly figure spoke of oiled baths, frankincense, and the more decorous pleasures of an abstemious harem. (*The Guardian*, 27 July 1970, on the deposition of Sultan Said bin Taimur).

> Unhappily, being a deeply religious man of a retiring and somewhat parsimonious disposition, he appeared chiefly concerned to conserve these reserves and to keep his people insulated against the spread of modern ideas and developments. (*The Times*, 23 October 1972, on the death of Sultan Said bin Taimur).

The Sultanate of Oman, a state of around three-quarters of a million people lying on the south-east of the Arabian Peninsula, has had close political and military links with Britain since the late eighteenth century. Although never formally proclaimed a colony, it was in effect under British colonial rule from the late nineteenth century until the 1970s. In the past decades this relationship has involved Britain in two significant wars in Oman, defending the reigning Al Bu Said Sultans against internal rebels. The first such operation was in the period 1957 – 59, when tribal and nationalist forces rebelled in the interior of northern Oman. The second rebellion took place in the southern province, Dhofar, in the period 1965–75. In both wars British forces were deployed against the rebels, almost totally in secret, along with local Omani troops and mercenaries from Pakistani Baluchistan. The focus of the discussion that follows is on the second of these wars, that in Dhofar, and on the manner in which news about this conflict was presented in the British media. It is a classic case of news management and control, and of press collusion in this process.

Whitehall news management of military matters was, of course, a practice developed to great effect during the two world wars.[1] The Ministry of Defence Press Office was originally founded in 1914, that of the Foreign Office in 1916. After the Second World War the Information and Research Department of the Foreign Office prosecuted the Cold War in the realm of information. The corresponding press attitudes – of discretion, respect for the hush-hush, loyalty, 'blind eyes', patriotism, battlefield and officers' mess matiness – also derive from wartime experience. In the period since 1945 Britain has fought a number of other wars, many of them counter-insurgency wars, in which, suitably adapted, the news management lessons of the world wars have been applied.[2]

When fighting did break out in Dhofar in 1965, it offered conditions that were almost ideal for news management. First, the level of British involvement was small – never more than 2000 men, compared to the many thousands involved in Aden and other counter-insurgency operations; and of these, only a minority were in the category that Whitehall had to admit to (i.e. *both* in combat *and* still serving in the British Army). By sleight of hand that will be discussed later, the degree of British military involvement was therefore made to look even smaller than it actually was. Secondly Dhofar, the area in which the fighting took place, was physically remote and virtually inaccessible. Only those vetted and guarded by the MoD could get into Oman, let alone into the war zone on the Sultan's side, and the only access to rebel areas was through the People's Democratic Republic of Yemen and then, by foot, into the guerrilla-held mountains. During the ten years of the Dhofar war only one British observer, myself, visited the guerrilla-held areas. It was possible for the news managers virtually to seal the war zone off – as was not possible in Vietnam or Cyprus, but was possible for the UK in the Falklands and for the Indonesians in Timor. Thirdly, the guerrillas in Oman, known during much of this period as the People's Front for the Liberation of Oman and the Arabian Gulf (PFLOAG), were fighting almost without international allies. They received some arms from China and, later, USSR, but virtually no support at the UN or in other fora where Third World issues have been publicised.[3]

The ruler whom Britain supported in Oman was a curious and quirkish tyrant, named Said bin Taimur. Born in 1910 he had become Sultan in 1932. Said bin Taimur had, during the course of his reign, become increasingly reclusive, and had, from 1958 onwards, decided to spend most of the year at his palace in Salala, Dhofar, 500 miles or so from the main part of Oman. He was a man who maintained a domestic retinue of slaves, and who sought to ban as much of the modern world as he could: there were only three primary schools in the whole country when he fell; spectacles were banned, as was most modern medicine. The result of his odious regime was that many of his subjects fled the country to seek work, while those who remained were victims of poverty, disease and ignorance. Yet while it was pretended that he was an independent ruler this was a sham: his army was officered and trained by British personnel, his Treasury, until the discovery of oil in 1967, was largely funded by Britain, and he was kept in power by British intervention, in the 1950s and again after 1965. A peculiar independent ruler, who had no embassies in any foreign country, whose interests at the UN were handled by Britain, and who allowed no foreign observers into the country. Oman was, in all but name, a British colony and Said bin Taimur a British client. All his main advisers were Britons.[4]

Throughout the period of his rule, this grotesque figure remained immune from criticism or investigation by the British press. David Holden, foreign correspondent of *The Sunday Times*, in his *Farewell to Arabia* (1966), gives a stark account of Whitehall's Omani press policy. Holden reports that after the one MoD press trip during the suppression of the Imamate revolt of the 1950s, and in the ten years up to the mid-1960s, only a dozen or so journalists were allowed into Oman.[5] There was, however, one notable exception to this restriction: a visit in 1955 by *The Times* correspondent, James Morris (later known as Jan Morris). This was positive coverage in style. Morris's visit was recorded in a later book, *Sultan in Oman*, which must rank as one of the more unctuous effusions of the imperial imagination. Early on in his account Morris meets the Sultan's slaves, who, he tells us, 'were it not for the matter of actual ownership, might better be described as retainers, so easy were their bondage and so cheerful their demeanor'. When Morris reaches Dhofar, the most oppressed and poverty-stricken of all the country's provinces, later to rise in revolt, it becomes 'a little backward paradise on the sea-shore, and the Sultan, who ran it like a private estate did not want to see it contaminated'.[6]

After giving his consistently benign views of the Sultanate, Morris then turns to the British officers who kept Said bin Taimur in power:

> It was a sad concomitant of fading empire that such openings for soldierly adventures abroad were getting fewer every year, for by a happy paradox nothing had done more to increase amity among peoples . . . The Sultan's private armies were among the last of their breed, still purveying the Small Arms Manual to illiterate peoples and tribesmen, and still managing to mould the most unlikely material into fine and faithful fighting forces. I liked them very much.[7]

This then was the most widely diffused, indeed the only, portrait of the Omani dungeon available when, in 1965, some of these self-same Sultan's solidiers, joined by others from British-trained armies in the Gulf, began a guerrilla war in Dhofar. A year later the loyalty so vaunted by Morris was spectacularly demonstrated when the Sultan's troops opened fire on him during a military parade in Salala, in an assassination attempt.

## The Dhofar War: 1965 – 70

The conflict in Dhofar, and the coverage of it, falls into four broad periods. The first is up to 1970: in this phase, fighting began in Dhofar and led to a situation, at the end of 1969, where the guerrillas controlled the whole of the province, with the exception of a coastal strip around Salala, where an RAF base and the Sultan's palace were located. The second phase was 1970 itself when, in the face of guerrilla success and the overall challenge they posed to the regime and the West's position in the Gulf, a *coup* was organised by MI6. After a shootout at his palace, the Sultan was overthrown, flown out of the country, and replaced by his son, Qabus. The third phase was from 1970 to the end of the war, in December 1975; during this phase, the British forces, supported from 1973 onwards by troops from Iran, gradually pushed the guerrillas back towards the frontier with South Yemen and, finally, reconquered the whole of the mountain territory. The fourth phase is that since 1975, during which the aftermath of the war itself and the continued British role in Oman have remained the object of considerable care by news managers.

For the first five years of the war, as the conflict gathered force, up to the July 1970 *coup,* not a single on-the-spot report was filed by any reporter from the British side in Dhofar. The number of articles appearing in the British press was insignificant. The Ministry of Defence and Foreign Office desks would appear to have put out almost nothing. It seems that no newspapers sought to investigate independently what was happening. There were no questions asked, and none answered. In March 1970 I was able to publish a first-hand report on the Dhofar war, and British involvement, in *The Sunday Times* (22 March 1970): but this was a report from behind rebel lines, beyond the control of the news managers.

### Phase two: The stage-managed coup

It was in July 1970 that the Ministry of Defence staged its first active publicity exercise in connection with the Dhofar war. The coverage of Oman had already begun to change perceptibly in the early part of 1970. For the first time since the war began, articles began to appear on the critical military situation. Such stories had the unmistakable tang of the background press briefing. Thus, the *Daily Telegraph* of 24 April 1970 wrote: 'If the Chinese-led intrusion of his southern provinces cannot be halted, the Sultan has intimated that he will leave his country to live in Europe.' *The Economist* of 18 July 1970 urged Britain to 'persuade [the Sultan] to go, before it is too late for an alternative ruler to hold the country together.' The Sultan had, of course, not intimated what the *Telegraph* ascribed to him and had studiously ignored all British advice: at one stage the British representative in the Gulf had considered turning up at Salala in a warship and coming aboard in full regalia to intimidate the Sultan, but this was, it was realised, a waste of time. *The Economist*'s urgings were more to the point: they smacked equally of the briefing room, since by 18 July the *coup* was all but carried out. It was to occur on 23 July.

Immediately after the Sultan was removed, the Ministry of Defence in London moved into action. First news of the *coup* was published a couple of days later and at once two delicate problems were finessed: one, who had organised the *coup*?; and two, if the *coup* were welcome and justified – a difficult thing to argue in such a philo-monarchical country as the UK – why had it not taken place earlier? Both were well handled in the press. Thus the *Financial Times* of 27 July 1970:

> Last night Whitehall denied that the British government had connived at the *coup*. The Foreign Office seemed genuinely short of detailed information. But there was evident relief at Sultan Said's deposition. The reactionary Sultan's inability to change his parsimonious ways has been the despair of the British government...

And, the same paper on 28 July 1970:

> No particular significance should be attached to the fact that the Foreign Office was in possession of information about the *coup* for nearly two days before it was released.

*The Guardian* told its readers on 27 July that 'the Foreign and Commonwealth Office were discreetly tossing their hats into the air', while *The Times*, a paper that had never criticised British policy in the period before the *coup*, now produced on 27 July an editorial of apparent relief: 'Change At Last in Muscat', it said, as if this is what it had been urging all along. Meanwhile its erstwhile Omani correspondent Morris was lamenting Said bin Taimur's departure – in *The Guardian*.

The news of the *coup* announced, it was time to fly selected correspondents out to Oman, courtesy of the RAF and in the charge of personnel from the MoD's press office. Fourteen in all were contacted, some of whom were unable to go. The result of this facility was a rash of articles putting out what the MoD wanted people to hear. First, the old Sultan was duly denigrated: his slaves, concubines and prisoners were paraded for all to see, to reassure readers that he did have to be ousted. Then, it was claimed that the population had rejoiced at the accession of the new Sultan. Describing Qabus's entry into the capital, Muscat, the *Daily Express* of 31 July 1970 reported: 'It was like Wembley Cup Tie day, Epsom Downs on Derby Day, and a fair-ground fantasy, all in one.' Thirdly, having taken care of the old Sultan, it was time to check any sympathy for the rebels who have revolted against his rule: these were, paper after paper told its readers, trained by Chinese officers. The rebellion had been taken over by fanatical communists.[8] No evidence for the Chinese officers was ever produced. There were none there. But it read well. Apart from Maoism and communism, the rebels were castigated for another activity which sprung from the briefer's clip-board; trying to emancipate women. *The Times* of 3 August 1970 delivered itself of a choice piece of garbled innuendo: 'There is also evidence that the guerrillas have begun to involve village women in their battle, and several cases of murder have been reported in the past three months.'

The 1970 press trip to Oman was a classic of its kind. None of those who went had ever been to Oman before. They were accompanied throughout by MoD press personnel. No independent witnesses or authorities were available in the country itself, and the British advisers who had helped Said bin Taimur were unavailable since they were 'on holiday'. They were probably in England, but no one could take the trouble to track them down, so near to home. Similarly, no one tried to get to Sultan Said who remained ensconced in a Park Lane hotel until his death two years later. Certain topics were discussed but not to be reported: the presence in Oman of SAS troops, British casualties, and of course, British responsibility for Said bin Taimur and his overthrow. Only one correspondent, Andrew Wilson of *The Observer*, suggested a prior British involvement. The crimes of the old Sultan had to be denounced without asking who had helped him carry them out: nameless Arabs, or perhaps *djinns*. The PFLOAG were crazed extremists – true, they had been right to revolt at first, but they were not right to do so later. Now that they were freeing women and reading Mao, they were beyond the pale.

**Phase three: winning the war, and the battle of information**
With their new Sandhurst-educated Sultan in power, the British officers running the Omani armed forces began to hit back against the guerrillas, and by the end of 1975 the war was over. The gradual improvement in the military situation, and the overall change in Oman following the lifting of economic restrictions, was reflected in the news coverage. Dhofar became a half-secret war, with a curtain selectively and occasionally lifted as, and to the extent that, the MoD wanted. The limits of this opening can be gauged from examining some sensitive issues on which coverage remained tightly controlled: the SAS, total British personnel deployed, casualties, counter-insurgency tactics and the role of the Iranians.

Reports of the SAS being in Oman began to appear in the latter part of 1970, but these stories, of official provenance, claimed the SAS was only *on training missions*. When in 1972 reports of SAS deaths appeared in the press, their combat role was half-admitted in standard vein:

Despite their official role as a training detachment, there is a strong suspicion in some quarters that the SAS are in fact fighting actively against the guerrillas. Local rulers are sensitive to accusations that they are receiving 'Colonialist' assistance. (*Daily Telegraph*, 1 January 1972)

Throughout the first years of the counter-offensive, the SAS remained part of what was referred to as BATT – the British Army Training Team. The official position was to deny a frontline role.

Mr Newens asked the Secretary of State for Defence what are the functions of the British Army training team at present serving in the Sultanate of Oman; and whether members of the SAS are part of the team.
Mr Mason: The British Army training team serving in Oman, which includes members of the SAS, gives training assistance to the Sultan's armed forces.
Mr Newens asked the Secretary of State for Defence if members of Her Majesty's Armed Forces not seconded to the service of the armed forces of the Sultan of Oman have been involved in hostilities in Dhofar; and in what capacity.
Mr Mason: The detachment of Service men operating the airfield at Salala and assisting in its defence have come under rebel attack from time to time, as have members of the team assisting in the training of the Sultan's armed forces. (*Hansard*, Written Answers, 30 April 1974)

The SAS in Dhofar were, as their chroniclers later proudly announced, a combat unit.[9] The treatment of the SAS was further obscured by the second sensitive item of the Dhofar war, the *overall number* of British personnel in Oman. The total number involved was never that high – 1000 – 2000 – but it was none the less too large for comfort in the UK. The result was that of four categories of British personnel, only one was ever officially answered for. Whitehall did admit to military personnel who still remained in the British armed forces and who were 'seconded' to the forces of the Omani Sultan. These numbered over 100 in 1974. But much larger numbers of personnel were not accounted for: serving British personnel not 'seconded', but guarding the RAF bases at Salala and on Masira Island (i.e. not part of Omani government forces): ex-army or ex-RAF personnel serving in the Sultan's forces but under British Command; and the members of the British Army Training Team, the SAS. An exchange in Parliament in 1974 exemplified how this sleight of hand worked:

Mr William Wilson asked the Secretary of State for Defence how many British Servicemen are seconded to the Sultan of Oman for service with the army and navy of Oman.
Mr Ian Gilmour: One hundred and twenty-three.
Mr William Wilson asked the Secretary of State for Defence how many

> British Servicemen are in Oman but not seconded to the forces of the
> Sultan of Oman.
> Mr Ian Gilmour: It is not our practice to disclose details of this kind.
> Mr William Wilson asked the Secretary of State for Defence how many
> British Servicemen are engaged in the British Army Training Team.
> Mr Ian Gilmour: It is not our practice to disclose details of this kind.
> Mr William Wilson asked the Secretary of State for Defence how many
> British Servicemen, either seconded or under contract, have died in
> Oman in the last two years.
> Mr Ian Gilmour: Three British Servicemen seconded to the Sultan of
> Oman have died in Oman in the last two years. Contract personnel are
> not serving members of Her Majesty's Forces and no figures are avail-
> able. (*Hansard*, 'Written Answers', 28 January 1974)

Everyone knew that the distinction between the 'seconded' and the other categories was factitious. The RAF personnel guarding the base were part of the combat operation. BATT too was on combat service. And the mercenaries were under British command and organised by recruiting agencies in Britain that operated with the support of the MoD. The trick of bulking up a fighting force by employing retired personnel is one that the Americans have used in Central America and Indochina for similar reasons.

Sleight of hand on numbers enabled Whitehall the easier to control discussion of a third sensitive item, casualties. Some individual reports of casualties were published after 1970, but as long as the war lasted no overall figures for British deaths in Oman were given, and the only totals were for the 'seconded' category. One listing published much later gives the names of 35 Britons who died in the ten years of the Dhofar war, of whom nine appeared to be contract personnel, and the remaining 26 'seconded'.[10]

Control of casualty announcements was achieved in various ways – by outright suppression, or by some standard subterfuges. When, in June 1972, some officers wounded as PFLOAG scored a hit on the Salala officers' mess were flown to a base in Cyprus, the hospital personnel were quoted as saying: 'This is very hush-hush. We have been told not to say anything'.[11] In 1974 an American reported from Salala that 'bodies have been flown back to Britain – in some cases listed as traffic fatalities, according to doctors here'.[12]

Controls of this kind applied to the conduct of the war itself. Official and semi-official mythology had it that the Dhofar war was a 'clean' war, a good old-fashioned bush war, one that soldiers could fight with a light heart; not a 'dirty' war like Ulster or Vietnam. Those wanting to get a rather less rosy and John Buchan-like view of the war did not have to exert themselves too much. American reporters visiting Dhofar gave examples of villages bombed by government planes (Jim Hoagland, in

*The Guardian*, 13 January 1975) and a graphic description of counter-insurgency tactics was given by one British officer, in the comparatively obscure columns of his regimental journal:

> We also burnt rebel villages and shot their goats and cows. Any enemy corpses we recovered were propped up in a corner of the Salala *suq* as a salutary lesson to any would-be freedom fighters.[13]

## Disinformation, and its accomplices

If news management involves restricting information in this way, and putting out upbeat coverage when available, it has an additional dimension, one also evident in Dhofar, namely disinformation, the spreading of false news to undermine the enemy and rally support for the cause. In the case of Dhofar, the press were more than willing to fall into line. The 1970 press briefings provide two fine examples of this – the claim that the guerrillas were led by Chinese officers, and the suggestion that they were extremists because they were altering the social position of women. It was not, however, sufficient to spread disinformation about PFLOAG, but also to do so about the Front's main backer, South Yemen. Thus, throughout the 1970s stories about South Yemen began to appear in the British press claiming there were Soviet bases there, and that the East German secret police had taken over in Aden.[14] Some of these stories originated in the right-wing Arab press, and some from the USA. But a significant number came via Oman, i.e. from British briefing personnel working there for the MoD or under some Omani government guise.[15]

A particularly delicate item in the news management was presented by the intervention in Oman of Iranian combat troops. They arrived in late 1973 and did a considerable amount of fighting in the last two years of the war. The arrival of the Iranian forces was at first kept secret, and the first news came only from rebel or South Yemeni sources.[16] This then prompted a series of organised coverage in the British press and later an official statement by the Shah to the *Daily Telegraph*.[17] There were, however, two particular problems about the Iranians. One was the evident scorn in which the British held them – the 'Geraniums' as they colloquially called them. The British mocked at the luxurious PX-type conditions in which the Iranian soldiers lived and suggested that many of their casualties were the result of their own careless use of firepower. Iranian casualties were also quite high. But the solution here was to keep reporters at a distance: no interviews with Iranian personnel or direct eye-witness reports of their actions ever came out. The UK government also tried to obscure the Iranians' use of RAF facilities.[18]

The other problem was that the Iranians were unpopular in the Arab world, and the Sultan paid a diplomatic price for this. Months after the intervention, in late 1974, Arab criticism of the Iranians increased. The news managers had the answer: stories were planted in the British press saying that the Iranians were leaving Oman. 'Persians Start Pullout', headlined *The Guardian* of 19 October 1974. 'The first phase of the gradual withdrawal of Persian troops from Oman is under way.... The Omani Foreign Ministry announced the withdrawal officially last week.' The *Financial Times* too, reported on 11 October 1974 that 'Iranian troops, which have aided local forces in fighting rebels in the Dhofar region of Oman, have begun withdrawing....' And, a month later on 15 November 1974, the same paper went further and stated that 'The Sultan's Armed Forces (SAF) are sufficiently confident of their position to have sent home the 2,000 man Iranian battle group dispatched to their aid by the Shah a year ago.' This was far from being the case. The Iranians were still in Oman. What had happened? An American reporter had the answer.

> Hoping to muffle Arab criticism of foreign involvement in the 10-year-old Dhofar war, ... Oman declared, before the Arab summit meeting in October, that an Iranian task force which had arrived in the country in December 1973, was returning.home. No mention of the arrival of a new brigade later that month was made, and its operations in the western mountains of Dhofar were not disclosed until last week. (Jim Hoagland, *International Herald Tribune*, 17 December 1974)

Iranian combat forces stayed in Oman until the onset of the Iranian revolution, in late 1978.

### Winning the peace: Oman and the press since 1975

News management of Oman did not cease with the defeat of the guerrillas in 1975. Rather, the mechanisms set up to deal with the press in the war period itself were maintained to serve other, peacetime, purposes. British military personnel continued to run the Sultan's armed forces, and the British bases were kept until March 1977. British personnel also still ran the Ministry of Information and the Oman Information Department, the Sultan's intelligence service.

One deft manoeuvre carried out by the news managers was to keep the Dhofar war alive once the guerrillas had been crushed. Having effectively defeated PFLOAG, it was now convenient and possible to claim that *some* guerrillas still operated in the mountains, and that a threat from South Yemen still existed. This justified the maintenance of tight security and news control, and encouraged Oman's new patrons, the Americans, to establish their commitment to Oman, supplying military aid and in 1980 taking over the British bases for use by the Rapid Development Force. Press coverage from the late 1970s onwards, therefore, portrayed Oman as somehow in the front line of the world fight against communism and as therefore deserving of substantial military support.

This piece of deception was particularly evident in 1979: the fall of the Shah and the overall crisis in the West Asian region provided Oman with an ideal opportunity to push its claims on the USA.[19] So a spate of articles stressing the threat to Oman from the PDRY appeared. There was no truth at all in the claim that South Yemen was somehow menacing Oman, but it suited the Sultan and his briefers to pretend this was so. Many were the journalists flown to the frontier positions near South Yemen, only to find a tranquil, inactive, mountain landscape. All this did not stop disinformation from appearing in the press. Thus, *The Guardian* of 14 June 1979 reported:

> Marxist guerrillas appear to be preparing for another effort to bring down the conservative Sultan of Oman, the ruler of an area of vital interest to the West.
>
> Diplomats said yesterday that the Popular Front for the Liberation of Oman began to regroup its forces soon after the overthrow of the Shah of Iran....
>
> 'Now that the post of policeman of the Gulf has become vacant with the departure of the Shah, it is only natural that there should be fresh trouble in Oman', one diplomat said. 'After all, Oman is too rich a prize to be left alone'.

There were, however, other items on the news management desk that had to be carefully handled. First, there was the matter of the Sultan's internal policies, 'democracy', and the absence thereof. When the new Sultan came to power in 1970, he had promised political change: but none had come. A government advertisement in 1972 had spoken of a 'calculated, Communist-inspired movement which proposes to crush existing democratic forms of government in the Gulf', without saying what these democratic forms were.[20] British journalists rarely commented on this subject, nor on the growing frictions between the Sultan and his advisers. It was left to the French press to offer a somewhat more realistic picture:

> Sultan Qabus who, on great occasions, likes to throw handfuls [of] silver coins from his balcony to the crowd of his subjects come to pay homage, is, similarly, faithful to tribal customs when he refuses to establish a state budget or to make it public. 'Why should I do it?' he told us, somewhat irritated by the question, 'this is a technical problem on which the vast majority of our subjects understand absolutely nothing. We take decisions which are in the interest of the country and it would be better that they be not questioned by ignorant people...'[21]

Even the *US News and World Report* (2 April 1979), the most right-wing of the major American weeklies, described Oman as 'lacking even rudimentary democratic institutions'.

Then, there was the matter of some of Oman's foreign connections. The war in Dhofar coincided with the conflict in Rhodesia, and with an official British policy of embargoing contact with that country. It emerged later that the British government had connived at supplies by British oil companies to Rhodesia throughout the period of UDI. It also emerged that similar connivance had operated in the case of Rhodesian – Omani relations. Direct flights between Oman and Rhodesia took place, supplying Rhodesian meat and other agricultural produce to Oman, in return for needed imports to the UDI regime in Salisbury. In 1978 Rhodesian helicopter pilots also trained in Dhofar (in terrain similar to that used by guerrillas on the Rhodesian – Mozambique frontier) and a number of ex-RAF, Rhodesian mercenaries, fought in the Sultan's armed forces. None of this could have taken place without official British knowledge. Yet it was only reported much later, by alternative press outlets in London.[22]

A third item of concern to the news managers was corruption. The flow of oil money into Oman and the economic opening after 1970 brought a flood of carpet-baggers and white-collar criminals into the country. John Townsend, economic adviser in the early 1970s, spoke of this in his 1976 book *Oman*. Some of these carpet-baggers were British, other Arab. Hardly a word about this corruption was to be found in the British press, even though two of the people most involved were operating under diplomatic cover from the Omani Embassy in London. It was left to the American press to highlight this and provide details.[23] A court case involving the arms manufacturers, Racal, did hit the papers, because it came to court in the UK. Later, in the early 1980s, when scandals broke out involving purchasing personnel in the Omani Ministry of Defence, the story was almost completely suppressed until one disgruntled British specialist, safely lodged in the USA, spoke his mind.[24]

There was, fourthly, the large and expanding intelligence operation in Oman. Part of this was American-run, a combination of free-market business deals and private espionage that Qabus set up soon after his accession to power.[25] No information, or names, involved in this operation, the details of which were widely known in Oman, were published in the main organs of the British press. Again, it was left to the US press and fringe papers in the UK to publish details of this espionage network operating in Oman.[26] Suppression of the intelligence dimension in Oman was especially noticeable in connection with one individual. Brigadier Tim Landon, a Sandhurst-educated cavalry officer and intelligence operative, later known as the 'white Sultan'. Landon had initially gone to Oman in 1965 and had formed a good working relationship with Qabus, then the heir-apparent, with whom he had studied at Sandhurst. It was Landon who, acting in liaison with MI6 and the MoD, organised the 1970 *coup*. He remained working there throughout the 1970s. Every diplomat, businessman and journalist who worked in Oman knew who Landon was, and what both his business and intelligence role was. Yet, until the 1984 Mark Thatcher case, his name did not appear in the mainstream British press.

## Mechanisms of control

The presentation of the news about Oman during the Dhofar war, and in the years preceding and following it, was therefore a fine example of information management work. This case study shows that management is not simply the result of one mechanism – censorship, or press collusion – but rests rather upon a layered complex of mechanisms. Four were of particular relevance in the case of the Dhofar war:

1. *The briefing process itself.* Studies of other news management operations, on domestic and foreign issues, have shown how this process works, and the customs and constraints involved. The Foreign Office, for example, operates a regular briefing system for correspondents – a private, individual series for diplomatic correspondents of the major British papers, a group meeting for more favoured correspondents, and a regular daily briefing meeting at which all foreign correspondents present in London can, upon receipt of accreditation, attend. Such briefings, like their domestic counterparts, are confidential and operate with the sanction that if the source is revealed, the briefing facilities will be withdrawn. In the case of Oman, of course, the briefing mechanism extended to the foreign country itself: correspondents visiting were chaperoned by MoD and Omani Ministry of Information officials (themselves 'seconded' from the Foreign Office).

An illustration of how the briefing system works was the 12.30 session of 4 January 1972, at which the reports of SAS deaths in Oman came up.[27] At this session, some non-British correspondents tried to press the Foreign Office briefers about what the SAS were doing in Oman. Archaic formulations were produced by the men in the front line: 'The SAS of course take action to defend themselves . . .'. 'We do not normally give information on troop dispositions.' When questioners persisted, a more senior official in the background bellowed: 'You're barking up the wrong tree, you know.' That, more or less, was that. The foreign journalists shrugged, and gave up. The handling of the 1970 *coup*, and the Iranian troop presence, were equally models of how the briefing system is used to befuddle and divert.

No account of the role of briefing in Oman would be complete without a note on the operations, and personnel out there on the ground. In particular, it is worth recording the many years of service in this particular domain of one Tony Ashworth, a personage known to every foreign journalist who has visited Oman since the middle 1970s and whose name no one has cared to print. Anthony Clayton Ashworth, born 1921, and until 1962 a serving member of the British armed forces, was from 1963 to 1967 First Secretary (Information) in the British High Commission in Aden, and then in 1968 became Director of the Regional Information Office for South-East Asia in Hong Kong. He later served in the British Embassy in Beirut, and in 1974 was 'seconded' to the Ministry of Information in Oman, where he remained for a decade. Ashworth was, by all appearances, a curious operative: his job in Aden included covert liaison with the guerrillas, as well as press work; he was in Hong Kong at a time when western disinformation against China, in the last years of the Cultural Revolution, was at its height and the Regional Information Office he ran was known to journalists in the Far East as the source of many anti-Chinese stories. In Oman, Ashworth oversaw the control of foreign journalists, and the disinformation campaign against PFLOAG, South Yemen and all who sympathised with them.[28]

*2. Censorship, and information suppression.* Censorship in the case of Oman was a reserve power, a sort of gold reserve or ultimate resort upon which the larger fiduciary issue of news management and self-censorship operated. Some aspects of the Oman operation pertained directly to British security and fell under the D-notice system: this included the fact that Masira was one of the points to which British V-bombers were to be dispersed in the event of a nuclear crisis. But others were imposed by the British officials running the war in Oman itself. Thus, special attention was given to suppressing news about the SAS: a 'World in Action' TV film crew who visited Oman in 1972 had to sign a written promise not to mention the SAS's combat role; a woman photographer, who in 1973 took a photograph of an SAS member with a kind of rifle she had never seen before, had the whole film confiscated.

An additional element of censorship was, however, present in the Oman coverage of one important British news outlet, and moulder of informed opinion, namely the BBC. For some years prior to the outbreak of the Dhofar war, the BBC had used, for its overseas transmissions, a relay station on the Omani island of Masira. While nothing was, it seems, written down, it was well 'understood' by the BBC that one of the conditions for continued use of this facility was that it did not publish broadcast material unwelcome to the Sultan of Oman. As the war progressed, listeners to the English and Arabic-language services of the BBC in Oman were increasingly struck by the Corporation's silence on the war, but attempts to nudge it forward by writing readers' letters, produced little response. The BBC's approach to Oman can be gauged from a report by one of its correspondents in 1966. He had visited Dhofar, and must have seen the war, the slaves, the poverty and the oppression. What he told his listeners was:

> The Sultan made it clear that the oil money will go for development. His present Development Department will be expanded to cope. He said he felt that in the interests of his deeply religious people changes should be gradual. He does not plan, at present, to borrow in advance on his oil revenue. The oil community, with their modern ideas, will be largely segregated from his people. From within, he told me, there is no agitation for change.

The BBC, of course, declined to tell its listeners anything different.

3. *Editorial ideology.* The efforts of the news managers would not, however, have had anything like the success they did, had they not been met half-way by the newspapers themselves. Here it is not so much a question of the failings of individual journalists, as of a whole ideology of news reporting, a set of practices, constraints, values and expectations which combined to make the press so compliant. Two practical constraints are simple enough: the need to get enough information to write a story and file by a certain copy date; and the restrictions of the law of libel. Both helped keep journalists in line in Oman. A third is expense: newspaper editors would think twice before allowing a journalist to spend extra time in a place as expensive as Oman even if they were allowed to. But these *material* components of the ideology of collusion were more than compounded by the *values* involved: the willingness of journalists to swallow what their briefers told them, and of editors to print it, and the lack of any critical activity on their part. It was obvious on many occasions that cover-ups and diversions were going on – from the total silence during the early guerrilla victories, and on the 1970 *coup*, and the SAS and Iranian combat roles.

Yet time and again British journalists simply reproduced what they were told. That this was not absolutely necessary was shown by those from other countries who visited Oman and wrote far more critical pieces – on the war itself, on the British involvement with the Sultan, on espionage, on corruption. Critical stories did appear on occasion in the British press, but they were not usually written by journalists who had gone to Oman. The majority of these appeared in fringe or low-circulation left-wing papers, or were stories by Americans reprinted in the British press (such as Joseph Fitchett and Jim Hoagland).[29] A fraction of the effort, time and expense put into chasing and doorstepping royalty, filmstars, high society adulterers and escaped train robbers would have yielded a very different picture of what was going on in Oman. The sickly comments of *The Guardian* and *The Times* on the demise of Said bin Taimur were not a result of official pressure, but of editorial decision, and preference.

The experiences I myself had in reporting on the war in Oman illustrate two sides of the argument on ideology: that the most effective block is the value-system of the British papers, *not* censorship, and that some alternative can, on some occasions, be put forward. In February 1970 I visited the guerrilla-held areas of Dhofar and on my return submitted an article to *The Times*. The article was taken, and rewritten to the point of emasculation by an editor who had himself served in the Arab world. Upon my protesting that, among other things, any mention of slaves had been removed, he looked up and said: 'Don't you know that all Arabs are liars?'. I withdrew the piece, took it to the *Sunday Times* 'Insight' team: there, one of the team, Lewis Chester, rewrote the piece and greatly improved it. It was then published.[30] Three years later when I again went to Dhofar, I submitted my piece on my return to the *Sunday Times* assuming on the basis of earlier experience this would be the place to publish it again. The piece was taken by the then foreign editor, Frank Giles. He decided it should not be published because it would need 'balance', i.e. a piece from the other side. This, of course, they did not have. So I submitted the article to *The Times*: the man then on the foreign desk, Nicholas Ashford, put the piece through, under the by line of 'A Special Correspondent'. It was duly published,[31] provoking some irritation from the Sultan's British cronies in the correspondence columns.

4. *The weakness of alternative sources.* These three mechanisms of control – briefing, suppression, ideology – would not have been so effective had there been a strong alternative source of information. It is true that even available alternative sources can be blotted out – as witness the debate on the arms race and the US – Soviet military balance in the late 1970s. In the case of Oman, however, the lack of autonomous observers on the ground was matched by their absence internationally. The lack of any sustained international criticism of the British role, with little of the clamour in the UN and the House of Commons that had accompanied the counter-insurgency in Aden, certainly made the job of the news managers all that easier. There was small external public pressure for a different press approach. A minority of MPs in the Labour Party, chief among them the committed anti-colonialist Stan Newens, did criticise Britain's role, and in December 1974 nearly 100 signed a motion condemning it: but this was as far as opposition got. British involvement in Oman never occasioned a debate in the House of Commons, or at a Labour Party Conference.

# Conclusion

The coverage of the mainstream British press on Oman can be contrasted not just with the facts as known from other, more critical, sources inside Oman, but also with the coverage in the press of other states. Thus, both the French and US press provided more material of a dissident nature on the military and commercial scandals of Oman than the British did, despite, or because of, the special British relationship with Oman. The Oman story is therefore a particularly striking case of press collusion over many years in a case where strategic interest, commercial advantage and publishing timidity interlocked.

Most suggestions on how to overcome the management of the news in Britain start with the supply side – the government and its briefers – and calls for changes there: more open government, the ability to name sources, freedom of information. These reforms are certainly desirable, but they are unlikely. Equal responsibility lies, however, somewhere beyond government control, namely with the news editors and reporters themselves, on the demand side. What is equally necessary, and far more possible, is a clear and resolute break with the conventions that have sustained the manipulation of news to date: a refusal to be silent on sensitive issues, a willingness to exert investigative power to delve into the facts, and a calm acceptance of the state's possible replies and pressures. It is the collusion of editors, as much as the cynicism of the news managers, that underlies the news management system. The state's news managers and censors are doing their job: it is time more editors and journalists did theirs. This, above all, is the information lesson of the Dhofar war.

# Notes

1. Michael Cockerell, Peter Hennessy and David Walker,*Sources Close to the Prime Minister*, London, 1985,Chapters 2 and 4.
2. The postwar record of British counter-insurgency is discussed in Julian Paget, *Counter-insurgency Campaigning*, London, 1965, and in my *Mercenaries:Counter-Insurgency in the Gulf*, Nottingham, 1977. In the latter I suggest that there were ten major such wars: Greece (1944-49); Palestine (1946-48); Malaya (1948-60); Kenya (1953-56); Cyprus (1955-59); Oman (1955-59); South Yemen (1963-67); Borneo (1961-65); Oman/Dhofar (1965-75); Northern Ireland (1969 onwards).
3. On the Dhofar war, see my *Arabia without Sultans*, Penguin, 1974, Part 3; *Mercenaries;* John Akehurst, *We won a War*, London, 1982; Ranulph Fiennes, *Where Soldiers Fear to Tread*, London, 1975.
4. On the Omani background, see *Arabia without Sultans*, Chapter 9, and John Townsend, *Oman*, London, 1976, Chapter 3.
5. David Holden, *Farewell to Arabia*, London, 1966, pp.218-19.
6. James Morris, *Sultan in Oman*, London, 1957, pp.13, 31.
7. Ibid., p.135.
8. *The Times*, 3 August 1970; *The Guardian* 3 August 1970; *Daily Express*, 29 July 1970; *Daily Telegraph*, 23 April 1971,etc. Later British accounts – Akehurst, Fiennes, Jeapes – make no mention of this *canard*.
9. Colonel Tony Jeapes, *SAS: Operation Oman*, London, 1980. Tony Geraghty, *Who Dares Wins*, London, 1980, Chapter 5.

10. Akehurst, op.cit., pp. ix-x.
11. *Daily Express*, 15 June 1972.
12. Joseph Fitchett, *The Observer*, 3 March 1974.
13. Captain N.G.R. Hepworth, 'The Unknown War', in *The White Horse and Fleur de Lys*, Journal of the King's Regiment, Vol. VI, No. 6, Winter 1970.
14. For example, on Soviet 'bases' in South Yemen, see *The Times*, 30 December 1970; later variations in Robert Moss, 'Threat to the Gulf: Soviet Buildup in South Yemen', *Daily Telegraph* 25 October 1978; Gordon Brook-Shepherd, 'South Yemen falls under heel of new Gestapo', *Daily Telegraph*, 5 February 1978.
15. Amongst the unattributed briefing material used by sections of the British press was a periodical called *South Yemen Report* which was mailed to journalists interested in the area from a fictitious *Post Restante* in Paris. This four-page publication, written in fluent English, contained stories of corruption, Soviet and Cuban interference, sexual misbehaviour and the like in South Yemen. Chunks of it appeared almost verbatim in newspaper articles. It was a low-scale but in its own way effective disinformation activity.
16. *The Observer*, 6 January 1974; *Le Monde*, 2 January 1974.
17. *Daily Telegraph*, 12 February 1974.
18. Hansard, *Written Answers*, 28 January 1974, where the Minister of Defence, Ian Gilmour, denied that any British facilities in Oman had been made available to Iranian forces. Yet Qabus himself confirmed a month later that the Iranians were using the Salala base (*al-Hawadeth*, Beirut, 8 February 1974).
19. For appeals to the USA see *Newsweek*, 19 February, 1979: in June 1980 the USA signed a defence agreement with Oman, under which it provided guarantees to Oman and acquired use of several bases in the Sultanese, including Salala and Thumrait in Dhofar.
20. *Financial Times*, 17 November 1972.
21. *Le Monde*, 30-31 May 1971.
22. *New African*, October 1979; *Time Out*, 5-11 October 1979. Also *The Observer* 5 February 1984.
23. Jim Hoagland, *Washington Post*, 17 September 1975, 'As Espionage, Profit Meet'. Townsend has some anonymous hints on this topic in his *Oman*.
24. *The Guardian*, 16 August 1984.
25. Hoagland, as note 31.
26. As note 24, and *New York Times*, 26 March 1985.
27. My own observations.
28. Ashworth was, in his later years, given to making wild claims that even his more credulous listeners found hard to swallow. Thus he told more than one visiting journalist that I was the head of KGB Information in Western Europe, and he had a way of accusing any people he disliked of being 'communists'. It is believed that the British Embassy in Oman became a little irritated by his conduct, but this merely reflected a conflict between different sections of the British state, not a conflict between the UK and an autonomous Omani bureaucracy.
29. These included *Time Out, Black Dwarf, 7 Days, Red Mole, Tribune, Morning Star*, and the Guardian Diary 'Open File', written by Martin Walker. One paper that did pursue the Sultan and Landon in the UK was the local paper covering the region where they bought their English estates (*Newbury Weekly News* 5 October 1978).
30. *Sunday Times*, 22 March 1970.
31. *The Times*, 13 May 1973.

# 10 The media and politics in Northern Ireland
## Paul Arthur

### 'The oxygen of publicity'

When BBC journalists, supported by their colleagues at ITN, went on strike on 7 August 1985 over the banning of a 'Real Lives' programme featuring Martin McGuinness of Provisional Sinn Fein (PSF) and Gregory Campbell of the Democratic Unionist Party (DUP), Peter Fiddick of *The Guardian* described it as 'the greatest consitutional crisis in the history of British broadcasting'. In Northern Ireland the issue was seen more mundanely. The NUJ picketed BBC headquarters and put on repeated showings of the banned programme for the passing public. Their reaction was mixed. A DUP councillor took photographs of the picketers; and a passer-by shouted, 'Parasites. If the journalists had come out ten years ago there would have been no troubles'.[1]

The precise meaning of the ejaculation – and indeed, of the politico-photographer's motivation – is not immediately obvious. The latter might conceivably be threat, and the former a reference to the BBC's role during the Ulster Workers' Council (UWC) strike of 1974 when the medium inadvertently aided the strikers by fulfilling the public duty of broadcasting news. Whatever the reasons, the Northern Ireland public were not concerned with the media's incestuous analysis of their own role. Locals could reach for their own sensitive, and selective, antennae. Censorship meant one of two things: the ban was yet another attempt to exorcise the 'risen people' in the shape of PSF, or it was an example of woolly-minded liberalism tilting at windmills: 'If the Government wishes to proscribe Sinn Fein and prevent them gaining access to the media, they should ban them totally and not just take off a programme', was the opinion of Gregory Campbell, a victim, of course, of the BBC Governors' decision.

In the wake of the strike several (short-term?) lessons emerged. Neither the BBC management nor its Board of Governors had covered themselves in glory. Management had not followed the peculiarly stringent precautions attached to documentaries concerned with Northern Ireland. The Governors had subjected themselves cravenly to the

Home Secretary's 'request' that the film be not shown and thereby illustrated that particular Board's political composition and its fears of
further government cuts into the BBC's finances. The decision to show
an amended version of the banned documentary complete with additional material on the effects of IRA violence, was little more than an
acceptance of the inevitable. The BBC's reputation had been damaged
– perhaps not irrevocably, but its enemies abroad were able to make
much of its alleged 'independence' and of its role as a propaganda wing
of government. Politicians fared badly too; their interference was re-
sented, and the Home Secretary, Leon Brittan, was moved in a government reshuffle a month later, the authentic sacrificial lamb of the whole
episode.

But the fundamental issues had not been decided. The distinction
between 'a request' and overt (or covert) pressure was still not clear. It
may be that that can be decided only piecemeal in the context of the
political climate of the day. The temporary ban had had the adverse
effect of turning the 'oxygen of publicity' on the IRA/SF beyond their
wildest dreams. A *Financial Times* leader (7 August) pointed to the
wider implications: 'On the political level the Government must make
up its mind about Sinn Fein, the political wing of the IRA. If Sinn Fein
candidates are allowed, even encouraged, to stand for Parliament and in
local elections, it is inconsistent to deny them air-time'. Hence, what
may have led to some telephone protests and innocuous questions in the
House, had the documentary been shown, was now transformed into
profound questioning of Britain's role in Northern Ireland.

For broadcasters the issues of self-censorship, of reference upwards,
of the relationship between the documentary and the news service, and
of the concept of moral neutrality, all of these still hung in the air. The
first two were perennials which tend to sort themselves out in the political bargaining of daily news coverage. The last two concerned themselves with growing professionalism and a change in the internal
balance in the BBC. Asa Briggs[2] puts the present crisis into its proper
perspective in a detailed study of nine historic occasions when there had
been obvious tension and conflict (and misjudgement) between the
BBC and the government of the day. He asserts that the rows took on a
new dimension in the 1960s when the separation of documentary features
from current affairs posed organisational as well as policy problems:

> It was in face of the increasing professionalism of the greatly extended
> news and documentary services that the Governors prodded by the
> Government, which was finding it increasingly difficult to govern the
> country, felt during the late 1960s and early 1970s that they ought to be
> more actively engaged in 'governing the BBC'.

The 'Real Lives' crisis may have brought this particular problem to a head. In another important respect, however, it seemed to have muddied the waters. In his original letter to Stuart Young, Chairman of the Board of Governors, the Home Secretary had stated, 'Even if the programme and any surrounding material were, as a whole, to present terrorist organisations in a wholly unfavourable light, I would still ask you not to permit it to be broadcast'. There seems little doubt that the documentary was *not* morally neutral.

Laurence Marks in *The Observer* (4 August) asserts that one 'would have to be historically illiterate not to catch the echoes of Nuremburg.... One comes away from the film more deeply repelled by the extremists of both communities than one normally does from routine slam-bang interviewing'. In this instance the producer was simply responding to the parameters laid down by a former BBC Chairman, Lord Hill, and a former Northern Ireland Controller, Dick Francis. In a letter to the Home Secretary in November 1971, Lord Hill accepted that there were limitations to broadcasting in Northern Ireland: 'as between the government and the opposition, as between the two communities in Northern Ireland, the BBC has a duty to be impartial no less than in the rest of the United Kingdom. But, as between the British Army and the gunmen the BBC is not and cannot be impartial'.[3] And in an address to The Royal Institute of International Affairs, Dick Francis stated, 'The experience in Northern Ireland, where communities and Governments are in conflict but not in a state of emergency or a state of war, suggests a greater need than ever for the media to function as the Fourth Estate, distinct from the Executive, the legislature and the judiciary.'[4] Leon Brittan's letter was no less than an attempt to set even more stringent restrictions on broadcasting.

Much, but not all, of the informed comment on the controversy ignored the impact of the decision on the daily lives of the people of Northern Ireland. They were aware that Martin McGuinness had been invited, in his capacity as an elected representative, to the official opening of Radio Foyle on 28 June by the Board of Governors. And they heard him being interviewed on *local* radio as to why he was being banned from the national network. They would have found little difficulty agreeing with *The Guardian* leader (1 August), 'To assert, with Mrs Thatcher, that he may be reported briefly at Stormont (if he turns up) but not on television, because he's a terrorist, is to get the broadcasters to rationalise a deeply hypocritical stance which the Government, for its own political reasons, does not wish to resolve'. Understandably, the local population responded with a mixture of cynicism, fatalism and introspection.

**A most contrary region**
Northern Ireland is a tiny segment of the United Kingdom with a population less than 3 per cent of the total and a landmass no larger than that
of Yorkshire. Formally British, it does not appear to fit into the usual
parameters of British political practice because 'in Ulster the great, permanent question of political philosophy – the moral basis of authority,
and of the right to resist authority, the relationship between law and
force and that between nationality and political allegiance – were being
debated.'[5] Of course, these fundamentals existed long before the outbreak of the present 'Troubles' in 1968, and hence, long before the
media took a sustained interest in the problem – for example, press
coverage increased 500 per cent between the first and second civil rights
marches in late 1968. And as the political violence continued and solutions disappeared in the mists of time, the media's conception of the
problem changed likewise.
    Originally it was viewed as 'part of the home country rather than a
colonial possession'. As late as 1972 reporters spoke of it as 'the biggest
home news story since the war'. Many of them may have taken on board
the advice of the fictional Lord Copper, Evelyn Waugh's press baron:

> What the British public wants first, last, and all the time is News. Re-
> member that the Patriots are in the right and are going to win....But they
> must win quickly. The British public have no interest in a war which
> drags on indecisively. A few sharp victories, some conspicuous acts of
> personal bravery on the Patriot side and a colourful entry into the capi-
> tal. That is *The Beast* Policy for the War.[6]

But the 'war' did drag on indecisively and it was not always clear who
were the Patriots and who the Traitors. Better to set it in an external
environment:

> As the possibility of British withdrawal entered the political agenda,
> newsmen tended to talk about it less as a home news story. Certainly, in
> broadcasting's output 'Northern Ireland' is very much a story category
> which stands apart from the rest of British coverage. It comes over as at
> best only ambiguously British, as violence is thought to be an un-British
> way of solving political problems.[7]

    If, in broadcasting terms, Northern Ireland has become less British,
that perception has not diminished the integrity of the quarrel. It may
stiffen republican resolve that 'the Brits' are on their way out, and Loyalist confirmation of perfidious Albion and the need to look to their own
defence. But it is unlikely that mainland coverage of events has shaped
in any fundamental sense attitudes in Northern Ireland. The historian,
George Boyce, rightly asserts that the province is 'a part of the world

where public opinion has, up to now, been born, not made'.[8]

The explanation lies in the communal nature of society. Frank Burton's study of a (republican) community under stress captures its hermetic quality:

> Precisely because the community manages to contain and disperse the troubles into its institutional framework, its normative structure and its symbolic universe, it manages to prevent the dominance of external social control. In turn, the community retains enough of its solidarity to allow the militant activists to continue the politics of violence . . . . The possibility of an IRA campaign is dependent in this respect on the social structure of its community being able to withstand the deleterious consequences that urban guerrilla activity creates.[9]

Northern Ireland is composed of an interlocking series of communities like 'Anro' – Burton's pseudonymous Belfast working-class community. The sense of territorial integrity is reinforced by a staple diet of self-imposed censorship: one read one's own, and where one had to rely on a 'neutral' source such as television, one brought one's own prejudices and interpretations. *The Belfast Newsletter* had an overwhelmingly Protestant readership matched on its side of the sectarian divide by the (Catholic) *Irish News*. Simon Winchester described them as 'the pepper and salt of Ulster journalism: they reported each day's events with about the coordination and agreement one might expect of the *Wall Street Journal* and the *Morning Star*.'[10] Only the evening *Belfast Telegraph*, both in readership and in content, held out the potential as a cross-community integrator.

These three large provincial dailies were supplemented by 30 or so regional weekly newspapers, all of them faithful to their readers' political outlook. In his semi-autobiographical account of life in the Bogside, Eamonn McCann writes of how the prevailing ideology sustained by the Church, the schools and the Nationalist Party was supplemented by the *Derry Journal*,

> bitterly anti-Unionist, passionately pro-Fianna Fail, reverently Catholic and hysterically anti-communist. It never wrote 'Northern Ireland', always ' "Northern" Ireland'; never 'Londonderry', always ' "London" derry'. Even the punctuation was patriotic.[11]

The outbreak of communal violence after 1968 led to a tremendous outgrowth of community newspapers and of political pamphlets, as if the usual sources of information were tainted. This flowering had the additional bonus of cementing communal solidarity. And where news-sheets could not be published rapidly enough, some localities turned to pirate radios. One, Radio Free Lough Neagh, was resurrected solely to campaign for the nationalisation of fishing rights in the largest lake in the British Isles. Others were more defensive and offensive. Radio Free Belfast was created in the Falls Road area in August 1969 and after a Loyalist incursion which the residents perceived as a pogrom. An early broadcast stated bluntly: 'We have not erected barricades to keep Catholic and Protestant apart', but 'because the people of the barricaded districts are terrified and must be protected against a possible repetition of the savagery of 14 and 15 August'.[12] Such idealism was soon dimmed when control of the radio station passed into the hands of an older Republican generation who were in the process of launching the Provisional movement.

The Shankill Road produced its own loyalist variant in Radio Orange which the Home Secretary, Jim Callaghan, considered to be 'far more pernicious'. It launched the careers of two voluble ladies, Orange Lily and Roaring Meg, who preached a daily hymn of hate against Catholics. Callaghan recalls one broadcast on 7 September 1969:

> While a fairly minor confrontation was going on in Percy Street, Orange Lily called on every able-bodied man to go to the area, which lies between the Falls Road and the Shankill. Protestants poured out in response to the appeal and the result was a full-blown riot during which our troops had to use CS gas.[13]

Of course, the more legitimate broadcasting medium was frequently open to the charge that it had induced riots through fulfilling its duty, but at least it had the excuse that that was an unfortunate and unwitting side-effect. Pirate radios were not prevalent but they could heighten communal polarisation and their existence was another instance of the necessity to rely on one's own interpretation of events.

Continuing communal conflict provided an additional insight into the role of the media in Northern Ireland – the ambivalent and the ambiguous status of the BBC. Rex Cathcart, historian of the BBC in Northern Ireland, delineates three strategies which the Corporation adopted over the past 60 years. The first occurred during the pre-war period when 'the BBC ignored the division and sought to prevent any of its manifestations from impinging on programmes. This was an abdication of social responsibility.'[14] In fact, Cathcart produces impressive evidence which demonstrates the extent to which BBC Northern Ireland was beholden to the Unionist establishment. He quotes the second Station Director, Gerald Beadle:

> When I arrived in Northern Ireland I was made to feel for the first time in my life that I was a person of some public importance...I was invited to become a member of the Ulster Club, where almost daily I met members of the Government; the Governor, the Duke of Abercorn, who was

immensely helpful and friendly, and Lord Craigavon, the Prime Minister, was a keen supporter of our work. In effect I was made a member of the Establishment.[15]

His successors were to enjoy the same acclaim with the result that the BBC was perceived by the minority as a propaganda arm of government. On such sensitive issues as the broadcasting of Gaelic sport results on a Sunday, of finding a place for the Irish language in the schedules, of cooperating in any manner with the Irish broadcasting service, Radio Eireann, on all of these issues, Belfast bowed to the wishes of the Unionist government. (In the light of the 'Real Lives' controversy it is interesting to note that as early as 1940 the Regional Director had established the principle of prior consultation before any commitments were made which might either directly or indirectly impinge on Northern Ireland.)

This strategy was succeeded in the post-war era by a desire to bring both sides of society together:

> The feeling that this should be done without provoking vociferous and possibly violent reaction from the unionist majority meant that the positive aspects of community relations were emphasised and the negative underplayed. A consensus emerged which had a false basis. When the civil rights movement attempted to give it a real basis, the BBC's strategy became irrelevant.[16]

In fact, it seems that it unwittingly contributed to the promotion of the false confidence which was to launch the Prime Minister, Terence O'Neill, on his reform programme. That, in its turn, led to the formation of the civil rights movement, uncontrollable tension inside the 'Unionist family', and the spiral of political violence which ensued.

It is not suggested that the BBC must bear prime responsibility for the outbreak of the 'Troubles'. The point is more delicate. In a divided society the BBC appeared to the minority to be part of an adversarial system when what was essential was a medium for promoting coalescent attitudes – not necessarily as a form of blatant social engineering but simply as a recognition of the realities of political division. Because the newspaper industry was not homogeneous and could reflect with a reasonable degree of proportionality the sectarian nature of society, it was not open to that charge. Some change in approach occurred in 1959 with the establishment of Ulster Television (UTV), the commercial channel, which could not afford (literally) to alienate an entire section of the population. But, as Cathcart points out, the BBC made haste slowly on the bandwagon of false consensus.

It is instructive to look at the example of Dutch television to see whether any lessons can be learned from a divided society which oper-

ated a form of consociational democracy. For most of the twentieth century the Netherlands operated a system of *verzuiling* whereby resources
were allocated in proportion to a community's political bargaining
power, and each political bloc organised its own destiny. The same held
for broadcasting until the introduction of a national television service.
The technology proved too expensive to set up several bloc television
stations. But that did not prevent cooperation:

> Until the mid-1960s there was only one channel on Dutch television.
> Every organisation had its own evening to broadcast documentaries,
> current affairs programmes, shows, church services – everything with
> its own Catholic, Protestant and Socialist flavour. With people watching
> every night, television broke the isolation of the pillars and opened the
> window to show how the other half lived. With only one channel, people
> were 'forced' to look at other ideologies and religions and were surprised
> to find that they were human too.[17]

By the 1960s it was too late for the BBC region to make this abrupt
change, and in any case broadcasting is part of the political environment. Power-sharing on the air would have been at odds with an adversarial political system. So the BBC's third and current strategy, honed in
the hostile environment of incipient civil war, has been 'to reflect the
whole of society as it is, in its negative and its positive aspects....The
price of the strategy is that neither community is satisfied, for each
manifests exclusive political and cultural attitudes, and harbours the
ultimate determination that the other side will not be seen or heard.'[18]
Cathcart may have overstated the case at this point. Since 1969 Northern Ireland has been governed by 'the politics of the last atrocity'; that
is, people react to the latest political violence rather than work at
reaching agreement through well-defined strategies. In so far as they
consider broadcasting policy it is along the lines of individual programmes – does it enhance or denigrate my cause? There is a feeling,
too, particularly among hardline Loyalists, that salami tactics are being
used in broadcasting as they are in the wider political sphere. Thus, just
as the politicians are attempting to impose power-sharing (by stealth if
necessary) so the broadcasters are undermining the 'purity' of Ulster's
cause. But the power of the broadcaster comes fairly low down the list
of priorities to save Ulster or to move towards a united Ireland. The
population has, it needs to be stated again, its own selective antennae.

### The Irish dimension

A proper consideration of the 'Troubles' on the media cannot be constrained within the bounds of the United Kingdom. Much of the debate
concerned with the principles surrounding the 'Real Lives' controversy
has taken place already in the Irish media. Besides, RTE (the Irish

broadcasting system) is in the unusual position that it suffers from the same asymmetry as Anglo-Irish relations; that is, as a small broadcasting system on the periphery of one of the most sophisticated media in the world it is conscious that it could lose its independence in a wave of Anglo-American culture – *and* it has the means to influence the debate within Northern Ireland by beaming in its programmes.

RTE was inaugurated in December 1961 through the Broadcasting Act 1960. It reflected a more authoritarian political culture by permitting the Minister for Posts and Telegraphs the right to appoint or remove from office the members of the RTE Authority (a statutory, independent authority responsible for all broadcasting) and the right to issue directives in regard to broadcast matter: in 1967, for example, an RTE news team was prevented from going to North Vietnam. The government made no secret of its ultimate authority. The Taoiseach, Sean Lemass, told the Dail in 1966, just as current affairs programming was coming into its own: 'The government reject the view that Radio Telefis Eireann should be, either generally, or in regard to its current affairs and news programmes, completely independent of government supervision'. Martin McLoone describes this as being more 'Gaullist' than 'Reithian' in its interpretation of public broadcasting.[19] Indeed, in 1972 the Minister sacked the whole of the RTE Authority over the broadcasting of a report of an interview with a Provisional IRA spokesman.

Dublin's more censorious attitude towards terrorism simply reflects the proximity of its threat to the stability of the Republic. (In May 1974 UDA car bombs claimed 28 lives in the space of three hours in Monaghan and Dublin – still the most horrendous single incident of the present Troubles). Hence in November 1971 the Minister issued a directive under section 31 of the Broadcasting Authority Act, 'to refrain from broadcasting any matter that could be calculated to promote the aims and activities of any organisation which engages in, encourages or advocates the attaining of any particular objective by violent means'. Another directive was issued in October 1976 forbidding broadcasts or reports of interviews with members of a number of republican organisations and of organisations proscribed in Northern Ireland by the British government.

The success of this policy is dubious in the light of Britain's ambiguous and inconsistent policy; and it is conceivable that censorship may have hardened republican determination. In that respect the evidence of a former Provisional to the New Ireland Forum (3 November 1983) is revealing:

> I believe that the operation of section 31 of the Broadcasting Act in the Republic has had an extraordinary effect within the republican govern-

ment. It has frozen out the moderate leaders and allowed the hardline Republicans from the Six Counties to gain total dominance.

The veracity of this opinion cannot be checked, and certainly it is unlikely to have little influence on the man who was responsible for the 1976 directive. Conor Cruise O'Brien was the Minister for Posts and Telegraphs in the Coalition Government between 1973-77. His period in office is noted for its singleminded campaign against all forms of support for terrorism. He particularly excoriated the attitude of mind which he described as '"unilateral liberalism" sensitive exclusively to threats to liberty seen as emanating from the democratic state itself' but 'curiously phlegmatic about threats to liberty from the enemies of that state'.[20]

Much of his considerable wrath was reserved for those broadcasters who indulged in a 'kind of neutral professionalism, indifferent to social consequences'. They unwittingly stood by the cause of terrorism:

> Just as violence is attracted to the camera, so the camera is attracted to violence; it is a case of love at first sight on both sides. This is of course due not just to the perversity of cameramen or broadcasters, but to the fascination which violence has for so many people – especially for people who can witness or hear about it happening to others from the safety of their own living room.[21]

O'Brien's crusade was not conducted solely at a philosophical level – witness the presence of section 31. Nor was he slow to criticise the BBC. During the UWC strike in 1974, he rang the BBC to ask whether Sir Charles Curran, the Director General, was aware of the nature of broadcasts during the strike. Similarly, in 1976, in an address to the European Broadcasting Union, and in the presence of Sir Charles, he castigated the role of the BBC:

> if the faces and words of the IRA Godfathers are wafted into our living rooms here in Dublin they come to us by courtesy of British broadcasting. The central purpose of the IRA is to 'break the connection' between Ireland and England. Yet it is only in virtue of that connection, in terms of broadcasting, that the IRA has access to the viewing and listening public in Ireland. And it has used that connection to try to win support for its fanatical and lethal anti-British campaign.[22]

It is a curious feature of contemporary Anglo-Irish relations that these pre-Thatcherite musings should emanate from Dublin. Surprisingly – with the exception of the media and the chattering class – they have caused little public debate in Ireland. It may be a more authoritarian structure or it may simply be a lack of national hypocrisy, a recognition that 'liberty' is divisible. Whatever the reason, it has removed from journalists and broadcasters the constraint of self-censorship and firmly placed the onus of responsibility where it should belong – with government. Its educative qualities are dubious, but no less so than the 'spontaneous' debates which arise from time to time in Britain when freedom of information is called into question.

The 'Real Lives' controversy is the last in a line of such issues, significant for the compliance of the Governors and the crude nature of the Home Secretary's request. But paradoxically it may have been less damaging to freedom of speech than the insidious growth of neutral professionalism in relation to Ireland.

## The lesson of Northern Ireland

It has not been the purpose of this chapter to draw up a moral ledger of the media's misdemeanours in Ireland. There are no shortages of such examples.[23] One immediately thinks of a deliberate policy of 'misinformation' which occurred when the Widgery Tribunal reported on 'Bloody Sunday'.[24] One recognises the growing professionalism of Army and RUC public relations policy. One appreciates that mistaken policies are pursued. Probably the most blatant was the BBC's coverage of the UWC strike which gave unintentional succour to the strikers, and which, according to Robert Fisk, 'undermined the authority of the state broadcasting service'. Three years later when loyalists attempted another 'constitutional stoppage' the BBC demonstrated that it had learned the lessons of 1974:

> It isn't sufficient where society is under threat to simply report incidents. The question is whether the threat is having any effect....It is not enough to go by the simple criterion of reporting abnormalities. It is just as important to give a measure of the situation in general.[25]

The fundamental weakness of the media's role in Northern Ireland concerns human nature, 'decontextualisation' and the limitations of the orthodox consensus.

Human nature speaks for itself – the reliance on official handouts married to a sense of distaste and despair at what appears, through British eyes, to be a nasty and incomprehensible civil war. Every serious journalist who has commented on Northern Ireland has noted the shortcomings of his profession. Thus, Andrew Stephen of the *Observer*: 'The lazy national newspaperman can stay in his hotel room and lift all his material from the comprehensive local radio and television news coverage and the *Belfast Telegraph* and still appear well informed.'[26] Journalists and broadcasters are probably no more venal than any other profession. It is, in general, their lack of context, which adds to their difficulties.

'Decontextualisation' must be seen at two overlapping levels. The most obvious is the alien environment and culture with which they are presented in Northern Ireland – 'alien' because on the surface it appears to be British but all one's training and instincts suggest otherwise. In a content analysis of the reporting of Northern Ireland in the press, radio and television reported in Belfast, Dublin and London prepared for UNESCO, Philip Elliott has two conclusions worthy of note. One concerns the predominance of violence or the enforcement of the law. Only one third of the reports dealt with politics and other subjects. Secondly, violence on the mainland received more attention in the British media

> which reflects a difference between the two societies. In Britain the leaders of the society and the forces of law and order mobilised in response to the threat. The reporting of the incident [the Guildford pub bombing in 1974] performed a function which might be termed *social cauterisation*. Each day the news media applied a new dressing to the wound society had suffered.[27]

The British media could not empathise with the people in Northern Ireland in the same fashion because they were not a united people and sympathy towards one was an act of hostility towards another.

At a more fundamental level the absence of context meant more than the overtly ahistorical nature of reporting:

> This concentration on the documentation of the present leaves little space for assessing the importance of the familiar, the old and the commonplace which happens all the time. Time and events take on a discrete quality. 'Context' also implies the cultural frame of reference that may be provided by history.

Burton explains this in the context of 'Anro' as being about different frames of reference. For the locals 'the cumulative phenomenon of oppression' is an everyday occurrence. It is not simply about gun battles but about a selective folk memory and the daily grind of existence.

More mundanely, individual incidents are recorded through different cultural lenses: 'within the community's context a construction of events takes place of which the reporter is either ignorant or feels is of no relevance for his own purposes'. This often leads to a lack of 'feel': 'The process of constructing the reality of an event from a particular frame of reference is also a process of creating meaning. Clearly the significance that is attached to incidents in the troubles is consequential for the continuation or cessation of the war'.[28] The local community has to perform its own social cauterisation which is usually at odds with that of the establishment. The reporting of events can broaden the divide irrespective of the good intentions of the journalist. In the present context the temptation to view Northern Ireland as a sideshow only enhances the nature of the polarisation by encouraging a sense of distance.

Distance, too, is to be found in the superficiality of much of the reporting. Philip Schlesinger has been the most searching critic of the media's relationship to the state. He stresses the integral links between the *internal* policing of dissent through mechanisms of control such as the media and the *international* dimension. The media's voluntary self-restraint permits it to retain their public credibility, and the 'state's ideological capital remains intact' by avoiding evident censorship. By representing terrorism as the initiating force, state violence can be seen as purely 'responsive', and draconian legislation such as the Prevention of Terrorism Act given a gloss. By presenting all forms of terrorism as irrational activity, it becomes much easier to woo public opinion. All of this is possible if decontextualisation reigns supreme.

In the local setting this is presented as the development of a 'public order' policy on Northern Ireland by the broadcasting authorities. It contains three elements:

> First, they generally support the efforts of the security forces in law enforcement. Second, they delegitimise 'extremism' and 'terrorism', especially that of the IRA, which is presented as the principal enemy and is the initiating cause of violence. Finally, there is a stress upon the evidence of 'inflammatory' coverage. The first two characteristics are shared by much of the press.

The result has tended to be 'an "affirmatory ritual", one in which press and broadcasting have emphasised the integrity of the social order'.[29]

It may well be more advantageous to support the 'affirmatory ritual' for the benefit of the whole of society. In the context of Ireland, O'Brien's 'repression' has at least the merit of being honest and consistent, and compromises the media less than stop–go voluntary self-restraint. In the context of Northern Ireland the affirmatory ritual harms the healing process because it identifies the media as part of a distant Establishment. The integrity of the Ulster quarrel rises above media manipulation.

## Notes

1. Cited in the *Irish Times*, 8 August 1985.
2. 'The right to know is of crucial importance', *Financial Times* 10 August 1985.
3. Cited in P. Schlesinger, *Putting Reality Together* London: Constable, 1978, p.212.
4. Cited in the *Irish Times*, 23 February 1977.
5. T.E. Utley, *Lessons of Ulster*, London: Dent, 1975, p.7.
6. Evelyn Waugh, *Scoop* London: Penguin Books, 1957, p.42.
7. Schlesinger, *op.cit.*, p. 236.
8. Cited in Y. Alexander and A. O'Day (eds), *Terrorism in Ireland* Beckenham: Croom Helm, 1984, p.168.

9.  F. Burton, *The Politics of Legitimacy. Struggles in A Belfast Community*. London: Routledge & Kegan Paul, 1978, p.10.
10. S. Winchester, *In Holy Terror*, London: Faber, 1974, p.35.
11. E. McCann, *War and an Irish Town* Harmondsworth: Penguin, 1974, pp.18-19.
12. P. Arthur, *The People's Democracy 1968-1973*, Blackstaff Press, 1974, p.131 and passim.
13. J. Callaghan, *A House Divided* London: Collins, 1973, pp. 102-3.
14. R. Cathcart, *The Most Contrary Region. The BBC in Northern Ireland 1924-84*, Blackstaff Press, 1984, p. 262.
15. Ibid., p.36.
16. Ibid., p.263.
17. K. Brants, 'Broadcasting and Politics in the Netherlands: From Pillar to Post', in *West European Studies*, 8, 2, April 1985, p. 110.
18. Cathcart, *op.cit.*, p. 263.
19. M. McLoone and J. MacMahon (eds), *Television and Irish Society*, RTE-IFI, 1984, p.6 and passim.
20. C.C. O'Brien, *Herod. Reflections on Political Violence* London: Hutchinson, 1978, p.38.
21. Ibid., pp. 122-3.
22. Ibid., pp. 149-50.
23. Perhaps a classic case of the checklist approach married to a conspiracy theory is Liz Curtis, *'Ireland: The Propaganda War. The British Media and the 'battle for hearts and minds'* London: Pluto, 1984. The title speaks for itself.
24. See Winchester, *op.cit.*, p.210.
25. Dick Francis, quoted in the *Irish Times*, 27 September 1977. On the UWC Strike, see R. Fisk, *The Point of No Return. The Strike which broke the British in Ulster* London: André Deutsch, 1975.
26. Quoted in Alexander and O'Day (eds), *op.cit.*, p. 179.
27. 'Misreporting Northern Ireland', *Irish Times*, 14 December 1976. Ken Ward in Alexander and O'Day, *op.cit.*, arrived at similar conclusions based on an analysis of the US network news coverage. There the interpretation was founded on the perception of American involvement in Vietnam.
28. Burton, *op.cit.*, pp.151-5.
29. See Schlesinger,'"Terrorism", the Media and the Liberal Democratic State: A Critique of the Orthodoxy', in Alexander and O'Day, *op.cit.*, pp. 213-32.

# 11 Media policy and the Left
## Denis MacShane

The media have arrived as a subject in the British political economy. Go into a university library or radical bookshop and you will see more books under a section probably headed 'Media' than say, on, South America or international trade. Media studies are now a substantial sub-branch of sociology. Media schools or centres have been set up at many of the major universities. The work of Hall, Curran, Seaton, Philo *et al.*, Tracey, Schlesinger and others is to be found on all self-respecting left-wing bookshelves. The same writers' articles regularly appear in the pages of left-wing journals: it is now unusual for *The New Statesman, New Socialist, Marxism Today* to carry an article on the media.

The *Guardian, Independent* and *Observer* publish regular media sections. In addition to academic investigation, the media – in this case particularly the national press – are the object of books aimed at the popular market. Some authors have returned again and again to the media, like Robert Harris with his books on the press and Falklands War, or his account of the Hitler diaries, or Michael Leapman who in as many years has produced three popular and informative books – on Rupert Murdoch, on the launch of TV AM and the decline of the BBC. As well as the excellent books by Henry Porter (on Fleet Street fibbing), by Linda Melvern (on Wapping), by Harold Evans (on his editorship of the *Sunday Times* and *The Times*), by Simon Jenkins (on proprietors) or the Goodhart/Wintour biography of Eddie Shah, there should be noted the more polemical works such as Tom Baistow's *Fourth Rate Estate* and *The Press and Political Dissent* by Mark Hollingsworth.[1] Over half the books mentioned above were published in 1985 or 1986 so the media continues to be important objects of analytical and political concern.

All that is missing in Britain is a really effective film or novel about the media. McEwan's *The Ploughman's Lunch* was too caricatural though taut on the political corruptibility of television journalists, while Hare's *Pravda* attacked the easiest of targets, an overwhelming and overweening proprietor and his fawning editors. Nevertheless, it was an attack which irritated many right-wing writers in the national press. *Defence of the Realm* offered us the journalist discharging his liberal mission, as an exposer of wrong-doings by the state. In English letters no one has improved on Waugh's fifty-year-old *Scoop*.

Hollywood has provided some sharply pointed films about the American media, with the journalist as hero of *All the President's Men* in the 1970s, turning into a much more ambiguous figure in *Jagged Edge* in 1985. From continental Europe, Boll's *The Lost Honour of Katherina Blum*, later made into a superb film by Schlondorf or Wajda's *Man of Iron* use journalism and media issues as the best available mechanism for passing on views about contemporary crises in capitalist West Germany, and communist Poland. Whether the journalist is portrayed as a crusader for truth and justice, or as a cog in a cruel media machine which traduces all human values, is beside the point. The journalist and the media are now mass entertainment subjects, almost as much as cowboys and the Wild West or military officers in the war features of the 1950s and 1960s.

For the Labour Party and the trade unions the media occupy a special place reserved for the Left's most hated demons. No major set-piece speech by a left-wing union or Labour leader is complete without an attack on media bias. Sessions at both the Labour Party and TUC conferences are set aside to debate the media. The TUC has set up a media working party on which sit senior trade union leaders.[2] The TUC offers a week's course for union officials, on using the media. Some of the media unions themselves (notably the NUJ and ACTT) have devoted internal resources and time to discussing the media – not in union economistic terms of employment, income and working conditions, but from an explicitly political perspective of concern about control and bias. This writer organised a one-day stoppage of all BBC journalists in 1975 in a pay dispute, but there was only a narrow majority for a strike and some journalists refused to walk out. By contrast, there was an almost unanimous endorsement of a strike ten years later in protest against government censorship of the BBC's 'Real Lives' programme about Ulster politics. Such was the enthusiasm for an overtly *political* strike that NUJ members employed in independent television and radio also stopped work.[3]

The dovetailing of political and economic ends in the media unions' discussion of press and broadcasting is an important element in clouding the debate on the media and one to which we shall return, but in general terms the media unions have debated and adopted more policies in the past decade on the ownership, control, purpose and role of the media than in the previous half-century.

This heightened interest in the media is further reflected in the launch and activities of such groups as the Campaign for Press and Broadcasting Freedom (CPBF), the Minority Press Group (MPG), the Campaign Against Racism in the Media (CARM) and the media-oriented publishing group, Comedia. The CPBF runs a full-time office in London, and employs a regional officer based in Manchester. A regular newsletter, topical pamphlets and full-length books[4] and a high level of membership involvement marks the CPBF as one of the better-known political campaigning groups in Britain. The more narrowly focused Freedom of Information campaign has succeeded in gathering all-party support, and under Des Wilson's vigorous leadership has given new life to the decade-old campaign for a reform of Britain's Official Secrets Act and the introduction of a public right to government and corporate information.[5]

This political, academic, union, journalistic and campaigning interest in the media reflects the important role that the media play in the country's economy. Both under the Thatcher recession and indeed during the general economic decline in Britain since 1973, the media industry has continued to expand. During the 1980s a new television channel, three new national papers, several dozen new radio stations, and 800 free newspapers were launched. Only the United States has a higher per capita ownership of video-recorders than Britain – some 8 million have been sold – and the provision of video cassette programmes has also created a new industry.

If one takes the national newspaper industry as a single entity, Fleet Street was, at least until 1985, the biggest private employer in the Greater London area, after Ford at Dagenham and Heathrow Airport. The British periodical industry with its 7,500 titles is booming as a quick look at the crowded magazine shelves in W.H. Smith shows. One hundred new magazines catering for computer owners alone have been launched in recent years. *Benn's Press Directory* records 11,151 newspapers and magazines on sale in 1985 compared to 7,351 in 1975.[6] Advertising revenue for newspapers has gone up from £347 million in 1979 to £677 million in 1984 and in television advertising revenue had increased from £471 million (1979) to £1245 million (1984).'[7]

Employment in the media is also rising – the NUJ's membership has increased by a third in the past fifteen years; the print and broadcasting unions, even with the NGA/SOGAT haemorrhage at Wapping, have not suffered the same loss of membership as most other TUC unions in the past decade. The de-unionisation of Wapping and the massive cuts forced upon the former Fleet Street print unions in the post-Wapping staffing agreements signed in 1986 open a new bleaker chapter for union organisation. Developments such as the arrival of desk-top publishing and swifter video shooting and editing further threaten traditional union strength in print, films and broadcasting.

Although unions may be under pressure as never before, media employment on a full or part-time basis is going up. If one takes the media in the broadest sense, press, broadcasting, advertising and publishing, nearly one million people are directly employed in a highly profitable industry. Although most attention is given to the political excesses and editorial interference of media proprietors like Rupert Murdoch, or Robert Maxwell, and although suspicions are raised at their ideological motives in supporting money-losers like *The Times*, it should not be forgotten that they are primarily businessmen, capitalists who have shown that, taken as a whole, their media businesses are profitable investments.

Growth and change in the British media is still in progress. Technological innovation in both broadcasting and print could extend far further the quantity of products currently produced by the media industry.

Full deregulation of broadcasting and overcoming print union power, (both demands have a priority place on the political agenda of a spectrum stretching from Thatcherite hard-liners to the SDP/Liberal alliance) would further increase the economic importance of the media. Add to that the possibilities offered by cable and satellite broadcasting, and the potential of electronic publishing if interactive computers become as commonplace as telephones, and the media, as an industry, can only grow in importance.

Early in 1985, a crucial milestone was passed in the United States. There is now more capital invested in each US office worker than in each industrial worker. The secretary or middle manager, behind a word-processor plugged into a corporation computer net, has more fixed capital at their finger tips, than an assembly line worker in a modern automated plant or a skilled craftsman controlling an expensive machine tool. The media as part of the material base of society are of increasing importance. Their political role is well known.

Yet the Labour Party still has no agreed policy on the media. If it formed a government at the next general election, there is no indication that the media would be the object of legislation. The most that could be expected are some civil servant-hedged changes in the Official Secrets Act and possibly a limited Freedom of Information Act.

The shadow Home Secretary, Gerald Kaufman, who is broadly responsible for media questions, has said he would not permit the BBC to carry advertising, if such a change is introduced following the Peacock Report on Broadcasting. Otherwise, Kaufman has been silent on any substantial reforms. Indeed, in the book he edited shortly before the 1983 general election which included a wide range of contributions from putative Labour ministers, media reform was not mentioned at all.[8] A deliberate mistake? Hardly. Kaufman is an unusually articulate

Labour spokesman, with a wide direct personal experience in the media, as a newspaper and magazine journalist, a writer for BBC TV's *That Was The Week That Was,* and press officer to Harold Wilson during the 1964-70 Labour government. If Labour had a media policy then Kaufman would promote it.

The problem is that Labour has no media policy. It has a handful of motions (as does the TUC) passed at annual conferences, but unlike areas such as education, local government, health, defence, and economic management, where there are coherent programmes which would stand some chance of being implemented were Labour to secure a majority in the Commons, the media are left without even programmatic intentions.

Why is this? In trying to answer this question, we may learn not only about the contradictions and difficulties in the Left's discussion of the media but, more importantly, learn something about the Labour Party's capacity to tackle contemporary issues.

Until the beginning of the 1970s the Labour Party in opposition or government had shown little interest in the media. There is no tradition of concern on which present-day policy-makers can draw. Although media matters – the arrest and subsequent release of the Communist Party's editor, J.R. Campbell, and the publication by the *Daily Mail* of the forged Zinoviev letter – contributed greatly to the fall of the 1924 government, the pre-war Labour Party did not treat the media as a policy issue.

Indeed, it was the Conservative Party that took the major inter-war government media decision when it set up the BBC. The BBC is one of Britain's first nationalised corporations and the curious form of arm's length state control and its swiftly established paternalism have proved highly seductive to many on the Left. It was Baldwin, a Conservative, rather than a Labour spokesman, who launched the most vitriolic attack on the press with his famous remark in 1931: 'power without responsibility, the prerogative of the harlot through the ages'. Again, it was a body outside the labour movement, the Political and Economic Planning Group, which in 1938 produced a report on the bias in the press and called for greater public regulation of newspapers. This resulted in the first Royal Commission on the Press, set up in 1947, which gave birth in due course (1953) to the Press Council, though in such an attenuated form that it has never had much effect in its two main aims: preserving press freedom and lifting journalistic standards by receiving and adjudicating on public complaints about inaccurate or malicious reporting. Otherwise the first Royal Commission on the press had little to say, and the 1945-51 government did not introduce any media reform. Conservative governments brought in radical changes with the setting up of commercial television and, later, after the Pilkington

Committee, BBC-2. The 1962 Royal Commission on the press produced nothing of note.

The 1964-70 Labour government did nothing save to charge the Monopolies Commission with the duty of investigating any proposed newspaper takeover referred to it by the government: again, a largely ineffective gesture as the buying and selling of titles and the concentration of media outlets in the hands of individuals like Rupert Murdoch shows. Wilson's only direct intervention in the media was to appoint provocatively a former Conservative minister, Charles Hill, as chairman of the BBC. It led to a clear shift towards the Right in the BBC's senior executives, culminating in the appointment of an overt Tory, Ian Trethowan, as Director-General.

It was again a Conservative government (the 1970-74 administration) that launched commercial radio and Thatcher's first administration that sanctioned Channel 4.

The Wilson–Callaghan government appointed two major commissions on the press and broadcasting. The former produced nothing of value (a minority report by two Labour members was ignored by the government) save for useful research work which has provided data for continuing analysis of press questions.[9] The Annan Committee on Broadcasting stepped back from radical proposals. The 1974-79 government also reneged on a manifesto commitment to reform the Official Secrets Act; and the Labour Home secretary, Merlyn Rees, and the Attorney General, Sam Silkin, took legal action against three journalists, Crispin Aubrey, Duncan Campbell and Mark Hosenball, which ended in judicial fiascos which were not only highly embarrassing to the government, but suggested that Labour ministers were anti-libertarian in outlook.

Yet the 1974-79 Labour government entered office with at least some ideas on media reform. In 1974, the Labour Party proposed a wide range of reforms, in *The People and the Media*. In addition, the Left had discovered the media as an issue. From the late 1960s radical journalists working with the Free Communications Group and then with the short-lived *7 Days* had initiated a fierce debate among more thoughtful and left-of-centre journalists about ownership, control and bias.[10] A high point of this debate was when *The Times* gave space in 1975 to John Birt and Peter Jay for their famous article on 'a bias against understanding'. The debate has continued into the 1980s. Major left-wing politicians, notably, Tony Benn, had begun making the media a major reference point in their speeches prior to the 1974 elections, but in office did nothing to press for media reform with their Cabinet colleagues. Since 1979, attacks on the media and calls for reform have been a major element in the public politics of possible future Labour ministers, including Michael Meacher and Harriet Harman.[11] This historical review indicates one reason why the Labour Party has no media policy: namely, that it never had one in the past.

A key moment, that in a sense was missed, is 1945. Most of the media reforms that were implemented in the Continental West European countries and that continue to underpin the plurality and access to printed media in France, Italy and West Germany, were introduced between the liberation and the outbreak of the Cold War in 1947. They were introduced deliberately because the role of the press in encouraging pre-war reaction and, in the case of France, in shoring up the collaborationist Vichy regime, seemed self-evident.

The Rothermere press of the 1930s had been openly pro-Nazi, but in 1945 the British press did not seem the problem it was across the Channel. There was a combined circulation of pro-Labour papers (*Daily Mirror, Daily Herald, Sunday Pictorial, Reynolds News, Daily Worker*) amounting to nearly 9 million. The popular *Picture Post* and the liberal *News Chronicle* were also broadly sympathetic. The BBC appeared an informational, cultural and entertainment counterpart to the partly nationalised welfare state then being created. For the Left, 1945 was not a moment when media reform appeared necessary or urgent.[12]

The Left were hampered by the lack of any classic socialist theory on the media. Superb journalists as Marx and Lenin were,[13] they did not address themselves to specific problems of a post-capitalist outline of publishing. Nor is there a revisionist policy on the media which in a Fabianesque way might have permeated into political thinking and party programmes.

In contrast, the attraction of a 'free press' has a massive cultural hold. Stretching from Milton's *Areopagitica* through the Enlightenment of Voltaire and Jefferson 'Were it left to me to decide whether we should have a government without newspapers, or newspapers without a government, I should not hestitate for a moment to prefer the latter'; the fight against Stamp Duty and other state controls in the nineteenth century, and the arrival of exposure journalism with Stead and Russell, down to the enshrinement of the press in the Watergate affair, the concept of press freedom is seen as central to any free society. For the Labour Party, with many of its roots in nineteenth century liberalism and with a libertarian element, admittedly small, but present none the less in its make-up, it would require a major change to turn away from the value and importance of press freedom.

A benchmark of the level of freedom in other countries has always been the state of the press. The development of totalitarian theory has as one of its unifying themes that communist and fascist regimes treat the media identically. The image of brave men and women (Jacob Timmerman in Argentina, the *samizdat* publishers in Poland and

Russia, journalists of all colours in South Africa) battling to defy repression and print the truth has strong current resonance. The perceived evil of state control easily, and usually deliberately, is elided into state legislation of any sort, on the media.

Of course, the Left argue that press freedom as defined by newspaper proprietors is a sham and that the state can enlarge press freedom in many ways. Theoretically this is true, but the 300-year-old tradition that any state involvement in media regulation has serious negative consequences places the Left at a disadvantage as it presents a case for media reform. It requires courage on the part of politicians seeking office to open the possibility by calling for even mild reforms, since they can then be depicted as attacking press freedom. As Michael Foot discovered when he sought to introduce labour legislation in the 1974-79 government which would have restored trade union rights to have a closed shop if their members voted for it, the suggestion that the NUJ might thus have its bargaining power strengthened was quickly turned into a major issue of press freedom by newspaper proprietors and television manangements. It was a false argument and directed more against what the employers and capital saw as a shift in favour of union strength. But in choosing press freedom as the terrain on which to fight the government they rallied much greater support than if they had simply defended managerial authority. Foot, with skill and considerable political courage, saw off the challenge and refused to allow the press freedom hullabaloo to deflect his support for labour law reform. Foot has an outstanding personal record as a libertarian journalist, and could more easily achieve this than most other ministers – there was simply no matching him in public or private debate on the issue. But it was proof to other Labour ministers that any legislative proposals that could be seen as impinging on press freedom would be the signal for effective, well-marshalled campaigning against the government.[14]

One has seen these same arguments developed very effectively at the international level in the campaign against UNESCO's calls for a more balanced flow of information throughout the world and some check to the imperialist designs of the Anglo-Saxon media transnationals that control or filter so much of the world's information.[15] Profit, power and principle have been so cunningly conflated that to build wide support for an alternative vision of press freedom and accountability, is a Sisyphean task.

No help is given to the Left by the example of the media in non-capitalist societies. The press and broadcasting media in the Soviet Union, as well as in those East European countries which had a tradition before 1939 of vigorous, political publishing like Czechoslovakia and pre-Nazi East Germany are a painful reminder of the incompatability of communist rule and even limited free expression. The disagreement over media control was one of the sharpest divisions between the Polish union Solidarity and the government during the union's period of legal existence.[16] Whatever claims are made about employment, housing, health or education in Soviet bloc countries, not even the most committed enthusiast suggests that their media are to be admired. The imprisonment of poets in Cuba and of the 'Democracy Wall' writers in China, provides one kind of warning. But in addition, the avid interest of people in all communist countries in western books and magazines, together with the huge audiences for the overseas broadcasts of the BBC as well as the more explicitly propagandistic stations, such as Radio Free Europe and Voice of America, all support a widespread set of beliefs that for the media, the overthrow of capitalism brings nothing positive in its wake.

Closer to home, the failure of the labour movement to sustain its own journals has not increased confidence that it has any justification to say that it can reform the media for the better. The *Daily Herald* closed down because there was insufficient advertising revenue despite a greater readership than the combined audiences for the quality press: a point always stressed by those who want to change the revenue basis of newspapers. But it also folded because it was dull and boring. This journalistic lifelessness was induced by the control that top union bureaucrats had over its editorial line. The dwindling circulation of the *Morning Star* – a decline already well under way before its formal take-over by pro-Moscow hardliners in the British Communist Party – was in part a function of its dreary editorial style.

Much has been made of the successful launch of the *New Socialist* and the new-look *Marxism Today*. Both journals are prominently displayed at W.H. Smith, (which thus hoped to head off calls for change in the distribution system in Britain aimed at obliging retailers to display all journals – a system which in France has helped to maintain a politically diverse press). Compared with, say, the 1970s it is interesting to see the range of left-wing journals: *New Socialist, Marxism Today*, the CND's *Sanity*, even on occasion, *Tribune* and *Labour Weekly* on sale in High Street newsagents in addition to the veteran *New Statesman*. But as with W.H. Smith's decision to sell *Private Eye* after nearly twenty years of refusing to do so, it is probable that the change in the newsagent chains' policy was determined by a wish to avoid any charge of censorship through distribution control. The aim was to defuse the pressure, such as there is, for a switch to the French system of compulsory display.[17] Yet limited High Street display has done very little for the circulation of the Left journals. Twenty years ago the circulation of the *New Statesman* was 90,000. Today, the combined circulation of the *New Statesman, New Socialist, Marxism Today* and *Tribune* does not add up to that figure. Every attempt by the Left to launch an alternative newspaper sympathetic to Labour ranging from the ambitious *Scottish Daily News* project to smaller affairs in East London, Hull and Nottingham, have collapsed, leaving a handful of exhausted journalists and pressing financial problems. As Sandra Horne of the ACTT observed in 1984 at a conference called to discuss the idea of a Labour daily newspaper:

> Shortly after coming to power the Labour government will nationalize this, denationalize that – all without the slightest bother. Every problem has a socialist solution that anyone of us could give in five minutes. However, when it comes to actually doing something like starting up a newspaper, we appear to be completely confounded by the economic and political problems involved.[18]

To a certain extent this problem has been offset by the rise in radical and alternative book publishing and the success of some magazines, especially for women or those linked to single-issue campaigns such as the peace movement.

So far we have been looking at external reasons to explain why media reform does not command any place in a future Labour government's legislative programme. But of even greater weight are difficulties inside the labour movement itself. The word reform is revealing because in the discussions that have been taking place since the early 1970s there has been great confusion about who or what the enemy was; what should be the extent of the demands, and what forces should be mobilised to achieve these never fully articulated ends.

Various reforms have been proposed. Major attempts to change ownership and financing, including the idea of an independent press authority with licensing powers, national and regional printing centres, a media bank, a levy on advertising to subsidise alternative publications, a limit on the number of newspapers any individual or company can own, are among the most canvassed proposals.[19] Indeed, both conferences of the Labour Party and the TUC voted in 1986 to debar foreign nationals from owning British papers. To protect the consumer a press council with teeth, an effective press ombudsman, the introduction of a legal right of reply and reform of the libel laws[20] have all been proposed.

Further calls have been made for a new system of distribution and a Freedom of Information Act. It should be noted that most demands refer to newspapers. The Left is generally silent on the broadcast media. Indeed it is trapped between its dislike of the BBC's anti-worker, anti-progressive bias and admiration for one important technically non-capitalist institution able to offer some limited resistance to Mrs Thatcher. As with the House of Lords and the GLC, the Church of England and the miners' dispute, and Oxford University's refusal to grant Mrs Thatcher an honorary degree, the Left is making its peace with some of Britain's most venerable and conservative institutions because of their refusal to bow before all the Prime Minister's desires. My enemy's enemy is my friend.

In terms of their impact, the broadcast media are more important than the press. Though it is important to recognize the extent to which broadcasting journalists follow an agenda laid down by the press.

Yet despite its greater importance there is even less clarity on what reforms should be called for in broadcasting. The Campaign for Press Freedom became in 1982 the Campaign for Press and Broadcasting Freedom. It has spent a great deal of time discussing community radio or whether access programmes should provide time for reactionary viewpoints. Both questions are important, but a body created originally to focus narrowly and, it was hoped, with targeted effectiveness on press reforms has become a diffuse organisation expected to provide a home to every concern and complaint about a very broad range of media.

In the 1970s, NUJ debates at its annual conferences calling for a specific reform of the media often used to attract far Left amendments calling for 'the immediate nationalisation of all the press without compensation under full workers' control'![21] These amendments were not adopted but they represent a further problem for the Left in its discussion on the media: whether one should talk about limited reforms under capitalism, or whether a fairer, freer press has to await a greater social upheaval. A fear shared by any proclaimed spokesperson for the Left is that in advancing proposals for media reform he or she will be greeted with the accusation, 'That does not go far enough' or 'You are only suggesting feeble palliatives';[22] to be outflanked on the Left has been enough to stop most leading left-wing politicians from endorsing a specific set of limited or modest reform proposals. On the other hand, the ferocity of some proposals as well as the tone of discussions has meant that media reform has become largely identified as a left-wing cause associated with certain factions in the Labour Party that became alienated from the governing establishment during the infighting of 1979–84.

Tony Benn is an interesting case in point. More than any other Labour politician, he has articulated the case against the present-day media. His famous closing speech as party chairman at the Labour Party Conference in 1972, in which he said that the liftman at *The Times* had a right to be involved in editorial decisions, may be said to be the moment when the media as a labour movement issue left the margins and became accepted as major occasion for polemic, discussion and policy. Benn was scorned for the remark — it was made at the height of his interest in syndicalist workers' control. He has been perceptive and witty in his analysis, particularly in his striking comparison between the power of late twentieth-century television and the Church in the past, both functioning as message bringers and interpreters of the world imperfectly understood by the people, and urging passive obedience to consensual authority.

As we acknowledge Benn's role in making the media a substantive issue, a major problem emerges. Nowhere does he specify in precise, detailed and unambiguous terms what reforms or more radical changes he would wish to see, to secure the improvements he calls for. He makes fairly generalised calls for a reform of ownership, for a right of reply, for democratisation of editorial control, for unfiltered access to the media by workers, anti-establishment campaigners like the peace movement, and minorities such as blacks and gays. But as you read his books and analyse his speeches, what are missing are concrete proposals, worked out as implementable Acts of Parliament.

James Curran has mischievously suggested that instead of all the public campaigning, it would be better to persuade a couple of highly placed future ministers and their key advisers to support media reform and through behind-the-scenes discussion, try to get change done on the quiet. It is an attractive proposition and probably better attuned to how things work in practice, but it is unlikely that one could persuade those uninterested in media reform to become involved unless they felt there was real party or public advantage in doing so.

Another problem has been the confused role that trade unions play in the debate. The media unions, in particular, have been instrumental in raising the issue of media reform and supporting bodies such as the CPBF. For the media unions, part of the demand for reform is to secure and improve upon current levels of jobs, pay and conditions. Thus the broadcasting unions have campaigned, for example, against any extension of broadcasting, first against ITV, then against commercial radio, and most recently against Channel 4, for fear that dislocating competition or reallocation of advertising revenue would upset the status quo. In a sense, it has, in so far that the commercial local radio worker is paid less than her BBC counterpart, while most Channel 4 production companies are the poorest of poor relations in the IBA.[23] The free newspapers (which unlike innovations in broadcasting, arrived unregulated on the scene and thus were not subject to union lobbying) employ far fewer people than their bought equivalents. In the form of the most dynamic of the free newspaper proprietors, Eddie Shah, they represent the thick end of the wedge for the disappearance of printers' jobs via new technology and a recasting of union organisation.

For media reformers and for all on the Left, most of the labour movement, and much of the public, it is Fleet Street – especially the popular tabloids – that stands as the symbol of that biased, pro-authority, sexist, racist and militarist sector of the media which most needs a thorough shake-up. Yet Fleet Street was, until the winter of 1986 and the dispute with Rupert Murdoch over his Wapping production plant, a virtual paradise in terms of pay, job regulation, employment security and a comradely, supportive, confident union structure close to the workforce rather than a remote bureaucracy. Naturally, part of the unions' demand for reform is to secure and improve current levels of jobs, pay and conditions. Yet this traditional trade union approach has also led them at times to be conservative and, to put it politely, cautious about innovation.

So it has been the broadcasting unions which have campaigned, for example, against any extension of broadcasting, for fear that competition would damage the status quo.

Print unions also successfully resisted, at least up to 1986, any major changes in national newspaper production that threatened their jobs.[24] Labour costs in newspaper production have never been the deciding factor in a paper's success or survival and the sustained campaign against the high wages and short hours of some Fleet Street printers was more an expression of right-wing fury that here was a group of workers, who, in every sense had it as good, if not better, than their bosses. Yet this powerful bastion of working class strength was never translated into an effective challenge to editorial content. This contradiction was seen during the 1985-86 miners' strike when Fleet Street workers were responsible for writing, printing and distributing a barrage of mendacious propaganda against the striking miners yet at the same time they raised £2 million for the families of strikers.

The printers, have, on occasion, refused to print a particularly disgusting cartoon or picture or demanded that the editor ran a balancing article or statement. But such interventions, though they are presented by editors as earth-shaking examples of censorship, are relatively rare – perhaps a dozen examples since 1970. For the rest of the time Fleet Street workers pumped out whatever their proprietors and editors asked of them, without much visible concern about anti-unionism, sexism, racism.

Cynics who looked at the campaign mounted by the print unions over the Wapping dismissals, noted that all the unions wanted was a return to the right of their members to keep on producing the *Sun* which had set new low standards in British journalism for attacking unions and the values they stand for.

If one listens to most speeches at labour movement events attacking the media one has the impression that the best contribution to improving the press would be simply to shut down all the national tabloids. Even given the reduced staffing imposed as many papers announced plans to leave Fleet Street during 1986, such a proposition would be bitterly rejected by the print unions. Jobs would always be given priority over a challenge to the system. One of the fascinating aspects of the 1986 upheaval and the reduction of staffing levels (*The Independent*, for example, contracted out all its printing requirements, which, combined with direct input by the journalists, meant it did not need to employ any NGA labour at all) is whether the disappearance of print union pay as the main locus of management-union confrontation inside newspapers, will be replaced by journalists and managers fighting over editorial issues. This does not seem to have happened in the United States and other countries where print unions were decimated. The arrival of new technology and disappearance of printers' jobs has not meant an extension in quality or quantity of the press, though profitability has increased. If *The Independent* succeeds in maintaining the quality of its first two months it might prove the exception to this rule, but the example of the Wapping newspapers, where even conservative commentators have noted the drop in quality of both the tabloids and upmarket papers, would appear to be the more usual pattern. But the events of 1986 support the argument that the print unions, when faced with a major challenge, respond by urging a return to the status quo.

A further area in which the unions have not had much success is attempting to improve press coverage through monitoring of stories, disciplining their own members or forcing editors to change policy. The NUJ has tried to use its internal complaints procedure, which allows members and the public to bring a complaint against a journalist who contravenes a clause in the union's impressive and toughly worded *Code of Professional Conduct*, as a means of highlighting examples of bad journalism. The NUJ here is caught between acting as a kind of professional regulatory body akin to the British Medical Association or the Law Society, while at the same time claiming to be a workers' union existing to defend its members' working conditions. NUJ members have preferred to stress the latter aspect of the union's function and have not been willing to comply with the proposition that their union should act as policeman, prosecutor, witness, judge and jury in an ethical case. The union has been innovative and flexible in trying to devise means to encourage and, if necessary, enforce better journalism. But enforcement has proved almost impossible to achieve. Paradoxically, the campaign for media reform may be hampered rather than helped by its close identification with union officials, who despite their knowledge and good intentions, are caught between the priority, on one hand, of representing their members' existing and pressing interests, and on the other, setting forth proposals for considerable upheaval in the way the media function and are organised.

This is further reflected when we look at the failure to settle upon what should be the instruments of reform. If the problem is ownership

– who or what should be the owner? The state? A state-erected but arm's length body like the BBC or the IBA? Private companies but severely limited in size? Should trusts or cooperatives be the model? If so, would this be for new newspapers or television/radio stations, or should employees be empowered to convert their company into a new ownership structure? Should the unions have a stake in ownership or the workers? And if the latter, what would happen to the unions?

If the problem is editorial control how should this be altered? Should power devolve only to journalists? To all workers involved in printing and distribution? What then of employees employed by the media company but not directly involved in production – do they have a voice in editorial control? Do readers or viewers have a right to a voice beyond the act of making a consumer choice? What should be the mechanism for improved editorial control? The election of the editor? The chief editorial executives? If editorial committees are to be set up, who sits on them – union nominees, elected workers' representatives or outside representatives of the community, readers, or public bodies? Should such a committee meet daily to exercise forward control or less often to look retrospectively at editorial performance?

If the problem is bias, lack of balance and misrepresentation of the position of workers or unions, blacks or women, or the peace movement, how exactly is this to be redressed? Who speaks for workers when there is disagreement between the rank and file and union leaders? Is Arthur Scargill or Eric Hammond the authentic voice of organised labour? Roy Hattersley or Ken Livingstone that of the Labour Party? If there is no bias, won't the resulting balance be bland and boring? If, in fact, what is wanted are vigorous attacks on existing order, crusading journalism against monetarism, militarism and multinationals, is that not simply the cry for the Left's biases and lack of balance to replace those of the Right?

The attempt to launch a left-of-centre Sunday newspaper may help answer that puzzling question: what exactly is a left-wing newspaper in terms of subjects covered, headlines written, pictures chosen, journalists hired, lay-out and subbing, etc? Is there a *socialist* way of covering important issues like the miners' dispute or black sections in the Labour Party where opinions are hopelessly divided?

If the problem is the right of reply, against what or whom should one have this right? Factual inaccuracy? An aggressive headline? Hard-hitting comment? Automatically whenever Bernard Levin or Woodrow Wyatt comment upon union affairs? Who should determine and grant the right of reply? A stronger Press Council? A judicial tribunal as in West Germany? A press ombudsman as in Sweden? A body internal to the newspaper or broadcasting station? To whom should the right of reply be extended? To Mrs Thatcher against say, the *Guardian*'s Hugo

Young? To the CBI against most left-wing and union journals? To those who want stronger policing? How fast can or should a right of reply process take? What should be the sanctions against an offending paper or journalist? And if compliance is refused, what further sanctions are available?

Many of these questions have been addressed in part by those campaigning for media reform but most remain only vaguely answered, or not at all. The failure to settle upon a broadly agreed package of reform, with priorities and limitations worked out and decided upon is perhaps the single most important factor holding back the media reformers in turning their necessary and legitimate claims into a campaign with enthusiastic labour movement endorsement and broad public support. If you do not know what you want or how to get it, you will not persuade others enthusiastically to follow your uncertainty.

There is another factor which needs to be mentioned and that is the close relationship between the establishment media and key sections of the labour movement leadership. Gifted politician-journalists like Roy Hattersley have to turn away invitations to appear in the mass media. In less than a decade Neil Kinnock has been transformed from an occasional (and extremely good) writer for fringe Left publications, into someone whose press secretary merely has to lift the phone to convey his views onto the front pages of the press. To associate with a vigorous campaign for media reform would be to jeopardise that access. Benn has never been so foully treated by the popular press (though he has almost unlimited access to the *Guardian* and cannot complain that his views have not been disseminated by journals, broadcasting and publishers) since he raised the standard, advocating media reform in the early 1970s.

The established Labour leaders know well that on forming a government, the media will turn against any but the most conservative Labour proposals. Nevertheless, the dissociation of the labour movement establishment from a media reform campaign is yet another severe obstacle to serious accomplishment.

## Conclusion

Six external, and six internal factors have been identified to suggest why, despite fifteen years steady growth of the media as a labour movement issue, there is little likelihood that a majority Labour government will introduce major media reforms. The six external reasons are:

1. No classic Marxist, Socialist or Labour tradition of media reform proposals.
2. No historic Labour government interest in media reform.
3. The weight of the free press cultural-historic tradition.

4. The miserable example of the media in post-capitalist countries.
5. The failure of the Left to sustain its own viable mass circulation media.
6. The lack of distinction between different branches of the media.

The six internal reasons are:

1. Lack of willingness to settle upon a limited, unifying programme.
2. Failure to treat media reform as a legislative priority.
3. Media unions' confusions between role as preservers of labour market status quo and advocates of hierarchical, editorial upheaval in the media.
4. Indifference of media workers, as opposed to union leadership/activists, to calls for media reform.
5. Identification of media reform as a hardish Left cause.
6. The relationship of the Labour Party establishment with the media and the consequent lack of interest in substantial media reform.

Some of these reasons overlap and others could be added, in particular the labour movement's insularity which prevents British socialists from learning from the successes in media reform carried out across the Channel: what a member of the Labour Party's NEC recently called 'all them continentals'.[25] But some tentative conclusions suggest that the media share with other areas of desired reform the fate of being on the list of political issues that to the labour movement are more a source of problematic uncertainty than the occasion for radical change. Like issues connected with women, blacks, nuclear power and white-collar workers, the media represent a political problem that is superficially easy to make speeches about, but difficult to come to terms with programmmatically.

They are modern problems in the sense that there is no theoretical guidance or historical administrative experience to steer by. They are modern problems in that classic nostrums such as nationalisation or major extensions of union power seem irrelevant or would make things worse. They are modern problems in that they pose most sharply the conflict between advocates of socialism from above and fighters for socialism from below.

Unlike issues such as jobs in the mining community or the welfare state which show Labour at its defensive, conservative (in the sense of conserving something worthwhile) best, the media, like other modern problems, demand offensive, innovative solutions rather than a preservation of past gains. They are about breaking and reforging the consensus rather than returning to a milder version of it. In short, they demand that the Labour Party becomes a vehicle for radical progress.

Media reform, as with substantial progress in the field of other problems, cannot fight its way onto an agenda fashioned to attract those willing to step on the Labour chariot, only on condition that the ride is smooth, comfortable, and inconveniences no one *en route*. But if these issues that in their way are as pressing today as other injustices that called into birth the labour movement a hundred years ago continue to be shunted aside, Labour will become a cause for disappointment rather than a source of hope. Worse, other groups or coalitions may pick up the torch of radicalism and Labour's necessary claim to be all-embracing with the courage and vision to give an answer to society's major problems, will take yet another substantial knock. If Labour cannot reform the media, what can it reform?

This is a necessarily pessimistic overview of the specific problem of Labour and the media, though I think it throws some light on the wider question of why the labour movement has difficulties in handling the important issues that have come to prominence since 1968.

If I have to make a personal choice of media reforms I would tend to avoid the setting-up of major new boards or authorities aimed at interfering structurally in the media. If they can be given the framework of support for reform, I believe that the workers – editors, managers, printers, technicians – in alliance with a concerned public can massively improve the quality of the media. Tom Baistow, in his marvellous polemic *Fourth Rate Estate: An Anatomy of Fleet Street*, suggests the following reforms:

- safeguards for the independence of editors and their protection from improper pressures from proprietors, advertisers, trade unions and other organisations
- the incorporation of a code of conduct based on that of the NUJ
- the investment of a reformed Press Council with statutory power to impose appriate fines on newspapers that knowingly breach the code of conduct
- the appointment to the boards of all national newspapers, popular and quality, independent directors without whose approval editors cannot be engaged or dismissed
- machinery for the consultation and involvement of editorial staff in the appointment of editors
- the appointment to all national newspapers of an ombudsman/woman, on the North American model, to monitor and to attempt to settle routine complaints from the public to obviate unnecessary resort to the Press Council or Right of Reply Panel
- the reference of all newspaper takeover bids to the Monopolies Commission for full examination of the circumstances, with special reference to applications from editorial-management consortia of the publications involved
- the restriction of ownership of national newspapers and their control, direct or indirect, to persons of British nationality and companies or

organisations whose headquarters are registered in the UK
- regulations requiring that all national newspapers and periodicals be made available on demand throughout the national distribution network[26]

Some of these need amending. Unlike Baistow, I would increase the responsibility of workers and unions by involving them in the running and direction of what they produce rather than leave them in a subordinate, oppositionist category. Any reforms too should extend to the regional press which is entirely monopolistic and right-wing. But overall, Baistow's reforms are located in what is possible and beneficial. Add to them a Freedom of Information Act (which although necessary and overdue, is not an automatic check on government arrogance or corporate power, nor on their ability to manipulate the media as evidence from the United States demonstrates – a country which has both a FOI law and the most right-wing administration and reactionary corporate sector this century) and a tiny levy on advertising to pay for some of these bodies (1 per cent on newspaper advertising would produce £6 million), and you would have a modest and implementable package of media reforms which should be able to attract public and cross-party support.

However, I am fairly confident – that is to say, after fifteen years' involvement in the campaigning arena of media reform, I am completely pessimistic that such proposals will probably not form part of the Labour Party's next election programme. However, if Labour wins, I venture to guess, it will be months, not years, before a Labour government rues its unwillingness to tackle media reform.

## Notes

1. A good bibliography of recent British publications on the media is to be found in J. Curran and J. Seaton, *Power Without Responsibility. The Press and Broadcasting in Britain*, (2nd edition)London: Methuen, 1985, which remains the best historical-analytical introduction.
2. Since 1980 the TUC has published a wide range of reports and pamphlets on the media. Some of them are of very high quality and it is a shame that they have not received wider public distribution.
3. See the NUJ's *Journalist*, July and August 1985.
4. The October 1985 issue of *Free Press*, the journal of the Campaign for Press and Broadcasting Freedom listed 33 recent publications covering the press, television, radio, racism, technology, civil liberties and women in which the CPBF had a hand in producing. This in addition to three videos and postcards (CPBF, 9 Poland Street, London W1).
5. See D. Wilson (ed.)*The Secrets File – the Case for Freedom of Information in Britain Today*, London: Heinemann, 1984.
6. *Benn's Press Directory, 1985*, p. 6.
7. Advertising Association, quoted in T. Biastow, *Fourth Rate Estate*, London: Commedia, 1985, p. 41.
8. G. Kaufman (ed.), *Renewal: Labour's Britain in the 1980s*, London: Penguin Books, 1983.

9.　See the Curran and Seaton bibliography, *op.cit.*, for details of the various Commissions on Press and Broadcasting. The Labour Party in 1977 published as a pamphlet the minority report of GMWU General Secretary, David Basnett, and *Daily Mirror* writer Geoffrey Goodman, who were members of the 1974-77 Royal Commission on the Press. It had no impact.

10.　Among the pioneers in this group were Neal Ascherson and Alexander Cockburn. The latter writes a coruscating column on the media in the New York *Nation*. Alas, there is no equivalent in Britain. Ascherson sometime gives space in his *Observer* column to shrewd comments about the press. As with others involved in the FCG or *7 Days*, their sheer ability and journalistic talent ensured that irrespective of their political views their writing skills would usually provide mainstream media employment. One of the problems with the later debate is that while political engagement and theoretical analysis were still manifest, a command of good, clear English was not always so evident.

11.　See Meacher's speech at the 1982 Labour Party Conference:

> What we lack is not policy in this area [the media], but the will to carry it out . . . Are we really serious about reforming the media? ...If we are, when are we going to appoint somebody in the next Labour government with a specific and direct responsibility for carrying out this policy?

Harriet Harman gave the keynote address at the 1983 annual general meeting of the CPBF. Since the election of Neil Kinnock as Party Leader and the realignment of the Left (*New Statesman*, 1 November 1985, p.12), Meacher and Harman have not been as prominent on the media issue.

12.　Curran and Seaton, op.cit., p.88. For international press see A. Smith, *The Newspaper: An International History*, London: Thames and Hudson, 1979; and M. Walker, *Powers of the Press: The World's Great Newspapers*, London: Quartet, 1982.

13.　See *Lenin on the Press*, Prague: International Organisation of Journalists, 1972.

14.　See *Press Freedom: A Proud Record*, London: National Union of Journalists, 1977.

15.　See O. Boyd Barret, *The International News Agencies*, London: Constable, 1985; and F. Halliday, 'The Cold War Takes to the Air Waves' *Tribune* 1 November 1985, pp. 6-7.

16.　See T. Garton-Ash,*The Polish Revolution*, London: Cape, 1983, p.203; and D. MacShane, *Solidarity – Poland's Independent Trade Union*, Nottingham: Spokesman, 1981, pp.112-13.

17.　See *The Other Secret Service – Press Distributors and Press Censorship*, London: Minority Press group, 1980.

18.　S. Horne, cited in *Labour Daily? Ins and Outs of a new Labour Daily and other media alternatives*, London: CPBF, 1984, p.18.

19.　The 1982 Labour Party Conference, for example, called upon a Labour government to:

> (a) introduce as a matter of urgency a legal right of reply, of equal weight to the original item, to apply to all victims of distortion by the press, television and radio;
> (b) introduce a national printing corporation to finance local alternative newspapers, as proposed by previous Labour Party documents and trade union policy;
> (c) introduce a system of distribution which allows small publications the right of display in all newsagents on a sale or return basis;
> (d) set up an independent press authority which would require the owners of the British daily press to adhere to a strict code of impartiality such as is required by the Independent Broadcasting Authority in the field of broadcasting.
> 　Conference proposes that steps should be taken for the Labour Party and the trade union movement to jointly produce their own daily newspaper.

See also J. Curran, *The British Press: A Manifesto*, London: Macmillan, 1976 and the same author's proposals in *The Future of the Left*, London: Polity Press, 1984.

20. See G. Robertson,*People Against the Press*, London: Quartet, 1983.
21. See NUJ Annual Delegate Meeting Final Agenda, 1973, p.18.
22. For an example of this, see Paul Foot's attack on the right of reply campaign in *Free Press*, November 1984, and ensuing correspondence.
23. John Foster, the NUJ's broadcasting organiser, claimed that some commercial local radio journalists were living below the poverty line in 1985, (*Guardian*, 4 November 1985).
24. See T. Baistow, *Fourth Rate Estate: An Anatomy of Fleet Street*, London: Comedia, 1985, pp.90-4.
25. Dennis Skinner MP at special Labour Party NEC meeting to appoint a Director of Communications and Campaigns, 24 September 1985.
26. Baistow op.cit., p. 109.

# 12 Newspapers and the new technology
## Brian Whitaker

In a contest to choose the person whose technological innovation has done most to change newspapers, the front-runner would probably not be Eddie Shah and certainly not Rupert Murdoch. It might well be a man who never even owned a newspaper: Samuel Morse.

It was Morse who, in the 1840s, developed the telegraph – an invention which had a profound effect, not only on the speed and efficiency with which newspapers reported the news, but also on the nature of journalism itself. Through using the telegraph reporters began the separation of fact from comment that is so familiar today. Telegrams were expensive; they had to be kept as short as possible and confined to the bare essentials. The managing editor of *The Times*, Mobberley Bell, told correspondents: 'Telegrams are for facts. Background and comment must come by post'. Previously accounts and interpretations of events had arrived simultaneously, often intermingled in the same article. But from then on there were likely to be delays between reporting news and commenting on it.

This distinction between comment and fact had important repercussions. At first it was simply a matter of the practicalities of telegrams versus letters. But before long it involved questions of objectivity and journalistic ethics. Only bad reporters, people thought, would allow their opinions to enter into stories. An important change had taken place: the concept of 'pure' news as opposed to opinionated despatches had arrived. It is an idea which is still very powerful in newspapers today, though more enlightened journalists recognise that facts are not necessarily any more 'objective' than openly expressed opinions.

In Morse's day Britain had many newspapers, all with extremely small circulations by today's standards. These were ideal conditions for a diverse and often outspoken press to flourish. The fact that most papers were regarded by the authorities as thoroughly subversive and undesirable is a tribute to the courage of their writers and publishers. But a few years after the invention of the telegraph, there was another development which transformed newspaper economics. It marked the start of the trend away from diversity and the birth of the mass circulation press, with fewer newspapers concentrated in the hands of progressively fewer proprietors. In 1855 the two-year-old *Daily Telegraph* was selling 27,000 copies after what then seemed a spectacular rise in circulation. By 1870 it was selling 200,000, which made it the largest selling paper in the world. Such a huge daily sale would have been unthinkable only twenty years earlier. So how had it been achieved?

The first big spurt in the growth of national dailies is usually attributed to the abolition of Stamp Duty (which made papers cheaper) and to the development of railways (which made distribution swifter and easier). But there was also a crucial innovation in printing: stereotyping. Without it, the growth of a national press would have been impossible. Developments in printing technology before the 1850s had increased the speed of presses. Even so, daily print-runs of hundreds of thousands or even millions, were out of the question. Circulation was limited by the speed of a single press.

The obvious answer was to run more than one press simultaneously, but that meant having more than one set of type, which normally would have meant typesetting each article several times and laboriously making up several identical pages. In the 1850s stereotyping neatly overcame the problem. In essence, the process is very simple. Once a page of type is complete, a *papier mâché* mould is made, from which any number of identical pages of type can be cast. The result was that for the first time newspapers could print as many copies as they wished, as quickly as they wished. They were no longer restricted by the speed of a single press; they could run any number of presses together, all printing the same newspaper. The system proved so successful that it is still used today.

These two rather ancient examples of technological change in newspapers may not immediately seem relevant to present-day changes. But they are. First, they show that there is nothing particularly new about 'new' technology; there is always new technology of some kind. When discussing the 'Fleet Street revolution' of the 1980s, it is important not to regard Fleet Street as a fossil that has suddenly sprung into life. There have been many changes in newspaper technology over the years, despite the much publicised reluctance of the print unions to accept some of them.

Secondly, the twin examples of the telegraph and stereotyping provide a context for the latest innovations. Both brought changes which can truly be described as revolutionary. One transformed the nature of journalism, the other transformed newspaper economics. A few years from now, will it be possible to say the same for Eddie Shah's paper rainbow or Rupert Murdoch's Wapping?

'New Technology' in the present Fleet Street context covers a variety of things, but mostly it refers to one part of the operation where technology has made many jobs unnecessary – typesetting.

A century ago all newspapers used the professional equivalent of a *John Bull* printing outfit. Compositors with tweezers picked individual metal or wooden letters out of a tray and assembled them into words. When printing was finished, they put all the letters back in the appropriate compartments of the tray. It was both fiddly and time-consuming.

In 1886 the *Linotype* machine was introduced. This has three basic elements: a keyboard, a lot of tiny brass moulds representing all the letters and symbols, and a pot of molten metal. Type is cast, a line at a time, as the operator taps the keys. The moulds are automatically returned to their storage slot after use, and the lines of type are simply melted down again when they are finished with. Apart from the savings in time, lines of type proved a lot easier to handle than loose type when making up pages for printing. Linotype machines are still used in many Fleet Street papers. The system is known as 'hot metal' to distinguish it from the newer system of 'cold type', or photocomposition.

The new equipment uses a keyboard with a display screen. This is linked to a computer which eventually produces 'bromides' – columns of type on photographic paper. The type is then pasted into position on a board, and when the page is complete it is converted, by a series of processes, into a metal or plastic plate for printing. Photocomposition is about 25 per cent faster than hot metal, partly because the operators no longer have to decide whether to hyphenate words at the end of lines – the computer does that for them. The resulting loss of jobs is considerable. There is also a far greater reduction in the skill needed to operate the system (apart from a few highly trained computer operators who keep it running). Photocomposition equipment uses standard 'qwerty' typewriter keyboards whereas the old linotype machines have a unique arrangement of keys (the vowels, for example, are grouped together). The old linotype keyboards offered useful job protection because only trained compositors could use the machines with any degree of speed. By contrast, any competent typist, given a few hours' practice, can use photocomposition equipment.

Photocomposition in itself is no longer a matter of controversy. The equipment is used by newspapers almost everywhere, with the notable exception of some Fleet Street papers. Where it has yet to be introduced, the trade union concern is not so much about the technology in principle as about the numbers of jobs to be lost, the redundancy terms and the new working practices. What is much more controversial is the question of who should type the words into the computer. In most British newspapers the journalists type their stories on a typewriter, the sub-editors make alterations and the stories are then keyed into the computer by members of the National Graphical Association (NGA) who used to work the linotype machines. In the old days this made sense because of the specialist skills needed to operate a linotype. But with photocomposition it involves unnecessary duplication of work. It also leads, unnecessarily, to mistakes creeping into stories because of the retyping. It is much simpler to let reporters feed their stories directly into the computer and for sub-editors to make alterations on a screen, without any retyping by compositors – what is known as 'single key-stroking' or 'direct inputting'. That has long been the established practice in many other countries, and now in Britain on *Today* and on the News International papers at Wapping. The savings from direct inputting are significant, but they are more important for 'heavy-weight' papers with a lot of text than for popular tabloids with large pictures and headlines.

For many years the NGA opposed direct inputting by journalists, mainly because of the job losses involved. Recently it has become willing to consider it. Even where journalists type their own copy straight into the system, the jobs of some compositors can be preserved. The stories still have to be assembled into pages, and there are articles from freelance contributors to be typeset, as well as some advertising copy.

From the journalists' point of view, direct inputting has many advantages and some disadvantages. Writing is generally considered easier. The keyboards have a lighter touch than a typewriter, which makes them less tiring. There are fewer cases of 'writer's block' because reporters can easily try out a few sentences on the screen then revise them if they want. Reporters working out of the office can write on a portable computer and feed their story straight into the office computer over the telephone. There are none of the frustrations of dictating a story to a typist who seems to mis-hear every other word.

The problems start with the sub-editors. Editing on screen is widely believed to be more cumbersome than on paper. But a more serious problem is that sub-editors, unlike reporters, have to spend almost all their working lives in front of the screen. It is difficult to devise new work patterns that meet all the recommendations of health and safety experts. Probably the most serious risk for sub-editors is an industrial injury called tenosynovitis, caused by repetitive movements of the fingers. In Australia, where journalists have been editing on screen for a long time, there are 100 or more sufferers. If treatment is left too late there can be permanent damage, which effectively makes the sufferer unemployable as a sub-editor.

The other important technological development is the growing use of 'satellite' printing plants many miles from the main centre of production. This saves the delays and expense of transporting bundles of newspapers over long distances. Already we have the first truly international newspapers: the *Wall Street Journal* is printed simultaneously in America, Hong Kong and Europe; the *Financial Times* is printed in London, Frankfurt and the United States. What makes this possible is facsimile transmission. Newspaper pages are broken down into electrical pulses by a light-sensitive scanner and transmitted to another machine in another town or country which reassembles the pulses into an identical page. The facsimile is then converted into a plate for printing.

Less ambitiously, the practice of printing in more than one part of an individual country has been around for a long time. The *Daily Telegraph, The Guardian, Daily Mail, Daily Express* and *Daily Mirror* have all been printed simultaneously in London and Manchester for years. Before facsimiles were available there was a lot of duplication. A reporter's story, written in London, would be sent to Manchester by teleprinter. It would be edited by two sub-editors (one in London and one in Manchester) and typeset by compositors in both cities. In the 1970s, two papers, *The Guardian* and the *Daily Mirror*, began sending completed pages from London to Manchester by facsimile. *Today* has facsimile transmission to three satellite printing plants, and there are plans for more.

Before long most Fleet Street papers will transfer their London printing works to the docklands or use satellite plants. Some will do both. There are several reasons besides simply replacing old presses with new ones. Some, for instance, want the facility for colour pictures like *Today*. Supplementary print-runs in Scotland, Ireland and the North can ease distribution problems. There is also a feeling that these new plants will be less vulnerable to industrial action, especially if they are run (nominally, at least) by separate companies. But the main reason is that it will provide an opportunity to cut the workforce drastically. Murdoch is the example they will seek to follow. His move to Wapping reduced the number of production workers from 5000 to just 1000. The largest number of jobs lost was not among compositors but among press operators and publishers (who fasten the papers into bundles).

It is important to recognise in the present situation that there are a variety of reasons for introducing the new technology. Introducing it simply because it is new and goes 'whizz-bang' is the worst reason of all. Even with union cooperation, there can be serious problems – which is why some managements have wisely held back in the hope of learning from others' mistakes. In the late 1970s, the *Mirror Group* threw away £5 million on a futuristic system designed to assemble whole pages electronically. It did not work, and after a few disastrous months the company switched to a simpler system. A more cautious view is that new technology should be introduced only when it is strictly necessary.

If it improves the quality of journalism or the quality of printing, fine. If it helps a loss-making paper to produce profits, fine again. Beyond that, what is the point? The fact that the *Sun*, before Wapping, employed several times as many people as it strictly needed – and paid some of them several times the national average wage – really did not matter. In any case the *Sun* made more profit than all Murdoch's American papers put together. The British newspaper industry may be grossly inefficient but while all the papers were equally inefficient it made little difference. In contrast to the engineering industry, for example, the newspaper industry has no need to compete in world markets. Its exports are negligible and, unlike BL, it will never be threatened by cheap imports of Japanese newspapers. What it now faces, however, is competition from within, in the form of several new papers, starting with Eddie Shah. His arrival signalled a rush into new technology. But more than that, new technology has become the cover for a union-bashing exercise of the most Dickensian kind.

Before the launch of *Today*, Eddie Shah was a small publisher of free-sheets in North-West England. He would probably have remained there but for an industrial dispute which hurtled him to national prominence. He employed a mainly non-union workforce which, if Shah is to be believed, was perfectly happy until he hired a few members of the print union, the National Graphical Association. A series of clashes followed, culminating in a strike by the NGA, who wanted a closed shop. In the autumn of 1983, Shah's Warrington printing works became the scene of battles between police and massed pickets attempting to stop lorries distributing his papers. The battle went to court, the NGA lost and incurred the largest contempt fine in legal history: £375,000.

Shah instantly became a hero to the Fleet Street proprietors and editors, who saw his struggle with the NGA in David and Goliath terms. Here was a relatively small businessman taking on the might of one of the most conservative print unions. It was something the Fleet Street bosses had not dared to do themselves because they had too much to lose from the ensuing struggle. Amid all the glowing articles about Shah in the Fleet Street press, one point emerged very strongly: his papers used the latest technology and were produced far more efficiently than the Fleet Street papers.

The comparison had an interesting effect on Shah. It was not long before he began to think of starting his own national newspaper – an idea encouraged particularly by Andrew Neil, the editor of the *Sunday Times*. (Shah reportedly invited Neil to take editorial command of the project but he declined.) Normally, Fleet Street managements would not have welcomed the prospect of a new competitor with different methods. But they quickly spotted that Shah was offering them an opportunity. They could use him as a weapon to beat their own print unions into line. Consequently, in the run-up to publication, Shah's *Today* got a very sympathetic press.

Shah also patched up his anti-union image by striking a deal, not with a traditional print union, but with the right-wing EEPTU, the electricians' union, which was noted for its flexible approach and which often found itself at odds with the main body of the trade union movement. This had devastating implications for the print unions but it was also logical: *Today* was going to be Britain's first electronic national newspaper.

Shah opted for technology which put *Today* among the dozen most advanced papers in the world. Instead of using computer terminals merely to set type and then pasting it into pages, Shah uses them to assemble complete pages, including photographs, electronically. After that, the pages disappear out of a dish on the roof of the office and reappear at the three printing works in West London, Birmingham and Manchester. Soon, two more plants, in Rotherham and Bristol, will join the network.

Certainly this has a novelty value. But, as the *Financial Times* put it: 'The man on the Rhyl promenade...doesn't buy a newspaper because it has been bounced off a satellite'. Initially, there were teething problems with the equipment. Pages vanished into the computer and refused to come out. The first issue was delayed for an hour and a half in order to include a smudgy colour picture of the Queen in New Zealand 'transmitted in seconds down a telephone line on an Israeli-made Scitex scanner machine'. For the first few days several other papers fought back with 'old technology' pre-printed colour pictures of a much higher quality. They won easily.

*Today* may well serve as a lesson in the dangers of technology as an end in itself. There is a limit to how long readers will marvel at news that has been fully computerised, digitised and siliconised on its way to the breakfast table – especially if the resulting product is just another rather ordinary newspaper. Shah launched *Today* with very clear ideas about how he wanted to produce it and manage it, but with almost no idea of what he wanted to do journalistically. The only real innovation was the coloured weather chart (and even that was copied from an American paper, *USA Today*). The first few issues of any paper normally have a lot of wrinkles, but *Today* was unusually bad. It was plain that the staff had spent so long trying to master the technology that they had overlooked most of the basic editorial tricks of a first issue: a few good old-fashioned scoops, a campaign or two and a blockbusting 'continued tomorrow' series designed to hold readers who bought the first issue out of curiosity. Within weeks, Shah had run short of cash. Tiny Rowland's Lonrho, owners of the *Observer*, came to the rescue and took over day-to-day control.

What could still be a serious difficulty for *Today* in the long term, is the paper's editorial pitch in the middle-market ground previously held by the *Daily Mail* and the *Daily Express*. This is the weakest sector of the newspaper market and one which Murdoch, interestingly, believes has no future. *The Express* is struggling and the *Daily Mail*, though much admired by journalists for sharp editing and technical excellence, despite its bigoted politics, is no gold mine. The *Mail*'s sister paper, the *Mail on Sunday*, is now selling well after a hugely expensive launch and relaunch. The best hope in this sector might be for a left-leaning counterweight to the right-wing *Mail* and *Express*, but *Today* is unlikely to provide that.

On 24 January, 1986 – little more than a month before the launch of *Today* – Eddie Shah was dramatically upstaged by Rupert Murdoch. After weeks of provocation, he finally goaded more than 5000 of his workers (members of the print unions Sogat and the NGA) into a strike. He dismissed them and abruptly transferred all his British titles, the *Sun*, the *News of the World*, *The Times* and the *Sunday Times*, to Wapping in East London, where a new workforce (members of the electricians' union) were ready and waiting. His journalists, vital to continuity of production, were offered £2000 plus free medical insurance to join in the move, with the alternative of dismissal for any who refused.

Wapping was planned in the late 1970s – long before Rupert Murdoch owned *The Times* and *Sunday Times*. It was originally intended as a printing works for the *Sun* and *News of the World*. The circulation of both papers was restricted by limited printing capacity in their cramped Victorian offices in Bouverie Street, just off Fleet Street. At that stage, Murdoch had no plans to move the editorial and composing departments to Wapping. In transferring the printing operation, Murdoch also hoped to reduce manning levels at the new plant – though he was unable to reach agreement with the print unions on this point. There was no immediate pressure to introduce photocomposition or direct inputting by journalists at the *Sun* and *News of the World*. The amount of text in them is relatively small, so any economies in this area would probably not be worth the aggravation they would cause. In any case, both papers were already highly profitable.

In the meantime, Murdoch bought *The Times* and *Sunday Times* from the Thomson Organisation which had suffered a long series of trade union battles caused, at least in part, by incompetent management. After a couple of serious clashes in which Murdoch threatened to close the papers permanently, industrial relations settled down to the Fleet Street norm. Photocomposition was introduced – well ahead of most other national papers – and Times Newspapers became profitable.

In 1984 detailed plans were drawn up for a computer system to be used by *The Times* and *Sunday Times* journalists for writing and editing. The rumour at the time was that this would at first be used to produce print-outs which the compositors would retype. At some point in the future, after agreement with the NGA this would become a direct inputting system. The NGA let it be known that they were willing to discuss direct inputting, and waited for management to approach them. But no approach came. A small computer system for journalists was brought in on trial, as well as a few word-processors, but that was all.

The following year things started happening at the half-forgotten Wapping. Murdoch announced plans for a new evening paper, the *London Post*, to be printed there. It seemed that he had given up trying to transfer the Bouverie Street printing there and instead was treating Wapping as a 'greenfield' site, where it would be easier to get agreement on the manning levels he wanted. An editor was appointed for the *Post* (Charles Wilson, now editor of *The Times*) and senior management and production executives from Murdoch's existing papers began disappearing 'to help launch the *Post*'. (Later on, others worked secretly at Wapping, pretending to be ill – a disease which became known as 'Wapping cough'.) But as the paper's launch-date approached, there were none of the usual signs that a new paper was in the offing. No journalists were recruited and there were no leaks of 'dummy' issues. During the summer, the police reportedly held 'training exercises' at Wapping, with officers helping imaginary newspaper lorries to thwart imaginary pickets.

It was not long before Murdoch secretly began hiring members of the electricians' union and training them to work the machinery at Wapping. Initially, they were employed on short-term contracts but, once the plant was ready, Murdoch threatened to follow Shah's example and make a permanent deal with their union if the print unions failed to agree to his demands for printing the *Post*. These demands were unusually tough, even for an opening shot in negotiations. But it soon became apparent that Murdoch was not interested in negotiating anything except the most minor alterations. He wanted acceptance or nothing.

As it happened, at one edge of the Wapping compound there was a quarter mile-long row of low-level warehouses – former rum stores. Murdoch would probably have knocked them down during construction if the GLC Ancient Buildings Department had not ordered them to be preserved for their old brick fan arches and interesting Queen Anne roof timbers. Suddenly Murdoch began equipping them as editorial offices 'for the *Post*'. What the unions did not discover until too late was that they contained hundreds of Atex computer terminals – far more than an evening paper could ever need. In fact, it was the largest editorial system in the world, enough for all Murdoch's existing British papers.

Unlike Shah, Murdoch had no interest in 'state of the art' technology. He wanted to be sure that everything would work. The presses were some which he had snapped up in the 1970s because they were going cheap. For the time being, at least, there would be no electronic page make-up. The Atex system was not the best, but it was well tried and used by many newspapers: a Ford Escort to Shah's Lamborghini. Murdoch's most advanced technology was outside in the barbed wire surrounding the plant – a vicious type with half-inch blades instead of thorns. It was the first time in Britain that anyone had used it.

Technologically, Wapping achieved nothing that could not have been achieved by negotiation with the print unions. The drawback to negotiation, from Murdoch's point of view, was that it takes a long time and costs money in redundancy payments. By dismissing most of his workforce during a strike, Murdoch was able to short-circuit the negotiations and by-pass union agreements on staffing levels, as well as those on compensation for redundancy.

In the long run-up to new technology in Fleet Street, there had been much debate among journalists as to how it would come about. Some supported the 'evolutionary' theory where new technology would be introduced in a series of painstakingly negotiated steps. Others thought there would be a 'big bang', with a head-on clash between managements and print unions, possibly with the whole industry shut down for a time. Until about 1984, most newspapers appeared set on an evolutionary course. There was a fair chance that it would succeed. The print unions were gradually becoming less conservative in their attitude to technological change and high unemployment made workers willing to concede ground rather than lose their jobs. Several Fleet Street papers brought in photocomposition and other new equipment.

At that stage, most managements lacked the confidence to attempt anything other than the evolutionary course. For a start, there seemed to be no way they could continue publishing if the print unions went on strike. Also, many papers had no money for new investment. But that situation was rapidly transformed. The Shah dispute demonstrated the power of the new industrial relations laws, especially on picketing and secondary action. In addition, the whole of Fleet Street had an unexpected windfall of cash. All the papers held shares in Reuters, the famous (but for many years, unprofitable) news agency. What they now discovered was that Reuters had grown, almost unnoticed, into a high-technology information service whose business had expanded well beyond the newspaper industry. Reuters was floated on the stock market, and suddenly those half-forgotten shares were worth millions.

As a result, what now looks like happening is a modified version of the 'big bang' – a series of explosions, starting with Murdoch, spread over a year or two. Most papers plan to move at least part of their operations away from the traditional Fleet Street area. After the shock of Wapping, the unions may make the transition easier for other papers.

The big question is what effect these changes will have. One view is that there will be a greater diversity of newspapers and of the range of opinions expressed in them. The other is that control of newspapers will become even more concentrated than at present.

One of the main criticisms of the British press is that it leans overwhelmingly to the political Right. The number of papers supporting the Conservative Party is out of all proportion to the party's public support at general elections. It has been argued that new technology will lower the entry fee to the Fleet Street club and may therefore lead to a larger number of newspapers and greater diversity in the views they express. In short, new technology may be good for press freedom.

There are two economic factors to consider here: the start-up costs and the running costs. New technology makes start-up cheaper. The reduced size of the workforce keeps down wage costs during the first few weeks before revenue filters back from sales and advertising. Computer systems are expensive but the money can be raised relatively easily against the capital value of the equipment. If a modest circulation is envisaged, there is no need to buy presses – contract printers can do the printing. On running costs, the smaller workforce helps again, so it should be possible for a paper to survive on a much smaller circulation than previously. As a result, the argument goes, the market could sustain several new newspapers catering for minority interests. Even so, the savings brought by new technology have to be seen in perspective. For instance, all papers – regardless of their technology – use newsprint, which typically accounts for 30 per cent of running costs. Wages are normally around 40 per cent, so a new paper with staffing levels that were 75 per cent below the norm would actually save only 30 per cent on total running costs.

*Today* was quickly followed by *The Independent*, an up-market broadsheet launched by Andreas Whittam-Smith, a former City editor of the *Daily Telegraph*. At about the same time, a new Sunday paper appeared: *Sunday Sport*, which specialised in full-colour pictures of bare breasts. Sunday papers are especially attractive because start-up costs are lower than for dailies, and there is more double-buying by readers (which should make it easier to establish sales).

The interesting feature of the new papers is that only one plans a radical departure from Fleet Street's political norm. This is the left-of-centre *News on Sunday*, backed largely by trade unions and local authority pension funds. It aims to be a popular, investigative tabloid selling around one million copies a week. A dummy issue was test-marketed successfully in 1985, and it was launched in April, 1987.

Even with the lower start-up costs brought by new technology, the sums needed are considerable. The cost of starting *The Independent* was £17 – £18 million, *News on Sunday* raised just over £6 million.

Despite the obstacles, now is probably the most auspicious time since the nineteenth century for new publishers to break into Fleet Street. But the success or failure of these newcomers depends partly on how quickly the rest of Fleet Street adapts to the changed circumstances. Murdoch is the key here. His four Wapping papers include three market leaders – the *Sun* among the popular dailies, the *News of the World* among the popular Sundays, and the *Sunday Times* among the up-market Sundays. All were hugely profitable before the move. Murdoch's weakest paper, *The Times*, trails third behind the *Daily Telegraph* and *Guardian* among the up-market dailies, but even *The Times*, post-Wapping, is said to be profitable. The unknown factor is what Murdoch will do with all this extra profit.

He is already in a uniquely powerful position in the British newspaper industry (and in the English-speaking world's information and entertainment media generally). He could, if he chose, use the Wapping profits to strengthen his position in Britain still further, possibly even to the extent of eliminating several competitors. He could do so by temporarily sacrificing his profits and reducing the selling price of his papers and the cost of advertisements in them. It would be very similar to what the big airlines did to Freddie Laker. Commercially, it is a frightening prospect, and the consequences for press freedom would be incalculable.

However, several factors suggest that this may not happen. In the first place, Murdoch will have only a short time to make his move before the other papers introduce their own cost-cutting new technology. At present, he probably does not have the printing capacity to cope with the sudden increases in circulation that would be involved.

Murdoch has never been a man to worry much about his public image, but it could become increasingly important. Wapping was achieved on the back of changes in trade union law introduced by the Conservatives. Now, even some Conservatives are murmuring that he has overstepped the mark and abused the spirit of those changes. The Conservative government began to worry about re-election and on the Labour side there were threats to ban Murdoch from Britain as an undesirable alien (technically feasible now that he holds American rather than Australian citizenship). Murdoch's dismissal of his entire workforce (except the journalists) would have been illegal in many countries not regarded as havens of trade unionism. If Wapping had been in South Africa, he would almost certainly have been condemned by the courts for 'unfair' industrial practices and failure to negotiate with the unions 'in good faith'. Murdoch may not appear to care about that, but his empire is still expanding rapidly and every new dent in his image adds to the controversy surrounding his next takeover. To follow up Wapping with predatory price cuts aimed at damaging or destroying his British competitors might be too dirty even for the Dirty Digger.

But possibly the most persuasive argument is the nature of Murdoch's empire, always expanding, always heavily borrowed. He needs the profits from Wapping to help finance his acquisitions in the American film and television industry. Rather than cut prices and advertising rates, he may simply not increase them, thus maintaining his own profits and at the same time squeezing competitors who have already budgeted for price increases. That in itself could be enough to spread panic along Fleet Street and hasten the stampede to dockland. After the shake-out, the stage could be set for a suicidal circulation war of a kind not seen since the 1930s, when newspapers thrust free encyclopaedias and clothing at anyone who promised to buy their product for a few weeks.

Amid the fallout from that there is bound to be radiation sickness. A few years of newspaper mania would be followed by closures and mergers. One early victim is Eddie Shah. His paper survives, at least for the time being, in the hands of corporate professionals leaving him to join Britain's heroic line of amateur failures: the Captain Scott of Fleet Street. For Murdoch, if history repeats itself and his friendship with Billy Graham does not turn him into a born-again Christian, there is the path well-trodden by earlier press barons. For them, in old age, the great leveller was insanity. And it is a path down which Lord Northcliffe, for one, chose to lead his papers.

# 13 Goodbye to *The Times*
## *Peter Kellner*

Rupert Murdoch is one of the phenomena of modern British news-papers. When he bought the *Sun* in 1969 he took on the flagging tabloid market, and won. When he bought *The Times* and *Sunday Times* in 1981, he took on a part of the British establishment, and won. At the beginning of 1986, when he moved production of his papers to Wapping, he took on the newspaper unions, and won.

For two years until February 1986 I wrote for *The Times* – not as a staff journalist but as a fortnightly columnist. When I was first ap-proached to write my column, Peter Stothard, the paper's features edi-tor, explained that the slot, opposite the leader page, was one where 'BBC rules' applied: that is, where some conscious attempt was made to provide political balance. The cast list and their publication days changed from time to time, but the general pattern stayed much the same. By mid-1985 the routine was that Anne Sofer, an SDP member of the Greater London Council, wrote on Mondays, Roger Scruton and Digby Anderson – both apostles of the free market – wrote on alternate Tuesdays, and I alternated with the Labour MP Jack Straw to provide a left-of-centre view on Wednesdays.

Until the end of January 1986 I enjoyed the challenge of writing in *The Times*'. On only one occasion was any question raised about the wisdom of publishing my column. In March 1985 I wanted to comment on reports in *The Times*' news columns about the paper's circulation and readership figures. I considered two particular stories – one in Sep-tember 1984, the other on 11 March 1985 – to be misleading. Since *The Times*, more than any other national newspaper, presents itself as a journal of record, it seemed a matter of legitimate concern to comment on its coverage of its own affairs.

My first column following the 11 March story was scheduled for Wednesday, 20 March. Knowing that my article was likely to touch sensitivities within *The Times* offices, I informed George Brock, the editor of the 'Op-Ed' page of my intentions the previous Wednesday. He told me it would help if I submitted my column earlier than usual –

on Friday, 15 March, rather than the following Monday, which would have been my normal copy day.

Brock duly received my article. On the Saturday evening he telephoned to say that *The Times* was unlikely to print it. He would, if I wished, submit it to the editor, then Charles Douglas-Home, but he doubted whether this would make any difference. In any case, Douglas-Home was ill, and it might be some days before he had a chance to see what I had written. Meanwhile, would I write an alternative column on another subject? I declined. To have written another column would have removed any pressure on *The Times* to reach a clear decision. I said I was happy to wait for the editor's verdict.

Douglas-Home was still ill when my column should have gone to press; instead an article by Francis Pym appeared in its space. By the end of the week, however, Douglas-Home was back at work. He saw my column. He said it should be published provided I agreed to minor changes. I accepted this. (None of the changes affected the substance of my criticism.) The column appeared a week late, on 27 March. It concluded:

> Truth is valuable for its own sake. It is not just another commodity like aftershave or Sellotape: it is special. But truth can be special only as long as those who trade in it respect it. For *The Times* above all papers truth, like charity, should begin at home.

That episode in my relations with *The Times* had a significant bearing on my actions almost a year later. When Murdoch transferred the production of his titles to Wapping and sacked more than 5000 of his employees, I decided to write a column about Murdoch and the unions. I argued that while the Left had indicted Murdoch for 'attacking the rights of printers and journalists, there is a more serious charge for him to answer: that he has attacked the standards of the newspapers he has bought.' I attempted to balance a critique of Murdoch with an analysis of how the newspaper unions carried some of the blame for allowing Murdoch's forms of journalism to flourish. On Murdoch's record I wrote:

> In each of the three countries in which he operates Murdoch has been rumbled. In Australia in the mid-1970s he was condemned both by the Australian Press Council and by a number of his own journalists for distorting the news in order to help Malcolm Fraser's Liberals win power.
>
> In 1980 the *Columbia Journalism Review* considered Murdoch's stewardship of the *New York Post*. It concluded that the paper turned 'white against black, the comfortable against the poor, the First World against the Third....The *New York Post* is no longer merely a journalistic problem. It is a social problem – a force for evil.'

Here in Britain Murdoch's experience of Press Council censure goes back to 1969, when he sought to revive the sales of the *News of the World* with Christine Keeler's revised account of her affair with John Profumo, the former War Minister, almost a decade earlier. More recently the Press Council roundly condemned the *Sun* for inventing an interview with the widow of a Falklands war hero.

Had these been isolated incidents, Murdoch could reasonably reply that everyone makes mistakes, so why pick on him? The answer is that they are not isolated events: they fit a pattern. Comments by the Australian Press Council and the *Columbia Journalism Review* apply equally to the *Sun*.

On the unions I wrote:

> The pre-Murdoch *Sun* supported the Labour Party. When the International Publishing Corporation decided to sell it in 1969 the print unions opposed an attempt to turn it into an independent non-profit-making-pro-Labour daily. Murdoch was preferred because he seemed to offer the prospect of more jobs and higher pay.
>
> In 1981, when the International Thomson Organisation sold Times Newspapers Ltd, there were strong grounds for referring the sale of the *Sunday Times* to the Monopolies Commission. John Biffen, the Trade Secretary, decided against referral, and *Sunday Times* journalists embarked on a law suit against Biffen.
>
> The point at issue was whether the paper was a 'going concern'. If it was, then reference to the Monopolies Commission should have been automatic, and Murdoch would probably have been denied the right to buy the *Sunday Times*. The journalists were advised by a senior partner in Cork Gully that they had an excellent case.
>
> Their action was set down to be heard. Yet when they discovered the possible costs of pursuing their case, they dropped it. At this point it would have been open to the NGA, Sogat or any other interested party to take over or finance the action. None did.

Clearly I could not be certain that *The Times* would publish this column. Yet the events of March 1985 surely demonstrated the merits from the paper's view of allowing a columnist, writing as an alternative voice, to comment occasionally on his paymasters? After all, *The Times* had been widely praised for publishing my column on the paper's readership figures. It had been cited by writers as diverse as Colin Welch in the *Spectator* and John Grigg in the *Political Quarterly* as a sign that *The Times* took seriously its commitment to open its pages to dissent. Moreover, the week before my column on Murdoch was due to appear, *The Times* had carried a lengthy article by Bernard Levin attacking the print unions. Had the paper asked its columnists to keep off the subject of Murdoch, Wapping and the unions, it could have claimed some consistency. Levin's column showed that no such rule applied.

Logically, if one independent columnist were permitted to express one view – which happened to support the proprietor's case – then other columnists should be permitted to express other views on the same subject.

*The Times* did not publish my Murdoch column and I resigned as one of its columnists. I set down my account of the events leading up to my resignation, and my reasons for it, in a letter on 11 February to George Brock:

Dear George,
I am writing this letter following our telephone conversation yesterday afternoon.

On Sunday I told you of my intention to write my column for tomorrow's *Times* on Rupert Murdoch and the unions. You said that this might cause problems, but that there were no general rules covering this kind of piece and that the article would be judged on its merits.

Your response to the article itself shows that this was not the case. When we spoke at 5 p.m. yesterday you made no criticisms of the article's construction, clarity, logic, accuracy, topical relevance or originality. Had you any such specific comments then you know from our relationship over the past two years that I would have been ready to consider any improvements you might suggest.

Instead you told me that there was no way the article could be revised to make it suitable for publication in *The Times*; that there was no point even referring it to Charles Wilson, your new editor, for a final decision; and that you knew of no other paper that would publish such criticisms of its proprietor. Your message was clear: legitimate and robust criticism of *The Times*' proprietor is banned from its pages.

I understand your position, but have these comments on it:

First, your statement that there was no point even referring my article to Charles Wilson demonstrates the oppressive environment in which Murdoch's journalists are now required to work. To fight and lose a battle for independent journalism is one thing; to work in a paper where it is no longer even worth fighting is quite another.

Second, your comments about criticisms of proprietors in other papers are wrong. You seem to have forgotten Donald Trelford's public criticisms in *The Observer* of Atlantic Richfield at the time of the paper's sale to Lonrho, and of Tiny Rowland during the dispute over Trelford's investigation of conditions in Zimbabwe.

During my own days at the *Sunday Times* when it was owned by the Thomson Organisation, I can recall two experiences that directly contradict what you say:

In October 1972, when I ran the *ST's* consumer coverage, I wrote a long article on the travel industry containing specific criticisms of Thomson's travel operations. No question ever arose within the paper of deleting or toning down the article.

In July 1978 I wrote a front page story for the *ST* reporting evidence that many of Britain's biggest companies were avoiding paying mainstream corporation tax. Harry Evans, then editor, asked me afterwards why I had omitted the Thomson Organisation from the list. My answer was that it was not one of the companies covered by the research I was reporting. He told me that I should have made a point of publishing Thomson's figures – even if they portrayed the company in a poor light – *in order to demonstrate that the editorial operation of the paper was independent of its owners.*

In a slightly different vein, the last edition of the *Sunday Times* before the 1978/79 suspension of publication carried a column by the paper's TV critic, Dennis Potter, that was highly critical of the paper's top management. During the course of a review of a *Panorama* programme on the dispute at Times Newspapers he wrote:

'How cruel of *Panorama* to demonstrate so conclusively that a pair of newspapers by no means free of the usual canting humbug about the plight of Britain or the wood rot of her industries should all the time have been pathetically worm-ridden examples of the very malaise they so ponderously curse in others..."Duke" Hussey [is] my idea of a catastrophic manager'.

My own comments about Rupert Murdoch in the column you decline to publish were considerably milder than that.

Elsewhere, the *New Statesman* has on a number of occasions published articles criticising the paper's board (you should look out Richard Crossman's piece in 1972 describing how he was sacked); the BBC gave ample room to critics of its Governors during the *Real Lives* row last August; and I was one of many people who appeared on Independent Television last year – in my case reading my own prepared 'What the Papers Say' script – to attack the IBA for banning the programme of Cathy Massiter's revelations about MI5.

I make these points not to complain or particularly to express surprise at your decision, but to point out that Murdoch is not like any other media boss. He is different, and worse, and has decisively broken the tradition that good journalists and their editors always strive to put the interests of their readers above those of their paymasters – even if they sometimes fail in the attempt.

As far as I can tell, the fight has gone out of many journalists at *The Times*. One consequence is that columnists like myself must write within rules that are unspoken but of the greatest clarity. It is fine for Bernard Levin to write an article making serious charges against the print unions – charges that may be true, but for which his article adduced not one scrap of testable evidence – while it is forbidden for anyone else to write an article quoting evidence critical of Rupert Murdoch.

Fine. It is his paper. Now we all know where we stand, you can seek and may find columnists willing to write according to these rules. I regret that I cannot be one of them.

And so *The Times* and I parted company. Brock's letter in reply to mine argued that:

you cannot frontally attack the newspaper and its owner and reasonably expect one of its journalists to enter into fine-tuning about the copy. Any paper which did print such a piece would be proving that it had reached the demoralised depths which you think that we have plumbed. To talk about the failure to 'fight' for such a thing is absurd.

Absurd or not, I remain convinced that my original calculation was correct: *The Times* would emerge with more credit had it published my column than it did by rejecting it. Other newspapers reported my resignation; the 'World at One' on Radio Four carried an interview in which I summarised my views about Murdoch, the *New Statesman* published the rejected column, and the *Guardian* commissioned an article in which I suggested some lessons for the Left from Murdoch's move to Wapping. Altogether *The Times* achieved the worst of both worlds: it acted as a censor, but in such a way as to ensure that my column received far wider publicity than it would have done had it been published in the normal way. Such, fortunately, is often the way in a democracy. Even behind Wapping's barbed wire and working in the tense aftermath of their move from Grays Inn Road, Murdoch's executives should have known better.

# INDEX

Abyssinian war, 159, 160
accountability, 68, 72, 86, 222
ACTT, 216, 223
Aden, 19, 184, 196, 198
advertising, 76, 106-7, 218, 223,
  232-3
agenda-setting, xiii, 61, 138,
  224, 231
Aitken, Ian, 83, 111
Aitken, Jonathan, 114
Aitken, Max, 169-70
Akass, Jon, 80
Al Bu Said Sultans, 183
*All the President's Men* (film), 216
Alliance parties, 49, 56
Allied Declaration, 164, 170, 171,
  176
'alternative news', xiv, 98-108
Amery, Julian, 169
Anderson, Digby, 105
Anderton, James, 105
Andropov, Yu.V., 15
*Annan Report* (1977), 64, 220
anti-Semitism, 155, 164, 168-73
appeasement, 141-50
Archer, Jeffrey, 19
Ashford, Nicholas, 198
Ashworth, Anthony Clayton, 196
Askew, Alan, 97
Atlantic Richfield, 252
atrocities (BBC reporting),
  xv, 154-79
Attlee, Clement, 120, 135, 140,
  147-8
Aubrey, Crispin, 220
Auschwitz, 155, 166, 173, 178

Bacon, Reginald, 120

Baistow, Tom, *Fourth Rate Estate*,
  215, 232-3
balance (broadcasting), xv,
  151, 229
  evolution of, 133-41
Baldwin, Stanley, 219
Balfour, Michael, 161
Balinsky, Count, 165
Barnes, G.R., 170
Bartlett, Vernon, 142, 165
Bauer, Yehuda, 164
BBC, 35-6, 69, 100, 215
  anti-Semitism and, 155, 164,
    168-73
  atrocity reporting, xv, 154-79
  Conservative Party and, 134-5
    138-40, 142, 149, 219
  labour movement and, 133-4,
    136-7, 142-51
  Labour Party and, 134-42, 144,
    146-51, 218-21, 224
  Lobby system, 113, 115
  Northern Ireland, 201-3, 206-8,
    210-11
  Oman, 196-7
  religious programmes, 173-5
  'Real Lives' dispute, 201-3, 207,
    208, 211, 216, 253
  *see also* Director-General (BBC);
    Director of Talks (BBC)
Beadle, Gerald, 206-7
Beaverbrook, Max, 119, 120
*Belfast Newsletter*, The, 205
*Belfast Telegraph*, 205, 211
Bell, Daniel, xi
Bell, Mobberley, 236
Bell, Tim, 4
Bellamy, David, 13

Belsen, 156, 157
Benn, A.W., 5, 6-7, 17, 21, 124,
    220, 225, 230
*Benn's Press Directory*, 217
Berelson, B., 45-6, 65
Bergson, Peter, 177
Bermondsey by-election, 61
Bevan, Aneurin, 72
Beveridge, William, 137
Bevin, Ernest, 142
bias, 32, 35-6, 77, 91-3, 229, 246
Biffen, John, 251
Birmingham Centre for
    Contemporary Cultural
    Studies, 36
Birt, John, 220
'Bloody Sunday', 211
Blumler, I., 35, 36, 41, 55,
    58-9, 64, 65, 71
Boll, *The Lost Honour of Katherina
    Blum*, 216
Bottomley, Horatio, 14
Bowe, Colette, 127
Boyce, George, 204
Boyne, Harry, 124
Bracken, Brendan, 120, 150, 172
Brailsford, H.N., 143
Brezhnev, Leonid, 15
Briggs, Asa, 202
British Army Training Team,
    189-90
Brittan, Leon, 127, 202, 203
broadcasting, 14, 218, 226, 227
    balance, xv, 135-51, 229
    *see also* BBC; IBA; radio;
    television
Broadcasting Act (1960), 209-10
Brock, George, 249-50, 252-4
Buchenwald, 156
Budget, 120
*Bund Report*, 166
Burnet, Alistair, 14, 18
Burton, Frank, 205, 212
Butler, D., 58, 67, 79
Butler, R.A., 122, 144-5, 146-7
by-elections, 19, 61

Cabinet, 13, 16

Lobby system, 110, 111, 117,
    118, 121, 126-8
Cadogan, Sir Alexander, 146
Callaghan, James, 4, 17, 83, 119,
    125-6, 206, 220
Cambodia, 155, 179
Campaign Against Racism in the
    the Media, 217
Campaign for Press and
    Broadcasting Freedom, 217,
    225, 226
Campbell, Duncan, 101, 220
Campbell, Gregory, 201
Campbell, J.R., 219
canvassing, 66, 83
Carr, Raymond, 159, 160
cartoons/caricatures, 80, 81
Carvel, John, 120
Carvel, Robert, 118
Cathcart, Rex, 206, 207-8
Cenotaph effect, 10
censorship, 136, 146, 148
    news management, xv-xvi,
        183-99
    'Real Lives' controversy, 201-3,
        207, 208, 211, 216, 253
    self, xvi, 196, 205
    at *The Times*, xvi, 249-54
Chamberlain, Joseph, 117, 143, 146
Channel 4, 50, 51, 220, 226
Chataway, Chris, 18
Chernenko, K.U., 15
Chester, Lewis, 198
Chicago studies, 65
Child Poverty Action Group, 12
'Children's Hour', 140, 142, 169
Church of England, 224
Churchill, Winston, 7, 17, 18
    BBC and, 134, 149-50, 163,
        173, 176
    Lobby contacts, 119, 120-21
Citrine, Walter, 136, 142-5, 147-50
*City Life*, 103, 104
*City Limits*, 101
Civil Service, 13, 16, 111, 116, 117
Clark, Fife, 119, 120-21
class
    integration, 39-41, 42

media role, xiii, 26-7, 31-9, 41-2
social identity, 27-31
structure, 25-6
*see also* middle class;
working class
CND, 12, 223
Coalition government, 146-7, 150
Cockburn, Claud, 160
Cohen, Israel, 159
Cold War, 184, 221
Cole, John, 113
collective/individual continuum,
16
collectivisation process (Lobby),
118, 119
*Columbia Journalism Review*,
250-51
Comedia (publishing group), 217
communication, interpersonal,
61-2
communist countries, 222-3
computer systems (newspaper),
243-4, 246
concentration camps, xv, 156-7,
172-3, 176, 178-9
*Congleton Chronicle*, 99
Conservative Party, 7, 12-13, 17
83, 246
BBC and, 134-5, 138-40, 142,
149, 219
media policy, xvi, 219-20, 247
Corner, J., 39
Corrigan, P., 36
corruption, xvi, 96-8, 102-4,
194, 197
Cosgrove, P., 82
counter-insurgency, 184, 188-92,
198
*Coventry Evening Telegraph*, 99
CPRS papers, 5
Cramp, C.T., 136
Crewe, I., 65
Cripps, Sir Stafford, 138
Crosland, Anthony, 19
Crossman, Richard, 121, 122, 156,
157, 161, 167, 178, 253
cruise missiles, 5-6
Curran, Sir Charles, 210

Curran, James, ix, 215, 226
Curtis, Liz, 99-100

D-notice system, 196
Dachau, 156
*Daily Express*, 57, 140, 187, 240,
243
*Daily Herald*, 99, 149, 221, 223
*Daily Mail*, 99, 123, 140, 219,
221, 240, 243
*Daily Mirror*, 100, 101, 103, 106,
168, 240
*Daily News*, 14
*Daily Telegraph*, 12, 118, 122, 124,
130, 149, 159, 186, 189,
191, 237, 240, 247
*Daily Worker*, 221
Dalton, Hugh, 19, 120, 142, 143-7,
149, 168
Dalyell, Tam, 5
Dawson, Geoffrey, 14
Day, Robin, 14, 18
dealignment (political), 46-8, 60-1,
86
debate (comparison), 74-5
decision-making, 13
decontextualisation, 211-13
*Defence of the Realm*, 216
Delane, John, 113, 116, 117
Democratic Unionist Party, 201
*Derry Journal*, 205
Dhofar War, 183-92, 194-9 *passim*
Dimbleby, Richard, 14, 157, 178
Director-General (BBC), 143-8,
167, 170, 175, 210, 220
Greene, Hugh, 156, 162, 164,
177
Reith, John, 134-8, 140-42, 163,
168
Director of Talks (BBC), 140, 148,
170, 171, 174, 175
disinformation, 191-2, 193, 196
documentary programmes, 32
Doig, Alan, 97
Douglas, M., 30
Douglas-Home, Sir Alec, 3, 17, 21,
123
Douglas-Home, Charles, 250

Downing, Sir George, 118
Driberg, Tom, 167
Dutch television, 207-8

Estham, Ken, 103
*Economist*, The, 186-7
Edelman, Maurice, 167
Eden, Anthony, 121-2, 173
Eden, Guy, 119-20, 122
editorials, 77, 80
EEPTU, 242
'effects' (media), 41-2, 47, 49, 64-5
elections
    campaigns, 26, 46-7, 50-52,
        55-9, 78-86
    changes, xiv, 64-86
    contestation
        arenas, 64, 66-72
        representation, 64, 66-8, 72-8
    *see also* by-elections; general
        elections; voters
Elliott, Philip, 212
entertainment programmes, 32-3,
    52
espionage networks, 194
Evans, Sir Harold, 119, 122, 215,
    253
*Evening News*, 126
*Evening Standard*, 118, 120, 126
Ewbank, A., 35, 36, 41
*Express Newspapers*, 13

Falklands War, 5, 19, 29-30, 82,
    99, 126, 215, 251
family (social identity), 29
Feingold, L., 168
Fenians, 116
Fiddick, Peter, 201
Field, Frank, 12
films, 215-16
*Financial Times*, 187, 192, 202,
    240, 242
Finer, Professor S., 130
Fisk, Robert, 211
Fitchett, Joseph, 197
Foot, Michael, 5, 10, 84, 222
Foot, Paul, 101, 103

Foreign Office, 123, 142, 144-6,
    155, 159, 167, 171, 173, 184,
    186, 195
Francis, Dick, 203
Fraser, Malcolm, 250
Fraser, Robert, 158
Free Communications Group, 220
free press, 221-2, 230, 246
Freedom of Information campaign,
    217, 218, 224, 233
freesheets, 217, 226, 241
Freud, Clement, 19
Frischer, Ernest, 175
Fyfe, Hamilton, 117

'Gang of Four', 5, 17
Gardiner, A.G., 14
Garlinsky, Joseph, 173
Garvin, J.L., 14
Gaudet, H., 46
*General Belgrano*, 5, 20
general elections, 3, 4, 10, 18, 67,
    118, 135
    1979, 77, 84
    1983, 56-7, 61, 84
General Strike, 134, 136
Germany, 142-3, 144-6, 148
    holocaust, xv, 154-79
Gilbert, Martin, 166, 173, 176
    *Auschwitz and the Allies*, 155
Giles, Frank, 198
Gilmour, Ian, 189-90
Gladstone, W.E., 116-17, 130
Glasgow Media Group, ix, xiii, 34
GLC, 15, 19, 224
Goebbels, Joseph, 48, 163
Goldie, G.W., xii, 69, 139
Goodhart, David, 215
Goot, M., 67
Gordon Walker, Patrick, 148
Government Information Service,
    120, 122
Granville, Lord, 113, 114, 116
Green Party, 15-16
Greene, Hugh, 156, 162, 164, 177
Greenham Common, 12
Grigg, John, 251
Groves, John, 121

*Guardian*, The, 51, 65, 100, 215, 230, 254
  Lobby system, 111, 114, 118, 122, 130
  new technology, 240, 247
  Northern Ireland, 201, 203
  Oman case, 183, 187, 191, 192-3, 198
guerilla warfare, 184-93, 196-8

Hain, Peter, 13
Haines, Joe, 119, 124, 125
Halifax, Lord, 145-6, 147, 148
Hall, Stuart, ix, 36, 74-5
Hankey, Maurice, 118
Harding, Gilbert, 14
Hare, D., *Pravda*, 215-16
Harman, Harriet, 220
Harris, Robert, 215
Harrop, M., 65, 66
Hartmann, P., 35, 36, 41
Hastings, Max, 130
Hattersley, Roy, 84, 230
Hayley, W., 170
Headey, Bruce, 13
headlines, 80
Healey, Denis, 84
Heath, Edward, 4, 17, 119, 124-5
Henderson, Nevile, 145, 146
Heseltine, Michael, 127
Hetherington, Alistair, 122
Hill, Lord, 111-12, 122, 203, 220
Hindess, Barry, 66, 70-71
Hinsley, Cardinal, 159
Hitchcock, Alfred, 157
Hitler, Adolf, 144, 145, 146, 215
  *Mein Kampf*, 163
Hoagland, Jim, 190-91, 192, 197
Hoare, Sir Samuel, 147
Holden, David, *Farewell to Arabia*, 185
Hollingsworth, Mark, *The Press and Political Dissent*, 215
holocaust, BBC and, xv, 154-79
Home Office, 147, 202, 203, 211

Home Service, 162, 165
Horne, Sandra, 223
Hosenball, Mark, 220
House of Commons, xii, 198
  Lobby system, 110, 114-15, 119-20, 126
House of Lords, 13, 69, 114, 224
Howard, Anthony, 112, 118
Hughes, Spencer Leigh, 118
Hussey, 'Duke', 253

IBA, 35, 226, 253
ideologies, 7, 197-8
image (politicians), xi-xii, 4-5, 76, 82-5, 86, 112
immigration, 7
*Independent*, The, 130, 215, 227-8, 246, 247
industrial disputes, 5, 35, 41
  General Strike, 134, 136
  miners' strike, xiii, 5, 19, 126, 224, 227
  Real Lives conflict, 201-3, 207-8, 211, 216, 253
  Wapping, xvi, 215, 217, 226-8, 237, 240-41, 243-5, 247-54
  Warrington, 241, 245
information
  battle of (Oman case), 188-91
  disinformation, 191-2, 193, 196
  election campaign, 55-6, 67
  formation, 67, 68, 69
  misinformation, 211
  new, 47, 59-60
  presentation (BBC), 154-61, 163-8, 175-9
  suppression, 196-7
informational programming, 32-6, 41
Ingham, Bernard, 4, 110, 119, 127-8, 130
International Brigade, 160
*International Herald Tribune*, 192
investigative journalism, xiv, 19, 97, 101-2, 106
IRA, 202, 205, 209, 210, 213
Iranian troops, 186, 188, 191-2, 195, 197

*Irish News*, 205
IRN, 115
ITN, 78, 81, 113, 115, 201
ITV, 226

*Jagged Edge* (film), 216
James, Henry, 127
Jay, Peter, 126, 220
Jellicoe, Lord, 19
Jenkin, Patrick, 110
Jenkins, Roy, 17, 18
Jenkins, Simon, 215
*Jewish Chronicle*, 165, 166, 167, 177
Jews (holocaust), xv, 154-79
Jones, Mervyn, 100-101
journalism, 228
    investigative, xiv, 19, 97, 101-2, 106
    Lobby system, xv, 4, 99, 110-28

Katz, E., 55
Kaufmann, Gerald, 218-19
Keeler, Christine, 251
Kellner, Peter, xvi, 249-54
Keynes, John Maynard, 137
Kilroy-Silk, Robert, 18
Kinnock, Neil, 15, 18, 21, 83, 130, 230
Klapper, Joseph, 45
Koestler, A., 159-60, 168

Labouchere, Henry, 117
labour movement, 10, 223
    BBC and, 133-4, 136-7, 142-51
    media reform and, 216-18, 222, 226-32
    *see also* trade unions; TUC
Labour Party
    BBC and, 134-42, 144, 146-51, 218-21, 224
    election campaigns, 56, 83, 84-5
    leadership, 7, 10, 12, 13, 17
    Lobby system, 118, 121
    media policy, xvi, 216, 218-33, 247
*Labour Weekly*, 125, 223

Lacqueur, Walter, 155, 164, 167, 177
    *The Terrible Secret*, 176
Lambton, Lord 19
*Lancashire Evening Post*, 97
*Lancashire Gazette*, 97
Landon, Brigadier Tim, 194-5
Lansbury, George, 138
Laski, Harold, 143
Law, Derek, 167
Lawson, Christopher, 4
Lazarsfeld, P., 45-6, 65
leaks, 13, 117, 120, 121, 127
Lean, Tangye, 162
Leapman, Michale, 215
Leeds study, 55
Lemass, Sean, 209
Levin, Bernard, 251, 253
Lewin, Lord, 19
Liberal Party, 5, 8, 10, 13, 49, 56
    BBC and, 134, 135
linotype machine, 238, 239
Lippman, Walter, 61
Liverpool, 111
*Liverpool Daily Post*, 123
Livingstone, Ken, 15, 19
Lloyd-Hughes, Trevor, 123, 127
Lobby correspondents, xv, 4, 99, 110-128
local politics, xiv, 90-108
Lockhart, Robert Bruce, 169
*London Post*, 244
London Transport Board, 141
Lonrho, 242, 252

McCaffrey, Sir Tom, 125-6
McCann, Eamonn, 205
Macdonagh, Michael, 110, 116
MacDonald, Gregory, 164
MacDonald, Ramsay, 134, 138
McEwan, I., *The Ploughman's Lunch*, 215
MacGregor, I., xiii
McGuinness, Martin, 201, 203
Machonochie, W., 174
McKee, D., 78, 81
Mackintosh, Sir Alexander, 117
McLaine, Ian, 161

McLeod, J., 59
McLoone, Martin, 209
Macmillan, Harold, 17, 111, 122, 147
MacNeice, Louis, 168
McPhee, W., 45
McQuail, D., 55, 56, 65
*Mail on Sunday*, 243
*Making of the Prime Minister*, 118
*Manchester Evening News*, 103, 106
*Manchester Free Press*, 102
*Manchester Guardian*, 14, 99, 140, 149
manifestos, 66
Marks, Laurence, 203
Marsh, C., 80
Martin, Kingsley, 14
Marx, Karl, 36
Marxism, ix, 25
*Marxism Today*, 215, 223
Mason, Max, 121
Mason, Roy, 189
'mass society', 25
Massiter, Cathy, 253
Matheson, Hilda, 139, 141
Matthews, Victor, 13
Maude, Sir Angus, 128
Maudling, Reginald, 19, 101
Maxwell, Robert, 14, 218
Mayhew, Sir Patrick, 127
Meacher, Michael, 220
media
    class culture and, 26-7, 31-9, 41-2
    content, 31-9
    credibility, 51-3, 56-8, 60, 65, 72-8
    effects, 41-2, 47, 49, 64, 65
    elections and, 64-86
    electors and, 45-62
    interest in, 215-18
    leadership and, 3-23
    in Northern Ireland, xvi, 48, 99, 201-13
    ownership, xi, 14, 90-91, 224, 226, 228, 232
    as political arena, 17-21, 64, 66-72, 86

reform, xvi, 216, 218-33
    representation role, 72-8, 86
Melvern, Linda, 215
MI5, 253
MI6, 186, 195
Mial, Leonard, 157
middle class, 36, 52
Midlands Programming Board, 142
military *coup*, 186-8, 195
Miller, W., 57
miners' strike, xiii, 5, 19, 126, 224, 227
Minister of Economic Warfare, 149
Minister for Posts and Telegraphs, 209, 210
ministerial broadcasts, 3
Ministry of Defence, 183-91
    *passim*, 195
Ministry of Information, 146-8, 150, 158, 162, 165, 169-70
    in Oman, 192, 195, 196
Minority Press Group, 217
minority programmes, 32, 33, 35
Mirror Group, 14, 240
misinformation, 211
Mitchell, Austin, 18
Mitchell, Colonel (Mad Mitch), 19
*Mo Jo* (US newspaper), 98
Moise, L., 168
Monopolies Commission, 220, 232, 251
*Morecambe Guardian*, The, 97
Morel, E.D., 143
Morley, D., 35, 36-7, 38-9
*Morning Star*, 223
Morris, J., *Sultan in Oman*, 185
Morrison, Herbert, 141, 143
Morse, Samuel, 236
Muggeridge, Malcolm, 14
multiple arenas, 17-20
Murdoch, Rupert, 218, 220, 236
    Kellner article, 249-54
    Wapping dispute, 215, 226, 237, 240-41, 243-5, 247-54
Murrow, Ed, 150, 156

Nasser, Gamal, 122

National Council of Labour, 137, 143, 146, 148
National Farmers' Union, 12
National Front, 21, 22
National Government, 138
National Graphical Association, 217, 227, 239, 241, 243, 244, 251
National Joint Council, 137
National Union of Journalists, 216, 217, 222, 225, 228, 232
'Nationwide', 36-7, 50
Nazism, xv, 154-79 *passim*
Neil, Andrew, 241
Netherlands, 207-8
*New Manchester Review*, The, 102-3, 106, 108
*New Socialist*, 215, 223
*New Statesman*, 14, 77, 99, 101, 215, 223, 253, 254
*New York Post*, 250
*Newcastle Journal*, 99
Newens, Stan, 189, 198
news
    'alternative', xiv, 98-108
    bulletins, 32, 34-6, 50, 51, 56, 59
    magazines (TV), 32, 36-7, 77
    management, xv-xvi, 183-99
    sheets, free, 217, 226, 241
    sources, 94-8, 101-2, 104-6
    'value', 138
*News Chronicle*, 221
*News on Sunday*, 246-7
*News of the World*, 243, 247, 251
newsagents, 223
newspapers, *see* press
NGA, 217, 227, 239, 241, 243, 244, 251
Nichols, B.E., 161
Nicolson, Harold, 159, 165, 168
Noel-Baker, Philip, 145
Noelle-Neumann, E., 61
Northcliffe, Lord, 248
Northcote-Trevelyan reforms, 116
Northern Ireland, xvi, 48, 99, 201-13
Nuffield studies, 65
NUJ, 216, 217, 222, 225, 228, 232

O'Brien, C.C., 210, 213
*Observer*, The, 13, 14, 106, 121, 188, 203, 211, 215, 242, 252
'off the record' reporting, 113, 121-2
Official Secrets Act, 116, 217, 218, 220
Ogilvie, W.F., 143-8 *passim*, 175
Olympic Games, 10
Oman, xv-xvi, 183-99
O'Neill, Terence, 207
*Operation Overlord*, 119
opinion leaders, 61
opinion polls, 55, 66-7, 76
    election campaigns and, 78-81
opposition leaders, 5, 7, 15
Orwell, George, 160
Owen, David, xiii, 10, 14, 15, 17, 18, 130
ownership (media), ix, 14, 90-91, 224, 226, 228, 232

Page, Bruce, 101
panel studies, 58
*Panorama*, 50, 126, 253
Parkin, F., 36, 38
Parkinson, Cecil, 6, 19
Parliament
    democracy in, 68-70, 71, 74-5, 119
    Lobby system, xv, 4, 99, 110-28
    televising of, xii, 68-9, 118
    *see also* Cabinet; House of Commons; House of Lords
Parris, Matthew, 18
party loyalty, 53, 56, 57, 59
    dealignment, 46, 47-8, 60-61, 86
    press partisanship, 48, 58, 77, 80-81
    *see also* political parties
Pateman, T., 67, 69, 75
*Peacock Report*, 218
*People and the Media, The* 220
People's Front for the Liberation of Oman and the Arabian Gulf, 184, 188, 190, 191, 192, 196
Perth, Lord, 145, 147

Philo, G., 215
phone-ins, 4, 6
photocomposition, 238-9, 243
Pickles, Wilfrid, 148
*Picture Post*, 221
Pilkington Committee, 219-20
Poland, 164, 167, 169, 172
  Solidarity, 222
  Warsaw Ghetto, 159, 165, 166
Political and Economic Planning,
  219
political issues, 90-91
  Northern Ireland, xvi, 48, 99,
    201-13
  representation, 64, 66, 67, 68,
    72-8, 86
political parties, 22
  broadcasts by, 3, 77
  Conferences, 20, 83, 135-6, 198,
    224-5
  loyalty, *see* party loyalty
  *see also individual parties*
*Political Quarterly*, 251
Political Warfare Executive, 164
politicians
  image, xi-xii, 76, 82-6, 112
  leadership, *see* leadership
  Lobby systems, 110, 113, 114
Ponting, Clive, 5, 127
Popitz, H., 28
populism, 82-3, 86
Porter, Henry, 215
Potter, Dennis, 253
Powell, Enoch, 7
press, 6, 74, 140, 205
  code of conduct, 228, 232
  conferences, 4, 84-5, 118, 125
  election campaigns, 56, 57-9, 76
  freedom, ix, 221-2, 230, 246
  Labour Party and, 56, 222-4
  local, xiv, 90-108
  ownership, ix, 13-14, 90-91, 224,
    226, 228
  partisanship, 48, 58, 77, 80, 81
  reinforcement thesis, 51, 52,
    57-8
  technology, xiv, xvi, 91, 93-4,
    107, 108, 226, 228, 236-54
  unions, *see* NGA; NUJ; SOGAT
  *see also individual newspapers*
Press Association, 127 *bis*
Press Council, 219, 224, 232, 251
press secretary, 123, 125-8, 130
pressure groups, 7, 12, 13, 16, 21
Preston, Peter, 130
Priestley, J.B., 161
Prime Minister, 3, 4-5, 16
  BBC and, 144, 146, 149, 150
  Lobby system, 111, 112,
    118-19, 128
  *see also individual Prime Ministers*
print unions
  NGA, 217, 227, 239, 241, 243-4
  SOGAT, 217, 243, 251
  *see also* Wapping dispute
*Private Eye*, 15, 101, 223
'privatisation', 27, 29
Profumo, John, 19, 122, 251
propaganda, 45, 156, 174, 223
  atrocity, 158-9, 161-2, 164,
    170-71, 176
  election, 55, 56
  Northern Ireland, 202, 207
Provisional Sinn Fein, 201
public opinion, 141
  *see also* opinion polls
publicity
  catapult effect, 19-21
  coverage, 7-13
  management, 20, 21
Pym, Francis, 17, 126, 250

Qabus ibn Said, 186, 187, 194-5

Raczynsky, Count, 172
radio, 51-2, 225
  commercial, 220, 226
  influence of, 138-40, 141
  pirate, 205-6
Radio Four, 8, 115, 254
Radio Foyle, 203
Radio Free Belfast, 206
Radio Free Lough Neagh, 205-6
Radio Orange, 206
Radio Telefis Eireann, 207, 208-9
*Radioactive Times*, 98

RAF, 186, 189-90, 191, 194
Rantzen, Esther, 14
Rapid Development Force, 192
'Real Lives' programme, 201-3,
    207, 208, 211, 216, 253
Redgrave, Vanessa, 10, 15, 16
Reece, Gordon, 4, 20
Rees, Merlyn, 220
Reith, John, 134-8, 140-42, 163,
    168
religious programmes, 173-5
Reuters, 245
*Reynolds News*, 221
Rhodesia (UNI regime), 194
right of reply, 229, 232
Robertson, D., 65
Rodgers, Bill, 17
Rohrer, Rob, 101
Roosevelt, F.D., xi, 57
Rose, Richard, 80
Rothermere press, 221
Rowland, 'Tiny', 13, 242, 252
Royal Commission on the Press,
    219-20
RTE Authority, 207, 208-9
Rucker, P., 146

Said bin Taimur, 183-8 *passim*, 198
Salomon, Sidney, 168, 174-5
*samizdat* publishers, 221
Sandys, Duncan, 17
*Sanity* (CND), 98, 223
SAS, 188-90, 195, 196, 197
'satellite' printing plants, 239-40
Saville, Jimmy, 14
Scargill, Arthur, xiii, 5, 19, 21
Schlesinger, Philip, 213, 215
schools programmes, 32
Scott, C.P., 14
*Scottish Daily News*, 223
Scruton, Roger, 249
SDP, xiii, 5, 10, 13, 17, 48-9
Seaton, J., 215
Selassie, Haile, 160
Seldon, Anthony, 121
Serjeant-at Arms, 113, 116
*7-Days*, 220
sexual indiscretions, 19

Seymour-Ure, C., xi, 53, 65, 70
Shah Eddie, 215, 226, 236, 237,
    241-3, 245, 248
Shah of Iran, 191, 192, 193
Sharf, Anton, 155, 168
Shawcross, William, *The Quality of
    Mercy*, 155
Shelter, 12
Shinwell, E., 17
Shore, Peter, 84-5, 127
*Shropshire Star*, 91
Silkin, Sam, 220
Silverman, Sidney, 167, 173
Sinn Fein, 201
skills and deskilling, 39, 40
Smith, Anthony, ix, 158
Smith, W.H., 217, 223
Snowden, Philip, 135
*Socialist Worker*, 98
Sofer, Anne, 249
SOGAT, 217, 243, 251
Solidarity (Poland), 222
sources (news), 94-8, 101-2, 104-6
*Sources Close to the Prime Minister*,
    112
Soviet Union, 222
Spanish Civil War, 159-60
*Spare Rib*, 98
Special Operations Executive, 149
*Spectator*, The, 99, 101, 251
Spence, J., 74
sport, 8, 10, 13
Stalin, Josef, 179
Stamp Duty, 221, 237
*Star*, 119
Stead, W.T., 14
Steadman, Ralph, 81
Steed, Wickham, 142
Steel, David, 8, 130
Steiner, George, *Language and
    Silence*, 182
Stephen, Andrew, 211
Stokes, D., 58
Stopes, Marie, 139
Stothard, Peter, 249
Strachey, John, 163-4
Straw, Jack, 249
sub-editors, 239

Suez crisis, 121-2
*Sun*, 80, 227, 241, 243, 247, 249, 251
*Sunday Pictorial*, 221
*Sunday Sport*, 246
*Sunday Times, The*, 185, 186, 198, 215, 241, 243, 247, 249, 251, 252-3
Swinton, Earl of, 120

talk-backs, 76, 83
talk-shows, 6, 21
Tatchell, Peter, 19
Tebbitt, Norman, 36
technology, 28, 218
  press, xiv, xvi, 91, 93-4, 107, 108, 226, 228, 236-54
television, 3-4, 139-40, 207-8, 219
  audience receptivity, 32-9, 41-2, 141
  election campaigns, 55-7, 59
  Lobby system, 113, 118, 119, 125
  in Parliament, xii, 68-9, 118
  as political arena, 18-22
  reinforcement thesis, 48-57, 59-61
  representation, 72-8
  viewing figures/habits, 49-50, 73
terrorism, 209, 210, 213
Terry, Walter, 123
*That Was The Week That Was*, 219
Thatcher, Margaret, 84, 85, 203, 220, 224
  image, 4-5, 7, 20, 82-3
  leadership, 7, 17, 20, 77
  Lobby system and, 110, 119, 125, 126-7, 130
Thatcher, Mark, 195
Thomson Organisation, 243, 251, 252-3
Thornton, Clive, 229
Thorpe, Jeremy, 19
Thurtle, Ernest, 150
*Time Out*, 101
*Times, The*, 215
  censorship at, xvi, 249-54
  Labour Party and, 218, 220, 225

Lobby system, 113, 117-18, 121-2, 130
Oman coverage, 183, 185, 187-8, 198
political arena, 12, 14, 19
technology at, 236, 243, 247
Times Newspapers, 243, 251
Timmerman, Jacob, 221
Tisdall, Sarah, 6
*Today*, 239, 240, 241, 242-3, 246
*Today* (Radio Four), 8
Townsend, John, *Oman*, 194
Tracey, M., 215
trade unions, 16, 36, 41, 134
  BBC and, 136-7, 142-51
  in media, 216-18, 222, 226-9
  print, *see* print unions
  *see also* industrial disputes; TUC
Trelford, Donald, 252
Trenaman, J., 55, 56
Trethowan, Ian, 220
*Tribune*, 118, 223
TUC, 10, 133, 136-7, 142-51, 216, 224
Tucker, Harold, 102-4
Tunstall, Jeremy, 99, 114, 121-2
turnout (electoral), 53, 58-9
TV AM, 215
'two-step flow', 61

Ullswater Committee, 141
Ulster Television, 207
Ulster Workers' Council, 201, 210, 211
*Undesirable Journalist, The*, 100, 106
unemployment, 28, 138
UNESCO, 212, 222
*US News and World Report*, 194
*USA Today*, 242
UWC strike, 201, 210, 211

Vanessa Redgrave effect, 10, 15, 16
Vansittart, Sir Robert, 144, 170-71
*verzuiling* system, 208
video recorders, 50 *bis*, 74, 217
Vietnam War, 100
viewing figures/habits, 49-50, 73

Voice of America, 223
voters
    floating voters, 57, 86
    reinforcement thesis, 45-62

W.H.Smith, 217, 223
Wajda, *Man of Iron*, 216
Walden, Brian, 14, 18
Waley, Daniel, 160
walkabouts, 76, 83
*Wall Street Journal*, 240
Walraff, Gunther, 100-101, 106
Wansee Conference, 156, 163-4,
    176
Wapping dispute, xvi, 215, 217,
    226-8, 237, 240-41, 243-5,
    247-54
Warsaw Ghetto, 159, 165, 166
Wasserstein, Bernard, 155, 168
Waugh, Evelyn, 204
    *Scoop*, 216
Webb, Beatrice, 134
Wedgwood, Josiah, 142
*Weekend World*, 18
Weeks, Reverend, 174
Weiner Library, 165, 166
Welch, Colin, 251
West, Richard, 118
Westland Affair, 127
*Westminster Lobby Correspondents,*
    *The*, 114
'Wets', 17, 110
'White Commonwealth'
    correspondents, 123

Whitehouse, Mary, 14
Whittam-Smith, Andreas, 130, 246
Widgery Tribunal, 211
Williams, Francis, 162
Williams, Marcia, 125
Williams, Raymond, ix
Williams, Shirley, 17, 82
Willis, P., 36
Wilson, Charles, 130, 244, 252
Wilson, Des, 12, 217
Wilson, Harold, 4, 17, 20-21, 83,
    119, 121-5, 127, 219, 220
Wilson, William, 189-90
Winchester, Simon, 205
Wintour, Patrick, 215
Wood, David, 118
Worcester, R., 65
Workers' Revolutionary Party, 10,
    16
working class, 7, 27-8, 34, 36, 38,
    55, 136, 137, 142
'World in Action', 196
World Jewish Congress, 172, 174-5
'World at One', 254
World War I, 158-9
World War II, xv, 154-79

Yemen, 184, 186, 191, 192-3
'Yesterday in Parliament', 115
Young, Hugo, 83
Young, Stuart, 203

Zinoviev letter, 135, 219

A porcupine's tail:
"Too *stickly-prickly*," she said.

An owl's tail:
"A lizard with feathers?"
she exclaimed.

"I don't think so!"

A turtle's tail:
"Too pointy," said Little Skink.

While all were fine tails,
not one was quite right for her.

Then one day as she
scampered onto her sunny rock,
her shadow caught her eye ...

Her shadow had a tail!

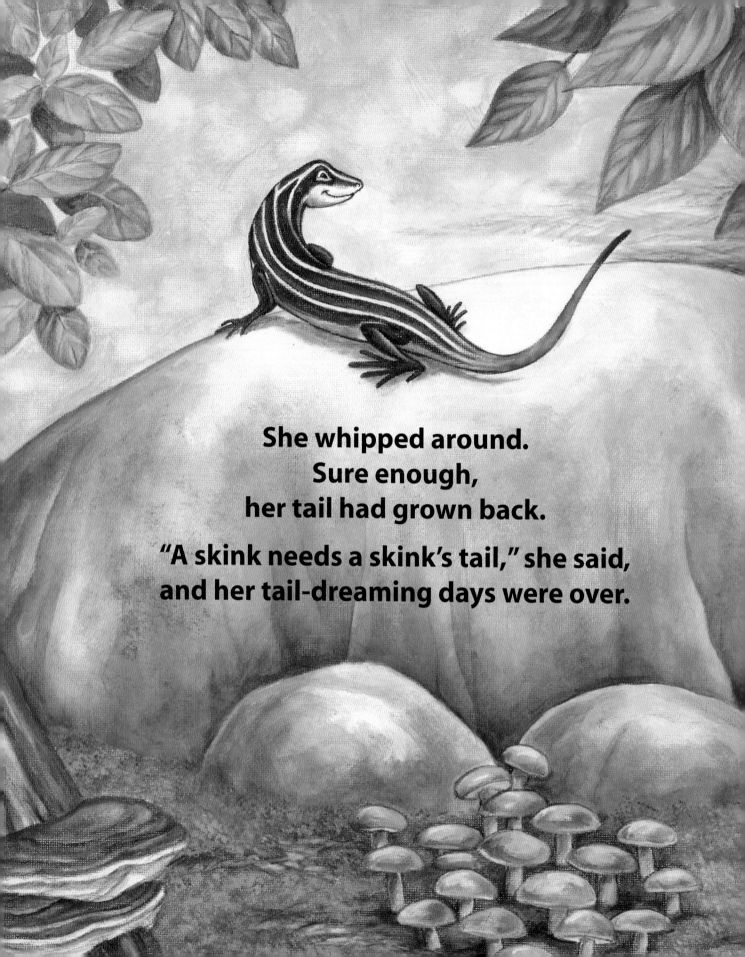

She whipped around.
Sure enough,
her tail had grown back.

"A skink needs a skink's tail," she said,
and her tail-dreaming days were over.

# For Creative Minds

For easy use, the "For Creative Minds" educational section may be photocopied or downloaded by the owner of this book from www.SylvanDellPublishing.com. Please do not write in the book.

## Footprint Map

Using the animal footprints as hints, can you identify where Little Skink saw the animals in the woods? Find the number and the letter of the box that identifies the animal tracks. For example, Little Skink is located in box 7, D.

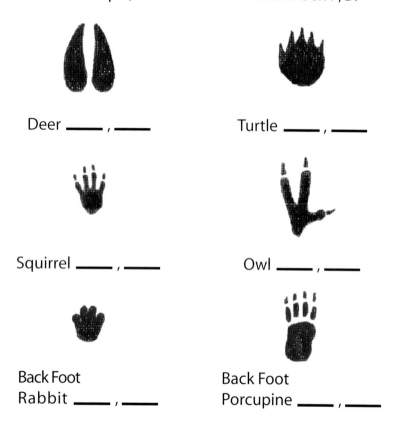

Deer \_\_\_\_ , \_\_\_\_

Turtle \_\_\_\_ , \_\_\_\_

Squirrel \_\_\_\_ , \_\_\_\_

Owl \_\_\_\_ , \_\_\_\_

Back Foot
Rabbit \_\_\_\_ , \_\_\_\_

Back Foot
Porcupine \_\_\_\_ , \_\_\_\_

1. If Little Skink starts at her rock (7, D), how many squares would she have to walk to find turtle and in which direction?

2. How many squares would turtle go to find porcupine and in which direction?

3. Which animal is to the northwest of Little Skink?

# Why Do Animals Have Tails? A Tail Matching Activity

Animals use tails in many different ways: to protect themselves, to balance or steer, to talk to other animals, or to attract other animals to them (either a mate or prey). Some animals can even store food in their tails or can use tails like a hand to hold onto things (prehensile). *Can you match the animal to its tail?*

1. _____

2. _____

3. _____

4. _____

5. _____

6. _____

7. _____

### a. Skink
*Little Skink's tail came off but kept wriggling in order to confuse the crow. That gave Little Skink a chance to get away: she used her tail to protect herself.*

### b. Cottontail Rabbit
*A cottontail rabbit's tail is dark on top and light on the bottom. A rabbit raises its tail when trying to tell other cottontails that there is trouble.*

### c. Squirrel
*A squirrel uses its tail to balance as it runs and jumps from one tree branch to another.*

### d. White-Tailed Deer
*A white-tailed deer raises its tail to warn other deer of danger.*

### e. Skunk
*If scared, a skunk will protect itself by raising its tail to release a stinky spray.*

### f. Porcupine
*A porcupine will rub its tail against an animal and release quills into the animal.*

### g. Owl
*An owl uses its tail to help balance and steer as it flies.*

Answers:
1.b; 2.f; 3.c; 4.g; 5.a; 6.d; 7.e